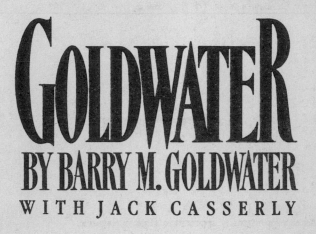

GOLDWATER

BY BARRY M. GOLDWATER

WITH JACK CASSERLY

ST. MARTIN'S PRESS/NEW YORK

To Peggy

An excerpt originally appeared in *Playboy* magazine.

Published by arrangement with Doubleday

GOLDWATER

Library of Congress Catalog Card Number: 87-38136

ISBN: 0-312-92000-8   Can. ISBN: 0-312-92001-6

Printed in the United States of America

Doubleday edition/October 1988
First St. Martin's Press mass market edition/January 1990

10 9 8 7 6 5 4 3 2 1

Acknowledgments

THIS IS TO EXPRESS MY GRATITUDE TO ALL WHO helped us on these memoirs, including President Ronald Reagan, my brother and sister, Bob and Carolyn, and my four children, Barry Jr., Michael, Joanne, and Peggy.

To Senators Sam Nunn, Paul Laxalt, Ted Kennedy, Pat Moynihan, and Dennis DeConcini, as well as Secretary of the Interior Don Hodel, Representative Morris Udall, and Supreme Court Justice Sandra Day O'Connor. Also, to my former colleagues Senator Paul Fannin, Senator John Tower, U.S. Attorney Richard Kleindienst, Presidential Counsel Dean Burch, Presidential Communications Director Pat Buchanan, Presidential Advisers Ed McCabe and Herb Stein, CIA Directors Richard Helms and William Colby, Arizona Governor Howard Pyle, and Phoenix Mayor Margaret Hance.

We especially wish to thank the following, who devoted an extraordinary amount of time to this work: Joy Ruth Casserly, former Ambassador Charles Lichenstein, Agnes Waldron, Carol Dickinson, Benjamin Schemmer, Robert "Rob" Simmons, James W. Smith, Doris Berry, James Locher III, Judy and Earl Eisenhower, Nick Bakalar, our editor at Doubleday, and Helen Rees, our agent.

A salute to U.S. Air Force colleagues, now retired,

who contributed: Generals Jimmy Doolittle, Chuck Yeager, Curt LeMay, G. P. Disosway, Jack Catton, Lieutenant General William Pitts, and Colonel Leon Gray. Also, Major General Don Owens. Retired U.S. Army colleagues who also assisted were Lieutenant General Harry W. O. Kinnard, Lieutenant General William Quinn and his wife, Betty, Colonel J. H. "Trapper" Drum and his wife, Betty, and Colonel Charlie A. Beckwith, as well as others, both active and retired.

A thank-you to all of my office staff who helped. In Washington: J. Terry Emerson, Ellen Thrasher, Jim Ferguson, Gerry Smith, Dick Clifton, Donni Hassler, Jim Horton, Dorothy Bryant, Mary Bouchard, Beth Jones, Melinda Kitchell, Marge Kraning, Luisa Ogles, Pamala Plummer, Annette Maglione, Dot Roberson, Twinkle Thompson, Scott Travers, and Dorothy Troutman.

In Phoenix: Tom Dunlavey, Bonnie Downey, Betty Jo Phillips, Michael Seitts, Bob Greunig, and Debbie Morrell.

In Tucson: Winifred Hershberger, Dolores Johnson, and Tiana Smith.

It's almost impossible to list the hundreds of people we interviewed throughout the country and who otherwise helped us. These are some: Ambassador Edward Rowny, Denny Kitchel, Bill Rusher, F. Clifton White, Harry Rosenzweig, Ed Feulner, Lance Tarrance, Dick Wirthlin, Vic Gold, Paul Wagner, Stephanie Miller, Ben Bradlee, Sally Quinn, Phil Jones, Daniel Schorr, Ron Crawford, Tony Smith, Dean Smith, Paul Weyrich, Morton Blackwell, Kemp Devereaux, Bill Schulz, Jonathan Marshall, Ralph Watkins, Jr., Delbert Lewis, Ollie Carey, Dr. Henry Running, Dorothy Yardley, Jerry Foster, Fred Boynton, Bob Creighton, Bill Wyant, Budge Ruffner, Bert Holloway, Bob and Merilee Thompson, Katherine Dixon, Charlie Coffer, and all my pals in metals and the other workshops of the U.S. Senate.

Thanks, too, to the many newspapers, magazines, and

books whose reporting and reflections jogged my memory.

For those we have missed, we also express our sincere gratitude. God bless every one of you.

BARRY M. GOLDWATER AND JACK CASSERLY

Contents

Preface

THESE RECOLLECTIONS OF MY LIFE ARE STRAIGHT
from the shoulder—a last salute before the flag is lowered
and the final notes of taps fade into memory. A man
stands up, says his piece, then sits down. Others must
judge his deeds.

We return to the American frontier—to my native Arizona when it was still a territory, to the sleepy town of
Phoenix, where a boy who liked radios, planes, and all
kinds of gadgets grew up. Then we fly with him around
the globe in World War II and walk the halls of Congress
when this virtually unknown Westerner is elected to the
U.S. Senate in 1952. We follow him on an unforgettable
—and to him unthinkable—journey. He campaigns for
the presidency in 1964 as the Republican nominee. He
loses in a landslide but returns to the Senate to fight
again. Finally, limping from time on the firing line and
gray with the years, he retires after thirty years in the
Senate.

My life parallels that of twentieth-century America—
raw energy amid boundless land and unlimited horizons.
A man rises from the ancient canyons of the Southwestern desert as his generation grows into the ages of the
automobile, airplane, atom, outer space, and supercomputers.

These remembrances are drawn from deep wells. They include my personal notes about people and events written throughout my career. Thousands of pages of official papers, other notes, and hundreds of hours of dictation were also used for reference. Innumerable letters to my wife, Peggy, and our four children helped to recall our sunshine and sorrow. Old memories were refreshed by thousands of letters written over nearly forty years to people all over America and the world—from presidents and prime ministers to pumpkinheads and fellows down on their luck.

I've recorded much of these memoirs on tape, talking for nearly two years with my friend Jack Casserly. He interviewed more than a hundred of my colleagues on Capitol Hill, personal friends, and acquaintances. Jack and I have known each other a long time, and I have great trust in him.

Our conversations have always been open, direct, and frank. Neither of us would have had it any other way. History is, after all, mostly spontaneous. My life was certainly that—without strategy or timetable.

You will meet some wonderful people—my mother, Uncle Morris, and Sandy Patch—who passed on to me their love of country, commitment to community service, dedication to the military, and interest in politics. Their personal example infused in me the courage to overcome my impulsive, independent youth. But Barry Goldwater always walked his own road, and I accept full responsibility for my life—as I do for these words.

My mother often said that humor should always find a home in our souls. So there are some funny stories about myself, my devoted brother and sister, Bob and Carolyn, and some of our friends and Arizona sidekicks.

Now, nearly a generation later, we'll go behind the scenes of my 1964 presidential race and analyze its place in the history of American politics. It's also time to make a candid appraisal of two tragedies of my time in the Senate—the Vietnam War and President Richard Nixon's involvement in the Watergate scandal. Some reflections about the role of the media are included in these events.

We'll light a few fires under some of the black hats in and around politics—from presidents and the peacocks who surround them to senators and some of the pretenders on Capitol Hill. Perhaps tomorrow's leaders may learn from their mistakes.

There have been white hats, too. Some of my colleagues truly followed in the footsteps of Washington, Jefferson, and Lincoln. I'll recall some of the most dedicated of my time, both Republican and Democrat.

We'll roll back time and try to get a perspective on some of the crucial Senate decisions of the past thirty years in which I played a part, from the turbulent days of Senator Joseph McCarthy to U.S. intelligence activities and the reorganization of the Department of Defense and the American military.

The Senate has changed considerably since my first day there on January 3, 1953—for the worse. We'll see how it has been weakened by its own mistakes and new forces it does not control. Finally, we'll look at the future of the Republican Party and the prospects for our nation in the twenty-first century.

Many people have graciously given of their time and remembrances, and I thank all of them—President Ronald Reagan, fellow senators and members of Congress, my staff, many in the military, other officials, and friends on Capitol Hill, as well as some of the Washington media. Also, longtime friends and acquaintances in Washington, Arizona, and elsewhere.

No words are adequate to describe one loss in my life —the passing of my beloved wife, Peggy, who died on December 11, 1985. We were married for fifty-one years. My life and home have been empty without her.

I still listen for her voice. When I do not hear it, I often look beyond the hills of our valley to where she's patiently waiting for me—as she faithfully did for so many years of our married life. This book is dedicated to her memory and our joyous reunion.

BARRY M. GOLDWATER

The Changing Congress

Now, in the twilight of my life, the past and future are struggling for my soul. My recollections of yesterday and hopes for tomorrow are at war.

This reflects the contrariness and contradiction that come with age and three decades of sweeping change in the U.S. Congress.

Nostalgia for old days and other times rises like the sun most of my mornings. I spend warm hours remembering them. But in the evening, when the cool desert air refreshes my spirit, my blood flows faster and I shake my fist at the present. I am not happy with what I saw in my last years in Congress—nor about today or tomorrow.

Yesterday's giant leaders no longer grace the floors of the Senate. Their eloquence is stilled in its hearing rooms and halls. These men were not merely lights of intelligence, the law, and language. Many acquitted themselves with elegant personal style. Above all, they were masters of a unique craft and tools—Senate rules and procedures.

Such a man was Richard B. Russell. The gentleman from Georgia with the homespun face and courtly manner was a brilliant legal scholar and historian. Russell nevertheless produced practical, down-home Democratic politics. He cared deeply about his native state and the South but also loved the U.S. Senate—so much so that no senator in history knew more about its rules and procedures.

Russell was as shrewd an individual as I ever met, yet well mannered to the point of allowing some colleagues to take advantage of him. He never demeaned a debate—no matter how much steam and smoke poured from the other side. The wily veteran would wait patiently, rise slowly to his feet, then demolish his opponent with a line-by-line refutation of what the challenger had said—all in a slow, easy Southern drawl.

Russell was almost the equal of another giant, Robert Taft, in his knowledge of bills before the Senate. The Ohio Republican, the GOP minority leader for many years, was a soft-spoken, scholarly man who practiced politics like a retired college professor. Taft simply overwhelmed us with his detailed understanding of the ultimate effects of each measure before us. Mr. Republican, as Taft was called, always had more answers than the questions raised. He was a brilliant legislator who lived in the shadow of defeat most of his political life. Yet perhaps no senator in history enjoyed greater professional respect.

Lyndon B. Johnson, who became the Senate's Democratic floor leader in 1953, was an old-style wheeler-dealer who used party discipline, political payoffs, and backroom horse trading to march his troops in proper formation down the Democratic road. By God, if Johnson wanted a roll call on a bill, no senator went home at 6 P.M. You stayed until that vote. Today, senators start grumbling about six o'clock and want to go home—or to some fancy shindig.

Russell said the Congress was passing too much legislation and should address only domestic problems. He saw mostly a budgetary role for Congress and deferred to the President on foreign policy decisions. Johnson's idea of congressional achievement was to pass a ton of measures with something for everybody. That was precisely the problem with his "Great Society." Johnson equated progress with how much social legislation he could flood through Congress.

My aim has always been to reduce the size of government. Not to pass laws but to repeal them. Not to institute new programs but to eliminate old ones. Whenever possible and practical, government should be at the local and state level—not in Washington.

The federal bureaucracy couldn't handle the runaway torrent of Great Society programs and money. Both have been badly mismanaged for the past twenty years, wasting billions of dollars while creating a rolling tide of false expectations. This has given rise to two new American classes—well-paid federal managers of poverty, health, education, and other social problems and masses of people who have accepted dependence on government and virtually turned their lives over to the bureaucracy. The result has been a managerial, financial, and moral monstrosity.

The nation finally discovered the simple truth that throwing money at problems doesn't solve them. Nor were the American people so rich that we could engage in unproductive and unresponsive giveaways—creating and even enforcing welfare addiction through a contradictory system of rules pitting husband against wife and family—while Johnson and Secretary of Defense Robert S. McNamara escalated a seemingly endless war in Vietnam.

Today, Johnson's onetime staff and other spending partners have joined those calling for changes and financial cuts in such programs. They are two decades too late.

Yet Johnson brought an era of discipline and work to the Senate. He makes the present Senate Democratic leadership look like pages rushing up and down the aisles delivering someone else's message.

Senator Everett Dirksen, the GOP minority leader at the time, was the antithesis of LBJ. Dirksen was a man of reason who built his power through intellectual persuasion. The old foghorn was a magnificent speaker. He towered above Johnson in debate, but his forces were smaller and the Illinois Republican detested political payola. Johnson saw it as an art form.

I'll never forget when Dirksen came to my Washington apartment one evening to try to talk me into voting for the 1964 civil rights bill. We had a drink, and he talked about history, Lincoln, and the gathering of all of us on the final day of judgment. It was as if he were singing "Amazing Grace." I was on the verge of tears. Then he said, "We need you, Barry. History awaits—but not for long. The river moves on. Time quickens."

I kept nodding yes, yes. Then I came out of his spell and said, "Hell, no, Ev. Two parts of the bill are unconstitutional. I'm going to vote against them."

He put on his hat and coat and, I think, quoted sacred scripture. It was one of the few times I couldn't hear his rich bass voice. He left, whispering as he closed the door, "I'm going to say a prayer."

There were other old-time giants. Senator Hubert Humphrey was among the greatest. I don't think I disagreed politically with any man more in my life. But Humphrey was a fair fighter, one of the most honorable men I ever met. The Minnesotan was not a show horse, as some suggested. Hubert did his homework, worked hard in the legislative process, and never gave an inch if he believed he was right. He had a terrific sense of humor and, of course, was an outstanding speaker—for ten to fifteen minutes. Hubert's weakness was the two-hour barn burner.

It's a new Congress today. A senator does not live or die on his legislative effectiveness, as in the old days. Appearances—media attention, staff-generated bills, and professional packaging like some mouthwash—often replace legislative tenacity.

Today's senators are more competitive with one another and assert their individual prerogatives more than ever. The younger members seem to know a little about everything but not enough about anything. Senate procedure is now geared to the individual, not the institution. The Senate floor today is often chaos. It's every man for himself, his personal agenda, not completing the business of the institution. This makes one senator temporarily more powerful but often renders the entire body powerless.

That is why I mentioned the old-time respect for rules and procedure. The basic reason for such decorum was to allow for adequate planning and scheduling of debate, to avoid the wild endings that have plagued Congress over the past decade. The agenda of Congress was the business of the nation as a whole, not the interests or reelection of the few.

Nevertheless, the Senate reflects the country. I don't believe the makeup of Americans and America is as solid as it was forty years ago. Society has become more selfish and, as a result, less dedicated to the common good. Millions hail a culture that is now more concerned with money and appearances than genuine accomplishment. I'm not saying people are not honest or productive. They are. But we've slipped as a nation.

Democrat Bob Byrd of West Virginia and Republican Bob Dole of Kansas are today's Senate leaders. Neither has mastered Senate rules and procedures or maintains the decorum of the past. The Senate floor is often a babbling marketplace of pet projects and personal promotion instead of measured debate on major issues. Neither man is within a country mile of Russell, Taft, Johnson, Dirksen, Humphrey, or others who served in the Senate over the past thirty to forty years.

In Dole's case, he doesn't have the leadership qualities that his job as GOP minority leader requires. He tries to make everybody happy. That can't be done. I and other Republicans were unable to harden his hide. The Kansan must become tough if he is ever to become a leader.

I remember a particular incident involving Dole that occurred toward the close of 1986. President Reagan had vetoed a bill the Democrats had pushed and passed—

reducing arms sales to Saudi Arabia. I knew we had the votes to approve a larger sale to the Saudis. So did Dole. But it was heading toward 6 P.M., and he was getting fidgety. Also, Byrd was threatening a Democratic filibuster. I wanted Dole to call Byrd's bluff. I was prepared to stay far into the night if necessary. Dole had wasted two or three hours fiddling around, deciding what to do. I got pretty sore, stood up and asked him, "Aren't you the majority leader?"

"Yes," Dole said.

"Well, why don't you use your power?"

He never did, and everyone went home early.

On the Democratic side, Byrd was speaking one evening I presided as acting president of the Senate. He was running for reelection that year. Byrd got upset and used some frothy language that wasn't particularly fitting for the floor. I can't recall exactly what he was excited about, but his anger poured out as though he had just finished a bad jug of West Virginia moonshine.

God, I said to myself, I've got to get a copy of that speech from the *Congressional Record*. He said some things that will really hurt him. We'll send it along to the Republican Party in West Virginia. The offensive remarks didn't appear in the *Record* the following morning, so I went back to the Senate reporter's room and asked, "Where's all that stuff Byrd talked about last night?"

"Oh," the reporter said, "he edited it out."

Today some senators operate regularly on this double standard—saying one thing on the floor to capture state or national media attention but deleting it from the official record so their precise remarks can't be held against them.

Old-timers stood on what they said. I knew of no senator who regularly sanitized the record. That's now common practice for some.

On another occasion Byrd also proved to be no giant. When the Republicans gained control of the Senate in

January 1981, I arrived early the morning we took over. I left my car at the parking spot on the street closest to my office to save me many steps on my bad right knee.

Later, Byrd's office phoned. Would I please move my car, since I had taken his parking place? I told Judy Eisenhower, my administrative assistant, to give Byrd's office the new total of GOP and Democratic senators. They could take the hint without us rubbing in the fact that the GOP was now in control.

Finally, Byrd himself got on the horn and in no uncertain terms told me I had taken his spot. I replied, "Bob, the Democrats just lost control of the Senate. You're out!"

In the Eisenhower era, when the Republicans won control of Congress, no question was ever raised about office space and other perks. The Democrats graciously turned over control. It was a simple matter of propriety and tradition. Those customs, sadly, are fading. It's every man for himself.

There are two major reasons for this—the staggering growth of personal and congressional staffs as well as support agencies, and an alarmingly selfish attitude among new senators.

When I first arrived at the Senate in 1953, I was given three small rooms in the Russell Senate Office Building and a personal staff of four people. When I left at the close of 1986, my Washington office had a staff of sixteen people and was spread across ten large rooms.

In 1953 we had fewer than a thousand employees on the personal staffs of senators and the Senate general staff. There are now about 7,500 persons working for the Senate. In 1953 the entire Congress employed a total of about 5,000 people. About 37,000 persons now work there! Instead of a few dozen committees, the two houses now have more than 250 committees with much larger and new support agencies.

In the early 1950s the entire Congress worked out of

six buildings. It's now spread across sixteen buildings, and there are plans to double this in coming years.

When I first arrived at the Senate, its annual legislative appropriation was about $77 million ($315 million in 1986 dollars). Congress, as an institution, now spends about $2 billion a year.

One reason for the explosion in staff was the Legislative Reorganization Act of 1970. This was meant to apportion more power to junior senators and to give each at least one good committee assignment. It eventually resulted in more subcommittees than anybody knew what to do with. Each has its own staff. The same "decentralization" of authority took place in the House. This was only a form of dispersing power. Staffs actually work mostly for their chairman, and their work is geared to his legislative goals, not those of the committee as a whole. Decentralization has become a meaningless waste of manpower and money.

The same waste is reflected in the larger personal staffs of Senate members. Some of these staffers are used for constituency work. This is good in principle but has become a major tool to win reelection. The work of some staff members is geared almost entirely toward their employer's reelection. Most members have at least one and often two public relations aides who spend their time grinding out press releases and getting the boss on radio or television. I issued very few news releases and made no effort to get on radio or TV. If something is news, it's news. In fact, I was often convinced that no news was good news.

I remember one day coming out of a secret meeting of the Senate Select Committee on Intelligence. A horde of reporters, cameras, and microphones waited on the Capitol steps. Phil Jones of "CBS News" and others kept firing questions at me about the U.S. mining of Nicaraguan harbors. I kept repeating, "It's classified. Don't you fellows understand English? It's secret!"

They wouldn't take no for an answer, so I finally blew

up: "Goddamn it, go find a leaker! I'm not a good leaker!"

Nicaragua was news, and they had every right to come after me. But secret intelligence meetings are not news in my book. Some of my colleagues leaked such information, placing themselves and their party above the national interest.

It's also not news when a congressman introduces five or ten pieces of legislation in one day that everybody knows are going nowhere. Yet he pours out press releases telling the special interests back home that he's taking care of them. That's cheap politics but expensive for taxpayers.

Congress is now sending out well over a billion pieces of mail each year. That's an average of four pieces for every man, woman, and child in the nation. At one point the cost soared to $96 million a year but has recently slipped slightly below that. This is an outrageous abuse of the franking privilege—to say nothing of taxpayers' money—particularly because many senators and congressmen use it primarily to get themselves reelected. California Senator Alan Cranston is the greatest offender, with about $2 million a year in postal bills. Challengers, of course, must raise their own mailing money. This junk mail is a form of congressional welfare.

I have other objections to today's Capitol Hill but none stronger than the sheer size of congressional staffs and support agencies. This balloon is likely to be filled with more hot air as staffs and agencies increase. Unlike U.S. corporations, which are trimming their fat to meet rising competition, the federal establishment is becoming even more bloated. Massive deficit spending and personal pay raises continue in Congress while millions of Americans, displaced by the current technological revolution, are struggling for economic survival. It's an incredible display of insensitivity to what is going on across the country.

The colossus we continue to construct in Washington is

now being threatened from within. The large staffs created to help Congress are now beginning to control it. I've long asked the question: Who the hell is running Congress, we or the staffs?

Each member obviously needs some personal staff. Committee staffs are necessary to do research, funnel basic information to members, arrange hearings, and provide other backup. In principle, all this is beneficial to congressmen and senators. The actual result is that the Senate, for example, is deluged with more than five thousand pieces of legislation each year. These are being whipped up day after day by personal and committee staffers. Some of us have long described this as a lawmaking assembly line. Instead of easing the load each member carries, these staffs actually make it heavier.

Neither Congress as a whole nor conscientious individual members can keep up with the work they have initiated or that has been created for them. The average congressman introduces three dozen or more bills a year. Members don't even pretend to know what's in them or what's happening on some of the committees they serve.

Congressmen are delegating more authority to their personal staffs. Chairmen are doing the same to their committee staffs. It has become a game of passing the buck on a grand scale. Some of these staff members now act for chairmen, discussing with many different parties what a bill may contain and even talking for the chairman with reporters. No one is really in charge.

This trend is dangerous because, to an ever increasing degree, Washington and the country are being run by people who have not been elected to office. The power on Capitol Hill, while not as faceless as the vast federal bureaucracy, is nevertheless fading from the duly elected to a nameless but central new political class. None of these people is directly accountable to the public. They often generate special interest bills in the areas in which they eventually hope to land big jobs. In Washington, power is money. These congressional power brokers later join

Washington law firms, become corporate lobbyists, and return to buy influence among their old colleagues, or they take on other lucrative positions.

There can be only one end to all this. The staffs, through interaction among themselves, will ultimately set the agenda for Congress. True, the President proposes the business at hand, and Congress disposes. Nevertheless, the agenda has many ways of shifting. Priorities are often lost in the shuffle as Congress deliberates. They are now set by strong-willed, activist staffers to an extent never imagined by the public, or even some members of Congress.

Senators, most of whom serve on four different committees, accept this weakness in order to polish their own image. Each member of the majority party becomes chairman of at least one committee or subcommittee. Many glory in the old Hill status symbol—the title of "Mister Chairman." In reality, many of these chairmanships are nothing more than a power trip.

One reason is that the work of one committee often overlaps and duplicates that of several others. Chairmen are constantly protecting their turf and fighting jurisdictional battles with other chairmen. There are dozens of ways, for example, that different aspects of the nation's commerce can be divided among committees. All this slows down getting anything done.

The massive congressional agenda forces important issues to be inadequately addressed. Some of the nation's most important business falls through the cracks.

Senators often don't know what they're voting on. That's a lousy way to run a lemonade stand, much less our national legislative process. My bill to reorganize the Department of Defense ran to 645 pages. I had a helluva time understanding everything in it myself. Multiply that several thousand times, and you begin to have some idea of the confusion in which Congress operates.

Worse yet, members often haven't the foggiest notion of the long-range implications of a law they have just passed. Members of the federal bureaucracy wind up interpreting and finalizing the law. No one elected them. They are responsible to nobody. So off they go into the wild blue yonder!

The final weeks of almost every session of the Congress now look and sound like a bargain basement sale. The trade-offs of one piece of legislation against another are tossed back and forth across the aisles like men's and women's undergarments that don't fit. We stay up half the night—sometimes all night—like sleepless taxi drivers looking for one or two more fares. Big budget decisions involving billions of dollars are rung up like a Dollar Day sale. Bills are passed so wildly that they often contain unprinted amendments. This means Congress is passing legislation it has never read!

Some argue that the world has become more complex, that we need more experts to help Congress. That is true in a limited number of scientific and other technical areas. But it does not justify multiplying committee staffs by eight and personal staffs by five over the past thirty-five years. We're not selecting experts; we're hiring more workers to keep the legislative ramrod line moving. If we reduced these staffs, we could, for example, help slash the thousands of superfluous bills introduced each year. I favor abolishing all subcommittees and reducing the number of standing and special full committees. Congress is not Disneyland.

Congressional reform can begin only when Congress recognizes that most of the country's problems cannot be solved by the federal government. It has to start believing that achievement lies not in the production of more and more legislation but in quality government.

A new breed of senator, born of a much more independent and self-centered attitude, walks the corridors of power today. These new senators are interested in doing a good job, but their mentality is different than that of most of their predecessors. The first priority of most is reelec-

tion. Genuine accomplishment in the Senate is secondary. It's quite a different priority than we had.

Ours was, first, the good of the nation and, second, the
good of our home state. Reelection was a distant third.
Today, freshman senators no sooner land in Washington
than they're raising money for their next campaign, a full
six years away. Their loyalty has been transformed from
their party to political action committees and their personal organizations back home. Many are less interested
in what good the position can accomplish than that it
become their property, their little family firm.

Reelection is the curse of Washington. For too many
senators, running for office has become a full-time job.
Campaign fund raising begins the very evening after Congress reconvenes following an election. That's no exaggeration. Night after night, fund-raising cocktail parties
roll all across town. I am challenging two things: the
importance senators attach to reelection and, equally
bad, their campaign emphasis on money over real accomplishment.

The sky won't fall on a congressman or the country if
he's not reelected. In fact, most of Washington forgets
one-term House members in forty-eight hours. Senate
one-termers are dismissed in two weeks. It takes about a
month to forget that a Senate two-termer ever hit town.
A fellow like me, who raised a lot of hell over three decades, Washington forgets in three months—one for every
decade served.

I spent about $45,000 in being elected to the Senate for
the first time. For my last campaign in 1980, we planned
to spend $750,000. However, my opponent, a multimil-
lionaire real estate developer, was spending three or four
times that much. So we had to up the ante to about $1.25
million. In the 1986 campaign, Senator John McCain,
who succeeded me, spent nearly $3 million.

The general cost of electioneering has soared out of
sight. In 1984, the last presidential election year, spending on national, state, and local campaigns climbed to a

record $1.8 billion. That was 50 percent higher than in 1980. Inflation and other factors, especially the price of television spots, have obviously increased campaign costs. But the acceptance of the necessity of spending so much money to be elected is an ominous development.

Just before leaving the Senate, I went to the parliamentarian and asked him how many U.S. senators we have had. He replied, "One thousand seven hundred and eighty-two." He added that only five individuals had been elected to five Senate terms. All of this is put in perspective by Goldwater's wisdom: Most are remembered for only a few months!

Should a senator think more of his own survival than accomplishing something for his country? The nation, God willing, will endure for thousands of years. The individual senator is a mosquito among our monuments.

Ben Bradlee, executive editor of the Washington *Post*, one day spoke negatively about the Senate to me, but directed his sharpest criticism at its leaders: "The Senate has changed. It's much less powerful. The leadership has gone to hell. Who are these fellows, Byrd and Dole? C'mon, Barry. Those guys couldn't draw a crowd serving Texas chili. The Senate today doesn't have strong, great men, like in the past. There's nobody over there with stature anymore."

To that, I add a quiet "Amen."

The same is true in the House. Thomas "Tip" O'Neill, in his decade as speaker, was much of the time unable to control a bunch of Democratic Young Turks over there. These ranged from those with a TV celebrity complex like Brooklyn Democrat Stephen Solarz to aging political rockers like California's Ron Dellums, whose behavior reflected the unpredictability of the Democratic Party itself.

In my thirty years in Congress, the most self-serving group was the black caucus, which thrived on charges of racism. It was unworthy of them in an institution where leadership and foresight were the hallmarks of innovative new solutions. Instead, they saw most black problems as civil rights issues, not questions to be solved in and of themselves. Black leadership in Congress still lives twenty to thirty years in the past. Men like Michigan's John Conyers, Jr., and Dellums peddle the past. Neither has had a new idea since he became a welfare pusher.

Times have changed for blacks and are still improving for them, despite rhetoric to the contrary. But competition is keen, especially from Asian-Americans and other minorities. Black leaders can no longer merely plead economic and cultural deprivation. It won't wash. The nation desperately needs new black leaders with ideas, ingenuity, and modern goals—not yesterday's pols who treat their people with contempt by addressing them with old slogans and tired promises of government salvation. There are about twenty hard-core leftists among the group. Some regularly spout the Marxist line.

Leadership is not the only reason why the Congress is weaker today. Members are less dependent on their party for money and other support. The majority raise most of their own reelection funds and maintain their own organization at home. Senators, in particular, have become political entrepreneurs—more independent and with bigger egos. I can see it in my own party. Certain Republicans repeatedly voted with the Democrats, men like Jacob Javits, Connecticut's Lowell Weicker, and Charles McC. Mathias of Maryland. Mathias was a person of sharply defined principles, so I understood some of his votes. But I never comprehended why others so consistently abandoned the GOP. Their only loyalty seemed to be to themselves.

Jack Kennedy jokingly used to say, "Washington is a city of Northern charm and Southern efficiency." If Jack were with us today, let me tell you he would be the first to admit that the South is a helluva lot more efficient than the present Congress.

The Senate generally works only three days a week, Tuesday through Thursday. That's to allow members at least three days of campaigning each weekend. They speak of staying in touch with constituents, but mostly that's a euphemism for electioneering.

I believe the Senate should put in a five-day workweek like the rest of the country. Members offer a horrible example to working men and women who are struggling to make a living. Who are they to bemoan low American competitiveness and productivity? Congressmen are far from paragons of productivity. If they worked a five-day week and limited legislation to our most important national interests, the sessions could be shortened while the electioneers could campaign to their hearts' content. And the nation would save money.

Another reason why Congress is in such disarray today is its media soapbox, particularly television news. Many congressmen view each TV appearance as free fund-raising or commercial time.

Senate policy is being made less and less on the floor and more and more in the radio-TV gallery. Also, since the Cable Satellite Public Affairs Network, or C-Span, began covering Senate floor debates a few years ago, more members are making more speeches. This has restricted Congress's work schedule even more. I could almost set my watch by the time certain senators would show up on the floor. We called it the "evening hour." This meant folks were home from work and the C-Span audience would increase.

Instead of sitting down, talking with one another, and carving out logical public policy—a long, hard, tough process—we have senators running upstairs to the radio-TV gallery in new three-piece suits, blue shirts with white collars, and blow-dry hairdos. A good number tell the nation what they think before they announce it to their colleagues. It's a damn farce!

One day, I saw Bob Byrd on the Senate floor and didn't recognize him. His face was covered with pancake makeup that ran down his starched collar. His hair was stylishly fluffed and tinged with silver gray. He looked like he was about to step onstage in some nightclub act. I took one look, walked back to my seat, sat down, and waited for him to pull out his fiddle. Byrd was dolled up for the TV cameras. On returning to the office, I casually mentioned the incident to Judy Eisenhower, my top assistant. She related that Byrd had been a customer of the Senate beauty salon for years. I was aghast and asked:

"Do you mean in there with you women?"

Judy laughed. "Of course, who else? He used to get his hair tinged with bluish gray. Now we call him the Silver Fox. He also gets his hair coiffed."

"Damn!" I said, shaking my head. I couldn't believe it. "I was right in voting against television in the Senate. Now we've got an actors' studio."

About ten members hustle about half of the Senate's television news attention. All one has to do is watch network television news for a few weeks, and the same faces will constantly pop up. Ted Kennedy, Pat Moynihan, Alan Cranston, and others love it. I wished to hell some of them would have given me more of the benefit of their knowledge in committee meetings.

TV news itself still has to grow up. Coverage of Washington and Congress seems to become more childish with time. "CBS News" comes to mind. Soon after President Reagan's 1986 State of the Union Address, the network's congressional correspondent, Phil Jones, asked me for an interview based on a CBS–New York *Times* national poll covering what the President had said. Jones is a good and fair reporter. He interviewed me for about forty-five minutes. I spent most of that time explaining and supporting the President's policies. Jones posed a question about blacks not having as rosy a place in the economy as Ronald Reagan's address had portrayed. I responded that I could understand such a viewpoint. However, if blacks thought they had problems, they should come out to our Indian reservations in Arizona. I'd show them squalor that would make blacks think they were living in luxury. CBS used about ten or twelve seconds of the long interview, a "bite." The snippet they chose attacked the President and his handling of minority problems. It was a complete distortion of what I had said for forty-five minutes.

After the program I phoned Jones and chewed him out. Yet Jones had had nothing to do with the final product. My interview had been incorporated into a larger segment handled by another CBS correspondent, Bob Schieffer. And Schieffer was being further sliced up six ways from breakfast by an editor whose job it was to package the reaction to the poll into ninety seconds or so.

I fired off a letter of complaint to the CBS brass saying my remarks had been taken out of context. Schieffer and Jack Smith, the CBS bureau chief in Washington, later came to my office and apologized about the editing. I took no comfort in their words, although I appreciated their courtesy. The fact is that all the TV network news programs use short takes or brief bursts of words in stories that run progressively shorter and shorter. Many complex Washington reports now run no more than sixty seconds on TV network news. This trend, which began about six years ago, is intellectually dishonest and outrageously unfair. Nobody's views can be responsibly summarized in ten seconds. Nor can most news stories on the federal government and other Washington developments be summarized in one minute—unless it's a few bars from our national anthem at the end of a big parade.

Network news is not supposed to be *Wheel of Fortune*. It's primarily meant to be a serious presentation of significant events. The networks would be much fairer to the individuals interviewed—even if they answered questions for an hour—if they broadcast nothing.

The instant news analysis on TV is no better. One glaring example was the Tower Commission Report on the Iran-Contra arms deal. I watched as copies of the study were handed to White House reporters. Within minutes, network correspondents came on the tube and said, in essence:

Here it is, you 45 million Americans who regularly tune in to network news. It should be obvious, if you've been watching, that we just got this report. We haven't even read it, but the brass want us to wing it. So here goes!

It's clear that more and more control of television news is being taken from the reporters—the people out on the street covering assignments and news beats—and shifted to anonymous production executives and money men in remote New York offices and elsewhere. With so many people getting much of their news from TV, the situation cannot be ignored.

The media believe their role and influence in Washington have increased over the past generation. I'm convinced they have lessened, as has congressional respect for reporters. When I ran for the presidency in 1964, about 1,650 journalists were accredited to Congress. Today, that number has grown to some ten thousand journalists from around the nation and abroad covering Washington. In the old days good reporters and newspapers had tremendous influence. They were more objective, with much less slanted reporting and writing.

Today, to avoid being attacked or harmed by antagonistic reporters, senators and congressmen use the media. They go over the heads of newsmen by doing their own thing—not even answering the questions put to them. Instead, they drive home their own views and agenda, often monopolizing radio and television time and not allowing newspeople to control it. Senators are now very adept at taking audiences away from reporters.

There are storm warnings on the national horizon concerning the First Amendment. It's not wise for the media to take refuge behind it so often. The average reader or listener really gets sore when newsmen leave the impression—and too many do—that they are answerable to nobody but their editors and producers. Indeed, they have obligations to the law and society in general. The media are not above the daily test of any free institution. Instead of whining about their First Amendment rights, the media must be more specific in answering the charges made against particular reporters and stories.

I like most reporters and have never considered myself a critic of the press. However, more and more I'm disturbed by what they do and say. So are many other Americans, whose litany of complaints boils down to these: inaccurate reporting, unfairness, bias, sensationalism, invasion of privacy, unethical practices, arrogance, and an overall preoccupation with bad news.

In defending themselves as guardians of the public interest, the media would do well to remember that they represent the public's interest, not their own. The First Amendment is not primarily a media defense. It protects every American. The media must pay a price for their right to know—public accountability.

Though the media issue is a big one in Washington, it's now being challenged for attention by another growing debate—the role of lobbyists. I've never had too much trouble with lobbyists. I scared them. From my first days in Washington, I told them that I was going to vote according to my conscience. I didn't give a hoot if it meant not producing an airplane engine in Arizona or closing a military base back home. If it wasn't good for the country, I didn't vote for it. One of my last acts in the Senate was to vote against my own state's interests. The Learjet is manufactured in Tucson. I voted against buying a dozen of them for the Army Reserve. It didn't need them, and besides, it's a luxury plane.

Political action committees (PACs) are now a dominant force in Washington. When I arrived on Capitol Hill, there were fewer than two thousand registered lobbyists. Today, there are about ten thousand. That's one hundred for every Senator and about twenty-three for each member of the House. The reasons for the growth of lobbyists are clear—the breakdown of congressional leadership and the seniority system, as well as the proliferation of committees.

Lobbyists have money, too. I always told them the same thing: If they wanted to contribute to one of my campaigns, fine. If they gave me campaign funds so I'd vote their way, they could get the hell out of the office. A lot of them never came back.

I was never put under greater pressure than by the Israeli lobby, nor has the Senate as a whole. It's the most influential crowd in Congress and America by far. The Israelis can come up with fifty votes or more on almost any bill in the Senate that affects their interests. They went to extraordinary lengths to get me to vote for them, even sending some of my dearest and closest Arizona friends, like Harry Rosenzweig, to lobby me in Washington.

The Israelis never raised the fact of my being half Jewish, but they stressed protecting Israel in the event of war. I told them over and over, "Without a treaty, we've already promised to go to war to protect Israel. And the United States is not getting all that much out of the deal. I think Israel is doing pretty well. I don't worry about Israel when I go to sleep at night. I worry about the U.S. Constitution, which I've sworn to uphold—not Israel's constitution, not that of Saudi Arabia, Lebanon, or anybody else in the Middle East or the world."

That usually shut them up, but they often went away mad because I was not about to support everything they wanted.

Lobbying is under a lot of fire in Washington today. The major reason is Michael Deaver. The former White House deputy chief of staff and longtime friend of the President apparently saw a new California gold strike. Deaver had hardly driven out the northwest gate of the White House than he was handling multimillion-dollar accounts from foreign governments and important American firms. There was only one reason he got those contracts. He knew The Man.

But Deaver made a mistake. He advertised his success. That's a big no-no among lobbyists. He was embarrassing the clan, so someone blew the whistle on him. Deaver was soon under criminal investigation and in court for alleged violations of conflict-of-interest laws. He was later convicted of some charges. The first rule of Washington lobbying is not to be blatant.

I happen to believe lobbyists perform a worthwhile function, but I don't condone all of their practices. They understand the issues better than most members of Congress because their interest is concentrated in a limited area. Congressmen are all over the map. I also have found most of them truthful. Because their interests compete, lobbyists also balance one another off.

I would like to see the present Ethics in Government Act more closely enforced. We should also be concerned that the country not lose the expertise of career civil service officials and military. Their technical experience cannot be easily duplicated. I've not found more federal regulation to be the answer to most problems, including this one. We need more personal ethics and greater concern about enforcing the present law.

Several organizations offered me lobbying jobs as I was leaving the Senate. I didn't accept because I'm too cussedly independent. But I don't condemn those who practice it.

To be frank, I'm much more concerned about the "lobbying" done by members of Congress. A disillusioning example came in the waning hours of the Ninety-ninth Congress, my last in the Senate. Senators Pat Moynihan and Alfonse D'Amato launched a last-ditch battle on the floor to have the U.S. Air Force buy a jet trainer aircraft that it clearly didn't want. Why were they trying to save the unneeded plane? Because it was being built on Long Island.

The New Yorkers launched their attack with the help of two of my friends, Senators Ted Stevens of Alaska and Dennis DeConcini of Arizona. The Senate was trying to act on a $576 billion catchall spending bill before adjournment. If the Senate didn't pass the bill, the federal government would have been forced to shut down for the fifth time since October 1 because it didn't have the authority to spend money.

House and Senate conferees had agreed earlier to fund the T-46A trainer, manufactured by Fairchild Republic Company at a plant in Farmingdale, New York. The bill released $170 million which had been appropriated in 1986 for the planes but withheld by the Air Force because it didn't want them. It also included $124 million for a dozen of the jet trainers in 1987 and $27 million for advance purchase of these trainers in 1988. In refusing the aircraft, the Air Force was trying to save taxpayers a total of $321 million. To top that, all of us were aware of a pertinent report by the Congressional Budget Office. It estimated the Air Force could save as much as another billion dollars by scrapping the T-46A and replacing it with a modified T-37, an earlier aircraft.

I've never approved of bailouts, whether it was New York City, a Long Island firm, or a company in my own state. If a city or a firm isn't hacking it, it should find a way to pay itself or declare bankruptcy, not ask for a U.S. bailout.

I voted, for example, against the bailouts of New York City and the Chrysler Corporation. Both were simply bad precedents. Where do such subsidies stop? I am against subsidies. Congress is not a bank or loan agency. In general the feds should stay out of state and local government as well as private enterprise. Otherwise, as we have seen, it will largely take over both. Neither state and local government nor business should operate on the notion that Uncle Sugar will pay for their mistakes.

I was shocked at the senators' action because not one knows which end of the plane goes down the runway first. At the age of seventy-seven I went out to California and flew the T-46A while they sat on their butts in Washington. It's not a bad plane, but the Air Force was right. We didn't need it, so why spend the money?

We argued all night—about twenty-four straight hours. Meantime, the government shut down for four hours because of lack of funds. Stevens really had no business in the discussion. I got furious because not only did Stevens not know what he was talking about, it was clear he was involved in some new political deal. A year earlier, he had pushed through a bill involving about $800 million in boats for Alaska. In exasperation with his charade, I finally took a shot at his double dealing: "You little bastard!"

The Senate TV microphones picked up the words, and so did the Senate Press Gallery. My sister, Carolyn, raised hell with me when she heard it back in Phoenix.

D'Amato used what we call prime time. He spoke in the evening when the folks out in Long Island could see him beating the Air Force over the head. In trying to gain Senate votes, he was really seeking votes for himself. D'Amato sounded like an idiot because all he knew about the plane was what he had read in Fairchild manuals. I got pretty mad at all the gibberish he was spouting and hollered across the aisle, "You're out of your head!"

He deserved worse, but I didn't want my sister calling me anymore.

D'Amato finally asked defiantly, "Aren't the engines for this plane made in your hometown?"

That was the reason, of course, why DeConcini had spoken for several hours in behalf of the trainer. He was lobbying for funds for his 1988 reelection campaign.

We finally worked out a compromise agreement with no additional T-46A appropriation for fiscal 1987. There will be a competitive fly-off for a future contract.

D'Amato represents what I've been talking about. He put himself and his home state ahead of his country. There wasn't the slightest doubt about it. So did Moynihan, Stevens, and DeConcini to lesser degrees.

My final hours on the Senate floor were a real downer.

I was frustrated and angry not only at this taxpayer rip-off, but at the fact that the $576 billion catchall bill was the largest appropriations measure ever passed by Congress.

The Ninety-ninth Congress was, as some members called it, "the ultimate horror movie." A number even wore buttons in their lapels describing it as "The Congress That Would Not Die" while others mocked, "Free the 99th Congress."

When we sent the fiscal 1987 budget back to the House for final approval, it weighed eight and a half pounds. The House passed it in two minutes.

I couldn't believe the headline when I picked up the Washington *Post* the morning after the record appropriation passed. It said, "Productive Congress Goes Home."

I arrived in the U.S. Senate calling for a reduction in federal spending. In my thirty years there, I don't think I accomplished a damn thing in terms of national fiscal integrity. I'm not at all optimistic about either balancing the budget or bringing the process under control. With all the excuses Congress still manages to come up with in support of big spending, the nation is headed for financial disaster. It's a damn disgrace.

The Congress has now put Americans about $2.5 trillion in hock. That's more than $10,000 for every man, woman, and child. It took the federal government two centuries—including the Great Depression and four major wars—to accumulate the first trillion dollars of national debt. The Congress raised those IOUs to more than $2 trillion in the first six years of this decade. American spending is out of control. The present One Hundredth Congress is speeding down the same road.

Federal entitlements—monies individuals are given by the government—have swollen beyond recognition. Since 1968, combined Social Security and railroad retirement payments have soared from $22 billion to more than $200 billion a year—an increase of 825 percent. Over the same period, federal medical care programs have skyrocketed some 2,000 percent, from $4.3 billion to nearly $100 billion. Federal employees' retirement benefits have climbed from $6 billion in 1968 to $55 billion today. The beat goes on.

Why don't I target President Reagan and other chief executives for Washington's continuous spending deficits? Because Congress has stripped the President of many of his budget powers. In 1974 Congress approved the Impoundment Control Act, which prevents presidents from refusing to approve unnecessary appropriations. Almost every chief executive from Jefferson to our times has fought spending such unneeded funds.

Congress now governs by continuing resolutions— catchall appropriations—that mix funding and policy legislation. This produces unpredictable, irresponsible results. The hands of the President are tied. If he vetoes the resolution, the federal apparatus is shut down.

Three quarters of each federal budget are now out of the President's reach. Congress did this by setting up a prodigious network of open-ended benefit programs. In the past twenty years, federal spending on these entitlements has climbed from less than half to three fourths of the annual budget. Only one quarter can be curbed. Congress has been unwilling to adopt amendments that would restrain these entitlements. The main reason is that each of these programs builds up a strong independent constituency. To help in reelection, members embrace them out of expediency or bow to pressure instead of voting according to their consciences.

The defense budget, because it is controllable, is always under widespread pressure to be cut. I have generally supported it but tried to reduce wasteful outlays—not only in the case of the T-46A trainer but in closing unnecessary military bases. In 1987 I publicly supported an amendment to the Defense Department authorization bill by Republican Representative Dick Armey of Texas. The plan attacked parochial politics by forming a bipartisan commission that would identify unneeded bases. About thirty of the 312 major military bases across the country could be shut down at an annual saving to taxpayers of $2.5 billion. I hope Congress closes all thirty of them.

Uncontrollable categories are not under similar financial pressure. Social Security, civil service pensions, railroad retirement payments, unemployment assistance, farm price supports, Medicare, subsidized housing, food stamps, and other public assistance remain untouched. Also unchanged are fixed costs, such as interest on the national debt, and outlays to pay off contracts already signed.

In the name of compassion, Democrats attack Reagan for cutting social programs. That's unfair and untrue. The President has tried to reduce the *rate of growth* of these benefits. They have actually risen under this administration. The truth is that today's Americans are living off the backs of their children and grandchildren, who must eventually pay for the present excesses.

These "uncontrollables," including farm price supports, deserve much greater scrutiny. U.S. farm policy is actually a massive public rip-off, not only of the American taxpayer but of the small farmer.

The policy ostensibly aims to preserve the average family farm. In reality, most benefits go to big family or corporate farmers. Less than one dollar of every three that Washington spends on such programs goes to farmers in financial trouble. The program has another glaring contradiction. It props up the prices farmers receive for producing specified commodities such as milk, wheat, corn, rice, and tobacco, which are already in surplus. Instead of discouraging such production, federal policy is actually adding to the surplus. Today, for all practical purposes, some farmers are part of the welfare system. They receive more income from the government than from selling their products. Both are hurt.

In the past two decades, entitlement spending has skyrocketed from $90 billion a year to about $750 billion a year. That's a 732 percent increase. The cost of one item, financing the federal debt, has jumped from $10 billion to some $145 billion a year, an increase of more than 1,000 percent.

If the nation is not to face financial ruin, Congress must recognize reality. It must reject narrow interests in favor of the nation as a whole. Above all, it must somehow become an example of sacrifice and leadership for the rest of the country. The congressman or senator cannot continue to be *numero uno*.

The example of Tip O'Neill illustrates the point. The Democratic Prince of the Poor had special legislation passed before he left the House so that taxpayers would finance an office, staff, and expenses for him in Boston to the tune of more than $115,000 a year. No former House Speaker in history has ever been so well taken care of by his poker-playing pals. Oklahoma Democrat Carl Albert cut a similar deal earlier. The O'Neill giveaway includes his cut-rate rent at the downtown Federal Office Building. He also has lifetime franking privileges, which senators with even longer service do not receive. It was a handsome federal handout—even by the sweetheart standards of north Cambridge and Boston—but a horrible last hurrah for the American people.

Congress also must restore a proper distribution or balance of functions between itself and the President. It should approve and send to the states, where it would be passed, a constitutional amendment providing the chief executive with line-item veto authority. Under such a veto, the President could reject political pork barrel programs. Congress would be forced to approve only funds that are essential to the national interest. The item veto already exists in more than forty states. It has been advocated by Presidents Roosevelt, Eisenhower, and Reagan.

The budget process is long and complex, and there are almost as many opinions about it as there are members of Congress. I don't claim to be the oracle who can bring order out of the present chaos. But it's certain we cannot let our present massive national debt stand. The world's stock markets are the most volatile indicators of that.

There are many ways to reduce both the annual fiscal budget and overall deficits. These range from subjecting entitlement programs to fixed multiyear spending levels and sunset legislation, which would expire after a limited time, to steps that would improve congressional discipline.

Congress ignores the time schedule for changing laws and achieving savings. Since the Budget Act of the mid-1970s, the Senate has approved 276 waivers of deadlines or budget-busting limits. Continuing resolutions—letting department and agency outlays stand as they were in the last budget—substitute for appropriations bills. The volume of continuing resolutions has climbed in the past six years from a few pages to about 250 pages.

If Congress is to reduce federal expenditures, it must start with its own budget. One of the worst ways members thumb their noses at the public is the expensive junkets they take to various parts of the world at taxpayer expense. Neither I nor most Americans believe their sanctimonious speeches about international goodwill. Only a limited number of such trips are necessary.

Another way members could exhibit some leadership would be to halt the underhanded way in which members give themselves pay raises. No group in American society has more fringe benefits and allowances than congressmen—with their subsidized shoe shines and haircuts, increased travel funds and staff allowances, and political contributions that may be used for special purposes. Congress also votes itself free medical exams and prescriptions with low room and care costs at three fine hospitals —Walter Reed, Bethesda Naval, and the Air Force's Malcolm Grow. Members have many tax breaks and rich retirement benefits.

I once paraphrased Mark Twain on the Senate floor— there is no distinctly native American criminal class except Congress. The conscience of the House once became so pained that members actually passed a resolution saying, "Your Congress is not a crook."

I've never believed in legislating morality or forcing members of Congress to be honorable through codes of official conduct. Such codes are just a salve for worried consciences. Our integrity must shine like a light from ourselves. It's that simple.

Arizona Representative and my longtime friend Morris Udall and I have talked about the problems of Congress many times. He has told me, "I don't know how to change our system except over time. It's self-correcting. But it often takes ten to fifteen years to change something. That's the price of living in a democracy."

In its appetite for more privilege, power, and financial control of the country, Congress is now trying to take over some of the authority of the presidency. I believe this is one of the greatest dangers facing our republic. This is not Democrat versus Republican, although some of that is present. The legislative branch is attempting to usurp the powers of the executive.

The fight is now focused on the continuing effort by Congress to determine and control U.S. foreign policy. Our founding fathers made foreign policy an executive branch responsibility. The Constitution provides Congress with the power to raise and support the armed forces. The direction of these forces and the daily control of foreign affairs rest with the President. The founding fathers well understood that Congress lacked the capacity for swift and decisive decision making that is essential to protect the nation in times of crisis.

The failure of Congress to grant humanitarian legislation that would have hastened the evacuation of stranded Americans and friendly Vietnamese civilians as Saigon collapsed to the communists in 1975 is one example of its inability to deal with critical foreign policy and defense needs as they arise. Five hundred thirty-five secretaries of state cannot make a fast, critical decision.

Our history clearly demonstrates that presidents have always exercised independent action on crucial foreign policy decisions. As a matter of fact, presidents have used American troops in hostilities more than two hundred times without any congressional declaration of war. That is important historical precedent. The United States has actually declared war only a handful of times.

In 1973 Congress passed the War Powers Resolution, which limited the President's ability to act in times of foreign crisis or conflict. The resolution was approved after a strongly worded veto by President Nixon, who argued that it was probably unconstitutional. The law stated that any time U.S. forces are engaged in hostilities outside the United States without specific legislative authority, these troops shall be removed if Congress so directs by concurrent resolution. If approved by both houses, the resolution does not need the President's signature.

The act says the President cannot keep troops in a hostile situation—whether in a shooting conflict or not—for more than sixty days unless Congress declares war or approves the action. An additional thirty days are allowed for troop withdrawal.

In my view, a 1983 U.S. Supreme Court decision took away Congress's power to command such a pullout. It can try to cut off money, but there will always be enough funds in the U.S. pipeline for the President to carry on such a conflict.

If the War Powers Resolution had been on the books in the early 1940s, Congress might well have nullified President Roosevelt's sending American troops to occupy bases in Greenland and Iceland in 1941. It's reasonable to ask whether Congress would have agreed with Roosevelt's action that same year to protect British convoys west of Iceland. Nor would it have authorized our lending long-range amphibian planes and eighty navy airmen to Britain, as Roosevelt did, to help the English sink the German battleship *Bismarck*. It should be remembered that Congress renewed the military draft in 1940 by only a single vote.

Foreign policy cannot be conducted by congressional amendments. That is precisely what has been happening. Members attempt to shape and even dictate what our policies may be through appropriations restrictions and other means. Congress consists mostly of foreign policy and military amateurs. These dilettantes are actually on a much more serious mission—control of the presidency itself.

This is not to claim the President is always right and the Congress is forever wrong. But I insist on a separation of powers rather than Congress's voting itself the authority to control the President, even in crisis. The Constitution does not give Congress that power.

There are notable cases in which Congress has created its own foreign policy. In 1986 the House voted to impose a one-year moratorium on all but the smallest underground nuclear tests. It also voted a one-year ban on the space tests of antisatellite weapons. To top it all off, the House passed a measure prohibiting funding of the deployment of nuclear systems that exceeded the expired SALT II limits, even though the Soviets had already breached these limitations and the treaty had never been ratified. It did the same thing a second time in 1987.

Ironically, these House actions have been harmful to arms control. In making concessions to the Soviets before and during periods of negotiation between Washington and Moscow, Congress encouraged the Soviets to wait us out and allow our domestic debate to help them obtain goals they would otherwise have to bargain for.

My criticism of Congress has nothing to do with partisan politics. I would offer the same defense in behalf of a Democratic administration. We have long sent the Soviets the wrong message—that America has an irresolute, divided leadership. As a result, the Russians have adopted a foreign policy of supporting uprisings on the fringes of big-power confrontation. One of their purposes is to keep the President and Congress—and the American people—at one another's throats over war powers. The War Powers Resolution should be repealed. It attempts to deny flexibility to the President in the defense of the nation.

None of this is to suggest that there should be no checks on the President. He must be elected and, if he seeks a second term, face the people again. The Senate must approve defense funds and the appointment of cabinet and other executive officers. Ultimately, the President can be impeached if Congress believes he has grossly abused his constitutional powers. But the President is the commander in chief—not Congress.

I'm worried that, because of the War Powers Resolution, the nation might be reluctant or unable to act at some future time of grave national need. In fact, I'm personally convinced that the law, as it now stands, is virtually certain to initiate a crisis between some future President and Congress. I believe the U.S. Supreme Court should decide this issue in the near future.

No one is more aware than I that these views will be attacked by the liberal left. That's fine with me. Perhaps some of this will smoke out their real intent—rule by the tyranny of the minority during crisis. That is my concern. In accepting their program of delay and compromise inside the country, we may be severely crippled by a united enemy striking from the outside.

If I could accomplish three things with the rest of my life, repealing the War Powers Resolution would be one of them. It would be on a par with balancing the national budget. If allowed a third wish, I would abolish the U.S. Department of Education.

Current federal education regulations would, if enforced, allow state and local school boards to do little more than police Washington's rules. The department is obsessed with race, sex, and numbers—not education. It has instituted racial quotas and mixed-sex classes and gym periods but ignored the "back-to-basics" wishes of most black and Hispanic families. The department has attacked standardized tests that indicate students' academic ability. It has tried to mandate bilingual instruction, forced universities to finance abortion, and pursued racism in reverse. It says, "Even though an applicant or recipient [of DOE grants] has never used discriminatory policies . . . [its] services and benefits . . . may not in fact be equally available to some racial or nationality groups. In such circumstances . . . [it] may properly give special consideration to race, color, or national origin."

Our educational system is a national disgrace, and just about everybody knows it. The Department of Education is playing a numbers game with virtually every aspect of learning in a bureaucratic bid to create "equality." Students are not all equal—just as not all mothers, lawyers, acrobats, or baseball players are equal. We cannot continue to drag the entire national system down to pull up the stragglers. The Japanese don't, nor do the Russians. The Vietnamese, who did not speak English and came here with a vast cultural bridge to cross, are doing exceptionally well in school. They haven't complained about race or of being culturally deprived or financially impoverished. None of them is asking for a quota system or other preferences.

It doesn't take a genius to answer our educational problems: Return control of our schools to local jurisdictions. If we elected more conservatives to Congress, we might just abolish the DOE and return education to teachers and parents.

As the last days of my Senate career turned over one by one, I reflected a lot about what I learned and about my stewardship over the years. The most persistent and powerful thought of all was that loyalty is the most important virtue in politics. Not intellect, not ability, not honesty, nor even hard work. If the personal cement of loyalty comes apart in political relationships—be it to staff or other politicians—the entire democratic system breaks down. I placed loyalty above any other quality in my staff members.

Ben Bradlee always insisted my staff "wasn't worth a shit." However, Ben never understood my method of doing things. Unlike others on the Hill, I never had anyone on my staff act or speak for me—never. I was elected. They were not. I never had a resident speechwriter, nor was my press secretary allowed to speak for me. We worked as a team and promoted from within. I retained staffers for fifteen, twenty, and more years, unlike other congressional offices, whose entrances were revolving doors.

I often sat down with the staff and discussed bills and other matters. When work was not done properly, I never minced words. I always demanded and expected the truth—not a ventriloquist and a dozen Charlie McCarthys in the office. Unlike other senators' staffs, only one member of my personal staff ever accompanied me to the floor to advise me. This was Terry Emerson, a fine constitutional lawyer, who helped me in that area. At times I did ask professional members of the Armed Services Committee to stand by in complex budget matters. No matter how tough a debate got, I never called on my personal staff to feed me information—except for Emerson on constitutional law. If I could put political heat on people, I could take it. I was never any different in public than in private except—and this was my biggest failing—I could be very impatient in private. In fact, I've been known to blow my top like an oil gusher.

I ran an open shop. My staff knew all my weaknesses: Dixieland jazz, big bands, fancy ties, and being a soft touch. Few things gave me greater pleasure than giving presents to Arizona Indian schools and libraries, to our Senate maintenance men, Capitol police, and the girls in the office. Being a soft touch has been one of the most enjoyable aspects of my life.

I was notorious for two habits—a clean desk top and regularly eating a cheeseburger supreme on that same desk for some fifteen years. The trick was to make them compatible. I came in about seven each morning and cleaned all work off my desk by 9 A.M. These two hours were the most productive of my day. I would be off to various committee hearings and discussion on the Senate floor throughout the day. If I didn't have a luncheon engagement, the cheeseburger—topped with a slice of raw onion—would be waiting for me at my desk. I cleaned up the crumbs immediately and did more work as soon as time allowed. I don't know if a spotless desk is the sign of a clean mind, but I was convinced that the smell of a cheeseburger supreme is not particularly conducive to airing official Senate business.

The highest reward of my public life was meeting and trying to help youngsters. I've received scores of awards —honorary doctor of law degrees, membership in the Aviation Hall of Fame, and the U.S. Medal of Freedom. None of them equaled—nor did I enjoy any of them more than—the exhilaration of giving graduation addresses at small elementary and high schools in rural Arizona. I never accepted any speaking engagement if it conflicted with the opportunity to address ten or twenty graduates at a small, out-of-the-way school. It was an incomparable thrill to go up north to Indian classrooms in particular. The students were poor, but their eyes seemed as big and appealing as those of young deer. It was the first time— and perhaps the last—that any of them would see a U.S. senator. We all knew that. It was total communion, a few moments none of us would easily forget. Nothing ever moved me as much, not even the cheers of the crowd when I received the Republican presidential nomination.

Warm, generous tributes were given me by my colleagues when I retired from the Senate. They run far too long in the *Congressional Record*. I was deeply moved by all of them. The finest words spoken about me came not on the floor but from Charlie Coffer, a Capitol Park police officer whose hero was Dr. Martin Luther King. He said, "Barry Goldwater always made me feel that it was an honor to be an American."

There were four relationships in Congress that meant a great deal to me—with the Kennedys, Senator Paul Laxalt, and two Arizona congressmen, Mo Udall and John Rhodes. With the Kennedys, patriotism drew us together. Jack loved this country, and I believe all the Kennedy brothers' lives were affected by losing Joe in World War II. The Kennedys returned the compliment. Ted expressed their view to a friend of mine: "I think my brother, Jack, liked Barry Goldwater so much because Barry was so good at poking fun at himself. I believe just about everybody in Washington likes Barry today because he came out of his 1964 loss with grace and humor. He started over."

Laxalt was the first public official in the West to support me for the 1964 presidential nomination. I never forgot that. Some Republicans were ducking me—not Paul. Laxalt is an open man. Through the years, we've always been able to say anything to one another. I knew, for example, that Ron and Nancy Reagan were upset that I supported Jerry Ford for the GOP presidential nomination in 1976. However, I still believe I never really had a choice. He was a Republican and the incumbent President. Paul, who is very close to the Reagans, went out of his way to explain my position to them: "It was never a question of not liking the Reagans. It was Barry's perception of the presidency. He took the Washington view. If a Republican President has done a good job, you support him."

My decision cut Ron and Nancy deeply at the time, but the hurt has healed.

Rhodes has been a friend, pure and simple. Udall has been that as well, but we've battled along party lines. Yet

Mo agrees with my view of Congress today: "We've allowed ourselves to do what no civilized group would do. Any idiot can get the floor and start talking—to hell with the priorities and business of the nation. Nowhere is this more evident than in the Senate. You've got a hundred egos. Fifty of them are grandstanders who know how to get a headline, but not how to get anything done."

In my final days on Capitol Hill, I gave away most of what I owned in the office to my staff, the U.S. Air Force Academy, the Arizona Air National Guard, and friends. This included dozens of model planes that I had made over the decades. On my final day, all I walked out with was a black felt pen.

I met with each staff member privately to say thanks and see if I could help find them new jobs. A few days before Thanksgiving, some of the young ladies brought in food they had prepared at home—turkey, a sweet potato casserole, vegetables, homemade bread, and various desserts. We sat around in my office and reminisced about old times.

On December 8 we had an open house in our office with Mexican food. People came from all over the Hill. It was a rip-roaring time with parking lot attendants, Senate shop workers, clerks, typists, and many Capitol police.

On December 11 I took my personal staff and their spouses to a candlelight dinner at Fort McNair in southwest Washington, where we had a roast beef dinner followed by chocolate mousse. We had humorous skits and readings, and a small band played dance music. Later, I took the majority and minority staffs of the Senate Armed Services Committee to a similar dinner at Fort Meyer in Virginia.

My staff gave me a present, a big Western boot filled with things I had left around the office—an old razor, shaving cream, combs, and other odds and ends. The committee staff bought me the chair to my Senate floor desk. The desk is permanent and passed to each succeeding senator. I had number XXV.

My last day was December 18. We had our annual Christmas party in the office. I wore Western boots and a bolo tie. The staff bought me an original 1848 Colt .44 with my name engraved on the strap and handle with two final words: Christmas 1986.

I rose early the following morning to drive out to Andrews Air Force Base for a flight to Wright-Patterson Air Force Base at Dayton, Ohio. I would later fly to Phoenix. When I got out of an Air Force car near the plane at 7 A.M., the entire staff was lined up on the tarmac. All were wearing T-shirts, hats, and buttons and carried signs from my presidential campaign. They formed an honor guard, and I shook hands with each of them.

As the plane took off, the sun was just coming up. I looked back and saw one large but faded sign above the rest: "Goldwater—A Choice—Not an Echo."

I was now an echo, going home for good.

2

Coming Home

THE SUN IS JUST RISING OVER CAMELBACK Mountain. Phoenix stands and stretches in the morning light. Looking out from our hill, I see that the old dirt roads and ditches where I played as a boy have disappeared. Arizona was a territory when I was born in this valley in 1909. We were about ten thousand people spread across the arid desert in farms of corn, cotton, and citrus. Small family vegetable patches dotted the city. The Salt and Verde rivers nourished the crops, cattle, and citizens. Because of our searing summer heat, parched dry land, and limited water supply, waves of migration passed us by, seeking richer dreams along the cooler shores of California. We were still a frontier town when, on February 14, 1912, Arizona became the forty-eighth state to enter the union.

Today, Phoenix is the nation's tenth largest city. It's one of the fastest-growing metropolitan areas in the country. I've been away for thirty years in the U.S. Senate, and my hometown and neighbors are, in many ways, strangers. The faces of many new homes, businesses, and people on the streets are unfamiliar. My companions for long hours these days are the doves, quail, and robins which flit across the ledge outside my study window.

My brother, Bob, and sister, Carolyn, are still here. So

is my lifelong pal Harry Rosenzweig and other old friends. But Phoenix, its people, and the times have changed—and so have I.

Some of my Senate colleagues told me: You can't go home again—not after three decades on Capitol Hill, the pinnacle of power. Listen to the advice of Thomas Wolfe and others. It'd be a big mistake. You'll twiddle your thumbs.

Since coming up the hill here, I've asked myself whether I made the right decision. Much of this is a new world. So much of the old is back in Washington.

I search the horizon beyond the Estrella Mountains, asking unfamiliar questions: What will you do with the rest of your life? Where are you going at seventy-nine?

After weeks of looking out the wide window of my study, the answer has finally come. It was drilled into me as a small boy by my mother: "Barry, all of us have to pay rent for the space we occupy on this earth."

I still have rent to pay to Arizona, my native state and home. Rent to America, my country. Rent to my family. To leave them some thoughts—one man's testament on his life and times. My mother did that for me all her life. So did my Uncle Morris during much of his. I need a quiet place to think about it, the place that has always been my home—Arizona.

The front doorbell is ringing. Lillian, my housekeeper, has gone to the door. I can hear her. She's talking with the hot tub man.

It's quite a change to go from reorganizing the Pentagon's military readiness and multibillion-dollar procurement system to taking care of hot tubs. From Senate debate on the nation's deficit spending to figuring out how to stop the robins from eating most of the seed before the doves and quail get to it. From juggling all the conflicting claims and issues about U.S. intelligence to cutting cactus in my backyard.

It's not easy to come home. I get an odd feeling going

out the door, knowing my destination is the cactus, the bird feeder, or the hot tub. My early morning journey these days is tapping my cane along the walk to the tub. A new artificial right knee now eases the ache there—the pain of twenty years finally became too much to bear—but the ache in my left knee lingers. Both came from football and basketball injuries. The pain seems to reach everywhere—my heels, shoulders, back, neck, both artificial hips, elbows, chest. A fellow comes to be philosophical about it after more than fifteen operations, including a triple coronary bypass in 1982.

Life has now come full circle. Today, people want me to give a lot of speeches. I guess some think old Goldwater has finally reached the age of reason. They give me testimonial dinners and hold public ceremonies. Arizona schools, military installations, roads, and kids are named after me. Defense Secretary Caspar Weinberger, the Joint Chiefs of Staff, and the Pentagon had a big blowout—a seventeen-gun salute, parade, and Air Force flyover. Frankly, there's been too much of this, and I'm glad it's over. It sure ain't the old days.

Three people—my mother, an uncle, and a teacher—finally convinced me that contributing something to the community was a lot pleasanter life than getting my britches burned in all kinds of trouble. My brother, sister, and some friends stood by my side when the going got tough.

My mother was a very individualistic woman, patriotic and dedicated to her community. Uncle Morris offered decades of public service to Arizona politics and the Masonic Order. Sandy Patch, one of my instructors at Staunton Military Academy, was one of the finest military officers this country ever produced.

My mother had a greater influence on my life than any other individual. It seems worth recalling some of those early years to see how and why the character of one person can leave such an impression on another. One of the things I remember best about Mun—the three of us always called my mother that—was our annual summer trip from Phoenix to the cool beaches of Southern California.

Mun and her three desert rats drove to California every summer because Phoenix was too hot. The trip across the Arizona and California deserts took about a week. Our car was loaded with gear spread across the seats into every corner of the car—bedrolls, tents, other camping equipment, cooking utensils, a first aid kit, a rifle, and a box of shells. The stuff that wouldn't fit hung from the front and back lights, door handles, even the windshield. This included two spare tires. We had about two dozen flat tires each way. My brother, Bob, and I patched the inner tubes in mostly 120-degree heat.

Mun wore knickers, leggings, and a beat-up old hat that she'd tilt at odd angles to make us laugh. She was about five feet four inches tall and a hundred pounds of double-barreled action. Mun was a tomboy who loved the outdoors—camping, hunting, fishing, and climbing. She was spunky and spontaneous, and she spoiled us rotten.

Dad was home minding the store. Outdoor exercise was not his game.

Mun had the uncanny ability of having fun and teaching at the same time. She kept her rifle cocked along the meandering route for coyotes, rattlesnakes, or any other critter that might bother her brood. We learned a lot about guns, camping, and protecting one another. Learning from her was never boring. None of us ever forgot those adventurous treks across the desert because she had so much time to pepper us with her wit and wisdom.

My mother taught mostly through example. One of her greatest lessons was patriotism. When Bob, Carolyn, and I were still in grade school, she used to hitch our horse to the family buckboard and drive us out to the Phoenix Indian School in early evening.

Ash trees and water ditches lined the dusty, unpaved four miles from our house to the school, located in farm country beyond Phoenix. Scattered buildings marked the corner of Central Avenue and Indian School Road, where the students studied, worked, and played on about eighty acres. The school, under the Bureau of Indian Affairs, opened in 1891. The grounds have since been enlarged to more than a hundred acres.

Some two hundred Indian elementary and high school kids from various tribes throughout the Southwest would line up around the flagpole in the late afternoon. One of the teachers would read from a book or offer a history lesson. The students would sing the national anthem. Then the flag would slowly be lowered as one of the boys blew taps on a bugle.

Mun saluted smartly as the flag was lowered. We and the handful of white families that came in those days also saluted. Everyone followed Mun's lead because she had such a distinguished bearing. Then the Indian kids marched off to supper, and we climbed back on the wagon and drove home.

When we arrived, mother lowered the flag on our front porch. She flew it every day. Mun folded it alone, carefully putting it away until morning.

She stitched the forty-seventh and forty-eighth stars on our flag when New Mexico and Arizona entered the union. I was only three years old at the time. She talked about that day for years.

My mother spoke a lot about our country when we were kids—our heritage of freedom, the history of Arizona, how individual initiative had made the desert bloom. Mun was a conservative Republican and proud of it.

She wanted us to know our state and took us everywhere—not only the cities, mountains, and rivers but the Navajo, Hopi, Apache, and other reservations. She would smile when we asked questions. I loved her smile. It was big, like sunrise over the Grand Canyon.

My mother took us to services at the Episcopal church. Yet she always said that God was not just inside the four walls of a house of worship but everywhere—in the rising sun over Camelback Mountain in Phoenix, a splash of water along the nearby Salt or Verde rivers, or clouds drifting over the Estrella Mountains, south of downtown. I've always thought of God in those terms, not in going to church every Sunday. I rarely, if ever, talk religion and never used it to appeal to people in politics. To me, religion is personal, private. It's an inner conviction and an inspiration to a better life. Mun lectured us a lot on our conduct toward others. She always said, "The other person may have the right to feel the way he or she does. Hear them out. You may learn something. They'll respect you for taking the time and are more likely to listen to your side."

Her words never left me. I often recalled them in Senate debates and smiled at the reminder. Some of my opponents must have wondered why I was smiling. I never explained.

Mun was a feisty woman. She smoked, drank now and then, and used a hearty "hell" or "damn" when she was at her rope's end. Mun wore flapper dresses at parties—sometimes she and Dad kept going all night—and knickers when hunting squirrel or playing golf. She was a fine golfer, played whenever she could, and won several local tournaments. Mun also liked hunting and was a good shot even in her eighties. My mother raced around town in a car and went camping in the wilderness when most women's biggest adventure was the daily walk to the grocery store.

After arriving in Phoenix on a caboose from Illinois, she became a nurse at St. Joseph's Hospital and later served as a volunteer at various hospitals. She was the first to help a neighbor in trouble, particularly kids.

Mun left our front door open to the entire neighborhood. Men would walk in on the way home from work, greet my mother if she were there, pour themselves a drink from my father's stock, and be on their way. Neighborhood kids would raid our icebox at all hours

and complain when Mun ran out of their favorite cold
drinks, fruits, or candy.

Our house exemplified her character—open, direct,
honest.

The miracle is that my father—impeccably dressed,
conservative, never drove a nail or car in his life, show-
ered twice a day and slept in fresh sheets, never a bedroll
under the stars, a man of measured words, tone and bearing—met, married, and loved my mother until the day he
died. Yet I've never met two more different people.

The two met in the Goldwater store and bachelor
Baron fell—hard. The couple married at St. Luke's Episcopal Church in Prescott, Arizona, on New Year's Day,
1907, during a snowstorm. My uncle Morris and his wife,
Sallie, hosted the wedding feast. I was later to meet my
own wife, Peggy, at the Goldwater store.

I was born at our home in Phoenix—their first child—
on my parents' second wedding anniversary, New Year's
Day, 1909.

In my terrible teens, I seemed to go from one scrape to
another, like wrecking my father's whiskey barrel. It was
the Fourth of July, my favorite holiday.

I tiptoed up to my mother's room, took her pistol from
under the bed, sneaked downstairs, and pumped a couple
of shots through the ceiling of our sleeping porch. One of
them ripped a hole in Dad's barrel of whiskey, which he
had put up there to age.

Don't ask me why I did it. It's too painful to remember.

First, it was only seven o'clock in the morning, a little
early to celebrate. Second, good whiskey was oozing out
the bullet hole, drop by drop, and blackening the white
paint on the ceiling. The whole barrel of the stuff was
soon lost.

My mother never strapped and rarely punished us, but
this time I knew I'd have to pay—and did.

She marched me into the living room and sat me facing
our grandfather clock. Mun told me to sit there until she

allowed me to rejoin the family. Those were strong words coming from her, and the tone of her voice wasn't any happier. I sat there all day, fidgeting and watching the hands on the clock, past the evening fireworks. I could hear my friends laughing and playing, but nobody talked to me. Mun brought me some sandwiches and milk, but, very unlike her, she never said a word. I was jailed for about sixteen hours.

That wasn't the first or last time I sat alone before the clock, but it was the longest. I learned then—and from all the hours later spent before those slowly circling hands—something about the value of time. It took on significance during my years in the Senate.

Perhaps a few words of explanation are needed, because my clock time influenced the rest of my life. I had a bad reputation as a senator—entirely justified—of starting hearings and other meetings on time. That's not the rule on Capitol Hill. Many representatives and senators make hardly any appointment on schedule—except votes. Not Goldwater!

My temperamental insistence on starting meetings promptly reached new dimensions a few years ago. We used to hold Senate intelligence hearings and briefings in S-407, a secluded, secure old room at the top of the U.S. Capitol Building.

A large electric clock hung from the yellowed wall at the back of the room. It was always ten to fifteen minutes slow, an excuse for senators and witnesses who didn't show up on time.

I had pointed out the clock's failing for several years, but nobody had ever done anything about it. Some of my memos to the Capitol's administrative hierarchy on the subject were hot enough to burn.

One day I arrived for an intelligence session about fifteen minutes early. A few staff members and several witnesses were already there. Goldwater was, as usual, the only senator present.

To the distress of the staff, I stood on a chair and pried

open the faceplate of the clock with a screwdriver from my office. It was a considerable pleasure to turn the minute hand fifteen minutes ahead before closing the faceplate. The startled staff and wide-eyed witnesses had never seen a U.S. senator climb a chair to fix a clock.

Little did they know. I still wasn't happy with S-407. The room did not have a single world map. I had quietly complained about the lack of maps for years, because we often discussed different parts of the globe. Goldwater reminded the brethren that our small-town school in frontier Arizona had had maps in the fifth-grade classroom. No one listened.

In a wonderful stroke of coincidence, someone sent me a fine batch of *National Geographic* maps covering all areas of the world. These were large, precise, modern pull-down maps used at universities and schools.

The old complainer happily arrived at S-407 one morning with some staff members helping him lug this good fortune. I carried a drill, hammer, and large screws.

As soon as I began drilling, all hell broke loose. No mortal drills into the hallowed walls of the U.S. Capitol without specified documents and other proper permissions. One functionary after another hurried in to tell me in hushed tones to stop in the name of God. God, in the case of the Capitol, is the official architect whose name I've used all my powers to forget.

I hung the maps.

If the architect will one day proceed to Room 350, the large, locked door of my old office in the Russell Senate Office Building, I have left an additional message for him and my successors. In the last months of my tenure, I fired my pellet gun a number of times, notching my remembrance into that door. The notches are Goldwater's mark that he was there—a way of carving my initials for my long love, the U.S. Senate. The marks also speak more eloquently than I ever could of my long frustration with the Washington bureaucracy, in the Senate and elsewhere.

The grapevine tells me that Missouri's Senator John Danforth has taken up residence in my old quarters and decreed that no one will fill or cover those notches. Anytime he wants to use my pellet gun, I'll be glad to lend it to him.

We were a happy family in a small town where folks had roots. It was easy living—not the stress that young people have today with drugs and other problems.

The biggest hardships and headaches were poverty among Hispanics, especially those coming up from Mexico, drinking among some of the Indians, and the intense summer heat, often rising above 115 degrees—and in those days we had no air conditioning.

When we weren't at the beach in California, Mun would put a mattress on our front porch and sprinkle a sheet with cold water, and we'd slip underneath, hoping a breeze would come up and keep the sheets cool. Much of the time, we'd wake up with the heat long before dawn. It often remained near 100 degrees all night and climbed as the sun rose.

The heat didn't bother me as much as it does most people. I've kept busy all my life—working, flying for thousands of hours, reading every kind of book, building hundreds of model planes and ships, tinkering with different cars, taking thousands of photographs and developing them, talking on my ham radio, camping, hiking, and canoeing across the West, assembling one new gadget after another, writing many letters, collecting and playing hundreds of Dixieland jazz records, swimming, and now soaking in the hot tub.

Radio is the oldest of those hobbies. When I was eleven years old, my father bought me a crystal radio receiver. There were no radio stations in Phoenix then, so I spent hours picking up music and news from as far away as Los Angeles.

Once I "borrowed" some parts from a mechanic—he later beat the hell out of me and I returned them—to build my own transmitter. In those youthful days, it seemed worth staying up all night to reach other ham radio operators. At the age of twelve, I helped Earl Neilson, a radio shop owner, set up KFAD, the first commercial station in Phoenix. Radios and gadgets have been part of my life ever since.

Leroy Essex, a wonderful black man who helped around our house, built a boxing ring above the garage and a miniature golf course on our property. He lived in a little house near ours and showed me many ways to work with my hands. Leroy introduced my brother and me to John Henry Lewis, a local boxing coach. His son later became light heavyweight champion of the world.

John put me in the ring at a local gym one day with Kid Parker, a professional fighter. The Kid was giving us a few lessons. I startled John, myself, and the Kid in the first round by walking up and hitting the fighter with a right to the jaw. The Kid was rocked back, but only for a second or so. He beat the daylights out of me. I never tried that again.

There was deep loyalty among family and friends in those days—even among some acquaintances. The devoted attachment among my brother, sister, and me has endured and grown with the years. So has my friendship with Harry Rosenzweig, a lifetime pal.

When Carolyn went out on one of her first dates, Bob and I waited up for her. We saw that this guy wanted to kiss her good-night on the front porch. I opened the door, walked out in my shorts, and pretended I was tossing my cookies, gagging and gasping for air. You should have seen this Douglas Fairbanks beat it down the street. Carolyn said she was going to kill me, but I winked and smiled—and she did, too. She knew her brother loved her deeply.

Another time, she smooched with some guy on the front porch, but I waited until she came inside. I told her people get TB from kissing. She called me a devil, but I gave her a big silly grin and she came over and hugged me. That was loyalty. Such personal allegiance, common among early Arizonans, was later to have a major effect on my political life. My long and deep affection for Arizona and the changeless, unspoiled nature of the land was deeply rooted in this same loyalty.

My brother and I were always playing pranks. It started when we were about seven years old and has continued throughout my life—at home, on trips with friends, in the military, during political campaigns, in the Senate, and just about everywhere else.

Not too many years ago, Bob bought me an old fire truck as a Christmas present. He drove the monstrosity onto our driveway, and when I woke up in the morning I thought for a moment the house might be on fire.

We pulled many pranks on others. The two of us once showed up for a local tennis tournament on roller skates. It was a hard court, and we played the practice round on skates. The other doubles team, which was heavily favored, was at first unnerved and finally laughed so hard that we beat them.

In 1929, at the age of twenty, I took up flying. Bob was what you might call my first victim.

I began slipping out the back door of the house about dawn. My mother later told me she had thought it was a sunrise romance with one of the town's fair maidens. Indeed, I'd found true love—the airplane.

Bob mentioned Mother's guess to me. It was time to confess. I said he could come with me some morning. Bob happily agreed. We had to make one stop first, at the small flying field southeast of town (now Sky Harbor International Airport) to look at a plane. When we arrived, I coaxed him into the passenger's seat and climbed into the cockpit. He hollered, "What the hell's going on?"

I took off and flew around Phoenix—and he has never completely trusted me since. My mother, finding out what happened, later said over breakfast, "Barry, why didn't you tell me you were taking flying lessons? I would have gone, too." She meant it.

Bob later got even with me. He gave a luncheon speech at a pro golf tournament near Los Angeles. He told the story of how his brother, Barry, was told he couldn't play a certain course because he was Jewish. Bob said, "So Barry told them it was all right—he'd play just nine holes because he was only half Jewish."

The story got a big laugh, but the incident never occurred. The truth is, Bob was called on to speak while still jotting down notes on what to say, and he made it all up on the spot. Both of us have taken a ribbing about that one for years.

I've also been kidded about an incident that actually happened. It was a weekend episode after Army Reserve Guard training at Camp Little in southern Arizona.

Two buddies—Paul Morris and A. J. Bayless—and I crossed the border at Nogales into Sonora, Mexico. At the time the United States had Prohibition. We decided to beat the law and wash down a few tequilas and beer on the Mexican side of the border.

The three of us were fooling around, sloshing beer out of coffee cans at one another. Somebody aimed too high. Half a can splashed across the mustache, chin, and shirt of a passing Mexican policeman. My pals dashed head-long for the border—and freedom. I had my leg in a cast from an earlier fall and landed in jail.

The Mexican cops saw I had a few bucks in my pockets, so we shot craps. I lost all my money and most of my clothes. We were getting to be *amigos,* so I asked them, as one old *amigo* to another, the price of the bribe to get out. The jailer said twenty-five bucks. With no more money, I asked him if an American check would be all right. They said it was fine among us *amigos.*

I had a blank check from a Phoenix bank. I knew Bayless had an account there, so I just signed his name to it.

Bayless, who became the owner of one of the state's

largest grocery chains, later had the check framed. It hung in his office until he passed away.

A lot of folks did their best to get even with us. One was Paul Fannin, a neighbor, who later became governor and a U.S. senator from Arizona. He once let a pig loose in our kitchen. My brother and I knocked over just about every stick of furniture in the house trying to catch it. The place was a shambles when Mun got home. She didn't just sigh at that one. There was hell to pay.

The Goldwater Arizona saga began in 1860. My grandfather, Michel "Big Mike" Goldwater, was the first of us to set foot in Arizona. Just before the U.S. Civil War, he drove a wagonload of merchandise—pots and pans, knives and other kitchenware, shirts and sweaters, as well as ammunition and tobacco—about 275 miles across the barren California desert from Los Angeles to Gila City, a mining camp nearly twenty miles east of Fort Yuma on the Gila River.

Michel was one of twenty-two children born to Hirsch and Elizabeth Goldwasser in Konin, Poland. Russia controlled Poland at the time of Mike's birth in 1821. The young apprentice tailor became a dissident in the Jewish underground after seeing some of the Czar's anti-Semitic pogroms—murder, arson, looting. Russian laws also denied higher schooling to Jews, and they were severely limited in their right to own land or prepare for most professions.

The teenager fled the pogroms and Poland, fearing arrest and conscription into the Russian army. He went first to Germany, then to Paris, and finally to London.

I never knew Big Mike, although my father and Uncle Morris described him as tall and good humored. They told me that Mike left Paris during the Revolution of 1848 and went to London, where he took up tailoring again. He married Sarah Nathan, who managed her father's prosperous fur business. Sarah bore two children while continuing to work. Michel set up his own tailor's shop, learned tradesman English, and Anglicized his name to Goldwater.

Joseph, one of Michel's younger brothers, later arrived in London. He soon began talking of stories in the newspapers about a big gold strike in California. Sarah scoffed at the wild tales, but Michel was intrigued. He dreamed of great wealth and, supported by Sarah's two brothers, embarked for America with Joseph. He'd send for Sarah and the children when he struck it rich.

In 1852 Michel and Joe arrived in San Francisco—a city blackened by fire over the two previous years. This was neither the spires of London nor the wide boulevards of Paris—not even the country charm of their birthplace. They were shocked at the run-down hotels, brawling saloons, loud gambling dens, and dimly lit whorehouses.

The brothers fled the chaos of San Francisco for Sonora, about a hundred miles east in the foothills of the high Sierra. It was another free-for-all—dreamers, drinking, gambling, whores.

They were lucky and found some European Jews who staked them to a couple of hundred dollars. Mike and Joe opened a saloon. Ladies of the evening did business on the second floor. Mike and Joe ran drinks upstairs but stayed clean themselves. It was bad to mix business with pleasure. They expanded their trade to small, general items—needles and thread, soap and combs.

Sarah and the two children, Morris and a sister, finally came to Sonora. She objected to the bordello, but the saloon was going well. Sarah had two more children but didn't want them to grow up in the wild atmosphere of Sonora. She moved back to San Francisco, which seemed less wicked to her. Mike and Sarah would be separated off and on for much of the next three decades. Mike was forever chasing rainbows, but their love endured. They eventually had eight children, including my father, Baron, the youngest. Mike retired in San Francisco when the last of his little luck ran out and his batteries began running dry.

Mike and Joe eventually went broke in Sonora and later in Los Angeles. That was the West in those days— boom and bust. They moved to La Paz, Arizona, after a gold strike there and then to the nearby town of Ehrenberg on the Colorado River.

I have a fond recollection of an afternoon in Ehrenberg during the Great Depression. Uncle Morris and I drove there in 1934.

My father had died of a heart attack five years earlier, when I was twenty years old. As the eldest son—my brother and sister were too young to assume such responsibility—I went to work in the family department store to learn the business. This meant I had to leave the University of Arizona after my freshman year.

That was the biggest mistake of my life. It would have been much better to somehow remain in school and graduate from college. I've long had misgivings about my education being cut short. My career would have been more fulfilling if I'd had additional history, economics, and other courses. Each of us, whether we go into private business or the business of government, needs the most education we can get. Both men and women are disadvantaged—I don't care what their other background may be—if they don't fulfill their intellectual potential.

I've tried to do that through lifelong daily reading. However, many economic, historical, and other basics are needed to obtain full value from later personal study and observation.

The recollection of Uncle Morris and me at Ehrenberg is important because Morris had become a second father to me. I needed a wise counselor who would teach and guide me.

Morris was not a formally educated man, but he read and improved himself all his life. He spoke fluent Hebrew and Spanish. His mind was very quick. It was also nimble because he was a founder of Arizona's Democratic Party and mayor of Prescott for twenty years. He also helped write Arizona's state constitution and was involved in other political roles for a half century.

Morris was not religious, although Big Mike and Sarah were Orthodox Jews. He did have deep, unshakable convictions. Morris became the Grand Master of Arizona Masonry and is still known as the "father of the Eastern Star" after sixty years in the state organization.

I invited Morris to Ehrenberg to talk about the family and our history. To know firsthand where I came from and who I was—from Europe to our house in Phoenix.

It was a hot summer day, and we arrived about noon. We got out of the car, and Morris pointed out the ghostly shell of the old family store. The two of us walked amid the ruins of the onetime clothing and dry goods establishment. It had been built in 1869. Most of the west wall still stood, but part of the north face had collapsed.

The faint outline of a glass of beer was etched on that part of the north section still standing. Scrawled in fading paint was "Beer 5¢." I guess that was a sideline venture.

We took strides to measure the store—about seventy-five feet wide and some 150 feet deep. I studied the storage loft and attic space that eased the searing heat of the summer sun. The windowframes were still firm and the doors strong. A freight loading dock boiled outside in the intense heat.

Morris walked to where the post office had once stood in the corner of the store and said, "Two of your great-uncles, Henry and Joseph, were postmasters here. But if a fellow didn't come here himself to get his mail, he might not receive it. Joe didn't always deliver the mail. Let's say he was a better businessman than a mail carrier."

We laughed.

I kicked at some boards and other debris. Some old, unopened letters lay scattered in the dust. One was written by Herman Ehrenberg's brother in Germany. Ehrenberg had been a mining engineer and friend of Big Mike. It was Mike who had actually founded the town after floods had washed out La Paz. However, he named it

Ehrenberg after Herman was ambushed and killed by mysterious assailants. Morris told me that Mike's loyalty to Herman's memory was common in those days.

Big Mike and Joe had been ambushed by Indians several times, but they managed to escape. Joe was shot once but survived. Indians stole our mules and burned our wagons, but Mike continued for years to haul wares for sale and supplies for the family across the California desert and Colorado River to Arizona.

The meandering 1,700-mile-long Colorado River divides Ehrenberg from the California desert. The river rolls slowly down to the Gulf of California, where, drop by drop, it dies.

The Colorado is part of my chemistry. No one can understand Arizona without appreciating the river's importance to the state. There are mightier rivers—the Amazon carries more water and has a larger watershed, and the Nile is longer—but the "Red Color," as the Spanish called the Colorado after watching its waters flow between some of the region's red soil and rocks, is the most-used river in the world. It has also been the center of the doggonedest water fights in U.S. political history. Arizona threatened to go to war with California over it earlier in this century. It's part of our lifeblood. As Mark Twain said: "Whiskey is for drinkin', but water is for fightin'."

Goldwater is an appropriate name in Arizona because water is gold here. The desert receives only seven and a half inches of rain a year.

I've returned to Ehrenberg many times. Our store is gone now. The two-mile main drag drowses in the sun much of the year. The population of about two thousand is mostly farmers and some retired folk living in trailer parks.

The local landmarks are a post office, an elementary school, a gas station, two bars, a pizza parlor, and a famous old cemetery that resembles the Boot Hill of Western movies.

All the early Goldwater men were involved in politics. Mike was persuaded—he was a big backslapper and had a lot of friends—to run for a seat in the eighth territorial assembly in 1874 but was roundly defeated. He never campaigned or even put the usual notice of candidacy in the Yuma newspaper—too busy working—but he had a finger in everything. Joe was elected as a school trustee in Yuma County's second district. Henry, one of Mike's sons, made national headlines. He blew the whistle on the "Star Route Scandal," in which several contractors and two U.S. senators were involved in postal fraud. Morris became the first Goldwater to hold public office in Arizona. His long political career was launched at the age of twenty-one in 1873, when he was chosen a part-time deputy clerk in Maricopa County's district court at Phoenix.

However, several years before that election, Big Mike had sent Morris back to San Francisco to learn the fundamentals of business. He worked in the store of a family friend. Morris returned to introduce San Francisco clothing styles and other fashionable merchandise when the family opened a new outlet in Phoenix.

He and Big Mike constructed two one-story adobe buildings with wooden floors and shingle roofs at Jefferson and First streets in the downtown district. The largest of the two structures was fifty feet by twenty-five feet —now large enough only for a barber shop. The store sold general merchandise—men's suits and shirts, ladies' dresses, and a wide array of other goods.

But business was poor, so Big Mike sold the store and recalled Morris to work with him hauling government grain and other freight.

The family struck gold in Prescott, the capital of the Arizona Territory. President Lincoln had created the territory in 1863. Big Mike opened a successful general store in the mile-high, central valley town in 1876, shortly after the nation's hundredth birthday celebration.

The store was a landmark for some eight decades.

Morris was mayor for two decades, and my father, Baron, got his start in the family business there.

Prescott was called the "The Jewel of the Yavapai." Yavapai is the name of an Indian tribe and now an Arizona county. Prescott is often described as "everybody's hometown" because it has always been known as a friendly place. It sits above the beautiful Verde Valley. The moderate climate is the best in the state—cool in the summer and mild in the winter.

In 1952, while running for the U.S. Senate for the first time, I launched my campaign from the steps of the Yavapai County Courthouse in Prescott's stately square. I did it because the town had brought luck to our family.

It was a nostalgic evening, and after the speech I walked across the square to old Whiskey Row. I made the rounds, shaking hands when my right arm wasn't busy. We talked about the old days when they had brewed beer in back of the Palace Bar and sold it for 12½ cents a glass. My campaign advisers later told me I had to quit such gallivanting because it would give me a bad image. Hell, let 'em gossip. That talk never bothered me. As a matter of fact, I'd vote for a candidate who openly walked into a bar and had a drink. It's the other type that I worry about.

Friends and I often return to Prescott. Whiskey Row has gone straight. Only a few saloons operate there now. Of course, the whorehouses disappeared long ago. The Palace Bar has gone modern with fancy meals and rock music. I once wanted to own the place. In fact, I thought Peggy was going to buy it for me as a present. The Palace, with its weathered walls and fading lights, seemed to be a kind of unpretentious heaven on earth. A fellow could sit there in the cool darkness of a hot summer afternoon, his cowboy boots up on an old wooden table, hoist a cold one, and spin long tales of Arizona history with the old-timers.

For more than fifty years, I've been studying that history, visiting all parts of the state and sometimes other states for more information on our people and places. I've gone to libraries, talked with thousands of natives, studied all types of documents—from city and county to state and federal files as well as personal diaries and other sources—and rummaged through whatever family papers were available. I've taken thousands of photographs of people and places. Maybe I've been looking for myself much of the time.

In opening my campaign for the presidency in 1964, I spoke from the same courthouse steps. And my political campaigning as a senator ended at Prescott in 1986 with a speech for Republican state and local candidates.

My political affinity for Prescott was simple—loyalty. It had been the Goldwaters' Promised Land.

It didn't seem that way at the beginning. On the very day Morris arrived in Prescott to begin his long career in the new store, tragedy struck. More than two hundred boxes of merchandise, purchased in California for the venture, were destroyed in a shipboard fire.

I've often reflected on the bad luck the family had. However, the more one comes to know the history of the West, the more such problems appear. We've been a region of boom and bust, not the romantic image of pioneers and cowboys conquering a boundless, bountiful land.

Uncle Joe was a typical example. He was involved in one of the state's saddest days, the Bisbee Massacre, and witnessed an old-fashioned frontier feud, the shoot-out at Tombstone's O.K. Corral.

Five bandits killed four innocent bystanders in a wild shoot-out after robbing Joe's store in Bisbee. And on October 26, 1881, while running a new store, Joe saw the shoot-out between his friends, the Earp brothers and Doc Holliday, and the Clanton-McLowry gang.

Joe later told Morris that the gunfight between Doc Holliday, the Earp brothers—Wyatt, Virgil, Morgan, and James—and Billy Clanton and the McLowrys—Tom and Frank—lasted less than thirty seconds. The McLowrys and Clanton were killed. Morgan and Virgil Earp were seriously wounded.

Joe, who married twice and had three children, had more than his share of bad luck. He finally died in San Francisco near Big Mike, who was living there in retirement with Sarah.

Uncle Morris was a Jeffersonian Democrat. Through the years many people have kidded me about that, especially his role in helping to found the state Democratic Party. Yet Morris was as conservative as I am. He never cared much about what party a man belonged to, as long as he believed in it.

Morris told me one time that politics needed more big-hearted people—"more knights and princes"—and more laughter. He recalled a territorial board meeting in Prescott. There was great tension about whether to raise taxes. To relieve the strain, Morris said, "Gentlemen, I think this board has to be reorganized. We have three Jews and two Mormons on it. What do you say about letting a white man serve?"

The laughter broke the tension.

Politics wouldn't be politics without a fight. However, I've always said that to disagree, one doesn't have to be disagreeable. My mother taught me that, and so did Morris by the example of his relationship with his longtime political rival, W. O. "Buckey" O'Neill.

Republican O'Neill and Morris clashed on just about every local issue. Buckey was a superstar of the time—a bare-knuckle brawler, frontier sheriff, judge, and commander of a company of Rough Riders in the Spanish-American war.

Buckey was killed at San Juan Hill. Morris immediately led a fund-raising drive, and, when the body was brought home, a magnificent statue was commissioned in Buckey's name. It still stands in Prescott's town square.

I had an eighteen-inch copy made of Buckey's statue. It sits in my study today. The bronze work reminds me of Morris's princely character.

I've tried to be more like Morris, magnanimous and more gracious in politics, as the years have passed. It has become easier with time and perspective.

The story of Morris and Buckey is recalled not just as part of the history of our family but in recognition of the fact that battles end. We grow older and, with luck, wiser. The important thing is to learn, become more gracious, and die as a gentleman.

On reflection, I'm now convinced that Morris was always edging me toward public service of some kind. His conversation was often about politics. He went out of his way to be straightforward and fair. Yet he was never cowed, for a vote or any other reason. He taught me something about personal and political integrity.

The Thirteenth Arizona Legislature said of my uncle on his eighty-fifth birthday, "Probably no man living has played a more interesting part in the history and development of Arizona, or more highly exemplified the life of a true pioneer and builder, than has Morris Goldwater."

Morris died in 1939 in Prescott, where his wife, Sallie, had passed away seven years earlier. He was eighty-seven years old. No building in Prescott was large enough for the wake and funeral of the little fellow, who was only five feet four. A Masonic memorial service was finally held in a big local theater. Morris had left instructions for his funeral and maintained his sharp wit even from the grave: "When I am laid out, do not go pussyfooting around, as if you are afraid to wake me. If I wake or hear you, the chances are I will not talk back."

Morris said he wanted to be buried as plainly as possible with no flowers, adding, "Do not spend much money on a tombstone. I may want to get up sometime and come back. A heavy stone might hinder me."

Morris was very frank with me about politics and money. He said an honest politician would never make money. The way he put it was, "A man can't butter his bread on both sides. If he doesn't respect honesty, he shouldn't go into politics."

I've never saved or paid much attention to money. My wife wrote all the checks and balanced the family books. Through the years, my family and friends have pushed me to invest in land and other projects, but I never did. There never seemed to be the time or personal inclination. Also, to be frank about it, I was always very sensitive about my position in the Senate and any conflict of interest.

I've never carried money in my life—literally. If anyone ever asked me to rub two nickels together, I couldn't do it.

My daughters, Joanne and little Peggy, are always lecturing me. Peg claims I never had a checkbook in my life. That's not correct, although an accountant actually pays most of my bills.

Little Peggy says my values are duty, honor, country—the motto of West Point—and I throw money away.

My childhood friend, Harry Rosenzweig, is constantly raising hell with me about becoming more aware of my own finances. We go on trips, and he picks up the bills. Rosie says that Goldy—that's what he calls me when we're on speaking terms—never worries about the bill because he never carries cash, a checkbook, or a credit card.

Peggy and I have met Rosie and his late wife, Sandy, in New York when I didn't have a dime in my pocket. I once asked a Manhattan cabbie, who recognized me, to send me the bill. Rosie was embarrassed and pulled out cash. The driver wouldn't let us out until I autographed the bill.

Dean Burch, once my legislative assistant in the Senate and later chairman of the Republican National Committee, claims Barry Goldwater is the worst money manager of any man he's ever known. He says I leave too many gifts along my tracks. Well, that may be, but what's the dough for anyway? As they say, you can't take it with you.

Dean tells the story about a Saturday morning in my

Washington office many years ago. I was leaving for New York and needed money, so I asked Dean to lend me fifty cents.

Puzzled, Dean asked how far fifty cents was going to get me. I said as far as the Washington train station in a cab. Somebody was meeting me at the other end in New York.

All my life I've given money away. The only time I got into hot water for it was when I borrowed $1,500 to buy land for a YMCA children's camp near Prescott. That was about forty years ago, when the money meant something. Maybe I shouldn't have done it, because we didn't have the funds. I sure heard about that from the family. All I said was that a helluva lot of people had helped me over the years.

My Dad—his nickname was Barry—was an outstanding businessman, but he spent no time on family investments, either. My parents did not own our home, and we rented the store. When Dad made money, he spent it. He was generous with charities, especially when St. Joseph's Catholic Hospital had financial problems near the turn of the century.

My father was always fashionably dressed. Some people called him a dandy because he wore pince-nez glasses and was elegant even when playing poker and billiards at the Arizona Club. However, fashion and elegance were his business. Goldwaters had a reputation for quality— the latest and best fashion, especially for women.

Dad was also a very private person. He confided in few people apart from our mother. However, he didn't always hide his feelings, especially about my comportment in high school. One evening at family dinner, he was looking down at me over his pince-nez like I was the two of spades. Dad may have liked cards, but not wild ones.

He didn't care that I'd been elected president of the freshman class or that I was good enough for both the football and basketball teams. His voice lowered as his eyebrows raised. My father said sternly that I was going to Staunton Military Academy in Virginia, and there wasn't going to be any back talk. I felt as though I'd just been sentenced to the state pen. It seemed the whole family was ready to form a firing squad—except my mother. She was worried about my being so far from home. Dad appeared to say, the farther away the better—until I learned some discipline. Then I could come home and return to school in Arizona.

I packed my bags. I'd shaken a lot of dust on people, and there was no use denying it. It would be difficult without Bob, Carolyn, Rosie, and my other buddies. But this fellow wasn't going to leave with his tail between his legs. They would see—all of them, Dad included—that I'd come back with medals. And the girls would love my new Southern charm. Just wait.

My father wasn't impressed. I knew he meant business —serious business—when he told me he was coming with me on the train to Virginia. He would continue to New York on a buying trip for the store.

The train ride East was the longest trip of my young life. Dad never lectured me. He was very calm. I looked out the train window and saw the land turn from brown desert to the green of grass and crops. It all seemed so big, so endless. I kept getting smaller, weaker, and more frightened.

My father went off to play cards with some of the men. I met Benjamin "Buckey" Harris. He was also a Staunton student. We began playing cards, too.

People played a lot of cards, checkers, and chess in those days. The train ride across the country took a week. Unlike on today's jets, you got to know some of your fellow passengers. Once Buckey and I became friends, he shared a secret with me: "Do you see that man in the dark suit and derby hat? He's a card shark. I can tell all those fellows. Stay away from him."

I whispered back, "Buckey, that's my father."

He turned red and ran to the toilet. I didn't see him for a few hours. He finally came back, and everything was all right. We've been friends ever since. Buckey now lives in Santa Clara, California.

My father's words rang crisp and final when I got off the train in Virginia. "You're on your own now, son. It's up to you."

The two-mile walk to the academy seemed endless. My bags were heavy, but my heart was heavier. I was about as alone as a scarecrow after crops are harvested—two thousand miles from home.

I was about to meet the man who would straighten my direction, stiffen my purpose, strengthen my mind, and show me a discipline I had never known before—Sandy Patch.

Major Alexander M. "Sandy" Patch was in charge of the Reserve Officers Training Corps and my military instruction at Staunton. He was Army from birth to death —and a native Arizonan. Patch had been born at Fort Huachuca in the southern part of the state and died of pneumonia at Fort Sam Houston in Texas. Like his father, who had lost a leg fighting Indians in the Southwest, he was career Army and eventually became a general. Both of them were West Point graduates.

Patch was about six feet tall, with blue eyes and reddish hair, weighing some 170 pounds, and light on his feet. The thing that marked him as a man and officer was his personal discipline. He wasn't tough or mean. He was calm. He never lost his temper, no matter what.

Behind those steel blue eyes was a taskmaster. If he said to be some place at 10 A.M., you had better be there on the dot. If he asked you a question in class, you had better be prepared with an answer. If you broke the rules, you paid the price.

Patch stressed basics. He was a painstakingly practical man. He always said we would use what we learned—in some way—for the rest of our lives.

I remember one evening when the class was fighting a mock Battle of Gettysburg. We were using a large sand-table model of the terrain.

Each cadet would start as a platoon leader. We'd work up to the problems facing captains and other officers. If anyone went off on the wrong track, the major would patiently allow him to go. He would let him dig his own trap. Then, he would stop and ask questions. He would slowly lead the cadet out of the trap but would make him find part of the way himself. The gentle but firm manner in which he did this was a work of art—like a master chess player. He was a gentle fox.

Sandy would always tell us to remember our basic orders, to keep in mind our original estimate of the situation. Not to just jump into a fight. Not to make big changes unless the battle shows the estimate was wrong. If you remember that, you may be able to avoid getting yourself and your men hurt.

After completing an assignment, I once asked Patch, "Major, is there any other way we can know our orders are right or wrong?"

He replied, "Son, you'll never know that until the enemy starts shooting at you."

Patch saw plenty of shooting in World War II. He organized, trained, and later commanded the Americal Division on Guadalcanal. He served in Algiers, the planning headquarters for the invasion of Italy and southern France. He replaced Patton as commander of the Seventh Army. That was after the famous incident when Patton slapped a GI at a military hospital and was recalled to England by General Dwight D. Eisenhower.

I've often thought of Sandy's teaching during visits to pilot training sites across the country. Pilots fly against "enemy" aircraft. When these men land and return to class, the dogfight is projected by film or tape on a four-column glass frame. You see American and "enemy" aircraft in action. The instructor can stop the projector at any time and either ask a pilot why he took an action—right or wrong—or explain what was good or poor in each performance.

You sure as hell have a much clearer picture of the

situation, as Sandy said, when you're being shot at. The trick is to figure out how or why you got there and the best ways to escape and come back on the other guy's tail.

At Staunton I was still a long way from being a deep thinker. Much of the time I was in trouble, walking beat. You put your rifle on your shoulder and march until you ache. The academy's rules were rigid. You couldn't run in certain areas, your bed had to be made a certain way, and everything about you and your room had to be clean. I could handle individual duties, but when the entire day's rules were added up, I was often on the short end.

As a Rat, a first-year student, I had to clean the rifle, shine the shoes, and make the bed of an Old Boy. That was understandable, but there were times when I barely had time to shine my own shoes.

Goldwater was late for formation. Goldwater's rifle was dirty. Goldwater ran out of toothpaste and tried to blow up an empty tube. Goldwater didn't brush his teeth. Goldwater was not present at bed check. Goldwater this, Goldwater that, Goldwater again.

I had only one fight. That was with my first roommate. I owed him money for something and paid him in silver dollars. He'd never seen a silver dollar and said it wasn't U.S. money. I'd never seen paper money, although we talked about it at home. So we put up our dukes and fought a financial war.

One semester I had so many hours of beat to serve that Colonel Ted Russell, the academy superintendent, told the student body, "If Goldwater goes one week without beat, I'll cancel all beats."

I finally did, to his astonishment and my own, and everybody got liberty.

It wouldn't be possible to write about Staunton without mentioning Frank Summers. He was our football coach and another taskmaster. I played in the line. Like Patch, Frank believed in basics. He said that on the football field it meant executing simple plays well. On the field of life, basics are good habits. Frank proved to me that you don't have to be ugly to be tough. He had class.

In my senior year at Staunton, I won the outstanding cadet award and was offered an appointment to West Point. However, my father was not well, and Mother thought it best that I return home.

It was a big mistake. I should have gone to the Point. To this day, I believe I was better equipped, psychologically, to be a military officer than a politician.

Politics is a life that is often out of focus, that rises and falls with the tide of events and everchanging public opinion. For the most part, the military has clear, singular goals. If I had my life to live over again, I'd go to West Point.

The concepts of duty, honor, and country are genuine to me. Patriotism is real. There's no greater service to this country than the defense of its freedom.

In these fading years of my life, the emblem and motto of West Point sum up what I've tried to achieve. In his address to the Point's cadets on May 12, 1962, General Douglas MacArthur also spoke for me:

"Duty—honor—country. Those three hallowed words reverently dictate what you ought to be, what you can be, what you will be.

"The unbelievers will say they are but words, but a slogan, but a flamboyant phrase.

"But they build your character; they mold you for your future roles as the custodians of the nation's defense; they make you strong enough to know when you are weak, and brave enough to face yourself when you are afraid.

"They teach you to be proud and unbending in honest failure, but humble and gentle in success; not to substitute words for actions, nor to seek the path of comfort, but to face the stress and spur of difficulty and challenge; to learn to stand up in the storm but to have compassion on those who fall; to master yourself before you seek to master others; to have a heart that is clean, a goal that is high; to learn to laugh yet never forget how to weep; to reach into the future, yet never neglect the past; to be serious, yet never take yourself too seriously; to be modest so that you will remember the simplicity of true greatness, the open mind of true wisdom, the meekness of true strength . . ."

Duty, honor, country—these are old words but not entirely forgotten.

3

A Double Life

THIS OLD-TIMER HAS LED TWO LIVES ALL THESE years, from my early days in school to my last in the U.S. Senate. The straight life—son and student, husband and father, military officer, businessman, and politician. And the sweet life—athlete, ham radio operator, pilot, car buff, photographer, gadgeteer, and all-around tinkerer with the gamut of electrical contraptions, model airplanes and ships, guns, woodwork, metalwork, plumbing, and other handiwork.

Show me a gadget, and you've found a handyman who'll be late to dinner. Lead me to a car engine or television set on the fritz, and you're talking with an amateur mechanic who just decided not to go to a party. Taxi a new military fighter plane onto a runway, and you've got an old jet jock who has tossed his day's schedule—sometimes even in the Senate—into a wastebasket.

Hobbies, from radio at the age of ten to satellite dishes today, have filled my years with just as much activity as my formal responsibilities. They often caused my public and private lives to crisscross, sometimes invading and other times complementing one another.

There has been both a plus and minus to all this. On the plus side, my love of flying took me into the Army Air Corps. Photography helped launch me as a politician.

Radio led me to propose regulatory and other changes in the U.S. communications industry. Hobbies have been an easy, natural way to get to know more people and make friends. These individuals have usually made me a better person. The places I visited have often given me a clearer perspective of myself.

My conscience has sometimes suffered because I took time and energy away from my family and professional life. Instead of flying or rapping in my radio shack, I might have been with the children or working behind my desk. Later, I'd try to make it up. We'd take photos on a camping trip or fly somewhere for a few days of vacation. A man with one or several hobbies often walks a fine line between family and job. Hobbies are good, but we pay a price for each of them.

Hobbies have been like two more arms—curiosity and adventure. They have kept me young and busy when my step slowed.

Most of us want to know what makes things tick, and what makes people tick. A person learns a lot about himself tinkering—in my case, my tendency to be impatient. My patience has improved by my using all my willpower not to cuss while tinkering. It has also gussied up my English.

There's tremendous satisfaction in working with your hands. A fellow can gauge headway with his own eyes. During my years in the Senate, it was often difficult to measure progress. For that reason, the job became frustrating at times. To weather difficulties and disappointments, I built model planes and ships and monkeyed with various new gadgets.

No one can ever know this fellow without getting his hands dirty with him, or jumping into a plane and taking off somewhere. Flying is my first love. It has been a hobby and part-time career. I flew in the U.S. Army Air Corps for about four years in World War II. After the war, flying was so much in my blood that I formed Arizona's Air National Guard. The government even paid me for it. That was the only time I ever beat the feds.

Over nearly sixty years, I've piloted about 15,000 hours and logged another 7 or 8 million miles in the air. It always seemed better than a lot of the hot air around Washington.

Most small boys dream about flying. Our gang watched the crop dusters and barnstormers around Phoenix. All of us heard about an Arizona air ace, Frank Luke, Jr., who had been awarded the Congressional Medal of Honor after being killed in France during World War I. Luke Air Force Base is named after him. Luke's statue stands before the state capitol in Phoenix.

I soloed in 1929. My father had died, and I was working at our Phoenix store. One of my first passengers was Joanne Strauss, a girlfriend of my pal Harry Rosenzweig. We were doing a tight 360 degrees at about two thousand feet over her house when, bingo, the plane snapped over and went into a spin.

Those early instructors rarely taught students how to get out of a spin. One of them once said jokingly to me, "If you ever get into one, let go of everything and start the Lord's Prayer."

That sure as hell wasn't going to solve my problem, so I grabbed the damn stick with both hands and instead took a deep breath to ease the tension. The trainer finally leveled out, and we landed. I took Joanne home and downed two shots of straight bourbon to stop my hands from shaking. I was back flying the next day—solo.

My four years at Staunton Military Academy were like a compass for me. In 1930 I was commissioned a second lieutenant in the Army Reserve and also received a commercial pilot's license. My hope was to parlay the two into military wings. For the next eleven years, I served part-time with the old 25th Infantry Division. Much of that was at Camp Little near the Arizona-Mexico border.

In 1932 I began courting Margaret Johnson, of Muncie, Indiana, who later became my wife. She said if

I'd quit flying and take up bridge, she'd marry me. I agreed. Those were the two biggest white lies of my life.

My proposals to Peggy would fill a good part of a long love story. She held out for a firm promise that I'd really ground myself. Her instincts were right. I never did. Peg finally accepted inside a Muncie phone booth. It was my twenty-fourth birthday—New Year's Eve, 1933. The booth was her idea—no trap. We were on our way to a dance, and Peggy called her parents to wish them a happy new year.

When Peg finally said yes, I opened the door of the phone booth. We were married in 1934, and I never learned bridge or left the cockpit.

My dream of becoming an Army Air Corps pilot lingered. The corps had rejected me as an aviation cadet before I was married for failing the vision test. But I never gave up the hope of wearing its wings. The store work meant only eating—flying with the corps would be living.

When war broke out in Europe, I was over thirty and we had small children. To my poor eyesight was added knee problems from old basketball injuries. However, the need for pilots soared.

It was time for a new try. I paid a courtesy call on Lieutenant Colonel Ennis Whitehead, commander of the Corps' Advanced Training School at Luke. Citizen Goldwater was acting in his official capacity as chairman of the Armed Services Committee of the Phoenix Chamber of Commerce. We discussed how the community in general and the Chamber in particular could assist Colonel Whitehead to carry out his many responsibilities. He would, of course, have our complete support. I let the word "complete" sink in because it seemed like very good protocol. People told me that protocol was the password to getting ahead in the military. Whitehead solemnly nodded. We got around to my reserve background, that I could fly, and that I liked the corps.

The colonel took the hint. He led me to a typewriter,

where I filled out an application to join the corps for a one-year tour of active duty. Within a month I was in uniform at Luke. First Lieutenant Goldwater became a ground school gunnery instructor. Peggy understood. It was flying.

When Congress declared war in 1941, I already had about two hundred hours of unofficial stick time in the dual-control AT-6 trainer. I parlayed my interest in photography into a seat in the cockpit. In exchange for photos taken of instructors and their planes, they allowed me to fly the AT-6. The pictures flew home to family and friends.

Despite more than a decade of flying, including the unofficial time at Luke, I was still on the ground when the Japanese attacked Pearl Harbor. The nearly-thirty-three-year-old hopeful spent the day mounting .30-caliber machine guns on planes at Luke. The young eagle inside me was screaming to fly.

My friend Fred Boynton was officer of the day at Luke on December 7, 1941. Fred was a big, rawboned pilot instructor, not big on protocol or ordering people around. He saw his main job that morning as making sure all the prisoners in the stockade were accounted for.

When the firehouse relief showed up about seven o'clock, they told Fred about a news report on the radio. It said Pearl Harbor had been bombed. Fred thought they were pulling his leg and shouted back, "Oh, yeah, what and where's Pearl Harbor?"

Despite his doubts, Fred decided to play it by the rule book. He phoned the commanding officer, related the incident, and was told it was probably only a rumor. The officer hung up. An hour later, the commander excitedly called back and ordered Boynton to round up every supply and ordnance officer and recall everyone on leave.

That meant me, and I rushed to Luke to find out as much as possible about the Japanese raid. This was not my choice, but it offered me the opportunity to fly, because we sure as hell were going to war.

A flying slot with the Air Transport Command eventually opened up. We were the Over-the-Hill Gang, which delivered aircraft and supplies to every American theater of the war. Later I became a command pilot.

Before going overseas, I was assigned to Yuma for aerial gunnery. First Lieutenant Goldwater had become a captain, and some buddies decided to throw a party before he left base. We had quite a saloon piano player in my pal Boynton, but no piano.

Fred wanted a big, loud one. As he put it, "Barry, get me one of those whorehouse pianos."

I called the madam at the biggest bordello in town. She obliged. "Anything for the boys."

We rolled out to her house with a big truck, hoisted the piano aboard, and rumbled back to base. The party roared like a bear in a barrel. Fred never could read a note, but we hummed a few bars of almost any song and he hit that piano like a roll of thunder. Everybody had a great time. I was a hero—briefly—until somebody told Whitehead where we'd gotten the piano. He fired this order from his office like a load of buckshot: The piano must return to its point of origin immediately.

The commander then declared the madam's place off limits. She was furious with me. But I was off to Yuma. It was great to soar again with the angels when somebody else was responsible for protocol.

Eventually I became operations officer of the 27th Ferry Squadron of the Air Transport Command at New Castle Army Base, Delaware. I was assigned as chief pilot of two operations, Crescent, operating out of LaGuardia Field in New York, and Fireball, from Miami. Crescent flew from the East Coast to the Azores, across North Africa to Karachi, India—now the capital of Pakistan. Fireball went from Miami to Brazil, on to Lagos, Nigeria, and across central Africa to Karachi.

In a stroke of luck, I was one of nine pilots to ferry the first and last group of single-engine P-47 Thunderbolts from the United States across the North Atlantic to

American units in Britain. We lost one plane at a refueling stop before landing in Scotland. The pilot survived. All single-engine aircraft were later sent by ship. These are a few words about my P-47, written in a brown spiral diary on July 16, 1943: "I am naming her *Peggy G* after you know who. She [the real Peggy] has led me through the best part of my life, so I figured I may as well follow her namesake across the Atlantic. . . . She is the sweetest, smoothest-running airplane man ever made, and she and I will get along as famously as her namesake."

While stationed at New Castle in Wilmington, Delaware, in 1942, some of us finally got leave. I phoned Dr. Henry Running, our family pediatrician, and asked him to bring our wives to Manhattan, where we'd have some fun. The girls and Hank soon arrived.

I didn't know anyone in New York, and they sure didn't know me. We called one of the fanciest restaurants in town for dinner reservations. The receptionist, in a charming, deferential whisper, asked, "Are you *the* Goldwater?"

"Honey," I replied, "the one and only."

We were escorted by the headwaiter to a good table and shown impeccable service. Strangers bought us drinks and came by to say hello. The four Westerners agreed these Easterners weren't so bad after all.

We later learned that a well-known New York philanthropist was named Goldwater. Several local institutions were named after him.

I saw no reason to allow a detail like that to dampen our spirits. It might be a long time before we were together again. So, with the traditional stiff upper lip of a good soldier, I continued on my merry way about town as *the* Goldwater.

Several months later, I had leave again and phoned Hank for another Manhattan jaunt with the girls. We stayed at the plush St. Regis. The place seemed a bit dull, so I went out and bought a rubber duck, a fancy decoy. It quacked when a rubber hose attached to it was squeezed.

I lay back in bed in our fancy room and began quacking the duck. It was loud enough to be heard above the traffic noise below.

Young women were sewing dresses and other clothes in a Hattie Carnegie workshop on the same floor across the street. A few came to the windows when they heard the quacking. None could see the duck, so more came to find the quack—not me, the duck. Production finally came to a standstill. One of the girls eventually spotted the duck on the tiny balcony outside our room.

Everywhere we went, from Central Park to Grand Central Station, where I caught a train to return to base, I carried the duck with its head sticking out of my flight bag. It would quack at the darndest times. People were splitting their sides laughing, but I kept a straight face.

After returning to New Castle, this squadron commander used the duck to assemble his men. The commanding officer became angry and eventually furious at what he considered making light of serious discipline. He told some of my men, "If I hear Goldwater's duck one more time, I'm going to kill somebody."

That did it, of course. I soon sounded the quack-quack of assembly over our loudspeaker. Needless to say, there was hell to pay.

I later flew in the China-Burma-India theater. We had shuttle runs over the Himalaya Mountains, known as the Hump, delivering arms, ammunition, and equipment to Chiang Kai-shek's forces.

The Americans had a running skirmish with Lord Mountbatten, one of Britain's theater commanders over there. I flew into Karachi with orders to get one of our C-54s airborne. The big transport was the first four-engine muscle that we had. It was a wonderful workhorse, but this one sat in a hangar with an engine falling off.

The Army flew over an engineer from McDonnell-

Douglas. But he was a civilian and wasn't going to get his hands dirty. This fellow took one look at me and seemed to say, "You're the grease monkey."

Looking at that giant loose engine, even this old gadgeteer was a bit shaken. But it was worth a try, so I started punching rivets.

The rivets held, but an even bigger problem came loose. The British passed the word—it eventually got to me—that this was now Mountbatten's plane. Our guys told me: Nuts to that.

Word came that Mountbatten himself was arriving. This was big. A lot of strings were being pulled. I was not going to be the yo-yo. So I jumped in the C-54 and took off. That baby bounced around nearly every Allied base in India with Mountbatten's boys on its tail. I'll never forget the tail number—444.

Our intelligence was pretty good, and we managed to keep one jump ahead of the British until they finally gave up. Hell, they could never have caught this old desert rat.

Some of us wished Mountbatten would have faced Curtis LeMay under those circumstances. LeMay, later to become a general and Air Force chief of staff, was a colonel in those days. I first met him at Kharagpur, India, after landing in a C-54. There didn't seem to be any equipment to unload my cargo, two replacement engines for B-29s. So I began looking around for someone in charge. This short, stocky officer, chewing on a cigar, finally heard me out. He said not to worry, but to stay with my plane and the cargo.

LeMay took off in a C-46, flew to Calcutta, and returned a few hours later with two forklifts. We've been friends ever since. He has always been a can-do officer.

If LeMay were in my boots, he never would have run from Mountbatten. The colonel would have greeted the British commander with a broad smile, his around-the-clock cigar in his mouth, and blown smoke rings in Mountbatten's face. I mean that. He wouldn't have said more than a pleasant howdy behind rings of zeros. Le-

May was that kind of guy. He was tough and you knew it, but he was class.

In Burma, I repeated one of my last assignments at Luke—helping train pilots—this time Chinese—to fly the P-40, our pursuit plane. We formed some fine friendships, which led me to support Formosa, later called Taiwan, after the Communists took power on the Chinese mainland.

After my tour in Asia, I was reassigned to Southern California to train pilots for combat duty in P-38 and P-51 fighters. It was ironic. I had always wanted to fly fighters in combat, but never got the chance. Nor did I fulfill my other major goal, piloting B-29s against the Japanese. I served in California until the end of the war.

The major political conviction I took from the conflict —one spends a lot of time thinking on long flying runs— was that it never would have erupted if the United States had remained militarily strong in the 1920s and 1930s. I'd never be an isolationist.

In November 1945 I was mustered out but soon formed the Arizona Air National Guard. I took a reduction in rank from colonel to captain to assume command of the guard's 197th Fighter Squadron. My first request was that the unit not be racially segregated. It was soon approved.

After I came home from the war, Hank Running phoned about three one morning. He asked if I'd fly him down to Sonora Province in Mexico. Hank explained that our Maricopa County Medical Society was donating penicillin and other emergency medical supplies to the Mexicans because of disastrous floods there. He had to go as the society's president. The Yaqui River was still pouring across northern Mexico with loss of life, injuries, and many homeless.

We took off from Phoenix in a single-engine Navion with a news photographer who hitched a ride to shoot photos of the scene, and ran into the angriest storm I'd ever seen over Mexico. The clouds were so thick I could barely make out my maps.

We finally landed at Hermosillo to gas up. The flood area was farther south. We were told the medicine was most needed at the town of Navojoa, below Guaymas. We took off again, but the storm was even worse. The photographer was shaking and white-knuckled. Hank kept looking at me nervously. The clouds were thick, and we couldn't see anything outside the plane.

There were some hills in the area, but we had to get down to see how close we were to Navojoa and where we could land. Suddenly, as the clouds broke, we were on a collision course with a smoking locomotive several hundred feet below. I pulled the plane up in a helluva hurry.

The ceiling was too low to find a landing strip, and there was no airport tower to help us. We decided to return to Hermosillo until the storm allowed more visibility. I landed and was pretty upset.

I showed Hank a sandwich he'd bought earlier at a Hermosillo restaurant. He'd given it to me on the plane. Hank and the photographer had eaten theirs despite the turbulence. They were hungry since no one had breakfast that morning. I said, "Damn it, Hank, I open up this sandwich, and what do I find in it—lettuce. Hell, you know you can't trust the lettuce down here. I'm not about to eat this sandwich."

I handed it to him and walked off. Hank hollered after me, "Here we are in a foreign country with fog, rain, and flood. We're wondering whether we're going to come out alive. You're inspecting a sandwich at the controls of a plane in a big storm. Now you're raising hell about a little piece of lettuce!"

We talked to the provincial governor about getting us more gas. He said okay and invited us to a local wedding to wait out the storm. Hank didn't want to go, saying we looked like bums. Nobody had shaved that morning, and we wore old clothes.

The governor started walking, and that was good

enough for me. I got into step, and the two others followed. A loud band played. The tequila had a terrific kick. I jolted one down and reeled back a couple of steps. The Mexicans were watching the *gringo.* I walked back to the bar, kicked it, and hollered, *"Bueno!"* They cheered. I belted down another to more cheers. Here was Goldwater, playing to the crowd, and he hadn't even started in politics.

After the sky cleared and we said *adiós,* I took Hank aside and said, "Down here, worry about the food and water—not the booze."

We delivered the medicine and other supplies and flew home. Hank never forgot that day. His tale of what happened has made Arizona air lore.

Hank never charged us or his other friends for taking care of our kids. I was determined to pay him back in a way that both of us would appreciate.

One day we drove out to Sky Harbor International Airport. I pointed to a new Air Coupe—a single-engine, two-seater prop job and said, "Hank, that's your new buggy."

His eyes bulged. Maybe he thought Peggy and I were planning to have seven or eight more kids. I told him not to worry about that.

He said, "Hell, Barry, I'm not worried about you and Peg. I'm concerned about myself. I don't know how to fly!"

Hank learned to fly and loved it.

The only air mishap I ever had occurred in that Air Coupe. It was a fluke. My brother's wife, Mary, and I were taking off from Navajo Mountain, about thirty miles northeast of Page, Arizona, when the wind picked up the plane and flipped it over onto a sandbank. Mary was learning to fly, and I was checking her out. We were slightly shaken up. The propeller and windshield were broken.

The Navajo medicine men nodded like sages. They told me the war gods who slept there had taught us a lesson for disturbing them. Some carried little pieces of that windshield around for a long time to prove it.

I bought Hank a new plane.

In those days, I did a lot of flying up in Navajo country. The tribe had some wicked winters. I'd collect food and hay and drop them to Indian families and cattle cut off by snowdrifts.

I've probably spent more time with Arizona's Indians than any other white man. It grew from an innocent boyhood interest in Indians when our family camped on their reservations. I had a trading post at the foot of Navajo Mountain with a partner, Bill Wilson, a great outdoorsman. This offered the chance to get to know many of the Navajo. All of us liked hiking and hunting. We were kindred spirits. Later, I collected the Kachina dolls of the Hopi tribe and other tribal artifacts. Finally, I crusaded for many Indian causes in the U.S. Senate.

After years of developing friendships, I began to understand Indian ways, needs, and causes. We used a Navajo name for our Scottsdale home. It's "Be-nun-i-kin," meaning "house on top of the hill." We had various aircraft during the 1964 presidential campaign, and each was given a Navajo name. The tribe gave me a Navajo name, "Chischilly," or the "curly-haired one." A tattoo on my left hand identifies me with the Smoki dancers, a Prescott organization that performs its own version of sacred Indian dances. A Kachina carving hangs from the front door of our Washington apartment.

Some of this may seem superficial. It isn't. These are outward signs of how something that began as a simple interest and historical hobby became an inner conviction and commitment. From my first campout in Indian country, the red man always seemed as much—if not more—a part of Arizona and America as any white or black person. No member of the U.S. Congress has worked longer or harder on their problems than I. They'll always be my brothers and sisters.

The Indians are the most significant example of how a private hobby—my interest in the history of the people and places of Arizona—completely invaded my public life. This became starkly clear in one of the saddest experiences of my life. In recent years, I had spent more time with the Hopi, a much smaller tribe than the neighboring Navajo. The Navajo number nearly 100,000 people on their reservation—another 72,000 live elsewhere—while the Hopi number only about 6,000.

My interest in the Hopi began when I started collecting their unusual Kachina carvings while still in my teens. Those first dolls were purchased with nickels and dimes, as well as in trade for different objects. Kachinas are religious symbols that represent the earth, wind, and other spirits. The Hopi are pantheistic.

Eventually, I purchased most of my collection of some seven hundred dolls from a Phoenix architect, John Kibbey. So the public might share in the lore of these multicolored dolls, we donated hundreds of them to the famous Heard Museum of Native American Anthropology and Art in Phoenix. A few still stand like sentinels in my home and radio shack.

Navajo leaders began an uproar in 1974, when Congress divided more than 1.8 million acres of disputed land between the two tribes. Their leaders and some tribesmen had argued over parts of the vast acreage for more than a century. Many of us in Congress had tried to settle the differences amicably, but every effort had failed. Old feuds had kept the area in turmoil. Tribal chairman Peter MacDonald and other Navajo officials blamed me and others in Congress for not swallowing all the claims coming out of their Window Rock, Arizona, home base.

The truth is that both tribes had a case. Since they were unwilling to settle it, Congress finally stepped in and divided the territory. To avoid future problems, it ordered that thousands of Navajo be relocated from the land apportioned to the Hopi. The Hopi also were to be moved from Navajo land. They were fewer in number and on smaller acreage. This was heartrending in some cases because families had lived in certain areas for as long as they could trace their ancestors. Yet it had to be done since neither side would guarantee the peace of the other. Those relocated were given new houses and land by the federal government.

Relocation still continues. The bitterness between the two tribes remains. It's not a perfect solution—there can't be with the many complex aspects of the land exchange—but Indian leaders have long used the endless feud between their tribes as a political poisoned arrow.

Anglo activists, most from outside Arizona, have adopted the Navajo as a social cause in recent years. These political and social engineers are still pouring kerosene on the old flames of tribal hatred and revenge. Most Indians and Arizonans have nothing but contempt for their invasion into what is totally an Indian issue. The Congress became involved because of its guardian or trust responsibilities.

The dispute is a personal tragedy for me—not a public fight—because there's no reason why the Navajo and Hopi should not live in peace as brothers and sisters. The outside world is cruel enough without fighting among the tribes themselves.

The Navajo-Hopi dispute became a public battle for me because it took national attention away from larger, more crucial issues facing the nation's 1.4 million Indians. I've long called for taking $1 billion a year away from foreign aid and using it to battle the dreadful educational, health, and economic problems among the 270 Indian tribes. This is not to suggest that continuing the federal dole to Indians is the answer. That long failure should be a further lesson to American society on the ills of the welfare state.

However, the Indians face immediate, overwhelming problems. Their dropout rate is greater than among any other sector of our educational system. Unemployment on reservations often runs 50 and sometimes 70 percent. Alcoholism is rampant.

Most Indians do not trust the white man, and with reason. The present federal welfare system breeds self-contempt and worse social problems. The Indians do not want favors. They want to rise or fall by themselves, but they have neither the necessary tribal leadership, in many cases, nor the educational and economic resources to aim for reasonable, realistic goals that will retain their basic cultural identity.

In many ways, the Indians are America's greatest tragedy.

Many of us are still hopeful they'll play an important role in Arizona's—and the nation's—future. One reason is that the state's twenty reservations cover a sweeping 19 million acres, more than 26 percent of our land. The federal government controls 44 percent, or 32 million acres. The state owns 9 million acres. Only 17 percent, or 12.3 million acres, is in private hands.

The cause of all Indians is a personal dream and a public hope in the crisscrossed lives of Barry Goldwater.

On entering politics, policy prohibited me from remaining in the guard. I continued flying in the Air Force Reserve and, when elected to the Senate, organized the 9999th Air Reserve Squadron, which was composed of congressmen and staff.

Before retiring as a major general from the Air Force Reserve in 1967 after thirty-seven years of active duty, I was in Washington for a painful bone spur operation. Feeling none too good, I happened to run into an old friend, Lieutenant General William Pitts, now USAF Retired. He had been the commander of the Fifteenth Air Force, Strategic Air Command. Pitts was taking an Air Force T-39 out toward Phoenix. Since I was on flying status, he could drop me off in time for Christmas. It was great luck.

However, it was difficult to know whether I'd hold up

on the flight because the pain from the operation was killing me. A friend said not to worry. He had the answer.

Pitts didn't know my secret as I struggled to get aboard the aircraft. It was a tight fit. Using a cane, I had to climb several steps that folded down from the fuselage. A narrow passageway led to the cabin.

Since I couldn't sit up, Bill removed the two seats on the right side of the aircraft. He put a mattress there. It was tough getting back to the cabin. I banged the heel that had been operated on and turned the air pretty blue. Sweat was pouring down my face by the time I made it to the mattress.

Bill took my cane and began to stow it up front. I coaxed him into giving it back to me. He climbed into the pilot's seat, and we took off.

Bill glanced back at the cane. He'd gotten the idea there was something special about it. There was. The length of the cane had been hollowed out and a flask fitted inside. Whenever I got the chance, I removed the top and took a swig of bourbon. Finally, about an hour into the flight, Bill caught me in the middle of a swig and asked, "What's that, Barry?"

"Bourbon!" I roared. That was my last word for the entire flight. No more pain. The tired and mellow passenger slept like a baby all the way to Phoenix.

Arizona is a large state, covering more than 72 million acres. My friend Jerry Foster and I have flown over almost every square foot of it. In the past twenty years or so, I've probably flown more with Jerry than anyone. Jerry started out on fixed wing and eventually became a helicopter pilot. He now flies and broadcasts for a Phoenix television station.

We don't use maps on these flights and don't talk much. Jerry toots a little about his knowledge of the terrain. One time we were headed to Black Canyon City, north of Phoenix. I pointed out an old Indian ruin on top of a mesa. Jerry said, "Hey, old-timer, I've flown over that area hundreds of times. There's no Indian ruin over there."

Jerry flew over, and we looked. Sure enough, there were the ruins. I said, "Hey, youngster, get a road map!"

We like to burn one another's butts on flying trips. About ten years ago, we rented two planes and took family and friends down to Mexico for Christmas. Jerry was loading up with maps. I said to forget it. This old pilot knew Mexico.

Three hours later, we were in a thunderstorm and running out of gas over Mexico. I mean, we were running right on empty. Jerry was bugging me on the radio: "Where are the maps, professor? How about a geography and geology lesson on good old Mexico?"

He was creaming me. We spotted a little town and landed.

"Hell, Jerry," I asked, "were you lost?"

I told Jerry not to worry—that my Spanish was *bueno*. Only the fellow in charge didn't understand me, and this *hombre* couldn't figure out a word he was saying. Jerry was laughing.

Ollie Carey, a longtime family friend and wife of the late actor Harry Carey, stepped up. In rapid-fire Spanish, she asked this guy where the aviation gas was. He beamed and rolled out enough fifty-five-gallon drums of the stuff to fly a DC-10 from there to Tokyo.

We took off and finally landed at a hideaway on Mexico's southern beaches. I walked over to Jerry and asked, "Were you lost?"

He shot me down. "Next time, I'll bring the maps."

That was his punch line to everything said for the rest of the vacation. However, I was to even the score.

When Senator Carl Hayden, an Arizona legend, died, President Johnson flew to Phoenix for the funeral. Hayden had served in the U.S. House of Representatives and Senate for fifty-seven years.

Johnson was flying by army helicopter from Sky Harbor International Airport to Gammage Auditorium at Arizona State University in Tempe. The memorial service was to be held there. Johnson was to land at the ASU football stadium a few miles away and proceed by motorcade to the auditorium.

Jerry was flying me and my pal Harry Rosenzweig to Tempe. I asked Jerry where he was going to land. He said next to the President's chopper.

I replied, "Oh, yeah?" and told him to land on the grass next to the auditorium. Jerry started arguing with me: "There's no space. Look at that mob down there. The lawn's filled with television cameras and photographers. See all those reporters and faculty? My God, there are the Tempe police and the state highway patrol. I'll bet the Secret Service are there, too. It's a zoo."

"Land!"

He was still arguing. "Where?"

"There!" I said, pointing to a patch of clear grass to the side of the auditorium.

"Aw, shit!" Jerry hollered, and put the bird down.

Jerry was right. The stuff hit the fan. It seemed every cop in town was bearing down on us—Tempe and university police, the highway patrol and Secret Service.

President Johnson's motorcade turned off Mill Avenue toward the auditorium. I stepped out of the helicopter and walked to greet the President in front of the building. The police flew by me to grab Jerry. I greeted Johnson, laughing so hard I couldn't stand straight. The President felt I'd upstaged him. When we'd arrived by helicopter, the crowd had turned our way instead of toward his motorcade.

I could hear Jerry shouting in the distance, "Go talk to Goldwater. He's the guy who did this. I'm only the pilot. See the senator, guys. Arrest him—not me!"

Jerry finally managed to convince the police I was the instigator. He avoided a Federal Aviation Administration citation. I never heard any more about it—except from

Jerry, who still taunts me from time to time: "So you finally beat Johnson! Yeah, you had to beat him!"

Jerry was another guy who was always on me for not carrying money on our trips. We flew to Los Angeles one time for a Johnny Carson roast. I was on the program.

We were picked up at the airport by a limousine with a real good-looking gal behind the wheel. We went to the roast, had a bite to eat and a few laughs, and returned to the airport with the same classy chauffeur. I said to Jerry, "Give her fifty bucks."

I could see the look on his face. He was dying. He elbowed me and whispered, "How about twenty?"

I said, "No, fifty."

He was stalling. "All I got is a ten."

I repeated, "Fifty."

He came up with his favorite phrase, "Aw, shit!" and handed her fifty. Jerry looked at me and finally said, "I'm not bringing any dough the next time."

"Neither am I," I said.

We flew home, and it was pretty quiet until we saw the lights of Phoenix. Jerry looked at me again and said, "Get a checkbook and a credit card, will ya?"

When my wife died in December 1985, Jerry was one of the first people I called. He said, "Let's go flying when you're feeling all right."

A few weeks later, he flew me up to Lake Powell on the Arizona-Utah border. Powell is one of the most beautiful lakes in the world. A magnificent stretch of red rocks borders the water for many miles.

We choppered from there to our old trading post. Then we flew to Rainbow Lodge, a hideaway my wife bought long ago. We walked around the place in silence. The only part left of the lodge was a section of cement foundation. Tears welled up in my eyes.

I'll never forget Jerry for that act of kindness. The trip took me back to our honeymoon. For an instant, the face of my beautiful young bride appeared in the emptiness of the lodge and my heart. Then she was gone. We flew home. But Peg was there—in the face of the desert and brown hills. My tears clouded the clear blue sky.

It has been fun flying with Jerry through the years. I've tried to combine the joy of flying with rediscovering my native state. This is an entry from my diary of April 17, 1981:

"Jerry Foster and I lifted off in the helicopter at 8:30 this morning from my driveway. We headed north, flying across the eastern edge of Black Mesa over the Verde River and valley. We landed on a flat slab of red sandstone near the Cathedral of Rocks.

"Jerry and I talked about how the area got its name, the geology and geography, and more about the history of the place.

"We flew to Flagstaff, where we refueled, and on to the lava beds east of the San Francisco Peaks, just south of Sunset Crater. I talked about the peaks, how they were named, and their elevation.

"We took off again for the Grand Canyon, and entered the gorge at Granite Falls. We proceeded downstream from twenty to fifty feet above the water. Finally, we circled Deer Creek Falls and landed. The creek flows out of Deer Valley from the northern rim of the canyon. It's a beautiful stream of crystal-clear water. The creek has cut through a hundred feet or more of red sandstone to where it emerges and becomes a waterfall. The water falls more than a hundred feet down into a beautiful pool, and later flows into the Colorado River.

"We spent considerable time there discussing the river, its history, and my first trip down the Colorado in the late 1930s. We enjoyed drinking the wonderful water and waded in the stream, which was extremely cold.

"We refueled at Grand Canyon Airport and flew back to Phoenix. It was simply a beautiful day."

Flying is a great adventure because it actually takes you there. Some of my most enjoyable moments have been discovering America from the air—naming mountains and rivers, picking out a city or landmark in the distance, watching clouds churning across the landscape like ships on a voyage to another planet.

It's fascinating flying at night, looking down at odd configurations of lights. Often I pick out a solitary light in the darkness and imagine it's a home with a family sitting down to dinner. One time it will be a farmer and his wife with a houseful of kids; on another occasion, a retired couple in the open countryside. I try to guess what they may be talking about, their cares and hopes. Finally, I close my eyes to better feel a kinship with these people. It's a search for the real America, far from the closed walls and some of the closed minds in Washington.

Flying has always been a natural high for me. I've never been afraid of it, although there have been some suspenseful moments. There's also suspense in driving a car or walking across a crowded city street. Flying often encourages a feeling of closeness and communication with God. Heaven is a slow, endless climb into clear skies.

People have asked more questions about one of my engineering enterprises than any other gadget. It's the electric eye I installed to raise the American flag outside our home when the sun rises and lower it at sunset. This device wasn't generally known when I began fooling with it. Now, of course, they're all over the country.

The experiment, it must be confessed, was ultimately a failure. Rain sometimes soaked the flag, making it too heavy to lift. Wind and other problems jammed the system. The headaches finally got the better of me, and the flag now rises and lowers with old-fashioned, dependable muscle power.

Some experiments were successful, some even humorous. I rigged a device behind the toilet bowl in the guest bathroom of our home. When an unsuspecting newcomer sat on the seat, a metal device tripped off a recording of my voice. It climbed up from the bowl in a not-too-inno-cent voice: "Hi, honey. How ya doin'? Can I be of any help?"

A few bashful gals have let out bloodcurdling screams. Others have dashed out dragging their britches. Some have done both.

Our mailboxes, especially in Washington, have always been full of gadgets to assemble. On many lonely eve-nings, without a wife and family there, I'd pull out a diagram to begin another project—from a musical door-bell for our apartment that played "Off We Go into the Wild Blue Yonder" to weathervanes and other gimmicks to spread a little more humor around. After my second term Peggy spent most of her time in Arizona. Her poor hearing, her wish to keep a closer watch on the children, and her dislike for the pervasive politics of the Washing-ton scene were all part of her decision.

We had a workroom off the kitchen of our five-room apartment. My handmade replicas of old black-powder pistols are still fixed to each cabinet door, a reminder of the Old West. Tools line the inside shelves. A worn sign hangs in the workroom: "Quit when you're tired!"

We've been lifelong subscribers to *Popular Mechanics.* Old copies still sit around the two bedrooms, tiny kitchen, and elsewhere. I often pick one up when at the apartment, always on the lookout for some new project to try.

In my Senate days, I'd pull out the orange juice and fix myself a peanut-butter-and-bacon sandwich—a favorite —or put a frozen dinner in the microwave to eat while reading a project's instructions. Two old bullfight posters from Spain, hanging from the walls, told one and all about a renowned matador, Don Barry Goldwater. It seems every tourist has one with his name on it.

This fellow goes to bed early, mostly by 9 P.M., and reads. A new Louis L'Amour Western is usually around. Two books from the Southwest are on the apartment nightstand now—*The Navajo Hunter Tradition* and

Southwestern Vocabulary. Many books on the military stand on the bookshelves. Two old ones still lie near my bed—*A Soldier Reports,* by General William Westmoreland, our former commander in Vietnam, and *Trident,* a study of the nuclear submarine. So does the book *Wall Street and FDR.*

I never went to sleep in Washington without seeing Arizona. Two large photos that I took decades ago—the Grand Canyon and an Arizona desert scene—hang from the wall above my bed. Scores of such photos and scenes from bygone political campaigns in Arizona and the presidential race line the walls of the apartment.

On most mornings, I climbed out of the rack about five o'clock, often to check my handiwork of the evening before. I was usually at my Senate office by 7:30 A.M. after reading the Washington *Post*'s latest liberal line. That rarely started my day well. There was some satisfaction in knowing the hours could only improve. It did since I then read *The Wall Street Journal,* the Baltimore *Sun, The Christian Science Monitor,* and the weekly news magazines when available.

For about fifteen years, before my triple coronary bypass in 1982, Judy Eisenhower, my secretary and later administrative assistant, brought me a cheeseburger with everything on it every workday. We had a standing order at the Senate dining room, depending on my schedule. This continued on our plane throughout the 1964 presidential campaign.

Some people found out about those cheeseburgers and began asking me about them. I merely replied, "I don't drink coffee and never have." I always felt the question deserved that kind of an answer—irrelevant.

I've never smoked, either. My mother told us kids that smoking and coffee would stunt our growth. The three of us have always said we were lucky she didn't say anything about booze.

This fellow was sometimes not at his best in the morning, especially if he'd caught some red-eye plane ride to return to the Senate. When faced with the cheeseburger and similar questions by dawn's early light, I often answered by pointing to a pencil sketch of myself on the office wall which showed my hair leaping out in different directions and my glasses cockeyed. Underneath a long, sour puss were these words: "When I woke up this morning, I had one nerve left, and damned if you ain't got on it!"

At the first opportunity many mornings, this old tinkerer would be off visiting one or more of the basement workshops in the Senate, usually to look for advice or help on some sideline project. The fellows in the paint, metal, carpentry, electrical, and even subway machine shop would see me coming and knew the fur was about to fly. We had some wild and woolly discussions. They were some of the happiest and most productive disagreements of my life.

I met Bill Davis, foreman of the Senate subway shop, for the first time in 1961. It was an informal and sometimes impossible partnership that lasted twenty-six years. Impossible because Bill's pal Barry was such a cantankerous old cuss who wanted to do things his way.

Bill loaned me a lot of tools, especially to retrofit parts. At one time, my office wall was overloaded with model planes. Bill and the others helped me cut the models smaller and mount them on plaques instead of picture wire. They once helped me build an organ.

I was a pain in the butt to Bill and his staff at times, but they always seemed genuinely interested in what trouble I'd gotten myself into lately. The senator from Arizona was sometimes seen on the Senate floor with grease on his hands or dirt on his pants or suit coat. Once in awhile, a fellow senator or page would give me a long, quizzical stare. I never gave a damn about it. My name kept cropping up on best-dressed lists.

Senate workers and I often talked shop in the halls. If my colleagues or visitors ever listened to some of those earthy conversations, they must have wondered whether

I was about to build a house or tear down the Capitol. The old tinkerer always remembered these craftsmen at Christmas because they had usually saved his neck on one project or another during the year.

It would get mushy if I said more about my long relationship with Davis and some of his staff. Bill had been around the Capitol most of his life—thirty years—starting with the ground crews at the age of twelve. It seems that I was the only senator who ever regularly came to the basement workshops.

Bill remembers the day I came into the shop wearing a new navy blue, pinstripe suit. I was carrying a piece of brass that needed buffing. Davis took one look at that suit and said he'd buff it. I said no, walked over to the buffing wheel, and was soon covered with lint. I finished, walked out, and never said a word. Bill now says, "He could be a stubborn man and cuss, but he always met you halfway."

In these last years, I've been on crutches and in a wheelchair a lot. It seemed almost as painful for them as it was for me. They'd watch me as I pushed along, but Goldwater was hard-nosed and never discussed his problems or pain. Neither did they. Davis says, "Now that he's gone from the Senate, I can mention the highest tribute we could give him. We called him 'Boss.'"

That was my underground life in the Senate. Above ground, I was a ham radio operator. Years ago, we organized amateur radio club station W3USS, the last three letters standing for the United States Senate. We had only a handful of members at the start, but today there are about twenty. I was the lone senator in the group. The others worked on various Hill staffs.

I had my own rig in the office, but we managed to get a larger one for the club. It had an amplifier and other equipment. We met regularly to rap about our rigs and exchange other information.

I talked a lot about radio with my friend Peter Huber, assistant superintendent of the Senate office buildings. We even examined some parts for my rig on the floor of my office one evening during a reception. No one seemed to notice. They were too busy talking politics.

My hobbies were often a relief from the daily pressures. Because of these different interests, our staff and the Capitol police used to say that I probably knew more people on the Hill than any of my colleagues.

Since coming home to Arizona, I've spent many hours in the ham shack beside the house. It's still a thrill to talk with people in different parts of the country and around the world.

After being defeated in the presidential race, I returned to this same ham shack. It was a good place to think. One day a friend, Herman Middleton, suggested we might do some real good for American servicemen in Vietnam. We could use my K7UGA station to help provide radiotelephone communication between servicemen and women in the war zone and their families in the states. I agreed faster than a jackrabbit on the run.

K7UGA—strengthened with surplus equipment on loan from the U.S. Air Force—joined Operation MARS to provide the free service. MARS stands for Military Affiliate Radio System. It's a network of ham radio stations around the world connected to similar facilities where our military are stationed. We called our operation the Bash Hal Ne Ae Club. That's Navajo for "metal that talks."

We had thirty-five volunteers in the operation. They manned the circuits around the clock. In all, we patched more than 300,000 shortwave radio calls from Vietnam into the U.S. commercial telephone system. GI families paid for connections between Phoenix and each hometown. I paid for all calls within Arizona. The operation eventually closed down in 1983 after more connections to other worldwide bases.

The crew received many awards. Some, from small groups of GIs in Vietnam, were homemade. They still hang in the shack. Among the awards and some long-ago letters of thanks from GIs in Vietnam, the other day I found a note I wrote to myself. It was dated December 24–25, 1972, after an all-night Christmas vigil at the radio. The simple words were an attempt to explain why I and the others had volunteered: "Life flows on its journey, and then we are gone from the river."

Some good remembrances from Operation Mars still return when I now begin rapping in the early morning: "The handle is Barry—Bravo, Alpha, Romeo, Romeo, Yankee."

Vietnam was an important part of the four years I spent out of the Senate—1965 through 1968. This old soldier went to Vietnam and gave many speeches about the war at the time—that we should fight it to win or get out. GIs had told me that during some of our radio chats and on visits to the war zone. On returning to the Senate in 1969, one of my first official acts was to return to Vietnam to observe the latest developments in the field firsthand. Afterward, I was doubly convinced that President Johnson's guns-and-butter policies—each weakening the other—were wrong. Time has unfortunately proved that judgment correct.

Amateur broadcasting has been one of the great joys and adventures of my life because—as in Operation MARS—it brings people together. Radio can be a very positive force among men and women in every land. I believe our country should take a greater lead in developing more agreements on direct, live, international programming.

Photography was one of my later hobbies. My wife gave me a little 2¼-inch reflex camera as a present. We had a small apartment then. It was necessary to use the kitchen as a darkroom. Peggy didn't like that because it smelled up the place.

A chance conversation got me into photography in a big way. Since I'd collected many books and historical records on Arizona, the Southwest, and Mexico, students at Arizona State University would stop by the house and use them for reference. One day a young fellow asked me if I'd ever seen a photo of Pipe Springs, Arizona. I'd been there but didn't have a picture of it. The chat made a big impression on me. It showed a need for local photographs. Obviously, there had to be many other Pipe Springs.

From then on, I carried a camera on every trip to take photos for the historical record. Later I bought a movie camera and filmed a rafting trip down the Colorado River in the summer of 1940. The 700-mile journey combined three hobbies—photography, rafting, and hiking.

I embarked on the six-week trip with five other men and three women in three boats. It was an exhausting forty-two days, filled with rapids, sharp winds, bug bites, and enough sand in different parts of my body to build a sizable kid's castle on any beach. Part of my diary on those days reads:

"Sleeping in the open under God's own sky is one of the most overrated of all acts of man or woman. Forty-two nights of huffing and puffing my lungs into the deep recesses of a rubber void, known as an air mattress, have convinced me that an innerspring has 10,000 advantages.

"Bugs of all sizes have promenaded over my body from top to bottom. Bugs with only a cursory interest have wandered over me and, with no more than a 'humph,' have let me be. Others, carrying knives, sabers, and broken bottles, have passed my way and left a diverse collection of tools of torture firmly implanted in my being. As a result of their nocturnal visits, I have as fine a collection of bumps and itches as any man ever supported. The lovely thing about these bites is they never itch until one is almost asleep."

I started showing film of that trip up and down the state, narrating it more than a hundred times. Those visits were a big help when I started out in politics. When Howard Pyle ran for governor in 1950, I knew people in almost every town we visited.

I developed my own film. At one time, I had more than 15,000 negatives and some twenty-five miles of film.

Much of that has already gone to Arizona State University. Some eight thousand negatives remain to be identified.

Photography began paying off around the country, too. Various galleries offered photo exhibits of my Indian work as well as Grand Canyon and desert scenes. More than 250 showings, including a good number in Europe, took the state of Arizona far beyond its boundaries. I eventually became an associate member of the Royal Photographic Society of London and had several books of photographs published. My scrapbooks show shots from Phoenix to Paris to Pakistan.

I spent a lot of time in Washington on my car, Spot. It's definitely unique. Some describe it less charitably. The 1969 Javelin AMX two-door sports car was called the "Slingshot" when it was introduced. The exterior is black with the inside black and red, my favorite car colors. Its Arizona license plate is K7UGA, my ham radio call letters.

For nineteen years I've been adding and removing different accessories at a cost of more than $110,000. The vehicle cost $5,000 new. It has so much wiring that an electronics engineer would have a tough time finding his way around it. Most of the car has been replaced except for the transmission and frame.

I've added more than sixty features, many of them special equipment, including the altimeter and exhaust temperature gauge from a jet fighter; a musical horn that plays sixty-four preprogrammed songs, including the *U.S. Air Force Fight Song;* a ham radio; an aircraft compass; a special stereo system developed by the Japanese; the first auto cellular phone in America and now the first voice-activated phone; custom-made Italian bucket seats; an ear-splitting alarm system; a beeper; an aircraft radio scanner; a special *Rebel Charge* musical horn; a unique fire extinguisher; and other extras.

I was driving home from the Senate on a summer evening a few years ago and stopped for a light. A well-dressed lady peered in at my dashboard. It looks like the cockpit of a jet passenger plane. She then glanced at the roof, a porcupine of antennas, and blurted, "An old man like you—you ought to be ashamed of yourself!"

A few winters ago, while home with a cold, I got to worrying about Spot. So, in a thin, old-fashioned nightshirt, this car buff went down to the basement of his Washington apartment building to check on her. Furious at my negligence, I read a long list of needed work and other oversights into my portable dictation machine. I felt much better and returned to work the next day.

Some of the staff gave me hell. They claimed I cared more about Spot than my health. Ellen Thrasher said, "That old car gives you so much trouble. Why don't you sell it?"

Ellen had just had a baby. I looked at her, shocked, and asked in a hushed tone, "Ellen, would you give up your baby?"

Nobody in the office ever criticized Spot again. Such is the sanctity of a senator's pet and hobby.

On another occasion, arriving at the office early, I forgot to leave my car keys with the staff. Spot was always parked outside the Russell Building, and one of them would normally drive it into the underground lot. That morning I was chairing a full Armed Services Committee on the 1985 Defense Authorization Bill. However, before the session began, the office and I finally straightened out the first crisis of the day—that I had the car keys. Someone would come and get them from me.

The hearing was crowded. Military brass, defense contractors, and reporters packed the place. Jim Ferguson, one of my staffers, entered through the back door of the hearing room. I spotted him and banged my gavel to interrupt the testimony. Jim was embarrassed when I motioned him to come forward. Everyone in the room was looking at him, wondering whether some emergency might halt the hearing.

"The keys," he whispered.

I handed them over and, as soon as he began to walk away, said, "Wait a minute, Jim. This is important."

I began to draw a diagram.

"What's that?" Jim asked.

"It's a diagram of a special screw," I replied. "There's no name for it. This is an exact diagram of it. You gotta see it to know it. And remember, it has to be galvanized."

"A what?" his voice seemed incredulous.

"*This* galvanized screw," I declared so emphatically that some in the audience heard me. I pointed to the drawing and demanded, "Buy one just like it. This one will secure Spot's dashboard."

The look on Jim's face said everything. No one in the world could have any comprehension of how much I cared about that car. He rushed for the exit.

My affection for Spot saved my mental equilibrium in a serious personal crisis. I received a call from our housekeeper, Lillian. She had just taken my wife to a Phoenix hospital. Peggy seemed to be slipping into a coma.

It was about 10 P.M. in early December 1985. The Senate was still in session. We were going through the annual ritual of late debate and roll calls to pass needed legislation.

A military flight out of Andrews Air Force base was available. Jim Ferguson accompanied me. We jumped into Spot and rolled. I was driving and very upset. The doctors had warned me after an earlier operation that Peggy was not entirely out of the woods, but she had a chance of making it. My wife had emphysema and other problems. One of her legs had been amputated.

My whole body began trembling. I had to get to her. Somehow I also had to calm myself. No husband could be good for his wife in such a condition. We sped down Suitland Parkway. I was trying to control myself and Spot. That was it—a flash. I said to Jim, "Got a pen and paper?"

"Yes," he said.

"Okay, here's what you have to do with Spot when I'm gone. First, fix the heater . . ."

Mentally, I took Spot apart from bumper to bumper—everything that needed fixing.

That was how I finally got control of myself. Spot and I have become family over the years.

Despite nearly two decades on the street, there are only 95,000 miles on the car. Some 35,000 are from the five-mile, twenty-minute drive between the Capitol and our apartment, in the Westchester Apartments at 4000 Cathedral Avenue, off Massachusetts Avenue. The rest were logged while motoring around the Washington metro area, and finally driving home to Arizona.

It's now time for this sinner to make a public confession. During evening rush hour for three decades, I made an illegal left turn at Wisconsin and Cathedral avenues to get to our apartment. Not only did this U.S. senator break the law over these many years, he was lucky enough never to get a ticket. That should destroy the image of the straitlaced conservative. By the way, I got plenty of blame for things I never said or did, so I never felt too guilty about not getting a ticket. Washington and I are about even.

My staff discussed my driving behind my back for years. The consensus was that I was not a speeder—true —but an "artful dodger" who impatiently gunned past the gawkers from Peoria and other parts and cut off little old lady drivers—not true because I still remember them with fondness from the 1964 campaign. Staffers also claimed I was always trying to outwit the other guy—only sometimes.

There's one more brief story about cars. It's worth telling because I love to burn Ben Bradlee, the executive editor of the Washington *Post*. I call it the *Post*-mortem because, if you manage to survive everything else in Washington, Bradlee and the *Post* will eventually get you.

Ben and his wife, Sally, invited me to dinner one evening. Sally's parents, Lieutenant General Bill Quinn and his wife, Bette, were also there. We were sitting down to eat when Ben's son, Dino, showed up. He'd just turned sixteen and had bought a 1974 Jeep. The lights weren't working, and there were a few other problems. The young man couldn't drive that evening unless the lights were fixed.

Dino and I went down to take a quick look. It took about an hour and a half to straighten everything out. We didn't know it, but everyone waited dinner. I showed up, said nothing, washed my hands for several minutes, and sat down to eat.

"Well?" Bradlee asked.

"Mark one up for Goldwater," I said.

It was the only time I ever got the upper hand on those guys.

It has been a privilege leading two lives. Perhaps, when all is said and done about the sweet life of these hobbies, I'll leave three legacies:

Ham radio operator—a lifelong friendship with many thousands of people whom Bravo, Alpha, Romeo, Romeo, Yankee has never met but spoken with around the globe. Some say those are the call letters of the world's best known ham. Let me say I'm not sure how to slice that.

Photographer—my photo books on Arizona are my last will and testament to my love for my native state. So are miles of amateur film and thousands of negatives that are being left to history.

Aviator—I leave the Barry M. Goldwater Visitor Center at the U.S. Air Force Academy in Colorado Springs, Colorado, to welcome new generations of military pilots, their parents, and all Americans. Peggy will also be remembered in the Western art and literature section of the academy library.

Part of my heart will always beat at the Smithsonian's National Air and Space Museum in Washington. Some of us spent years, after the museum was authorized by Congress in the late 1940s, trying to have the project funded and built.

Finally, during the nation's bicentennial in 1976, that magnificent monument to America's pioneer aviators was opened to the American people. The Wright brothers' plane, Charles Lindbergh's *Spirit of St. Louis,* and other historic aircraft and memorabilia are now seen by as many as 15 million people a year. The museum is the most popular in the United States and the world.

Since we're still pioneering in the skies—with the space shuttle, the Boeing 707, the Concorde, and other leaps into aviation's future—let's hope the nation will open a second such museum.

Now, as this old bird begins the descent for his final landing, it's an honor to salute the pilots I've known—fellows like General Jimmy Doolittle, Brigadier General Chuck Yaeger, General Jack Catton, General G. P. Disosway, and so many others whose wings touched mine in space and time.

My family will never forget Jimmy and Chuck saying that, for many years, every pilot in the military knew they had a copilot up there flying with them. His name was Barry Goldwater. He did his damnedest on the Senate floor to get them more flying time and better planes.

A plaque hanging from my Senate office wall reminded me each day of my obligation to our younger generation of military pilots. It carried me through some heavy thunderstorms on Capitol Hill.

The plaque was found by my friend Bill Quinn at a small shop in Seoul, South Korea. It reads:

A Pilot's Prayer

God grant me the eyes of an eagle,
The radar of a bat,
And the balls of an Army helicopter pilot.

My life and career would have been better spent in the uniform of my country. There is no greater duty or honor than defending America's liberty.

Freedom is what life and flying are all about—the will of men and women to climb above themselves, to soar with the angels, to find their own destiny. We fly higher and faster in search of greater freedom.

If, one day, someone walks into a room somewhere in these United States and finds my six-foot frame stretched out on a bed—no longer blessed with life—I want that individual to ask me if I have anything to say. I assure you that I will reply:

"Air Force—all the way!"

4

The Politics of Plain Talk

WHEN WORLD WAR II ENDED, I RETURNED HOME
more restless than ever. China, India, Burma, Britain,
and other lands had opened up new horizons. The United
States was a giant that had been awakened by the war. It
was a wide world and a big America.

Phoenix was booming. Thousands of GIs who had
been trained in the state and liked the sunny climate returned. They introduced their young wives to the open
spaces and small town atmosphere. It seemed everyone
was starting a family or a new business.

In the decade between 1940 and 1950, the town grew
from a population of 65,000 to more than 107,000. Surrounding Maricopa County soared to 332,000 people.
Our valley population had more than doubled. Yet
Arizona's sweeping 114,000 square miles contained only
750,000 people.

We were small potatoes compared to other cities and
states, but this was the big time for Phoenix. People had
money and spent it. The good times rolled with wed-
dings, baby christenings, new homes and furnishings,
business openings, job promotions, and parties galore.
Goldwaters celebrated with record sales. I was back at
the store, greeting old friends and making new ones. On
weekends, Peggy and I joined the fun. I played the trom-

bone and washboard, sang "Peg o' My Heart," and counted my blessings.

America was king of the hill. We were the guys who helped put her there. The Axis was on the ash heap of history. Freedom and democracy were safe. Jobs, kids, big hopes—we had it all. No wonder Peggy and I were so happy. And she was as gorgeous as ever. Hell, what more could anyone expect of life?

Yet I was reaching out for more—a mark, an accomplishment, something worthwhile that I could share with people in my own hometown. Not something for China or Britain, but for Arizona and America.

More and more, I was slipping away from the store to make that mark. First, it was to organize the Arizona Air National Guard. That in itself was almost a full-time job. Next, I was appointed a member of the Colorado River Commission. We in Arizona hoped the commission would help win congressional approval of the giant Central Arizona Project. The project would bring much-needed water from the Colorado River to the central part of the state. Also, I led a get-out-the-vote drive on a big local labor issue. Arizonans approved a right-to-work law. Union membership was no longer mandatory.

A half dozen projects were crowded into a day, but I stayed on at the store. The business experience was good training. I was proud of Goldwaters. It was a second home.

I first went to work at the store in 1929, after my father died. Sam Wilson, the veteran manager, became chief executive. He told me I had to learn the business from the ground up. Sam started me at $15 a week as a clerk in piece goods.

The Goldwaters stores in Phoenix and Prescott grossed about $400,000 a year in those days. We had fifty-five employees. Sam moved me from section to section. I once set a record with more than two hundred sales in a single day. Sam then moved me up to office work and finally to buying for the store. I became president in 1937, after Sam left us.

We were a quality operation—"The Best Always." Goldwaters prided itself not only on the latest and finest merchandise but on constant business innovation. We had the city's first elevators and introduced a pneumatic tube system for cash transactions.

I put in the city's first electric-eye door at the store. Crowds would stand on the sidewalk gawking, waiting to see if the eye would fail. They expected some customer to hit the closed plate glass and land on his or her rear end. It never happened.

The pneumatic tube was also a crowd-getter. Customers clogged the aisles as they watched it swoosh overhead. To loosen up the place one afternoon, I put a live mouse in one of the tubes. It shot up to our chief cashier, Clara Mains. When the tube hit the barrier at her station, the blow momentarily stunned the mouse. Clara lifted out the lifeless creature, thinking it was a toy. The mouse soon began to wriggle in her hand. Clara, a dignified, middle-aged lady, got her dander up, stood and started shouting, "I'm going to get you for this, Barry."

She didn't hesitate. I was always the culprit. Clara spotted me in an aisle and began chasing me with the wriggling mouse in her hand. I dashed from ladies' apparel to the cosmetics section, from men's suits to shirts and ties. Clara raced in hot pursuit. Customers scrambled for cover, unclogging the aisles. Finally, in exasperation, Clara threw the mouse at me. She missed. It scampered off, apparently none the worse for the adventure.

We built our reputation on being exclusive, but the staff and management were a very informal group. We worked hard, but there was never a boss-worker relationship. My brother, the finance manager, and I, on the merchandising end, were always available to talk with anyone about anything. The place was run as a family business where everybody was a neighbor. We bought a twenty-acre farm where everyone could socialize. It had cattle, chickens, a swimming pool, and some lively parties where all of us became better acquainted. Some employees cultivated victory gardens there during the war to get fresh vegetables.

I introduced a lot of sales promotions at the store—a new advertising symbol called Little Pedro, fashion shows, and even men's night on Fridays before Christmas. We stayed open late for husbands and boyfriends and served free drinks. Pretty girls modeled women's clothes and other presents. If Sam Goldwyn liked girls with good-looking legs in his Hollywood movies, why not the same for Goldwaters' customers in Arizona?

When Sam Wilson left us, Bob and I were faced with managing the operation during the Great Depression. No employee was ever let go, although everyone, including Bob and me, took pay cuts. We also reduced other expenses. Goldwaters managed to break even, although some of our friends were not so fortunate. It was a very rough time. Everyone was deeply concerned about the future.

Our employees and customers were incredibly loyal. Goldwaters and Phoenix were lifetime neighbors. I drew a lesson from that experience—that loyalty is an endless circle of goodwill. That conviction dominated my personal life and was to have a major effect on my political career, especially during the 1964 presidential campaign.

Bob ran Goldwaters after I went to war. He moved the downtown operation uptown. The store is now in the heart of the city's Central Avenue financial district. Bob continued to run the store after I came home, although he insists I was in charge. The place was that informal. We simply got together and made decisions in short order. Bob and I were always in tune. We've never gone through an entire day upset at each other. The same is true of our sister, Carolyn. To this day, we're extremely close. A few times, however, for ten or fifteen minutes, my house or theirs has sounded as though the Apaches were back on the warpath.

My interest in the store increasingly slackened. Putting on spectacular promotions and other sales stunts, like antsy-pants shorts for men, left me empty. My mind could no longer focus on merchandising. It turned to wider forums. I became a member of the U.S. Interior Department's Advisory Commission on Indian Affairs and the Arizona Interstate Stream Commission, whose decisions would affect our critical water supply. My sister, Carolyn, was already well known for her community service. She'd begun charitable and other works after graduating from the University of California at Los Angeles.

I kept expanding my community activities—the Phoenix Chamber of Commerce, Thunderbirds (a Chamber adjunct involved in charitable causes), Boy Scouts, YMCA, Masons, and Community Chest campaigns. The impetus to take on even more public service came from two developments in 1949. The local advertising club named me Phoenix Man of the Year, and people began urging me to seek public office—perhaps a seat on the Phoenix City Council.

Phoenix was not rising from the ashes, as the Greek legend would have it, but burying itself in one political scandal after another. There were about twenty betting parlors downtown. It was as easy to place a bet on a horse as to buy a sandwich. Phoenix had always been a town of live and let live. A lot of people viewed gambling as a business, like selling shirts. So the bookies were riding a comfortable horse at a friendly track. Gambling was illegal. The bookies were openly—flagrantly—defying city and state law. They were obviously paying protection money to somebody.

About forty different whorehouses were scattered throughout downtown. Women detested them. This hurt legitimate business because some refused to shop downtown. The police chief was telling the city manager that we had a clean town. The American Social Hygiene Association paid us a visit in 1949 and said, in effect, that we had a blind police chief. The police vice squad made one concession. They told the girls to turn off their lights at night. I guess the payoffs were easier that way, too.

Phoenix had other, even larger problems. The city changed its manager thirty-one times in the thirty-five years before 1950. Under our manager-commission form of government, the commission could fire the manager for almost any reason—and did. It played musical chairs, constantly shifting blame. The police chief was fired or quit eleven times from 1940 to 1950. Some may have pocketed enough to retire. At one point, gambling and prostitution were so uncontrolled that the military declared Phoenix off limits.

The city was in hock. Funds were diverted to meet each crisis. It was a wheeler-dealer government of cronies and endless payoffs. We knew it had to be cleaned up. Phoenix was no longer a horse-and-buggy frontier town, but a city of 100,000 people.

About a hundred of the city's most prominent people —old-timers who were independent of the politicians— got up a charter government committee. The idea was to elect a city council that would enforce a charter and to find and support a strong city manager.

My pal Harry Rosenzweig was one of the crusaders. He agreed to run for a council seat. A lot of people approached me to run, but I declined. The reason was that I still felt a commitment to my brother, Bob, and the store. It would be difficult to break away.

Harry invited me over to his house for dinner one evening. He pulled out a bottle of bourbon and poured some stiff ones. It was old times, old jokes, and a bunch of old lies. My head began to reel, but Harry was as smooth as silk. He was serving and tossing back those bourbons like we were drinking lemonade at a Sunday picnic. And he was stroking me like I was a prize hunting dog.

Dinner wasn't served until about nine o'clock, and the bottle looked like it had been passed around at a St. Patrick's Day parade. Harry began talking city politics at dinner, still soft and smooth, slowly laying down a velvet carpet toward City Hall. I was feeling mellow but began to smell a rat. I looked at my watch, and it was after ten. I rarely kept late hours, so I finally forced the issue: "All right, Harry, what the hell do you want?"

He said, "The boys want you to run for city council."

I replied, "Is that all you want? What the hell, I'll do it."

That was it—that quick. It wasn't the booze, nor because I could still be impulsive. Day by day, subconsciously, I'd been moving into politics. The question and answer just happened to coincide with the right time, the right place, and the right person asking me. The appearance of a fast draw was deceiving. Months before Harry asked me, I'd known I'd sooner or later crank up my political engines and fly.

Harry got off easy. I had to write a letter to my brother and Bill Saufley, our store manager, who were away at the time. It's a letter some of my old pals call "classic Goldwater"—whatever that means. The contents have followed me all my political life—for better or worse:

Dear Willie and Bob:

You both will probably think me seven kinds of a dirty bastard when you hear that I have decided to run for councilman with Harry.

I don't think a man can live with himself when he asks others to do his dirty work for him. I couldn't criticize the government of this city if I, myself, refused to help.

I don't know if we can win but, if we do, then I know Phoenix will have two years of damned good government that I hope will set a pattern for coming years and generations.

There has always been one, and sometimes two, Goldwaters who are damned fools enough to get into politics. They always did it with service in their minds. . . .

The city needs help more than any of our governments. Maybe we can give it to them. Maybe we will suffer in doing it but, in our minds, we will be doing what Americans should always be doing: helping each other.

Don't cuss me too much. It ain't for life, and it may be fun.

On November 8, 1949, out of a field of twenty-seven candidates, I was elected to my first political office—vice chairman of the new seven-member city council. I was forty years old. Our nonpartisan, broad-based cleanup crew—Christians, Jews, Mormons, and a woman—swept every precinct. More voters than ever had gone to the polls. I won a larger share of the 22,353 votes cast than any of the other candidates. The reason—straight talk.

I said that the bookies and other hustlers were cheating on taxes and robbing us blind. Some people in positions of public trust were taking payoffs. I didn't ask anybody to drive the bookies and whores out of town. My aim was to clean up city government itself. It was a question of fairness.

James Deppe, the city manager who had been widely criticized, refused to resign. He claimed his resignation would only give more ammunition to those who accused his administration of graft and corruption. Deppe stood in the doorway and wouldn't budge during our first council meeting on January 3, 1950. Finally I'd had enough. I asked him if he'd read the newspapers in the last two months—if he had any idea what the election was all about, that he'd gotten a vote of no confidence. I gave him one of those my-dog-is-gonna-bite-you looks, which he deserved, and I said, "Now, Jim, don't gum up the works here anymore."

He left, and the council appointed a new city manager.

We drove crime underground and balanced the city budget. Indeed, we had a surplus of more than $275,000 after one year in office. Phoenix received an All-America City Award for 1950 from the National Municipal League.

I raised hell in those council meetings. It never occurred to me to do otherwise. People rarely said what they meant. They beat around the bush, and it took hours, days, and weeks to get to the bottom of a problem. I really disliked that, because it was such a waste of time. So, to get people to the point, I would say in exasperation, "You're a liar" to a businessman accused of overcharging the city for library furniture, or "You're using Gestapo tactics. Get the hell off this woman's property." I said that to city housing officials who were attempting to force a woman out of her home to clear the land for a subsidized housing project.

One of my colleagues on the council bored us to sleep with his long-winded speeches. So I went to a store and bought a set of toy teeth. I put them in front of him as the next meeting was called to order. Those windup teeth started chomping just the way he always did. It brought down the house. But he never learned to shut up.

Other council members knew we wasted a lot of time by not getting to the point. But the local folk were not in a rush in those days. Wasting time was my pet peeve, so, meeting after meeting, I demanded we get to the point, take action, and move on. Sometimes I should have shortened my own speeches, especially those on local history.

Westerners often admire a man more for standing tall than being right. That might not appear to be the most politic thing to say, but it's the truth. The real trick is to stand tall and also be right. I stood tall on city spending and the budget. I tried to cut so much out of it that some folks thought I wanted representation without taxation.

We had many a Western showdown over contingency funds. I saw them as a shell game, a way to build in permanent spending without accountability. So I tried two techniques—playing dumb for a week or two, then on the attack for the next several weeks.

You'd be surprised how much can be accomplished by playing dumb in politics. No speeches are needed. You just shut up and shake your head sadly. I did it in some of those council meetings and later in the U.S. Senate. It upsets opponents. They're wondering why you're so silent. Sometimes they feel a tightening noose around the neck. That's when you hit 'em.

For the most part, I blasted the council spenders in off-the-cuff speeches. Harry would sometimes kick me under the table so I'd stop talking. I paid him no mind most of the time. Later, in the Senate, no one tried that. They knew I might kick them back.

I tried to put some of the sacred cows on the chopping block in those days. Once I told fellow merchants they should not ask the city to furnish them with free street parking outside their stores. Parking meters were needed in crowded districts and would provide income to the city. The nicest thing they said to me for weeks was that I was candid. During this time I fortified myself with a secret: "This is great fun, but I may walk away."

However, I wouldn't—and perhaps couldn't—walk away.

Few who have worked the political streets for a long time can ever call it quits. I still hop to my feet while watching a hot Senate debate on television.

A few months before I retired from the Senate, our old gang from those early city charter days held a private dinner reunion in Phoenix. Some thirteen of us who had served a term or more during the 1950s met at the home of Newton Rosenzweig, Harry's brother. With spouses, we were about two dozen people. Now in our seventies and eighties, we savored the golden moments of victory over dragons like gambling, prostitution, and those big spenders before charter rule.

We were full of a fine meal and good wine when it came time for me to say a few informal words. An odd incident—one that I hadn't thought of in more than three decades—came to mind. I recalled that, after we had closed the brothels, a madam asked to see me. She and many of her girls shopped at our store. This particular belle had been running the largest place in town but was worried about hard times in the future. So she asked if I would intercede with my fellow council members and other city officials to get her a liquor license.

This was a hot potato, so I proceeded prudently. I introduced the madam to the other members of the council so she could plead her own case.

One member, Frank Murphy, asked the chief of police what kind of record the applicant had. The chief mentioned there had been a few "incidents." Murphy insisted on knowing how many and on what charges. The chief repeatedly maintained there had been "a few." Murphy finally demanded to know exactly how many. The chief blurted out, "Seventy-two arrests—for the usual."

I gulped. In fact, I almost fell out of my seat.

The madam was quite upset when she didn't receive the license. She told me she'd never vote for reform again, adding, "We and the bookies got you elected, and you fellows put us out of business."

It was the first time I'd heard that one. There was apparently some truth to what she said. Some of the higher-class operators had bet on us because they thought we would run the lower class out of town—not those with select clientele.

The moral of the story is: Beware of political promises —even those you never made.

I was about to undertake a big political promise. A fellow by the name of Howard Pyle and I teamed up in 1950. Howard was a veteran newsman who had covered World War II for a Phoenix radio station. He was a strong Republican.

Both of us came home from the war curious about the future of Phoenix. We were soon captured by the town's new dynamism, new business, new people.

Most of the newcomers were from the Midwest and upper-tier states—Republican territory. We thought it might be time to introduce the two-party system to Arizona. Registration was ten to one Democratic in some

areas, six to one in others, and three to one Democratic
in the most Republican districts.

Up to that point, in the thirty-eight years since Arizona statehood in 1912, only two Republicans had been
elected governor and only one had managed to win a seat
in the U.S. House of Representatives. (That dominance
has now been reversed. Only one of Arizona's five-mem-
ber delegation in the U.S. House is a Democrat, the veteran Morris Udall, and our two Senate seats are split
between Dennis DeConcini, a Democrat, and John Mc-
Cain, a Republican, who succeeded me. The state had a
Republican governor, Evan Mecham, before he was removed.)

But in 1950, even some Democrats didn't like the odds
—strictly one-party power. They were willing to vote Republican if we came up with some good candidates and
programs.

One spring morning in 1950, the state's young Republicans were holding their annual convention in downtown
Phoenix. Pyle had addressed them with an old-fashioned
fire-and-brimstone speech characteristic of early Western
politics. Though not then a candidate, he lit a political
bonfire and eventually won the nomination for governor.

I was aching to take on the Democrats in a good fight.
So the next morning, I went over to the radio station
where Pyle worked and offered him my congratulations.
The news had come over my car radio the previous night.
On hearing it, I'd driven straight back from the desert,
where I'd been shooting photos. I was so excited that I
hadn't gone home to shave or change clothes.

Neither of us was convinced the GOP could beat the
Democrats for the governorship. They were very strong
and had nominated Anna Frohmiller, who for years had
been unbeatable as state auditor.

Yet there was some chance we could win. Pyle was well
known throughout the state from his many years in
broadcasting. He was a good, intelligent man. We'd work
our butts off, and maybe the Democrats would get cocky.

Pyle said he needed $50,000 to run. I told him that if it would help, I'd serve as his campaign manager and fly him around the state. We shook hands and took off.

Two of my hobbies, flying and photography, began to pay off. I knew folks in just about every town, since I'd flown into most and had shown films and photos in the others.

We invoked the names of every good public figure in Arizona history, from Governor George W. P. Hunt to U.S. Senators Henry Fountain Ashurst and Carl Hayden —all Democrats. Pyle and I said we were fair-minded citizens and would ally ourselves with any good Arizonan.

I was to invoke all their names many times in the future, particularly Hayden's, because we were good friends. His bust now sits on a pedestal in the Russell Senate Office Building, where I had my last office. Hayden was a representative in Congress from 1912 to 1927 and a U.S. senator from 1927 through 1969. He spent fifty-seven years in Congress, longer than any other individual.

Pyle and I would go into a bar and shake a few hands. I'd say, "Just put the governor's drinks up here on the bar."

I called Pyle "governor" to get a little respect and let folks know we meant business. Then I'd say, "If the governor doesn't get to the drinks, I'll personally look after 'em. No waste in this administration!"

That always got a good laugh and loosened folks up. The word would get out, and we'd start walking around town. Sometimes a kindly local would drive us. We'd finally get a crowd at city hall, in some park, or at a baseball field. That was Arizona politics thirty-five years ago. I loved it because I liked to shake a man's hand and look him in the eye.

My confidence in winning grew as Pyle and I traveled around the state. We flew down to Bisbee for an evening rally. That was the home of the Lavender Pit, a copper mine named after Harry Lavender, who ran the Phelps-Dodge Copper Company.

The rally was in a park across from Lavender's house. Of course, he heard Pyle's speech over the public address system.

After the talk, I said we should pay a courtesy call on Lavender. What the hell, he might as well meet the new governor.

Well, Lavender and I didn't see eye to eye. He said we didn't have a Chinaman's chance of winning. I told him to put his money where his mouth was. Of course, Lavender did. At that moment, I knew we would win. I really had to be confident to make that bet. This fellow is not a gambler.

To me, it was always crucial to show confidence. Never let the other guy see you look down or hesitate. Let 'em know you're in there to win. But make sure you back that up with twenty hours of campaigning every day. I introduced Pyle to the twenty-hour day. He was glad when the campaign was over, but I was just getting my engine warm.

Pyle won in an upset by fewer than three thousand votes. I was jubilant. The Republican Party was coming of age in Arizona. Maybe we were finally on our way to becoming a two-party state. None of the Democrats was too big. I was ready to challenge their giant—Senator Ernest W. McFarland, the Democratic majority leader of the U.S. Senate. At the close of 1952, McFarland was completing his second term. He was very popular throughout the state. My friends said if I ever opposed him, he'd saw me in half.

Senator Everett Dirksen, the Illinois Republican, came to Phoenix in 1951 to address state Republicans. Peggy and I attended a cocktail party for him on the terrace of the old Adams Hotel in downtown Phoenix. The state legislature had met for years at the Adams, the scene of more deals than any pawnshop in town.

Midway through the reception, Dirksen called us off to

a corner and quietly urged me to run against McFarland. The Wizard of Ooze, as the senator came to be known for his flowing orations, was a man of considerable charm and persuasion. I felt overwhelmed. Here was a veteran national politician coming into my home town, and he not only knew my name but suggested I run to help him in the Senate.

Who had told Dirksen that this political newcomer might defeat the veteran McFarland, the Senate majority leader? If a single person besides Dirksen ever believed that possible, I never heard from him. I would be at least a fifteen-to-one shot, and that's a lot in a two-horse race. Yet I wasn't scared. I wanted to challenge McFarland. I was fed up with President Franklin D. Roosevelt's New Deal, especially the ballooning federal government and its increasing invasion of our lives, and President Harry Truman's no-win policy in Korea.

There was one big hurdle to leap before running—Peggy's O.K. My wife was a private person who preferred life with her husband and four children—not out in public.

We had a long talk. Peggy expressed reservations. She said the Democrats were strong in the state. They also controlled Washington and had a strong grip on the entire country. Any Republican would have a long and difficult battle, not only in Arizona but after he got to Washington. For a nonpolitician, she was very perceptive.

On the personal side, Peg said I was too direct and candid to be successful in politics. She said I'd get hurt and disillusioned with the endless promises and compromises needed to survive. She didn't want to see me harmed.

Peggy expressed doubts about picking up the entire family and moving us into the twenty-four-hour whirlwind of Washington politics. Also, she explained, I could not myself be certain that I would like such a life, more than two thousand miles from longtime friends and the quieter, more informal outdoor life of sunny Arizona.

State and national politics would invade our family privacy, she insisted, and I was so happy at home among old friends. Peggy had clearly seen our conversation coming. She had prepared all her ammunition. She was emotional, yet quietly logical. Finally she asked, "Are you really sure you want to do it?"

"Yes," I responded.

Peg replied with the calm graciousness that always characterized her, "All right, Barry, if that's what you want."

Peggy often sacrificed—for me, the children, friends. She was the most charitable, compassionate, loyal human being I've ever known.

One of my first decisions in the race was to support Dwight D. Eisenhower over Senator Robert Taft for the GOP presidential nomination. That upset some old-time Republicans, to put it mildly. About half the regulars protested. Some indicated they might not support me. I felt that Ike was a fresh political personality, he could win, and the party needed a new beginning.

McFarland apparently thought I was a loser. The summer polls showed he had such a large lead that it would take a miracle for me to win. So McFarland remained in Washington, and Frank Beer, one of his aides, campaigned for him. Beer had one speech—that I was a country club Republican who knew more about being a playboy than I did about politics.

I went on the attack around the state in the summer and fall of 1952. At every stop, I said I was not a "Me Too" Republican who rubber-stamped the latest whims of the country's Democratic majority—especially Harry Truman.

I used a lot of one-liners about McFarland because that seemed to get us more publicity— "the darling of the Truman Gang" and "the junior senator from Arizona." Although he'd been in the Senate for a dozen years, McFarland was still a pup compared to Senator Hayden. Truman had many political liabilities, including corruption charges surrounding some appointees. So we put up signs along the state's highways with a ditty like those of Burma Shave:

> Mac is for Harry;
> Harry's all through.
> You be for Barry
> 'Cause Barry's for you.

I fired away at America's new super state—burgeoning federal spending and a bloated bureaucracy. The next speech assailed our weak conduct of the war in Korea. McFarland tried to defend the conflict as a "cheap" war. That was a big mistake. It wasn't "cheap" with American boys dying. The State Department was another target— an outfit that had more wishbone than backbone in facing the menace of international communism.

I called for a balanced national budget, greater self-reliance across the spectrum of American life, more power to local government, a mightier military, and stronger, better-directed opposition to communism.

These issues may seem like clichés today, but I was talking a new politics. It offered new national and international policies and direction—a clear-cut alternative to the New Deal.

For sentimental reasons, I opened the campaign on the Yavapai County courthouse steps in Prescott. I knew Big Mike and Morris would be there watching from the shadows. Nonetheless, Buckey O'Neill, the longtime political opponent of Morris, must have been around, too. The podium lights suddenly disappeared in the middle of my speech, and I had to finish by flashlight.

I read the speech because Steve Shadegg, my campaign manager, didn't want me to talk from notes any more. He was worried about some of my spontaneous one-liners. Shadegg cautioned that an unfriendly reporter might try to play up a phrase or two out of context. I was to learn that bitter lesson later.

The campaign went well, with long hours making up
for a lack of funds. McFarland rushed home for the last
three weeks of the campaign when it appeared that a
political miracle might be in the making.

The AFL-CIO tried to save him. That was because I'd
helped pass the state's right-to-work law. A few days before the election, flyers were distributed showing a carica-
ture of Josef Stalin winking and asking: "Why Not Vote
for Goldwater?"

I immediately went on television, to explain that we
hadn't done it. Someone connected with labor hoped to
show that we had put out the flyers to win sympathy for
ourselves. We finally learned that labor activists had
printed and distributed the flyers.

I rode to victory on Ike's coattails and McFarland's
overconfidence. The win spelled trouble with big labor.
Most of the Republicans who had fought it hard around
the country were defeated. I won against a Senate leader
after directly challenging the union bosses. They never
forgave me.

Harry and I went over to the Rosetree Bar in downtown Phoenix after the vote was counted and collected on
a few bets. I never looked on it as a gamble. It was a way
of showing confidence against the political odds. They
had a blackboard showing the odds in front of the bar,
and at one time the odds had been higher than fifteen to
one against me. We placed our bets then. In the final days
of the campaign, the contest was about even money.

It was a close race—a seven-thousand-vote victory—
but still miraculous by Republican standards in Arizona.

Pyle was reelected governor, and John J. Rhodes, who
was to serve with distinction for the next three decades in
the U.S. House of Representatives, eventually rising to
minority leader, also won in a three-way GOP triumph.
Arizona had indeed become a two-party state.

I arrived in Washington on New Year's Eve of 1953 to
begin work in the Eighty-third Congress. It was my
forty-fourth birthday. Peggy and my mother were with

me. It was a historic occasion for Mun. She wanted to see the swearing-in ceremony with her own eyes.

On January 3, my friend Carl Hayden accompanied me to the well of the Senate chamber for the swearing-in ceremony. Standing there amid the shadows of past senatorial giants, I felt overwhelmed by my own inadequacies. I was not a scholar or even an experienced legislator. Not an urbane sophisticate, wise in the ways of power and political manipulation, or even one of those slow-talking but shrewd country judges from the South.

I took comfort in the oath to support and defend the Constitution of these United States. I was at home with the Constitution. I told myself that enterprising America, in the surge of new nations around the globe, was a good representative of rising expectations. Our Declaration of Independence and Constitution were reshaping the notion of government in the emerging countries. Political institutions would be responsive to popular opinion and not encroach on the personal liberties of their citizens. We were the world's real revolutionaries. Our principles were lighting political fires never dreamed of by Lenin or world communism.

Watching my colleagues take their oaths of office, I thought about my own goals in the Senate. They centered on my campaign theme and were to dominate my entire political career.

I had little interest in streamlining government or in making it more efficient, for I meant to reduce its size. I did not undertake to promote welfare, for I proposed to extend freedom. My aim was not to pass laws but to repeal them. It was not to inaugurate new programs but to cancel old ones that do violence to the Constitution, or that have failed in their purpose, or that impose on the people an unwarranted financial burden.

I would not attempt to discover whether legislation is needed before I determined whether it was constitutionally permissible. And if I were later to be attacked for neglecting any constituent's interests, I would reply that I had been informed that their main interest was liberty and in that cause I was doing the very best I could.

The moral framework of the Constitution was my conscience. These thoughts, old and new, were my intellectual and spiritual roots. They were the basis of my political vision. The future would depend primarily on proven principles.

I never believed that anything I said publicly about the conservative philosophy was particularly inspired. I was born and raised a conservative. I didn't know any other way to think. As I grew up, I began to read and discuss new conservative literature. These "conservative doctrines" seemed to me to be as much a part of life as walking down the street or watering your horse. I never understood people who described such beliefs as unique or novel. But then, I never bought FDR.

My wife and mother witnessed the ceremony—simple, brief, but inspiring—for the second Republican senator from Arizona since it had become a state.

On February 18 I spoke for the first time as a senator. My speech, which was not much longer than my oath of office, was against federal price supports for the cattle industry. On May 12, four months after assuming office, I delivered my first major speech on the Senate floor. It was a long attack on federal price controls. President Eisenhower sent me a three-word accolade through a White House aide, "Atta boy, Barry."

I had hoped to be named to the Senate Armed Services Committee, but as a freshman I was named instead to Labor and Public Welfare and to Commerce and Banking.

There were few conservatives in Congress during those days. Although Dwight D. Eisenhower had become the first Republican president in twenty years, the nation was still moving left. Liberalism dominated not only the country's political and educational lives but the media. It was extremely difficult for a conservative to be heard, much less understood.

From those early days in the Senate, I never accepted the notion that conservatism was a primer for the past—that we did not have a vision of or faith in the future. We saw tomorrow in the hands of the many, not the self-anointed few.

For forty years, the nation's liberals had conjured up false conservative, capitalistic stereotypes—of selfish people with inordinate wealth, intellectually rooted in a dead yesterday, a contradiction to the challenges of the new atomic age.

Instead, liberals would plan our lives for us under the banner of Democratic administrations and the ever greater flow of federal largesse. They would build the Great Societies of the future.

Behind all the promises of the planners lay a cynical contempt for the individual freedoms which make Americans different from most of their contemporaries around the world. My political mission was to restore the emphasis on those individual freedoms despite the welfare state. It was also a private promise to one man—Barry Goldwater. And maybe to those beleaguered souls who shared another vision of America—not the New Dealers who would legalize their direction of our lives under the guise of economic grants and other giveaways, but conservatives who would free us from the grip of federal bureaucracy and inspire us to control more of our own destiny.

I sought no less than a new order and direction for American society. It seemed at the time like a cry in the wilderness. My aim was to make it a national cause. In a phrase, conservatives wanted to free the country from Roosevelt's economic, social, and political engineers.

In 1988 these are respectable political views. In 1953 they were revolutionary rhetoric.

Despite the hopes of the freshman senator from Arizona, these high-minded thoughts quickly floated down from the political clouds to reality. Ohio's Senator Bob Taft, the GOP minority leader, wanted a businessman—

citizen Goldwater—on the Labor and Commerce committees. It was that simple.

The decision was a stroke of fortune. In 1955 the labor issue would propel me into national attention.

I began attacking big labor's sweeping influence in Congress. The rank-and-file membership of unions was being forced to contribute to Democratic Party candidates. I criticized the political slush funds of the bosses, not the trade union movement or its membership. Various kickbacks and other abuses of union welfare funds began to surface in Congress and elsewhere. Union leadership tried hard to keep the lid on, but Congress launched the Select Committee on Improper Activities in the Labor or Management Field. The media later dubbed it the McClellan Rackets Committee after our Democratic chairman, Senator John McClellan of Arkansas. Senator John F. Kennedy was on the committee. His brother Robert became chief counsel.

The national television networks began broadcasting the hearings live after dramatic confrontations erupted between the eight-member committee and union bosses Dave Beck and Jimmy Hoffa. The hearings disclosed how Beck, the West Coast chief of the International Brotherhood of Teamsters, had stolen hundreds of thousands of dollars from the union. They also revealed his kickbacks to certain large companies and other similar maneuvers. Beck was later sentenced to prison on graft and corruption charges.

The Kennedys took on Jimmy Hoffa, the Teamster kingpin himself. They attempted to link him with beatings, intimidation, even killings.

I questioned both Beck and Hoffa at length, but the Kennedy-Hoffa fight was merciless. It was a battle of ruthless tactics, mutual threats and bitter personal exchanges. Bobby Kennedy had every top enforcement weapon of the federal government at his command, from the FBI to the Senate's own investigators, and he used them without mercy. Bobby and Jimmy Hoffa didn't like one another. They exploded in sharp exchanges inside and outside the committee—in corridor confrontations and phone calls and through emissaries. The personal vendetta would have made some legendary Western gunfights seem like children's bedtime stories.

Bobby was right in seeing that Hoffa was giving the entire labor movement a black eye. Hoffa ruled the union by muscle and employers by threats—and acts—of violence. Bobby was doing the labor movement's dirty work, cleaning up its house for them. It was only after Bobby beat Hoffa at his own game—the bully on the block—that Hoffa and his men were expelled from the AFL-CIO.

I and other GOP members of the committee tried to fire up a similar investigation of Walter Reuther's United Auto Workers. The Kennedys, because of Reuther's strong financial and other support of Democrats, backed away from investigating the UAW in depth. It fell to me to do it.

I went into Detroit, the UAW's home territory, and made two speeches assailing how unions in general and the UAW in particular were abusing the workingman's trust. Reuther blasted back by calling me a "fanatic" and the country's "number one anti-labor baiter."

The battle made national headlines for a year. The hearings, with more than 1,500 witnesses filling forty volumes of testimony, outraged millions of Americans. In 1958, when I came up for reelection, organized labor named me its number one enemy. They poured men and money into an all-out fight but failed to defeat me. Their funds and manpower had little or no effect because organized labor had long been viewed with suspicion in Arizona. Convictions for corruption among its leaders and a growing number of criminal charges against them also hurt their campaign against me.

In 1959 President Eisenhower and most senators supported a labor reform bill written by Senators John Kennedy and Sam Ervin, both Democrats. The bill passed, ninety-five to one. I was the lone opponent, calling the measure ineffective. That was the most significant vote of my first term in the Senate.

President Eisenhower took me aside at a White House reception and asked why I had voted against the bill. His aides had advised him it was a reasonable compromise. I told Ike the measure was a fraud for three reasons: It did little to reverse the control of unions by organized crime; it was too weak and ineffective to deal with union corruption; and, finally, it provided no real protection against secondary boycotts. Unions not involved would battle employers to aid their colleagues and would expect similar help when they wanted it.

The President asked his staff to check out the proposal more thoroughly. They did and agreed with my conclusion. To his credit, Ike went on national television and attacked the Kennedy-Ervin bill as weak and inadequate.

The Senate took up the measure again and did a flip-flop, voting ninety-five to two against the Kennedy-Ervin bill—one of the most stunning reversals I ever saw in the Senate. The Landrum-Griffin bill—a still inadequate but tougher version that had been adopted by the House—was finally approved. I voted for it as something better than nothing.

I learned a lot about the Kennedys during the maneuvering on those bills. I kicked myself for not having recognized what they were doing earlier. They had backed away from delving into Reuther's questionable use of UAW funds and similar activities because the nation's top labor boss could hurt them politically. None of us on the committee knew it at the time, but the Kennedys were already laying the groundwork for Jack's run for the White House in 1960. Reuther had to be let alone at all costs.

That is one reason why I eventually considered running against Kennedy for the presidency. One big battle would be over the changing role of organized labor in American society. The broad corruption of union leadership was masked by a self-serving loyalty to Democratic candidates. Union bosses were bribing the Democrats with millions of votes so they could not only hold up employers but steal from their own members. Events have justified my concerns, but I was hit with a lot of personal and political abuse at the time.

In the years that have passed, unions have increased their financial help to the Democrats. They have every right to do so, but the pervasive influence of such money is making reelection to Congress even more of a spoils system. Another development appears even more significant. Union leadership has manipulated the union apparatus so that it has taken on more and more of the operations of a political party. This is not merely peer pressure to vote Democratic but phoning voters, driving them to the polls, and other work that is constantly increasing.

Unions are always prepared to offer campaign funds and receive support as an organized, militant constituency. They still strike fear and foreboding into politicians because they have effectively been the third most powerful political party in this country for the past half century.

The power of unions has clearly diminished and continues to fall; membership is smaller and its political muscle weaker.

To a significant degree, the effectiveness of union leadership pressure on members to vote Democratic has lessened. So, too, has the unions' ability to hide how they spend their money.

I was convinced it was necessary to fight unions in the trenches—no surrender and no negotiated peace. In those days, unions were tough. When they fought, they went to war. I respected that. I did the same.

My fights with unions have never ceased. Various union leaders have accused me of all kinds of nefarious deeds over the years, the most notorious being the claim that I was personally involved with union racketeers.

On the morning of November 4, 1955, a man by the name of William Nelson started his truck, and it exploded outside his Phoenix home. It was soon discovered that Nelson was really Willie Bioff, a convicted labor racketeer. He had previously turned state's evidence and sent other underworld figures to prison.

Bioff had been a muscle man for unions in Chicago, New York, and Hollywood. He began to receive national attention when some film studios accused him of forcing payoffs under threat of union trouble. Bioff later admitted he had extorted more than $1 million from movie producers alone.

My acquaintance with Bioff began during my senatorial campaign in 1952. My wife's uncle Paul Davies brought a man named Bill Nelson by our store to meet me. The two apparently knew one another fairly well. After I was elected, Nelson returned and asked if I remembered him. I said that I did and recalled he had sent a check for $1,300 to my campaign headquarters.

Nelson said, "My real name is Willie Bioff."

I knew the name vaguely from the newspapers but didn't connect it with any illegal union activities. Bioff seemed a pleasant individual and asked me out golfing and to his home. My wife and I saw nothing wrong in it, although we didn't know him well. Her uncle had mentioned that Bioff often played golf with members of the FBI, and that at least one judge went to his home.

I met Bioff several times over the next few years. After we got to know each other socially, he began to explain how unions used enforcers to get what they wanted from their membership and various businesses. That's when the red flag went up. I asked him how he knew all this. Bioff said he had worked for various unions, but he didn't reveal his background. Needless to say, with all the battles I was having with union leadership, I found these discussions more than interesting. I didn't break off the talks but decided to find out more about him. Peggy and

I didn't see Bioff and his wife again until a chance encounter one night at the Las Vegas airport.

We had gone there since I was a speaker at a convention of the American Mining Congress. When we met, Bioff mentioned they were having trouble getting back to Phoenix since their commercial flight had been delayed by mechanical problems. He asked how we were returning. I said we had rented a plane, and I was flying it back. They asked to hitch a ride, and we said okay.

I realized how it might look—here was the crusader against union abuses chauffeuring a union racketeer out of Las Vegas. So I phoned columnist Westbrook Pegler, who had written a lot about Bioff, and explained what had happened. Pegler dismissed the incident as unimportant. As best as I can recall, he never wrote a word about it.

A book *(The Green Felt Jungle)* later attempted to establish a close link between me, my friend Harry Rosenzweig, Bioff, and Gus Greenbaum, a Las Vegas racketeer. Greenbaum was stabbed to death with his wife at their Phoenix home in 1958.

The fact is, as major Phoenix store owners and political figures, Harry and I knew many people in the city. Greenbaum had operated a Phoenix grocery store before taking over a Las Vegas casino. We'd met him at various civic functions. He was, after all, a local resident.

In 1976, after Phoenix newspaper reporter Don Bolles was killed when his car blew up, out-of-town newsmen dug into my "association" with Bioff and Greenbaum. Bolles had been investigating organized crime just before he died.

My brother, Bob, and Rosenzweig had often gone to Las Vegas to gamble. Both knew reputed mob figures there. Neither has ever denied it. However, *The Green Felt Jungle* and subsequent newspaper articles tried to link me to these figures simply because my brother and a friend knew them. Presumably, I might be guilty of something.

In all these years, despite the book and similar innuendos in the press, the media have been careful to avoid a specific charge that I have obtained any favors from Nevada gambling operations. They write by suggestion. Some have even suggested I may have chased Las Vegas showgirls. Again, innuendo and implication, never a charge. That is one of the rotten aspects of journalism, publishing rumor and then burying corrections in a few lines of type or seconds of broadcast time that rarely receive equal prominence. I believe the media should live by a more honorable code. They should publicly apologize for errors that reflect adversely on anyone, explain how or why they made the error, and offer that retraction in a position of equal prominence in the print media or the same time slot for radio and television. They should be forced to live by the same accountability as do all public figures.

Other union allegations in the book and other media were a crude attempt to embarrass me as a Jew. It was claimed that Phoenix had a Jewish Mafia that was closely linked to the Nevada underworld and other vice.

My family and other Jews who came to Arizona established a long, clear record of hard work and exceptional public service in the state, far beyond their small number.

Jews began arriving here in 1854, at the time of the Gadsden Purchase, when the United States bought some thirty thousand square miles of Arizona and New Mexico for $10 million from Mexico. They came to Arizona from New York and Philadelphia, Illinois and Kansas, as well as Colorado and California, like my grandfather and uncle.

They became cattlemen and timbermen. Some traded with the Indians. Many forgot their heritage—their Jewishness—because they were more concerned with hitching up their wagons and gunbelts in the raw territory.

There was never a Jewish group of any kind in the state until the Tombstone Hebrew Association was formed in 1861. Only about five hundred Jews lived in

Arizona in 1907. By 1920, when I was eleven years old, there were fewer than 1,200 Jews here.

Jews were elected to leadership posts throughout the state without any real alliance among themselves or a single report of anti-Semitism among those early settlers. In addition to my family, other Jews elected to public office in those days were Emil Ganz, twice elected mayor of Phoenix, and A. Leonard Meyer, who served in the same post. Jews were also elected to top offices in Tucson and other towns. Harry and Newton Rosenzweig have held virtually every public service post in the Valley of the Sun over the past fifty years.

Jews always mixed in the community. There was never a Jewish ghetto in Phoenix or any other Arizona city. The Valley of the Sun has been remarkably free of anti-Semitism or similar intolerance, although there have been a few exceptions.

When I came home from World War II, there were about three thousand Jews in the Phoenix area. They had two temples with one rabbi at each. The valley now has about 45,000 Jews with eighteen synagogues and twenty-four rabbis. The Phoenix metro area ranks nineteenth in the country in Jewish population. Nearly half the Jewish residents have arrived in the past decade. Jews now settle in Phoenix in larger numbers than any other group.

Neither my father nor any of our family ever took any part in the Jewish community. We never felt or talked about being half Jewish since my mother took us to the Episcopal church. It was only on entering the power circles of Washington that I was reminded I was a Jew.

I never got used to being singled out in that way. My answer was always the same. I'm proud of my ancestors and heritage. I've simply never practiced the Jewish faith or seen myself or our family as primarily of the Jewish culture. In the jargon of today's sociologists, we've been assimilated. We're Americans.

The allegations about Jews were part of a larger political war. If even a vague rumor could be floated that I, my family, or some Jewish friends might be enriching ourselves through the underworld, union bosses might be able to put a leash on the old bulldog from Arizona because he'd be compromised. It's one of the oldest political tricks in the book. I'm surprised that some reporters were that gullible.

I haven't enriched myself either in the U.S. Senate or in private life. I have never taken a dime of payola. I don't know how to be any clearer than that. In fact, odd as it may seem, money has never had any particular attraction for me.

Peggy and I were unable to make ends meet on my Senate salary. Over the years, we spent about $1 million of my and her savings to pay our bills. Part of that came from my share in the sale of the three Goldwaters stores to the Associated Dry Goods Company of New York in 1962. We had been grossing some $7 million a year since the early 1960s and had about six hundred employees. The new owners kept the name Goldwaters, so we were pleased.

Neither of us ever viewed spending these savings as a personal loss, nor did we discuss it outside the family. The two of us simply chose to live our lives as we did.

We built a big home in Phoenix because we had a large family. We collected some fine Western art. Also, we purchased an apartment in Washington. The money involved was relatively little by today's standards. The property has increased in value over some thirty-five years to perhaps $3 million today. All of that will go to our four children and ten grandchildren.

If I've made money from organized crime, or even from a legitimate business investment, such as real estate, I'd like some prospector to come up on my hill and find it for me. I can put the funds to good use.

I believe the old union bosses and the Mafia, wherever they may be, would consider me a financial flop. I wouldn't argue the point with them.

I look back on my battles with the country's union

leadership as worthwhile. There have been major changes in union operations, from the handling of pension funds to greater accountability by their officials.

My fight was never with rank-and-file membership. I am not and have never been antiunion and indeed have been a union member myself. I'm against some of their crooked officials and the manipulation of their membership for the leadership's own purposes, particularly political regimentation.

Organized labor has lost some 3 million members in the past decade. The sharp decline occurred while the total number of American workers increased. The downward spiral actually began in the late 1950s. There are many reasons for the drop in membership, from the decline of U.S. smokestack industries to the rise of nonunion firms when the transportation industry was deregulated. Foreign imports are a big factor, as is the increase of less well organized service industries. In my view, the corruption and arrogance of union leadership have also played a role.

Friends have asked me why I waged some of the wars. Many of the senators around me were so much more seasoned and capable of taking on powerful opponents—established leaders like Walter George and Richard Russell of Georgia, Everett Dirksen and Paul Douglas of Illinois, John Stennis and James Eastland of Mississippi, Homer Capehart and William Jenner of Indiana, Henry Jackson and Warren Magnuson of Washington—to say nothing of standouts like Hubert Humphrey of Minnesota, John Sparkman of Alabama, Mike Mansfield of Montana, Lyndon Johnson of Texas, Sam Ervin of North Carolina, Harry Byrd, Sr., of Virginia, and George Aiken of Vermont.

This is not to suggest they didn't wage major battles too. They did. But the young senator from Arizona was an upstart. I wasn't in their class. Many of my colleagues considered me a wild Westerner. I simply felt I was right.

I was to learn that integrity and fairness wear no party

label. Hubert Humphrey, with whom I disagreed across the entire political spectrum, was one of the most honorable men I have met in my life. We respected one another in the common realm of human decency, so much so that each of us often joked about the other in public.

The day of Humphrey's funeral I was barely able to walk because of an operation, but I would not have stayed home even if I had to crawl. Hubert was a clean fighter.

One of the big question marks in my early Senate life was my relationship with Dwight D. Eisenhower. I was grateful to Ike from my first day on Capitol Hill because I had ridden into the Senate on his coattails in 1952. I genuinely liked Ike and saw him as the leader of new and big change in the country.

However, my unwavering support of his leadership changed on April 8, 1957. It was a promising day. Weeks earlier, I had been invited to the White House not only for lunch but also cocktails to discuss my 1958 reelection campaign. It was also the day I attacked Ike's new federal spending plan. I was shocked by Eisenhower's proposed $71.8 billion annual federal budget. It was the largest peacetime budget in history.

Like President Reagan, Ike was immensely popular with the American people. My speech on the Senate floor attacking the proposal was a big risk. I also had mixed emotions about the remarks because they criticized a friend.

Some of my GOP colleagues in the Senate passed the word that they couldn't figure out me or the speech, but there was nothing mysterious about what I had said. I had declared that Ike's budget "weakens my faith in the constant assurances we have received from this administration that its goal is to cut spending, balance the budget, reduce the national debt, cut taxes—in short, to live within our means and give our citizens the maximum personal benefits from their endeavors."

I just didn't understand Ike. During the 1952 campaign he had said, in the clearest terms agreeing with Ohio Senator Robert Taft, that he'd reduce federal outlays to $60 billion by fiscal 1955. Yet he proposed to spend nearly $11 billion more than that in 1957. We were not at war, nor did the country face any national emergency necessitating such spending.

I mentioned giving the address "with the deepest sorrow." Headlines proclaimed that Goldwater had broken with Eisenhower. That wasn't true. I wasn't about to pass up a White House lunch and cocktail party, and didn't. The word over the hors d'oeuvres was that Ike was upset with me.

We conservatives were determined to reverse the policies of "moderate" Republicans who were little more than "Me Too" Democrats. Eventually, frustrated because Ike and the "moderates" would not cut back their spending policies, I called the Eisenhower administration a "dime store New Deal" because of its expanding programs. It was quotable stuff and made more headlines.

My fiscal policy differences with Ike were important. This was the start of a long public debate and the eventual conservative break with the party's so-called moderate wing, which was headed by New York's Governor Nelson Rockefeller, Senator Jacob Javits, and others. Rocky and Javits, the "Me Too" Twins, claimed I was "alienating" liberal Republicans and was outside the American political mainstream—as defined by them. I waved a political good-bye to Javits and his fellow liberals by suggesting that Jake "go straight" and join the Democrats. Rockefeller was more circumspect in his attack. I knew we would eventually clash head on. He was only biding his time.

That dispute with Ike and fight with the moderates led to three significant developments over the next thirty-year period—my presidential nomination, the movement of Republican Party power from the Eastern seaboard to west of the Mississippi River, and finally the full flowering of the conservative movement during the two terms of President Reagan.

The GOP is now undergoing further change. I have been, and am still, a traditional conservative, focusing on three general freedoms—economic, social, and political. My crucial difference with the Moral Majority is this: they are dividing Republicans, separating them into a host of single-issue groups that will ultimately do more to split than unite the party. That's precisely how the Democrats have wounded themselves.

One of the enjoyable aspects of being a Republican, from the time I entered the Senate in 1953 to today, has been the fact that the conservative movement has constantly expanded its intellectual base. During my early years in the Senate, I was much influenced by the work of Professor F. A. Hayek, author of *The Road to Serfdom.*

Russell Kirk's *The Conservative Mind,* published the year I entered the Senate, was also important to me. Kirk gave the conservative viewpoint an intellectual foundation and respectability it had not attained in modern society. He assailed the planning mentality of the times. Kirk rightly said it undermined the role of the family and community. He declared that religion, family, and private property and its yield, as well as law and order, were the foundations of a conservative society.

Kirk emphasized that social planning reduced the preeminence of the family and community. He also saw such planning as undercutting the rightful role of religion in attempting to solve many human problems. It substituted a humanistic, impermanent set of rules and aims that would, inevitably, make society unstable.

I had long been disgusted with the liberal belief that earning a profit meant abusing workers. That employing a thousand workers was a form of exploitation, while planning the economic and other aspects of the lives of the same people was somehow a new holy calling. Hayek said it well: "Whoever controls economic activity controls the means for all our ends and must therefore decide which are to be satisfied and which are not. Economic control is not merely control of the sector of human life which can be separated from the rest. It is the control of the means for all our ends."

Of course, liberals do not admit these stark terms. They disguise their state-controlled plans and programs with vague promises.

That was the high-flown rhetoric of all the New Dealers from Roosevelt to Truman, from Kennedy to Johnson and Carter. The aim of every one was the same—they would take your money and freedom to save you from yourself.

In the 1950s my criticism of the New Deal was political heresy, despite President Eisenhower's being in the White House. The Democrats even claimed Ike was not really a Republican. They saw his election as the triumph of a war hero. In other words, the Republicans were still out of mainstream America.

Conservatism was more than a cause. It was my creed, my life. Victory—control of both houses of Congress and the White House, which the Democrats had enjoyed for so long—was a distant trumpet, perhaps to be heard only in my dreams.

Yet conservatives were making progress. *National Review* was begun by William F. Buckley, Jr., in 1955. The lively, intellectual, often irreverent magazine burst on us like a spring shower, proclaiming that the liberals were all wet.

World-class economists like Milton Friedman and writers like Ayn Rand opened a new conservative horizon. The weekly newspaper *Human Events* and the monthly magazine *The Freeman* lifted conservatives from the doldrums of defeat to new hopes of recapturing some of the nation's political high ground.

We were sowing the seeds for the breakup of the Republican Eastern establishment, which included most of the Wall Street crowd and corporate executives, as well as their old boy network, which extended throughout much of the Midwest. Conservatives no longer accepted being sent up and down the corporate elevator while the board chairmen and presidents decided whom to run on the party ticket.

It was an incredible feeling. We had a voice, a chorus of articulate new voices challenging not only the Democratic Party but also what had become a GOP political dynasty.

It has always been difficult for me to comprehend why the media never understood the conservative groundswell in the decade from 1953 to 1963. Some have suggested that reporters centered their attention on Eisenhower's "moderation" and saw no conservative undercurrents. I believe the media simply blew the real story, primarily because they had become lazy in covering the GOP and biased toward the Democratic Party, which had held power for so long.

But the signs of change in the GOP were evident. Governor Rockefeller, after announcing his candidacy for the Republican presidential nomination, was the principal speaker at the Western Republican Conference in Los Angeles. He delivered a "Me Too" speech—more of the New and Fair Deals—to polite applause.

I took the stage with an all-out attack on the liberal voting record of the Democrats and "Me Too" Republicans. The Democrats were still dispensing their old "something for nothing" syrup, the patent medicine of the past. The speech was important because I made no concessions to the Republicans who had joined the Democratic parade to the public trough.

The attack on Rocky and his so-called moderates could not have been clearer: "My kind of Republican Party is committed to a free state, limited central power, a reduction in bureaucracy, and a balanced budget."

I sat down, and the crowd stood up. The ovation was thunderous. We were sending a message: Conservatives were going to fight the liberals and moderates for the soul of the party. The revolt on the right had begun.

5

Revolt on the Right

FIVE SIMPLE WORDS TELL IT ALL—NO ONE WANTED
the job. So in 1955 my GOP colleagues chose me—with
only two years' experience in the Senate—to be the new
chairman of the Republican Senatorial Campaign Committee. The post opened the way to the GOP presidential
nomination. I had no idea of what was being set in motion—which turned out to be perhaps the most turbulent
clash in Republican Party history.

We were living in an era of enormous expectations.
There was no end in sight to building America and recon-
structing the free world. Some called it the new Industrial Revolution. Others referred to it as the atomic age.

The world was witnessing the birth of new nations
faster than it could spell their names. But the Iron Curtain was now a permanent wall separating East and West.
Much of the East was still in ashes. Part of the Soviet
Union had been destroyed. The new heirs of Stalin were
bent on further destruction, suppressing freedom in Russia and among her neighbors. China's leaders had un-
bound the feet of millions of women but bound the
masses—hundreds of millions—to communism through
threats and terror.

The Communists launched the Korean war in 1950 to
test the American and free world's staying power in Asia.

That faraway battlefield left more than 50,000 Americans dead and political bitterness here at home.

We did not try to win the war in Korea. It was the first time in U.S. history that an American President sent men into battle and tied their hands.

The open, expansive American character began questioning itself and its motives: Why had we gone to Korea? Was it only a "conflict," or was it really a war? Why hadn't we won—or at least tried to win? If America's age of innocence ended with the War in Vietnam, it began disintegrating with disillusionment in Korea.

America was riding the crest of sweeping change. A baby boom exploded. Millions of Americans left rural areas and migrated to the big cities. Millions more moved from the Northeast and Midwest to the West and South, changing the population and political patterns of the country. GOP conservatives slowly began to emerge as a voice in the party and country. Senator Joseph McCarthy and the ultraconservative John Birch Society caused party feuds and other divisions. Ultimately, they became an excuse for many liberal Republicans to split from the GOP. President Truman's no-win policies in Korea spilled over into Vietnam. Finally, conservatives and liberals fought a fierce party battle for control of the GOP. Now, looking back more than three decades, the memory of that beginning still makes the old ticker pump faster.

No wonder my colleagues ducked the senatorial campaign chairmanship. It was a grueling, unrewarding, unglamorous job. The exhausting two-year responsibility was spread across the country—raising funds, rallying the party faithful, exhorting conservatives in particular to remain steadfast in the hope of better days, and blasting the Democrats in a GOP bid to retake control of the Senate and House. Eisenhower carried us to power in the Senate—the GOP already held the House—as a result of his sweeping 1952 presidential victory over Illinois Governor Adlai Stevenson. Unfortunately, we lost control of both houses in the 1954 elections.

My aim was to strengthen the party in general and our Senate chances in particular. It was also a good opportunity to get to know our grass roots leaders, our problems and strengths, and see if we could move the party in a more conservative direction.

It would be foolish for me to suggest that my own fate wasn't tied to strengthening the conservatives. I was paying my dues to the party—paying rent for my space—and the future would take care of itself. As the old saying goes, "You play the cards dealt you."

The thought of taking names of or notes on people who might later be personally helpful never occurred to me. To my knowledge, no previous chairman had used the post as a political launching pad to higher office. It would also have been wrong. Goldwater was sent around the country to blow not his own horn but that of his colleagues and the party in general. However, the Senatorial Campaign Committee chairmanship in both parties was to become more important as a result of my upgrading the post.

The travel and hours were incredibly long. An iron man would barely have had enough strength to keep going. I'd sometimes wake up not knowing what city I was in or whom I was speaking to that morning, noon, or night. At times, my greatest hope was that my stomach and weary bones would survive the endless travel, tasteless meals, and lonely hotel rooms.

My strength and spirit were sometimes so low that I questioned whether the party in general and we conservatives in particular were making any progress at all. There were few of us in those days. Republican liberals had accepted many of the New Deal's reforms of the 1930s and 1940s as permanent. We conservatives agreed that there were major differences with the Democrats, but we were disappointed that there was not more emphasis on big cutbacks in liberal spending programs. For the GOP, the issues were the threat of communism at home and abroad, corruption within the administration of President Harry Truman, and Truman's no-win policies in Korea.

Despite Eisenhower capturing the White House and the GOP controlling Congress, many Eastern Republicans continued to concede the New Deal changes of bigger, wider government. The Eastern GOP establishment was a pale imitation of the Democratic Party.

It's important to understand who and what constituted this network. The establishment was centered in the boardrooms of virtually all major companies and businesses—banks, insurance firms, financial institutions, steel and auto companies, the works. If you were a chief executive officer, trustee, or board member of one of these companies, it was generally assumed you were a Republican.

The biggest movers and shakers were an East Coast elite. Those from the heartland who rose in Republican circles—Tom Dewey from Michigan and Wendell Willkie from Indiana—did so only when they went East. Dewey became identified with big business and most of the New York establishment, while Willkie was a Wall Street lawyer. Dwight D. Eisenhower of Kansas became president of New York's Columbia University, but he didn't rise through party ranks.

On the social side, Republicans were club members—country clubs and other exclusive private groups. In those days you could not climb the heights if you were not from an Ivy League university or a member of some exclusive set.

Other analysts of the political scene, such as Theodore White, saw the Eastern establishment in more specific terms—Wall Street, international finance, Madison Avenue, Harvard, the New York *Times*, the Bankers Club, and Ivy League prep schools. These observers set the Easterners apart in three ways: wealth, executive ability, and professional responsibilities.

White and others claimed we conservatives living beyond the Allegheny Mountains misunderstood these leaders—that they were men from all parts of the nation who had worked hard and had not changed their basic beliefs after ascending to the pinnacle of U.S. corporate and financial power. White and others were dead wrong. These men had changed—drastically. They represented big business, not our new populist movement.

White argued with me face to face that these bankers and other Eastern interests could no longer command the GOP because the Eastern establishment was not centralized. It was true that these men were divided in their competitive business world, but they were united in their politics—and their large campaign funding. They wanted a GOP nominee who focused on big business interests, not someone like Barry Goldwater, who was taking the party in an entirely new direction.

Many of these establishment types had planted their feet in both camps—Democratic and Republican. They would, for example, support federal white collar welfare while condemning welfare waste among the poor. More and more, they were joining the Democrats and bigger government for a larger slice of the federal pie. They called themselves Republicans but sought a GOP-run government not to lessen its intrusion on all our lives but to control more of how the federal establishment spent its funds. These old-line Republicans were abandoning the middle class and vast majority of Americans, especially the growing West and South. They wanted the big to get bigger and had abandoned the rest of us.

I could not have cared less about their country clubs. My message was, if you work harder, you deserve more than the other guy. The test was not whether you were Ivy League or a corporate officer, but whether you cared deeply about individual initiative and individual rights.

The double standards and selfishness of the Eastern establishment excluded most of the nation. These had to go if conservatives were to rebuild the GOP from the grass roots up and broaden our base into mainstream

America. That is precisely what I intended to do—remake the party.

In 1953 and 1954 there seemed to be little or no movement of the country in a more conservative direction despite GOP control of both the executive and legislative branches of government. This seemed outrageous to us. Liberals still dominated broad national thinking as well as a majority of local and state governments, not to mention the media and academia. This was to continue, to a large extent, until Ronald Reagan was elected president in 1980.

The mid-1950s were very tough days for a conservative. What kept me going? Mostly the young people I met along those highways and byways. I saw myself in them, with their hunger for new ideas instead of the old handouts in social thinking and public programs. If there was one sentence which inspired these young people, it was this: Any government which can promise you everything you want can also take away everything you have.

I traveled hundreds of thousands of miles. It seemed I always had one eye on the audience and another on my airline schedule. One ear was cocked for news of any important Senate vote that would make me hurry back to Washington. Another listened for my wife and children. There were times when, if anybody asked me much more than my name, I would have blabbered to please call the fellows in the white coats because it was time to get back inside for a rest.

I wasn't anxious to take on the job for another two-year term, despite another upset victory over Ernest McFarland in Arizona in 1958. Frankly, all the travel was very tiring, and it was time to give more of myself to my family. But friends conned me by saying Senator Jacob Javits, a liberal New York Republican, wanted the post. Javits was everything in a Republican that I was not—he opposed President Eisenhower and his own party at virtually every turn and flaunted his liberalism at the struggling conservative movement. He was a provincial New

Yorker, mesmerized by Israel, who tried to pass as a great internationalist.

Rockefeller operated with the same double standard toward conservatives. It was only a matter of time before we fought one another. These intraparty differences wouldn't strengthen us in Congress or in a run for the White House.

Rockefeller sensed that the Eastern establishment might be losing some of its grip on the GOP, but he was not sure what to do about it. His intuition was right for two reasons: The country itself was changing, with major population shifts away from the East and Midwest to the West and South, and a new conservative movement was beginning to emerge.

In those fifteen years, the population living west of the Mississippi River rose from about 32 million to 45 million. Many GIs who had seen the West from military training bases during the war flocked back to new jobs as Western industry and other work expanded, especially in the electronics and aerospace fields.

Unlike the Midwestern farmers who had dominated previous migrations West, many of the new workers were well educated and highly skilled. Most of the retirees were relatively well off. The biggest increases in population were in California and the Southwest, including my home state of Arizona.

Liberalism and its rhetoric had dominated American politics for most of this century. But the political winds were almost imperceptibly beginning to change. So was the Republican Party. More Republicans were calling themselves conservatives. The right had begun to stir. William Rusher, a New York attorney and political activist who later became publisher of *National Review,* invited me to address the state's young Republicans. His colleagues were not impressed, but Rusher threatened to resign if I were not invited. They finally agreed, but Jake Javits, the liberal New York state attorney general, also was asked to speak in a trade-off. This was a firsthand manifestation of the growing split among New York Republicans.

After a two-year layoff in 1957–58, I again accepted the senatorial campaign chairmanship for the two-year term of 1959–60. It was against my better judgment and tough for Peggy and the kids. We had hoped to retake the Senate on a conservative upswing. It would be a political miracle, but Barry Goldwater's two Senate victories in Arizona had also been miracles.

Without fully realizing it, I was tapping into a growing conservative reservoir across the country. In the late fifties and early sixties, none of us could see the bottom of that reservoir. Nor did I comprehend how much it would affect me. If anyone had said in those days that I was the symbol for a massive new conservative movement, I would have asked for a thermometer to measure their fever. Tony Smith, a former newspaperman who became my press secretary in 1960, said to me, "There's more at work out there than Barry Goldwater's enunciation of conservative doctrine. It's also his personality—speaking frankly. This is good for conservatives. We've been dull for too long. Goldwater being Goldwater—unpretentious and unpredictable—is hot news."

To which I replied, "Baloney!"

One unexpected incident at the 1960 Republican National Convention in Chicago created a strong bond among GOP conservatives. We were angry because Vice President Richard Nixon had met secretly with Rockefeller in the governor's New York City apartment before the convention opened. The meeting had taken place despite a personal promise to me by Nixon that he would not ally himself with Rocky and other liberals in the party. In what was later called "the Treaty of Fifth Avenue," Nixon agreed to make the party platform more liberal in return for Rockefeller support. I called it "an American Munich," a surrender by Nixon to appease the GOP left. South Carolina placed my name in nomination for the presidency. It was seconded. However, 1960 was premature for a fight. We would have lost; the party would have been divided, and the resulting bitterness would have weakened the GOP chances of beating Kennedy.

I went before the convention, withdrew my name from nomination, and suggested that those who would support me cast their votes for Nixon. Those impromptu remarks, spoken from the heart, have been called the "Grow up, conservatives; we'll be back" speech. This is what I said:

"We've had our chance, and I think the conservatives have made a splendid showing at this convention. We've fought our battle. Now let's put our shoulders to the wheels of Dick Nixon and push him across the line. Let's not stand back. This country is too important for anyone's feelings; this country in its majesty is too great for any man, be he conservative or liberal, to stay home and not work just because he doesn't wholly agree. Let's grow up, conservatives. Let's, if we want to, take this party back—and I think we can someday. Let's get to work."

I lived up to my word, giving more than 125 speeches in twenty-six states for the Nixon–Henry Cabot Lodge ticket. They lost, but the conservatives won. We were now determined to take over the party.

Representative Morris Udall, an Arizona Democrat and my longtime sidekick in Congress, said it was the finest speech I ever made. He believes those few simple words were the beginning of the nation's conservative upsurge.

Others suggested it might have started with a book. In 1960 a thin 123-page publication with a red, white, and blue jacket slipped quietly out of the sleepy little town of Shepherdsville, Kentucky. It blew a fresh breeze across the American political landscape. *The Conscience of a Conservative* (Victor Publishing Company) was an attempt to explain the conservative philosophy in practical political terms. It spelled out conservative principles in everyday language—from states' rights to the U.S. Supreme Court, from labor to education, from the cold war to foreign aid.

The work was adapted by Brent Bozell, an editor at *National Review* and longtime Republican activist, based on speeches I'd given and his own research. Sales of the book soared beyond our wildest hopes. The book became a symbol of a new political consciousness.

The Conscience of a Conservative was the college student underground book of the times. It was virtually ignored by the media, most college professors, and other liberals, who had long held a monopoly on the information flowing to the American people. That first printing was ten thousand copies at three dollars each. Eventually, more than 4 million hardcover and paperback copies were sold. The book is still in print.

The book was an unpretentious introduction to conservative thought, not a dissertation. Nevertheless, it became a rallying cry of the right against three decades of Franklin D. Roosevelt and the liberal agenda.

In the book I said that the liberal agenda for the country was not working. I criticized increasing state paternalism at the expense of individual self-reliance. With new decentralized government, individual liberty and economic initiative could flourish. Collectivism and the welfare state were our greatest enemies at home, while communism had become our foremost enemy around the world. Either could destroy us. Some of my other conclusions were:

• The basic difference between conservatives and liberals is that conservatives account for the whole man while liberals tend to stress the material man. Liberals tend to regard economic satisfaction as the dominant mission of society.

• Conservatism puts material things in their proper place, subsidiary to the spiritual side of man's nature. The primary concern of conservative political philosophy is the enhancement of man's spiritual nature.

• The most sacred possession of a man is his soul.

Only a philosophy providing different potentialities for each person is in accord with natural law.

• No man or woman, if politically enslaved, can be economically free and efficient. People are responsible for their own spiritual and material development, and these should not be dictated by outside forces such as government.

• The conscience of a conservative opposes all who would debase the dignity of the individual. Freedom requires the establishment of order, but political power is limited and must be kept within its proper bounds.

In its simplest terms, conservatism is economic, social, and political practices based on the successes of the past. It rejects socialism, fascism, and other ideologies of failure. These principles have a long history, adapted and refined with the passage of centuries.

Conservatism was an intellectual movement with few organizational roots. After Richard Nixon lost the 1960 presidential race to John F. Kennedy, it seemed to many of us that we were ready to become not just an intellectual but a political movement. We were still several years away from creating a structure that could organize a movement and take over the party.

This new movement would be composed not of members of the board and Eastern old boy networks, but average Americans with strong beliefs in conservative principles, people with a cause, a creed: crusaders.

They would be mainstream Americans—the farmer in North Carolina, the rancher in Colorado, the oil prospector in Texas, the housewife in California, and the small businessman from as far away as Alaska. The new party would include people from an emerging new America— the Sunbelt, the South, the West, the Middle West, and some of the East, but there only the people who were willing to cast off the party's narrow-minded, short-sighted past.

My office was deluged with letters—from two thousand to, eventually, as many as eight thousand a week.

We were also receiving more phone calls and mail from the media than we could handle. I had worked directly with the media since arriving in the Senate. As a concession to the times, I hired Tony Smith to be my press secretary in 1960.

The reaction of some people to *The Conscience of a Conservative* was extraordinary. Many said I must carry its message across the country. I began writing a syndicated newspaper column, directly addressing specific public issues.

Our staff of thirteen people was in turmoil because of the volume of mail as a result of the book and some later speeches. Tony selectively read letters, discovering some from the president of U.S. Steel and other large companies. I also received requests from state and national GOP officials to speak at Republican fund-raising rallies and dinners. Other important letters, which we had not answered in the past, came to our attention. There was no way we could answer all the mail. It was left entirely up to Tony and the staff. If they found some letters that I should answer, that was fine. If not, forget it. There was only one rule: Answer all correspondence from constituents in Arizona.

Despite my promises to myself and my family to spend less time on the road, I was still giving many speeches around the country in 1960. It was a merry-go-round. Tony kept slipping into my office, showing me letters from people saying I should run for the presidency. I pooh-poohed the whole thing. Answer the Arizona letters, I would say, and, "Tony, we're doing all right just pooping along."

At staff meetings, Tony would mention the continuing volume of mail and media requests for interviews, saying, "We've got to get some organization into all this. We've got to answer these people. We just can't poop along any longer."

The mail and interview requests were just unnecessary

noise as far as I was concerned. It would all begin to disappear next week or a month from now.

I passed up the interviews because they would take time away from Senate participation and party work. We were still not answering most of the mail. Tony was a quiet bulldog. He'd return from lunch and say his desk was covered with messages to return calls from the media. Thirteen different magazines were doing cover stories on me at one time—all without an interview. These included *Time, Newsweek,* and even *Popular Mechanics,* which had heard I was a gadgeteer.

Finally I agreed to some interviews. *Time* came, and they interviewed me for hours, asking all kinds of silly questions, like how it felt being the golfing partner of Sammy Snead in the 1940 Phoenix Pro-Amateur match. They wanted to make a big deal out of the fact that I played in army boots and a beaten-up T-shirt while Snead was his fashionable self. The boots helped cushion the force that shot up to my wobbly knees when I hit the ball, and the T-shirt got dirty while I was working. I told the reporter I'd only given a damn about one thing: winning the tournament. That was the truth—and we won.

That *Time* photographer must have shot everything in my office. The whole thing was worse than an afternoon at the dentist. It seemed a senseless, depressing waste of time.

We never heard a word for six weeks, and I needled Tony, "I told you so. This is all smoke."

I was wrong. *Time* finally came out with a cover story on June 23, 1961—a big splash. But the article wasn't at all what I thought it would be—a typical *Time* takeout about an Arizona cowboy in the Senate. Instead, it was a big trial balloon about my running for the White House in 1964 as "the hottest political figure this side of Jack Kennedy."

It was a very unpleasant, unhappy experience. The senator from Arizona didn't want *Time* or anyone else floating his name as a candidate for the White House. What

would friends and the folks back home think? Had Barry
Goldwater become an arrogant, strutting peacock in
Washington? And people around the country—wouldn't
they think the article made me look like some country
bumpkin whose head was swollen by sitting in Washington? I detested the implication that I was jockeying to
become a front-runner for the GOP nomination. I was
angry. This was worse than smoke. This was fire.

I was a salesman. That's all. That's what my people
were. Goldwater wasn't the big enchilada. Just a guy
with a smile and a speech about freedom, opportunity,
hard work, and hope. Hell, I was out there to wipe away
the conservative stereotype—stuffed shirts in celluloid
collars and cuff links who combed their hair the wrong
way.

Some conservatives had another view. At a Chicago
meeting in 1961, Bill Rusher, F. Clifton White, the upstate New York public relations man, John Ashbrook, an
Ohio congressman, and others began secretly building a
Draft Goldwater Committee. They did it with no approval and no help from me. The whole bunch refused to
take no for an answer.

White was a pro, much more than a mere political
public relations man or college instructor in political science. He had been a GOP party worker since his twenties
and was a very experienced technician. No one in the
Republican Party knew more about the mechanics of putting a political machine together. He was now taking on
the role of a tactician, winning delegates on the basis of
issues and ideological commitment.

White was a likable, studious gentleman. I never
viewed him as a man of deep conservative conviction. He
was a professional political organizer, and an extremely
good one.

Rusher was well known to me—an unswerving conservative, dedicated, highly intelligent, a fine writer, a
real mover and shaker.

I was 100 percent against a draft and was never coy

about it. The White House was far from any of my plans, personal or political.

In 1962 Rusher and White asked to see me privately. The two came to my Senate office and said they wanted to change the Republican Party into an instrument of conservative politics. No conservative could disagree with that. I'd been trying to do it for more than six years. They began describing me as the party's conservative leader and symbol. The meeting became uneasy for everyone. It smelled like the start of something I'd not be able to control, much less want. The two left with one clear idea: I wanted no part of what they were launching.

Few people have ever understood my fierce resistance in those days to seeking higher office. I got damned mad about it because the whole idea was so silly. Not only did it seem preposterous, but I had never even jokingly considered the matter. And, to dismiss the notion entirely, I stressed that Arizona was a very small state with little or no political muscle.

Tony Smith insisted it was important that he become an informal liaison with the draft group, in order to know what they were up to and to offer reasonable replies to questions from the press. I kept putting off an answer.

He kept telling me about the letters, the pile of speaking invitations sitting on his desk, the phone calls from reporters asking for interviews and other information. Tony said, "Someday we'll have to deal with it."

I replied, "Baloney. Don't con me, Tony. We don't need any publicity in New York, Chicago, Atlanta, Dallas, or Miami. We want it in Tucson, Flagstaff, and Kingman, Arizona. How are we doing there?"

Tony was no yes man. He'd reply that sooner or later we'd have to face up to the fact that I was becoming the country's leading conservative spokesman—that it looked as if I would give 250 speeches during each of the next four years, through 1963. He warned that I would have to start watching every word I said.

Tony was well aware that I sometimes said things for

immediate effect, to get people on my side by making them listen or laugh. And I made too many joking references, like "lobbing one into the men's room of the Kremlin." (Boy, did I pay for that offhand quip!) It wasn't funny anymore. Tony was right. I'd have to watch the quips. It wasn't like back home in Arizona. A lot of these reporters had no sense of humor. And many didn't like conservative Republicans.

Tony and others wanted me to read more speeches, but I never liked speaking from a piece of paper. A text is sometimes necessary for precise meaning, but to this day I'm not comfortable with one. It always seemed more natural to me to share my immediate feelings with the people sitting nearby. An unwritten speech based on a clear outline is usually much closer to an individual's true convictions. But some of my off-the-cuff quips hit the evening television news or national headlines the following morning. I had to be more careful.

Reporters began to pay attention to my speeches, not because they had developed an interest in conservative principles but because they were looking for some colorful quote or incident. I responded to their questions with no rigid set of memorized answers. That was because I always tried to answer the specific question. Some politicians today—indeed, many members of Congress—spend considerable time memorizing twenty- to thirty-second answers to the diverse and often most difficult questions. Senators like Ted Kennedy, Pat Moynihan, and Alan Cranston have large staffs which grind out answers for them on almost every issue facing the country.

With these snappy, twenty-second answers, members of Congress aim to do two things at one time—twist their response to meet almost any question on a given subject and grab a quick headline on network radio and television news. It's now obvious that too many members of Congress are victims of the network syndrome—one quick burst to fit into the brief segments of news programming. I've never stage-managed myself this way.

What you saw was what you got—quips, jokes, cussing, and all. To me, however, the important part of any speech or interview is its central or overall message, not humor or a throwaway line taken out of context. Unfortunately, many editors in all media think otherwise.

This isn't to say I didn't shoot from the hip—or lip. I did. In rapid-fire exchanges with newsmen on perhaps a dozen or more subjects, I would even wind up saying some question was asinine. I wasn't the most patient politician in the world.

It was always my feeling, and still is, that a man's main message should be headlined—not the fact that he may have fallen off a horse at the county fair. Any damn fool can do that.

Paul Healy, of the New York *Daily News*, was the first Washington correspondent to "discover" and brand me. Healy wrote an anecdotal piece that made me into a rootin', tootin', shootin' Westerner who spoke his mind as few politicians in generations had.

That was quite a mouthful because we've had a lot of colorful characters in Congress. Healy put me right up there with some of America's top guns, from Teddy Roosevelt to Harry Truman. Editors and reporters were apparently looking for a maverick. That's news.

These newsmen were liberals to a large extent and uninterested in exploring conservative beliefs. Many of them ignored Senator Bob Taft as much as they could. Yet Taft may have been the most intelligent individual ever to have served in the U.S. Senate. He actually read every bill introduced in Congress. He was the Henry Clay of his time. But Taft was—by their odd measurement—dry, dull copy.

By their same odd view of what was significant, Goldwater was hot stuff. At the same time, conservatives wanted somebody who would talk back to the liberals, to all the media. Someone with moxie.

I plead guilty to firing back at some of our liberal critics. My aim was to win loyal converts to conservatism based on our principles. Contrary to any other perception, that was always my goal. Despite some national attention and more speaking invitations, I was never personally convinced I had started a bonfire to light a national conservative movement. That was still my hope, but it seemed years away.

I was being pounded mercilessly by the media and even members of my own party—the liberal wing—who suggested I was allied with the "fanatical right." Liberals often described the John Birch Society in such terms. Our critics began a concerted effort to link all conservatives with the Birchers and other extreme right-wing groups. The linkage was, to say the least, weak. Most conservatives didn't agree with the strong opinions of Robert Welch, founder of the society.

Welch had come to see me in Phoenix when he was writing *The Politician,* a book accusing Dwight D. Eisenhower of being either a dupe or a conscious agent of worldwide communism. I knew little of Welch but saw him as a favor to his brother, who lived in Phoenix. Welch pulled a copy of his manuscript from a brown paper wrapper and asked me to read it. The encounter seemed innocuous at the time. Views of all types constantly flow into the offices of most politicians.

After reading part of the manuscript, I returned it to Welch, saying his conjecture about Eisenhower and other matters was inaccurate. I suggested he not print the work because he could harm not only himself but the anticommunist cause. Welch never sought my advice again.

Throughout the early 1950s, both the John Birch Society and Senator Joseph McCarthy carried charges of Communists in government and other places to extremes. Our opponents, both Democrats and, eventually, liberal Republicans, tried to use this to thwart the rise of conservatism.

The Birchers numbered at most some 60,000 members. Their actual membership, mostly in the South and West, may have been much lower. The total was never made public. The overwhelming majority of conservatives were not members and knew little of the organization or Welch's private beliefs about a national Communist conspiracy.

In time, by simply ignoring them, we shook the Birchers from our coattails. I disagreed with some of their statements but refused to engage in any wholesale condemnation of them. The last thing conservatives needed was to begin a factional war by reading small minorities or individuals out of our ranks. We were struggling to strengthen ourselves, if not merely to survive. Our efforts would be better spent on strengthening U.S. defenses and those of our allies against the totalitarian threat rather than attacking small groups of fellow Americans.

Liberals blamed conservatives for years for the most extreme statements of both Welch and McCarthy. We became "the radical right," yet the overwhelming number of conservatives could hardly be considered radical. I said publicly in a letter to *National Review* that Welch's views were "irresponsible" and did not represent those of most members of the society. The letter called on Welch to resign. Despite this well-publicized statement, the left still linked me and conservatives with the "radical right." It was a tactic the liberals had long publicly scorned—guilt by association and slander, better known as McCarthyism.

In historical terms, Democrats in Congress had, as powerful committee chairmen, been investigating U.S. communism since the late 1930s. Such hearings peaked with the disclosure that Alger Hiss, a former member of the U.S. State Department, had engaged in espionage activities. This was revealed before McCarthy was elected to the Senate.

The sellout of freedom at Yalta was on our minds. Hiss had been on the U.S. delegation at Yalta. We were also concerned about the fall of Chiang Kai-shek. Despite his faults, Chiang was surely more faithful to the cause of liberty than Mao Tse-tung. Some Americans, however, saw Mao as a brighter hope for China.

We were disturbed by the long liberal lock on the White House, Congress, and the U.S. Supreme Court. The Eisenhower administration broke the lock momentarily, but it was mostly made up of passive Republicans, not a conservative majority dedicated to major changes. We hoped to curb the concentration of power in the hands of the few and spread it out among the states.

For the most part, the liberals ignored what Bill Buckley, Barry Goldwater, and other conservatives were saying. Rather, Bill and Barry were guilty of consorting with all those extremists out there. The truth is that liberals did not relish direct combat with us in speaking arenas across the country. They had long grown fat in government, academia, and the media by monopoly.

The left, which controlled most of the nation's large Eastern media, had monopolized public thinking for so long that it saw any challenge as heresy, if not ideological fanaticism; in a word, fascism.

This was symptomatic of the liberals' greatest fault. They had never learned, as the Republicans had had to, how to lose. They feared us—the challenge and the combat. One day we would prove that fear justified.

In examining Joe McCarthy, it's important to place him in the temper of his times as well as the perspective of today. The Wisconsin Republican did not act alone. He was backed by many respected people, including Joseph P. Kennedy. I supported some of McCarthy's investigations after arriving in the Senate in 1953. There was, for example, considerable evidence to back his charges that the Institute of Pacific Relations and *Amerasia* magazine were Communist front organizations. McCarthy found others to be either active members of the Communist Party or sympathetic to the cause. These included some leaders and advisers of the Electrical Workers and Steelworkers unions. Similar evidence concerning other groups was produced in various parts of the United States, Europe, and elsewhere.

U.S. atomic spies like Julius and Ethel Rosenberg and British spies like Guy Burgess and Donald Maclean, Kim Philby, and others were clear examples of Soviet attempts to steal the highest secrets of Western democracies.

For all his personal problems and excesses, McCarthy's central idea was on target—that not only was world communism a threat to this country and the free world, but its bloody repressions in the Soviet Union, Eastern Europe, China, and elsewhere could not go unanswered by civilized men and women. Those murders, purges, repressions, and jailings of tens of thousands persist today in Communist countries. From the Soviet Union to Poland, from China to Vietnam, from Castro's Cuba to Nicaragua and elsewhere, we're dealing with the perpetual persecution of freedom.

McCarthy's personal weaknesses—drinking, exaggeration, and unwillingness to compromise—washed him up. Even so, I tried, in a compromise move, to save McCarthy from Senate censure. Several Southern senators approached me during the censure debate on the floor in 1954. They said the South would vote against censure if McCarthy would apologize to two senators who felt he had publicly insulted them.

I drove out to suburban Bethesda Naval Hospital with McCarthy's attorney, Edward Bennett Williams. We explained to McCarthy what had happened and handed him two letters of apology drafted by Williams. Both were brief, mild expressions of regret about discourtesy to fellow senators. Neither admitted any serious guilt.

McCarthy cursed and threw the pen at us. The outburst caused the nurses to come running, and we were ordered to leave the hospital for disturbing a patient and not return without permission, or we would be arrested by the Shore Patrol.

I voted against censuring McCarthy for several reasons. Liberals themselves were guilty of excess in their sweeping castigation of conservatives. There was, in fact, some limited liberal involvement with communism. Both McCarthy and the conservatives had the right to challenge that involvement. A number of media attacks and other charges against the senator were just as crude and cruel as some of McCarthy's own statements.

Joe McCarthy was the most contentious, controversial, and stubbornly cussed character that I ever met in my life. He also was a very sick man physically and needed treatment. Few people knew how sick Joe really was. He used to invite me over to his house near the Capitol. He'd go out in the kitchen with the excuse of making me a drink and would have four or five shots, then return with our drinks. Unfortunately, Joe became a real booze hound—the worst. Without telling anyone, including Joe, I went up to see Francis Cardinal Spellman in New York and told him that someone had to have a fatherly talk with McCarthy. The cardinal did, but McCarthy never changed.

No one but I knew why Joe was admitted to the Bethesda Naval Hospital. He had invited me up to Milwaukee to make a speech for him. When I arrived at his hotel room, Joe was gassed. He fell and hit his elbow on a glass tabletop. It later became infected.

Once Indiana Senator Bill Jenner, several other senators, and I tried to help him. We took McCarthy to Spanish Key, an island in the Bahamas owned by a Texas family, to try to talk some sense into him and get him to quit the booze. We had made strict arrangements that no liquor would be available where we stayed. When I got there, Joe was already bombed and had a storehouse of the stuff. Everything went downhill, and we came home.

Knowing his illness—and many senators did—I wanted to offer McCarthy mercy. Some disagreed with that. But I said you pray for people who need the prayers —good or bad. If the Lord is willing to give him a hand, let us give him a hand. Other senators said he deserved the same as he'd given others. I didn't blame them for that view. However, I believe a man can be put out of action without a public lynching. The mood among Senate liberals was to lynch McCarthy. I was probably wrong in defending him, but I didn't want any part of it, especially in the respectful setting of the Senate. It was ruthless behavior in both cases. After the censure, Joe drank himself to death.

I've never spoken this candidly about McCarthy before because it's not part of my character to harpoon people. However, McCarthy was a very important part of our generation, good and bad. And that's just how I felt about him—very mixed feelings. He recognized the Communist menace, as many of us did, and conservatives recognize him for that. But McCarthy went overboard in his investigations because of his inability to handle power and alcohol. Joe became enamored of power. That's what really made him sick and changed him into such a drinker. He was off in an unreal world of self-importance and self-indulgence. Joe retaught us a very old lesson: Power corrupts.

As 1961 began, my good friend John F. Kennedy became President of the United States. His personal charm and eloquence lifted the spirits of millions of Americans.

Conservatives were not, however, happy with what we saw and heard. Communism had solidified itself around the world. Most Americans were ignoring the danger in a headlong national rush for money and the material rewards of the postwar economic upsurge. We conservatives were saying that power was too important to be left to the politicians. Too great to be held by the big corporations and big unions. Too costly to be wielded by an enormous and growing federal bureaucracy.

That was my message in those days, mounting an intellectual and spiritual challenge to a society whose goals seemed only to be more and more of everything. In my long travels, I'd often wonder whether I was relating to the young people who had come to hear and ask questions. It seemed self-serving and presumptuous that I should pretend to speak for them. It was more important for me to hear how and why they were motivated to learn more about the conservative movement. I listened a lot to what the young conservatives of those early years had to say.

Lance Tarrance, based in Houston, is now one of the best-known Republican pollsters in the country. He was attending Washington and Lee University in Lexington, Virginia, when *The Conscience of a Conservative* was published. The book was passed around as campus underground reading.

Tarrance was a senior, majoring in European history. He recalls, "It was one of the few times that I read a book that did not have a liberal direction. I became so fascinated by it that I missed a Friday night beer bust for the first time since going to college. Granted, it was a basic, simplified expression of what the conservatives were all about. I began to get a much clearer picture of how government worked, especially the nearby federal establishment in Washington."

Tarrance had never been active in politics. On graduation in 1962, he went home to Texas and began inquiring about what he might do in the GOP. The young Texan was disappointed by what the old-timers said, that his only role would be to lick envelopes and help at rallies. That was all right with him, but he wanted more than the spirit of politics. He wanted to discuss the substance.

Tarrance didn't join the Texas Republicans. He kept talking with other young conservatives and reading, especially the writings of Ayn Rand on the concept of individual liberty. In 1964, after I announced my candidacy for the presidency, Tarrance joined the Republican Party. He became a volunteer in Texas for the Goldwater-Miller ticket.

Vic Gold was an Alabama Democrat. In the mid-1950s, he heard about this fellow Barry Goldwater. Gold was having doubts about his political beliefs. He asked a lot of questions, listened to me and other conservatives, and read *National Review* and other literature. In 1964 he became my assistant press secretary on the campaign trail, saying, "I discovered a political identity that I never knew existed."

Gold had grown up in the era of the New Deal. Americans didn't have the opportunity they have today, with a more balanced presentation of viewpoints, to discover their own political identities. That was one reason why we adopted our slogan in 1964: "A Choice—Not an Echo." Vic worked in public relations and later became press secretary for Vice Presidents Spiro Agnew and George Bush. He still writes extensively on political and social issues.

Dr. Edward J. Feulner, Jr., is now president of the Heritage Foundation, a public policy research institute in Washington. In the early 1960s he was a student at the University of Pennsylvania in Philadelphia. Feulner supported the Goldwater-Miller ticket. On an Eastern campus in those days, that was treason. He became a real traitor—a volunteer working for the GOP ticket in 1964.

Pat Buchanan was a student at Georgetown University in the nation's capital in 1961. One of his fellow students asked Pat about his politics, and Buchanan made his first public confession—but only after the other student made his. They both liked "this guy Goldwater."

Pat is one of those who committed a good part of his life—and a salty dash of journalism—to politics, as a speechwriter for President Nixon and communications director for President Reagan. In 1962, while a graduate student at Columbia University's journalism school, he led a contingent of friends to hear me and other conservatives speak at a rally of Young Americans for Freedom in Madison Square Garden. Conservatives packed the place. It was an emotional evening and, in terms of numbers, a rousing success—especially as we did it in an off year and charged for tickets.

The program ran late. My talk was moved back into

the morning hours. No one left. I gave 'em hell, and the
thunder rattled the Garden and a few in the liberal media. They reported that something was brewing among
young Republicans. None except conservative publica-
tions took the time to understand what was happening,
that the growing numbers and increasing commitment of
conservatives might be a force to be reckoned with in
1964. The story of the rise of the right would prove to be
a classic example of journalistic failure. Even today,
many in the media still don't understand how badly they
missed the significance of events that unfolded right before their eyes. Their failure ranks with Washington reporters' general ineptitude in unraveling the major events
behind the Watergate mess. Congress and a single newspaper, the Washington *Post,* did most of the real work.
Pat later said, "Barry Goldwater just reached in and
touched our minds and hearts. He brought whole new
classes and groups of people into the GOP. He was the
wedge—the man who brought the South and West, the
young and energetic into Republican circles."

Tarrance, Gold, Feulner, and Buchanan—four names
representing several hundred thousand young people who
joined the ranks of conservatives in the late fifties and
early sixties. Not Republicans—conservatives. More than
a half million Americans would participate as volunteers
and in other ways in the 1964 GOP campaign for the
White House.

Unlike many of their liberal counterparts in the later
sixties and early seventies, most of these young conservatives did not tune in, turn on, and drop out of the political process. They stayed active in the GOP.

After 1960, the party was in complete disarray. We had
no national leaders. Ike had retired, Nixon was a defeated
man, and Rockefeller's liberalism had alienated many
conservative Republicans.

Although I didn't view myself at the time as leader of
the conservatives, my name began to be mentioned
around the country as a possible conservative presidential

candidate. The 1960 GOP convention had left a sour taste in our mouths. Nixon and Rockefeller felt they could outmaneuver the conservatives, whom they looked on as political amateurs. The Eastern establishment still appeared to dominate the party.

Conservatives and many younger Republicans, especially those just out of college, were furious at the way we were being brushed aside by the old-line leadership. Bill Buckley and Bill Rusher had formed and helped build a new national conservative youth organization, Young Americans for Freedom. The YAFs were to transform conservative ideas into political action.

In that unsettled background, Rusher and F. Clifton White convened nineteen of their onetime Young Republican crowd—distinct from the YAFs—and three others in Chicago in October 1961. That was the beginning of the national Draft Goldwater Committee.

Their goal was simple: conservative control of the GOP. But their plan was unconventional: to achieve victory by aligning the East Central states—Ohio, Indiana, Illinois, and Wisconsin—with the South and West.

They conceded only fourteen states to Kennedy and figured we would sweep the solid South. We yielded the traditional battlegrounds of presidential politics—New York, Pennsylvania, Michigan, and possibly California.

Such a coalition had never defeated the liberal East and its allies—New York, Massachusetts, and Pennsylvania, plus smaller states in the East, Middle West, and Northwest.

The GOP had already cracked the solid South in Eisenhower's campaigns. The increasing shift of population to the West had made the old Republican combination and Democratic coalitions highly vulnerable. The Young Republicans' convention of 1959 had already demonstrated that. Rockefeller had sent his representatives to the Denver meeting, and a coalition of the West and South had defeated his moves.

Rusher and White saw that the old Eastern establishment GOP was now only a shadow group—Rockefeller, his staff, and his personal fortune. It was a good time to move. I wasn't aware of their meetings, nor did I authorize them or any other group to work for my nomination. In reality, a Goldwater draft was under way.

This was a genuine draft, perhaps the only true one in American political history. As Rusher put it, "We were like a roving band of samurai that emerged from the forest and said: 'Hey you! You are our candidate!' "

Another group of samurai were about to capture the nation's attention. On a chill April morning in 1961 I was adjusting my straps in the cockpit of an F-86 fighter plane at Andrews Air Force Base outside Washington. It was April 15, Uncle Sam's Christmas. I was about to fly to Luke Air Force Base outside Phoenix to maintain my proficiency rating as a member of the active reserve.

A sergeant climbed onto the wing and said the President wanted to see me as soon as possible. I changed into my regular clothes and drove to the White House. It was a busy Saturday shopping day in the Maryland suburbs. Families crowded malls and supermarkets. The streets of federal Washington seemed almost deserted by comparison, except for buses filled with tourists.

In driving across the city, I had a foreboding about the meeting. I began to suspect the reason for the President's summons was the invasion of Cuba. The coming mission was known on Capitol Hill, and there was already speculation about it in the media. Why would he call me unless there was trouble? There was only one reason he needed me—to support him publicly.

There might not be much time with Kennedy. My views had to be clear, concise, firm. The longer I thought, the clearer my position became. It was one word: will—political and moral will.

Truman's no-win in Korea policy had been wrong. We could not adopt a no-win policy now that we were involved in a military operation against Cuba.

The White House seemed quiet, even somber. That seemed to be the President's mood when he entered. He seemed preoccupied, although he walked briskly. We were relaxed in one another's company because of years of private chats in the Senate. He bantered, "So you want this fucking job, eh?"

I laughed and replied, "You must be reading some of those conservative right wing newspapers."

Kennedy grinned but quickly came to the point. He said grimly that the first phase of the invasion of Cuba by anti-Castro Cuban forces had not gone as well as expected. Fidel Castro's air force had not, as planned, been completely demolished on the ground. Eight B-26s flown by Cuban exile pilots had made their surprise attack but had destroyed only half of the Cuban Air Force. Three planes flown by the exiles had been lost.

Sixteen bombers were to have made the run, but this number had been slashed in half. The State Department wanted to be able to officially deny our support of the exiles. The United States had furnished the planes. The State Department had told Kennedy it would be easier to defend the cover story that anti-Castro forces had obtained eight B-26s. However, it would be much more difficult to explain how and where they had gotten sixteen such bombers. The United States would certainly be blamed.

Kennedy was clearly having second thoughts about U.S. participation in the action. He was questioning the planning for the invasion and further involvement. The President finally said he thought the whole operation might fail. He turned, sitting on the edge of his desk, and faced me directly. Kennedy then asked what I would do in the situation.

I was stunned.

The President was not a profile in courage, as portrayed in his best-selling book. He projected little of the confidence and lofty resolve of his eloquent speeches. Kennedy was another man now that we were, in effect, on the shores of Cuba. He did not seem to have the old-fashioned guts to go on.

Kennedy could see the shock on my face. There could be no turning back now. Nearly 1,500 men would soon be on the beaches at the Bay of Pigs. We had helped put them where they were. The commander does not abandon men he has sent to fight. The President had a professional and moral responsibility to those men.

I grimaced when Kennedy recalled a statement he had made at his news conference a few days before—that no American forces would be used to invade Cuba. Kennedy now said nervously that the mission would fail unless the freedom fighters received U.S. air support.

Slowly, so the words would sink in, I reminded the President that our Navy and its fighter planes were standing ready in nearby waters. They could be launched to protect the next attack of B-26s. We must destroy all of Castro's planes on the ground. Then the exiles could fight their way from the beaches and spread out across the terrain.

I told Kennedy that our action was moral and legal and would be understandable to the entire free world. The United States could not tolerate Soviet nuclear missiles in Cuba. Every great nation must be willing to use its strength. Otherwise, it's a paper tiger. Whether we agree or not, power belongs to those who use it.

Kennedy still seemed to equivocate. I didn't understand how the President could, or why he would, abandon these men. They would be killed or captured without a chance of accomplishing their mission or even defending themselves.

I remember the moment well. Kennedy continued to search my face and eyes for an answer. This was also a crucial moment for me. For the first time, I saw clearly that I had the toughness of mind and will to lead the country. Others might be more educated or possess greater speaking and social skills, but I had something that individuals of greater talent did not have. I had an unshakable belief in, and willingness to defend, the fundamental interests of my country. My heart was pounding now as my mind became more convinced. I had the will—once the options were considered and a reasonable plan was agreed on, as in this instance—to carry out such a mission. It was not a boast. It was simply a matter of personal principle.

If world opinion were was so important to the President now, why hadn't he stopped the operation in the first place? The State Department be damned. I told him we didn't have to deny anything. And if, as the President said to me, Ambassador Adlai Stevenson had phoned him that morning threatening to tell the entire United Nations that we were behind the invasion, let that two-time loser tell them. Then I'd fire him so fast he'd barely have time to get his coat and leave the U.N.

I didn't have to remind the President that the American people had twice turned Stevenson down for the job that Kennedy now held. What made Stevenson think he could now go over the head of the President to the United Nations? Neither world opinion, nor the United Nations had stopped the Soviet tanks in Hungary and other parts of Eastern Europe. The self-interest of the United States, including the protection of the American people, was above the United Nations, above world opinion, and above Stevenson. I told the President, "I would do whatever is necessary to assure the invasion is a success."

I repeated, "Whatever is necessary."

I never suggested that the President drop a nuclear bomb or use such a device on anyone. We had conventional air power, and I felt he should use it to help the Cuban exiles advance from the beaches and take on the Castro forces. I finally told Kennedy that the American people and every free nation would thank him for ridding the world of Castro.

The President seemed to relax. My voice had risen. It

was clear and emphatic. Kennedy replied, "You're right."

I left the Oval Office fairly sure that the B-26s, escorted by U.S. Navy fighters, would soon blow holes to lead those freedom fighters off the beaches toward Havana. I was wrong.

The brigade left Guatemala. The B-26s were first to destroy Castro's air force on the ground and then support the landing group with air cover. Kennedy gave the go-ahead for the first air strike with the B-26 bombers launching from Central America. Then, for reasons he never explained, the President canceled the follow-up air attacks. U.S. Navy jet fighters, ready to support the B-26s from the nearby U.S.S. *Boxer,* never launched their attack. Kennedy clearly had lost his nerve. The brigade was routed. Some three hundred were killed, and the rest were imprisoned.

The President backed away from the counsel of all his top advisers when he refused to support an all-out attack and invasion of Cuba. Kennedy allowed the Russians to remain on the island on condition that they withdraw their nuclear missiles. The fact is, instead of the eyeball-to-eyeball victory the Kennedy administration claimed over Nikita Khrushchev, the President actually made concessions to the Soviet leader. These included removing U.S. missiles from Turkey. The decision not to attack Cuba was disastrous. We are still paying for it.

In the end, Kennedy's big lie in the 1960 campaign, that the Soviets enjoyed a large missile superiority over the United States, had returned to haunt him.

The Bay of Pigs ultimately allowed the influence of Castro and the Soviet Union to rise in the region. It was to spread to Nicaragua, El Salvador, and other parts of the hemisphere.

It's important to reflect on the political results of Kennedy's failure. Conservatives were convinced that the American people were genuinely shocked and dismayed by their leader's lack of political and moral will, especially in view of his rhetoric. The President's ability to lead the country had clearly become a political issue, not only at home but among the leaders of the Soviet Union.

Kennedy's indecisiveness in our private meeting caused me to begin reevaluating my unwillingness to run for the presidency. I did not, however, mention this to anyone.

Kennedy was a strong commander in chief publicly, yet equivocated privately not only regarding Cuba but in other crucial matters as well. Vietnam is a case in point.

The President sent a total of 17,000 American troops to Vietnam—with orders not to shoot back. Kennedy told me that Eisenhower had first sent troops there. In shifting blame for the U.S. presence there, he was technically correct. Ike had, however, sent only five hundred military advisers there. Kennedy was engaged in semantics to cover his rear end in the event of serious trouble. The real thrust into Vietnam was made by Kennedy. He equivocated again on Ngo Dinh Diem, President of South Vietnam. The President allowed Diem and his brother to be murdered in a military coup by South Vietnamese officers. Kennedy's people had approved the coup.

The President's continuing pattern of vacillation again stirred my private musings on whether to seek the GOP presidential nomination. I was convinced, because of his wavering on foreign policy and his worn-out domestic spending programs, that Kennedy was vulnerable and could be defeated in his bid for reelection.

Many people say today—and said then—that Kennedy would have defeated me. I'm not so sure. *Time* magazine and some of the polls clearly indicated he was slipping in national support. Kennedy himself admitted that. It was a major reason he went to Dallas in November 1963.

A Kennedy-Goldwater clash would have been quite different from my campaign against Lyndon Johnson. It would have been a direct and continuing attack on Kennedy policies, with much less time spent on irrelevancies.

Kennedy and I informally agreed—it seems a pipe dream in looking at some of today's negative campaigning—that we would ride the same plane or train to several stops and debate face to face on the same platform.

I was convinced I would do well because of my deep commitment to the conservative cause. Kennedy was a Democrat by accident of birth; he was more a pragmatist than a Democrat. Kennedy spouted the liberal line but was cynical about much of it. I was a conservative by personal conviction.

Issues were important, but more than that was at stake. I wanted to talk about a national will and direction that would replace Kennedy's vacillation and weak pragmatism. It was my hope that our direct confrontation would make it clear to the American people that genuine commitment and principles are necessary to sustain all great countries. Even if I lost, the race would have been well worth it for another reason. The conservative cause would gain because of the American people's exposure to our beliefs.

It was not until 1963 that I privately decided to oppose Kennedy by seeking the Republican nomination. The decision came quietly, matter-of-factly, in talking with my wife and a few friends. I said nothing publicly but sat back and waited.

Earlier, in 1962, it had seemed certain that Rockefeller intended to become a presidential candidate. The tip-off came when he gave several speeches stressing Republican orthodoxy, abandoning his penchant for New Deal phrases and policies.

Perhaps, I said to myself, there is hope for Rocky yet. We began to discuss party and policy problems on the phone and during breakfast and several dinner meetings at his palatial house on Foxhall Road in Washington.

We had more in common than we had realized—a distrust of Nixon as a politician, general agreement on greater fiscal restraint by the federal government (although Rockefeller was far from a fiscal conservative), and a tough stand against communism. Rockefeller left little doubt in my mind: He had moved to the right.

By the early fall of 1962, it appeared likely that Rockefeller, Michigan Governor George Romney, and perhaps Nixon—depending on how his race for the California governorship came out—would run for the 1964 GOP nomination. I preferred Rockefeller.

It was obvious that the vast majority of conservatives didn't share my views about the governor. Many were downright hostile to him, but I did my best to keep my mouth shut.

Nixon was to lose the 1962 governor's race against incumbent Democrat Pat Brown in California, apparently excluding himself from the presidential sweepstakes.

The media and many top members of the party made Rockefeller the front-runner for the nomination. He had been reelected governor. One potential problem—the fact that Rocky had divorced his wife—seemed to have disappeared from public consciousness. There wasn't much public support for other GOP candidates, except speculation about Barry Goldwater among conservatives. Rocky's lieutenants crisscrossed the country, extolling his newfound conservative virtues. The Rockefeller bandwagon was rolling.

Meantime, I told anyone who would listen that I wasn't seeking the nomination. The door wasn't closed. I simply hadn't made up my mind about whether to run. I told a persistent reporter, "A man would be a damn fool to predict with finality what he would do in this unpredictable world."

Peggy did not want me to run. However, she enjoyed the political jockeying and other antics. She often joked about them.

On a breezy Saturday in May 1963, the telephone in our Washington apartment rang. Peggy answered it because her old television repairman was up to his old fix-it tricks on the roof of the building. Unhappy with our television reception, I was fiddling with the antenna. A man's voice said, "Hello, this is Nelson Rockefeller."

"Hello yourself," Peg answered. "This is Mamie Eisenhower."

Peggy loved to tell that story and, in later versions, said she told Rocky she was Dinah Shore.

Rockefeller finally convinced my wife he was the genuine article, not some prankster like me. She hailed me down from the roof, and I picked up the phone. Rocky's dead-earnest tone cut through the miles of line separating us.

The governor said he had been married that afternoon to Mrs. Margaretta "Happy" Murphy. He wanted to tell a few friends and close associates about the wedding before it broke in the national media.

The message was clear but the meaning confusing. Why call me? I asked myself. Finally I wished him happiness, put the receiver down, looked at Peggy, and asked, "What the hell's going on?"

She joked, "You tell me."

"Rockefeller just got married," I said with a touch of wonderment.

"Bully for him!" she laughed.

This was no laughing matter. Rockefeller was not a man who made idle phone calls around the country. He was telling me something, but I couldn't figure out what.

Rumors had floated in and out of gossip columns for months about Rocky dating a married New York woman. There also was some talk in political circles. Many of us had never paid any attention to it. I detest such gossip. In fact, it makes me a little sick to my stomach. I never sniped at anyone behind his back. If the time came that it was needed, I let them have both barrels between the eyes from a few feet away.

The mail hit Capitol Hill and Rockefeller's office like a May snowstorm, totally unexpected. The writers were mostly women and some clergy. There were two complaints—that Rocky had been dating a married woman and that her husband, a physician, wanted their four children.

The governor had been leading me nearly two to one in the Gallup presidential poll. That was reversed within a month. I rose from 26 to 40 percent while Rocky fell from 43 percent to 29 percent.

This was a delicate moment for conservatives. It bolstered their view that Rockefeller could—and should—be beaten. The sudden reversal pushed me into a spotlight and put new pressure on me to make a firm decision about running.

The pros of both parties said the remarriage had been poorly timed. They claimed Rocky should have waited at least until after the GOP nomination and more likely the presidential election. Yet there hadn't been a ripple of dissatisfaction when the governor was divorced, so it had been impossible to anticipate the uproar about the marriage.

I was very uneasy about these developments. In fact, I was genuinely unhappy about them. The country needed a campaign of national and international issues, not personalities and moralizing about private lives. Many conservatives saw the matter as a victory of sorts over the GOP's leading liberal. I didn't view it that way at all. The campaign was getting out of focus. We had to get it back on the issues.

The names of a half dozen viable new GOP presidential candidates began to surface. The media were saying there was a vacuum in GOP party leadership for the first time in a generation. There were rumors that Eisenhower, contemplating at his Gettysburg farm, might endorse Pennsylvania Governor Bill Scranton for the nomination.

Of the four candidates most prominently mentioned—Rocky, Romney, Scranton, and myself—three had the blessing of the liberal Eastern GOP establishment. I was the only conservative. Two questions were raised: Who would the liberals choose, and would the conservatives try to veto him?

Tony Smith then showed me a poll done by *Congressional Quarterly* among delegates to the 1960 Republican National Convention. The questionnaire had been distributed both before and after the Rockefeller marriage. The before-the-wedding poll reported that nearly 65 percent of those questioned thought Rockefeller would be the nominee, with about 26 percent voting for me. However, the after-marriage poll said that 46 percent of the delegates preferred me, compared to the governor's 34.5 percent. The pressure on me to become a candidate intensified. I was still not absolutely firm about running and played down the possibility.

Meantime, the political rumor mill was still grinding away. Word filtered out from Rockefeller and his people that I might somehow be involved in the public heat he was taking over his remarriage. I brushed it off. My relations with Rocky were better than they had ever been. It would have been a low tactic to turn on him for such a reason. This was dirty stuff, not my style.

Still, I tried to determine how he could possibly have come to such an opinion. I thought back to the phone call on his wedding day. Would he really call me because he thought I was the type of guy who might lead a conservative moral crusade against his remarriage? That was ridiculous, I concluded. I had never uttered a single word, not a hint of disapproval, about his personal life. To this day, I still have no idea who might have spilled such poison. But Rockefeller had apparently concluded that I and other conservatives were the source of some of the personal nastiness in the media and the cause of his fall at the polls. Frustrated and angry, Rockefeller dropped a political bombshell. In a speech billed as his Declaration of July 14, he bitterly condemned the party's "radical right." The governor declared the conservatives were guilty of "subversion" by undermining Republican

articles of faith—equal opportunity for all, freedom of
speech and information, home rule under the federal system of government, fiscal integrity, and the free enterprise system. He referred to a "real danger" from
"extremist elements" in the GOP and said they were engaged in a "ruthless" effort to take over the party.

Rockefeller described these "extremists" as being involved in "threatening letters, smear and hate literature,
strong-arm and goon tactics, bomb threats and bombings,
infiltration and takeover of established political organizations by Communist and Nazi methods." There was absolutely no doubt about those he was referring to—
Goldwater supporters.

The governor spoke of the danger of a coup led by a
band of well-financed young people who had attended the
recent Young Republican convention in San Francisco.
He referred to "tactics of totalitarianism" that were being
used in the campaign by "Birchers and others of the radical right lunatic fringe."

Rockefeller also said the right was abandoning blacks
and other minorities and trying to build political power
through immoral segregation. He said the right was
walking away from the nation's big industrial states in
favor of electoral votes in the West and South to create a
racist sectionalism in the nation. The governor concluded
that real Republicans must save the party from the radi-
cals.

I was shocked and saddened by the declaration, especially since I had received no advance warning from
Rockefeller. It had seemed that we had developed a reasonably good relationship, maybe even the beginning of a
personal friendship. The memory of those breakfasts and
dinners at his Washington home was still warm. He had
spoken of Republicans once again running the nation in
an atmosphere of unity and fellowship. It turned out that
Rockefeller had airmailed a copy of his speech to my
office over the weekend. It did not arrive until our Monday mail—after the remarks had been made.

My hands began to tremble as I read the full text of the address. It was particularly upsetting to realize that the party would inevitably be weakened by a split. Astonishingly, that seemed to be Rockefeller's intention.

Rather than digging the wounds deeper with a detailed reply, I merely said that the speech seemed to be Rockefeller's declaration of candidacy for the GOP presidential nomination. Rocky no longer invited me to his home. I would not have accepted anyway. Our staffs broke contact.

Well, I consoled myself, at least he had spared me personally by not implying I might be an extremist. Wrong again. A few days later, Rockefeller came very close to calling me just that in saying I was a dupe and a puppet of sinister right-wing forces.

That was too much. I fired back, saying we should be more concerned about the radical left inside government than anyone outside it. However, it was no time for him, me, or anyone else to start kicking people out of the party. Indeed, I had no power to do so.

During the first week of August 1963, Rocky threw a knockout punch at me. The governor said he would not support me as the GOP nominee against President Kennedy if I were "a captive of the radical right."

It was now time to decide on whether to run. Rocky had declared war on conservatives in general and me in particular. It was now a question not only of breaking up the old boy network of the party, but of honor and principle. I had never walked away from a fight in my life. There was no backing away this time either. We'd seize control from Rocky and the liberals and take on Jack Kennedy.

From the historical perspective of an Arizonan and Westerner, there was another element in the battle to win control of the GOP. I had no qualms about taking on the Eastern establishment, whether it was Rockefeller, the banks, or the large corporations, because we had long been dominated by these interests.

For a century, the West had been a colony of big Eastern money—a boom when they had invested and a bust when they had pulled out of various mining and other operations. We had been left with ghost towns and holes in the ground where gold, silver, and large mineral deposits had been discovered.

It had begun with the gold rushes of 1849 in California and elsewhere in the 1860s and 1870s. Then they petered out. Silver later rose but came tumbling down in 1893. Copper prices hit rock bottom in 1921 and again during the Great Depression. Eastern companies, syndicates, and banks bled the region of these natural resources, then abandoned us as soon as the riches ran out. Easterners did help open up the region with investment and jobs—as well as federal tax money—but they reinvested little or nothing in the West. Instead, they built libraries and other monuments to their charity in the East.

Washington still holds half the spread in the West—hundreds of millions of acres—and often dictates how such land may be used. Individual states are not trusted to manage it well environmentally. That is because some states historically have not done a good job of land management. Times have changed. Nevertheless, the feds still want a grip on our reach into the future.

Today we are still under pressure from national companies and the Washington bureaucracy as to how we may use our land and other natural resources from copper to tungsten, uranium, oil, coal, shale, and forests.

The federal government and large corporations tried to wipe away state and local laws as late as the 1970s, when big oil and other companies came West in the name of saving the United States from an energy crisis caused by the Organization of Petroleum Exporting Countries (OPEC) and later Iranian oil embargoes. The companies wished to use our scarce water—vast amounts were needed to develop shale and other energy—while Eastern members of Congress argued to halt many Western reclamation projects.

I wanted not only a new GOP but an Administration more representative of its people and a Congress more attuned to demographic shifts and changing political winds.

In the late summer of 1963 I quietly asked Denison Kitchel, a Phoenix lawyer and close friend, to open a campaign office at the Carroll Arms Hotel, a few blocks from the Capitol. Kitchel, who still looked like a choir-boy despite a sprinkling of gray hair, amiably told inquir-ers he was handling my 1964 reelection run for the Senate. He said we needed time together for planning purposes. Few people believed that, but the answer was accurate—as far as it went. Denny had officially become head of my Senate campaign several months earlier.

Kitchel had no political background. I had chosen him through a twist of fate. In the spring of 1963, at a meeting of Arizona Republican leaders in Phoenix, Dick Klein-dienst had stepped down as state party chairman: he was considering running for governor. The party leaders had informally selected Denny, who had been our general counsel for years, to take over as state chairman. I had flown to Phoenix for the meeting. Denny had come to my home the evening before the meeting for a private chat. He'd said, "Barry, I don't want this job. They told me that I had to take it. Everybody says he's behind me. But I don't like the work. I wouldn't be any good at it. I've never been much good with politicians. Think of some-thing—anything—but get me the hell out of it."

All of us had lunch the next day, and the Kitchel deci-sion came up. Everyone said Denny would have to be-come state chairman. No arguments. I said, "Wait a minute, fellows. You've got to find somebody else. Den-ny's going to handle my senatorial campaign."

Everybody asked, "Is that so?"

I replied, "Certainly."

Everyone then looked at Denny, who showed a bit of surprise but quickly responded, "Yes, yes. That's right."

Timing was a factor in the choice, but there were many

more important reasons to bring Denny on as my right hand. We were old and very close friends. I totally trusted him. He was reserved and cautious. As a corporation lawyer, he was studious, intelligent, and conservative. Born in Bronxville, New York, Kitchel was graduated from Yale and later Harvard Law School. As a student, he worked on ranches in the West, and he came to Arizona after completing his studies. Denny was a longtime Arizonan.

Our understanding was very simple. He'd come to Washington, keep his powder dry, and listen—to everybody. We'd take until the end of 1963 to evaluate the political situation.

Denny made it clear he was no politician. He knew no one on the national political scene. Nor was he known in conservative intellectual circles. While I was the outspoken voice of a growing rebellion in the Republican Party, he was, in many ways, my antithesis.

Denny listened. It seemed that everyone in the party was soon bending his ear—congressional representatives, my GOP colleagues in the Senate, leaders of the Draft Goldwater Committee, and political veterans like Ed McCabe, a Washington lawyer and longtime White House aide to President Eisenhower, and William J. Baroody, Sr., head of the American Enterprise Institute, a nonprofit think tank he founded in the nation's capital.

The Draft Goldwater Committee, which had moved from New York City to new headquarters on Connecticut Avenue in Washington, continued its relentless hunt for convention delegates across the country, not only at state meetings and conventions but at the county and even precinct level. Clif White and his people seemed to be everywhere. They had already garnered delegates in some forty states. They did not yet have a steamroller under way, but they certainly had a grass roots fire burning.

Peter O'Donnell, an aggressive young Texan, turned up the heat from the draft committee. He argued with Kitchel over strategy and other moves to win the nomination. Denny politely but firmly rebuffed him, as I had instructed him. We weren't ready to make a formal announcement. The committee was eager to have such a commitment so it could pass the word in the hunt for more delegates.

The pressure from conservatives in Congress mounted with letters and phone calls. Eight hundred to a thousand letters a day poured into my Senate office from conservatives around the country, all urging me to run. Conservative intellectuals said that the right had found a new respectability and that we deserved a chance at major responsibility in the country.

Bill Buckley and Brent Bozell, of *National Review*, wanted to organize a committee of college professors as intellectual support for a Goldwater campaign. They discussed it at dinner with Kitchel, Baroody, and Dr. Charles Kelley, who was doing research work for Denny. All agreed to think further about the proposal. The New York *Times* soon revealed the meeting but inaccurately described what happened. The *Times* said that Goldwater advisers had "repelled a boarding party" of the "far right"—referring to Buckley and Bozell—which wanted to join his organization on a policy planning level.

All of us knew the story was false, but it raised a serious question. Who had leaked it to the *Times?* The question was extremely important because it had a major repercussion on my presidential campaign. The *National Review* crowd felt excluded from the workings of the campaign.

I'm convinced today that Baroody leaked the report. So are Kitchel and others. Bill has since passed away, so it's impossible to know with absolute certainty. The record is, however, important. None of the others present at the dinner spoke with the *Times* about the conversation.

If that is true, why would Baroody divulge a slanted version of what occurred? Bill had become the dominant figure among a small group of advisers around Kitchel—Dr. Kelley, Mike Bernstein, who had worked with me on labor law in the Senate, and McCabe, Ike's former aide. This small group was to grow and become an informal brain trust during my run for the White House. Baroody dominated these advisers for the entire campaign. I was simply too busy to keep track of who was saying what to whom in these issues and strategy sessions. Since Denny was neither a political tactician nor a hard-nosed issues man, he depended heavily on Baroody.

Bill saw the Buckley-Bozell gesture as a bid to gain access to the inner circle. Kitchel and I are now convinced that Baroody quickly slammed the door because he saw a possibility that he might have to share power with the two men, both of whom were highly intelligent and very political. In any event, neither Buckley nor Bozell could take a full-time job with us. They simply wanted to be helpful from time to time.

Buckley and Bozell, who married one of Buckley's sisters, saw the *Times* leak as a rebuff by the inner circle and perhaps by me. They were offended. The truth is, I would have welcomed both into the campaign with open arms. It had been impossible to do so earlier, for this reason: *National Review* supported the Draft Goldwater Committee at a time when I wanted to remain distant from that group. The entire situation was confused by the *Times* story, and both groups drifted apart.

Buckley, Bozell, and Bill Rusher were virtually shut out from any significant campaign assistance. It was an undeserved, unconscionable act on our part. All are men of the highest integrity and solid conservative views. They should have been on board, talking with me and others and offering feedback on issues, strategy, the media, our opposition, everything. Later, realizing what had happened, I was heartsick about the matter. But what could I say? What could I do? It was too late.

Dean Burch, my former administrative assistant and a Tucson lawyer, joined Kitchel as his administrative assistant. I knew Dean well and liked and trusted him.

On November 2, 1963, the Associated Press took a poll

of GOP state and county leaders. An overwhelming majority, more than 85 percent, chose me as the "strongest candidate" against Kennedy. Rockefeller had less than 4 percent; Nixon about 3 percent. More than 64 percent believed I would receive the nomination.

As the November winds cracked across the Capitol a year before the 1964 Presidential election, the GOP presidential sweepstakes lined up as follows:

George Romney rolled up his sleeves and climbed into the presidential ring. The Michigan governor had proved to be an exciting, surprising, unorthodox politician. But Romney was a liberal spender, and that didn't wash with conservatives.

Pennsylvania Governor Bill Scranton eased inside and outside the presidential ropes. Few people knew whether to take him seriously or not. The Pennsylvania governor leaned toward the conservatives on fiscal matters but embraced the left on many social issues. His Eisenhower connection was important. The Scranton family also were long and traditional Republicans, and he could not be dismissed, at least as a vice presidential possibility.

Nixon's defeat in the California gubernatorial race seemed to rule him out, but he began to make backstage noises about running again in case there was a deadlocked convention.

A few Easterners mentioned Henry Cabot Lodge as a possibility, but his acceptance of the ambassadorship to South Vietnam was a big handicap. He had his hands full in a faraway post.

Rockefeller still seemed the man to beat. No one appeared likely to defeat him except me. The Draft Goldwater Committee was kept waiting.

On November 22 the waiting was over. Within a few days, I knew that the bullet which killed Jack Kennedy had also shot down my chances for the Presidency. I told Kitchel to pass the word: I would not run.

Others tried to convince me differently. Kitchel mentioned a news report which said that the last words Kennedy had spoken to Johnson when they left their Dallas hotel that morning had been, "Well, Lyndon, I guess we can carry Massachusetts and Texas."

Obviously, that was just a Kennedy quip. However, we knew from GOP polls that the President's political fortunes were not as bright as Democrats had attempted to portray them. In another move to convince me to run, Clif White sent word that the "Goldwater train is running down the track toward the nomination at 120 miles an hour." Boston's Richard Cardinal Cushing, a friend of the Kennedy family, had been quoted as saying earlier that the President might not win in 1964.

To me, this was now all noise. I would not be a candidate. The idea of running against Lyndon Johnson was abhorrent to me.

Walter Cronkite of "CBS News" sealed my decision. When Kennedy was killed, I was escorting my mother-in-law's body from Phoenix to her funeral and burial in Muncie, Indiana. My wife's brother Ray met me in Chicago, where we had to change planes. He asked me if I had heard the news about the President. I hadn't. Ray told me Kennedy had been shot. I was shocked because we had been so personally close. By the time we arrived in Muncie, the President was dead.

Cronkite came on the air and, in the course of the "CBS Evening News," said I was off giving a political speech in Indiana and would not be present for the wake and funeral. The inference was clear. I wasn't showing the proper respect to the slain President and the office. I was never so angry in my life, and I phoned Cronkite to say, "Mr. Cronkite, I don't know you. I've always respected you. But you just told CBS viewers a blatant lie. I'm not here in Indiana to make a political speech, but to help bury my mother-in-law."

Later he apologized on CBS. Experience has shown that these corrections never undo the damage they cause. Some CBS spokesmen talked about a scrap of paper from the United Press International wire floating around

Cronkite's desk, and it had somehow gotten on the air.
They never offered a credible explanation. This was the
first in a series of major errors made by "CBS News"
over the course of my candidacy for the Presidency. I
accepted Cronkite's apology and, to this day, hold no
rancor against him. He's a personable and honorable
man. At the time, however, I turned to Peggy and said,
"That does it. I'm definitely not going to run!"

For the first time since her mother's death, the faint
glow of a smile creased her face.

The overwhelming reason for the decision was my personal and political contempt for Lyndon Johnson. Johnson was a master of manipulation. He solved tough
public issues through private plotting. His answer to almost everything was a deal—an air base here, a welfare
project there.

If conservatives were to plead their case before the
American people, the air had to be clear and clean. There
had to be a line of battle where principles and beliefs
clashed openly for the public to see. Johnson was the
epitome of the unprincipled politician. He would assume
the Kennedy legacy and be consumed by the sorrow of
Jack's martyrdom. I couldn't and wouldn't run against a
man like that.

I made none of these thoughts public, although there
was speculation in the media about my desire to run
against Kennedy. I spoke well of Johnson in public for
one reason: to help unite the entire country behind the
new President at a time of sorrow and crisis. I was an
American first, a Republican second.

I also was convinced that the American people were
not ready for three presidents in little more than a year.
They were not likely to support Johnson-Kennedy opponents. That would be the Democratic ticket in 1964, no
matter who Johnson chose as Vice President.

The so-called radical right was being blamed for assas-
sinating Kennedy. The Draft Goldwater Committee
closed its Washington headquarters because of threats.

Senator John Tower and his family moved out of their home to a hotel room because of phone callers who threatened their lives. Conservatives around the nation reported similar incidents. Lee Harvey Oswald's Soviet, Cuban, and other Communist connections soon surfaced, but that did not deter some liberals. There were quotes on television interviews and elsewhere that Texas had right-wing kooks who didn't like Kennedy and might have shot him. Some of the silly conclusions drove me nuts. There was clearly genuine sorrow among conservatives at the time, and some of the liberal sniping at us was unworthy.

December opened quietly. Mercifully, a turbulent year would soon close. It would be great to be with all the family at Christmas. I wanted to go home to Arizona.

Within a month, I made a complete turnaround. Under tremendous pressure, I agreed to run against Johnson.

On December 8, at Kitchel's insistence, there was a small meeting of some GOP leaders in my Washington apartment. I was very uncomfortable as the group assembled in the living room. They were Republican Senators Norris Cotton of New Hampshire, Carl Curtis of Nebraska, and Bill Knowland of California. Bill Baroody, Jay Gordon Hall, a veteran Washington lobbyist who had long been regarded as one of the savviest political analysts in the capital, and Kitchel were also there.

One by one, as casually as if we were talking about a Sunday afternoon pro football game, they brought up the GOP Presidential nomination. Each maintained that I had to reconsider my decision to drop out of the race.

I got damned mad at all of them. Jack Kennedy was dead. It was over. There would never be a battle of issues. No battle about the liberal agenda. Johnson was a dirty fighter. Any campaign with him in it would involve a lot of innuendo and lies. Johnson was a wheeler-dealer. Neither he nor anyone else could change that. That's what he was. And Johnson was treacherous to boot. He'd slap you on the back today and stab you in the back tomorrow.

Moreover, LBJ was dull. He was a lousy public speaker. The man didn't believe half of what he said. He was a hypocrite, and it came through in the hollowness of his speech. LBJ made me sick.

The last thing Lyndon Johnson wanted to do in life was talk political principles or beliefs. He wouldn't do it. LBJ never believed in either. His only political dogma was expediency. Things were never right or wrong. Most problems in the country could be fixed with cunning and craftiness.

He never cleaned that crap off his boots. It trailed him from the Senate to the vice presidency and into the Oval Office itself. There's an old saying out in Arizona: If you get down in the manure, you come up smelling like it.

The room was silent after I finished.

Finally, one by one, each of the senators spoke. It was like an echo chamber:

"This is the conservative hour—it's now or never. . . . The party needs you. Rockefeller, Nixon, Romney, Scranton, and Lodge are not the answer. . . . Think of those hundreds of thousands of young Republicans out there—the YAFs, the college crowd, all those young people who came to hear you speak over the last nine years or so. . . . You gotta do it, Barry. It's too late. You can't back out now. The Draft Goldwater Committee and too many other people have gone too far for you to walk away from them . . ."

All of this set the scene for Cotton. The New Englander was as eloquent as a modern Thoreau or Emerson. Cotton compared me with former French President Charles DeGaulle. He spoke of the decline of wartime France and its rebirth in postwar Europe under the general's guidance. America was getting soft. It needed a new commander. The nation's direction must be changed in slow, reasonable steps. That's the conservative mission. That's what we're all about. No one in the party has your mass appeal—the vision, the character, the will to turn America in a conservative direction. This is the hour. This is destiny. If only you'll give the command!

Cotton's emotion and eloquence overwhelmed us. Tears welled up in our eyes. Everyone was silent, looking at me, waiting. I needed time to think—to sleep on it. We should all sleep on it, I felt. Quietly, one by one, each shook hands with me and walked out into the fading afternoon. I asked Kitchel to remain.

Neither of us spoke. We sat alone for a long time. I finally stood and watched the darkness descend across Rock Creek Park and up along Embassy Row on Massachusetts Avenue. Neither of us turned on a light although the living room was now almost dark.

It meant leaving the Senate if I ran. I could never be like Johnson, who ran for the Senate while campaigning for the vice presidency. Lord, I really didn't want to run.

I turned on a lamp, walked over to the liquor cabinet, and poured Denny a bourbon and water, a plain bourbon for myself.

Finally, sitting down after pacing up and down the living room, I asked Denny, "What do you think?"

He retorted, "What do *you* think?"

I replied, "Well, I'm impressed by the sincerity of those fellows. They've obviously gone out on a limb for me. I think they're great guys. But, Denny, this isn't the time for a conservative Republican to run. The country doesn't want three different presidents in a year's time. I can't win. In the process, we could harm the conservative cause. I'm not inclined to do it—for all those reasons and the simple fact that I don't like or trust Lyndon Johnson."

Denny sipped his drink calmly. I edged closer to him. He was my friend—low-key, cool, thoughtful. Denny would never mislead me, never lie to me. He finally turned, looked directly at me, and said, "Barry, I don't think you can back down."

The words were like the shot at Concord Bridge, like the start of a revolution. Denny was talking war. It would be an all-out, bitter battle in any campaign against LBJ.

Denny explained that perhaps we had been wrong in setting up our little campaign office here in Washington. Sure, we were thinking Kennedy, but all that had changed. But nothing was now different to the others. They thought we were going to go. So they had gone a long way down the road. All of them were good friends. They would feel that Barry Goldwater had left them holding the bag if he decided not to run.

I had expected a lawyer's approach from Denny. He was viewing the decision more on a personal basis. I said, "But everything has changed. Jack Kennedy is dead."

"Yes," Denny responded, "but they didn't know your thinking on that."

He pointed out that they saw my running as the conservative answer to what was going on in the country—period. Kennedy was only a part of that, not the whole Democratic Party and its philosophy. Cotton and many others were thinking only of the conservatives—where were *we* going? What would *we* do?

He talked of millions of conservatives around the country who had made a stand in favor of Barry Goldwater and concluded: "You could lead this country. You've got to try it."

Instinctively, intuitively, I knew that the commitment —the bond I had made to so many conservatives and they to me—was virtually unbreakable at this point. It was all over. I said, "All right, damn it, I'll do it."

The fateful words came out in a flash.

I told Denny to tell no one but the three senators. "I don't care how you do it, but no one else must know!"

Kitchel phoned them the following day.

The decision seemed final. It wasn't. There was one more river to cross, but I kept that to myself.

* * *

Christmas was wonderful—Peggy, all the children, old
friends. In the background, several private meetings with
Arizona Republicans followed. These included Representative John Rhodes, former Senator Paul Fannin, Burch,
Kleindienst, and others. I asked Peggy, as a special favor,
to do something she never did—sit in on some of the
talks.

Then I spoke with her privately.

She had not changed her mind. Peggy did not want me
to run. She repeated many of the reasons she had not
wished me to run for the Senate twelve years before—
that I was too open and would be savagely attacked in a
national campaign, much more than running for the Senate in Arizona; that our family privacy would be invaded
and she was a very private person; and, finally, that she
didn't want to see me get hurt.

I told Peggy something I've never—to this moment—
told anyone else in my life. I said I didn't want to run. In
my gut, there was never a burning desire to be President.
I just wanted the conservatives to have a real voice in the
country. Many of us were damn tired of the Democrats.
They'd eventually wreck the economy and bring the
whole country down with them. Someone had to rally the
conservatives, take over the Republican Party, and turn
the direction of the GOP around. There was no one to do
it but me. We'd lose the election but win the party.

It was only after making that confession to Peggy that
I firmly and finally decided to run. Also, out of respect
for my family and native state, I wanted that decision to
be announced at my home in Arizona.

For the past twenty-five years, people have speculated
that I ran unwillingly. That's all it was—pure speculation. I never said that to a single soul—only Peggy. She
kept my secret, and how much it pained her. Only she
could understand what was in my mind and heart as
1964 began.

6

The Road to San Francisco

JACK BELL, THE WHITE-HAIRED CORRESPONDENT OF the Associated Press—tough, fair, taciturn—was a model of the Washington press veteran. He leaned back comfortably in a chair in my living room, sipped a drink, and said, "I came here in the 1930s of President Roosevelt. Barry, I've covered everything in this town. In all these years, there's only one man I never understood—Bob Taft. I never understood a word he said. In fact, I don't understand you guys most of the time—all you conservatives."

The conversation took place about thirty years ago, long before a conservative from Arizona considered running for the Presidency. Both of us lived in Washington's Westchester Apartments. We'd met at the elevator, and I'd invited him to our place for a drink. Bell added, "I listened to you today in the Senate, and I didn't understand you either."

That conversation made a lasting impression on me. Bell was saying something most conservatives had not grasped. We had long thought the media were unfair to us, but we had not sufficiently understood the reasons. Bell was spelling out one of them. We were simply not being understood. Why? Was it that many, like himself, were either too steeped in Roosevelt's New Deal to appreciate what we were trying to explain, or was it our own fault—for whatever reasons—that we weren't getting our message across?

On January 3, 1964, as I slipped into an old shirt, a pair of blue jeans, and slippers to greet the national media, I remembered that chat with Bell. The message of our campaign had to be crystal clear. It could not be misunderstood. Still in pain from surgery, carrying crutches, my right foot in a walking cast, I announced my candidacy for the Republican Presidential nomination from our home in Phoenix. These words spelled out our campaign as simply as we could: "We'll offer a choice, not an echo."

I would not be a "Me Too" Republican, an echo of the Democrats' liberal agenda. I would offer the nation a new national direction. We were going to explain to the American people the meaning and the opportunities of conservatism. That, as events have turned out, has been the mission of my entire political career.

It's important to recall our basic principles—greater national respect for and support of individual initiative, fiscal responsibility by the federal and other governments, more power in the hands of local citizens, and a strong national defense.

The 1964 campaign was to be a beginning. My first objective was realistic: to create an understanding of conservative beliefs among more Americans—millions more. However, that hope was dampened almost immediately.

My announcement created two storms in the East. In the first, the media pros said Goldwater was a fool to hold such a conference in Phoenix. They argued that any such statements should be made in Washington or New York, where the candidate would receive greater news coverage. The media were right, from their point of view.

We made the decision against all advice. It was a sentimental gesture to the state where I was born and which I loved. The announcement also sent a message to the Republican Party, to my fellow conservatives, and to the country: I was going to be my own man, not packaged for the voters by Madison Avenue and a lot of other slick professionals who made me very uncomfortable.

The announcement also had a deeper, much more significant implication. No one except Kitchel, Baroody, and I knew it at the time, but we had already made a crucial decision: For better or worse, I would be myself—a straight-shooting, down-the-line conservative—for the entire campaign.

The second storm was much larger. The nation's political pros described my choice of top campaign staff as a disaster. All were political unknowns from Arizona—Denison Kitchel, general director; Dean Burch, assistant director; Mrs. Emory Johnson, director of the women's campaign; and Richard Kleindienst, director of field operations. They were soon called the Arizona Mafia. The media attacked them as amateurs. Political pros were not any kinder. None of the top members of the Draft Goldwater Committee, all experienced campaign veterans, had been chosen.

All these years, the media and others have speculated about the group. They said the candidate wanted to be comfortable with friends around him. He feared being manipulated or controlled by outside political pros. Both observations were true but were not the major reason for my decision. The reason was my own conviction that, barring a political miracle, I'd lose the race against Johnson. The American people would not accept three different presidents in little more than a year, and the certain conservative-liberal fight for control of the GOP would leave the party on the ropes in the national election campaign. I could honorably ask friends to walk down a dead-end road with me because I'd do the same for them. They would benefit because the campaign would be a big challenge and an unforgettable experience. It would be unrealistic and perhaps unfair to ask outsiders to accept a large responsibility in a doomed campaign.

I didn't hide these feelings from my friends. I finally

confirmed what I had told Peggy. Before the announcement, scores of them had gathered in our living room. It was bedlam. The media had taken over the house and patio with camera cables, lights, and sound equipment plugged into every available electric socket. A dozen friends had gathered around me, and we chatted. Turning to Arizona Governor Paul Fannin, who would run for my vacated Senate seat, I said, "It's a damn shame things turned out like this, Paul. I don't think we're going anyplace at all. Frankly, I don't know why I'm doing this. I'll be damned if I want to run against Lyndon Johnson. I wanted to run against Jack Kennedy. I want all of you to know from the start that I believe it's a lost cause."

It was the closest I ever came to telling anyone, apart from Peggy, that I was running unwillingly. I wanted them to know the plain truth—that the odds against us were overwhelming. I wanted that to be crystal clear.

In all these years, neither Fannin nor any of those standing with me ever revealed that conversation. It was somewhat sad to be that frank, but I was upbeat from another viewpoint. I added, "There are a lot of young people out there. We can't let them down. Someday they're going to pick up where we leave off. Others are relying on us too. First let's take over the party. Then we'll go from there."

We were going down a road together as few men ever do. We never viewed ourselves as victors, a new White House team, but as people who believed in one another and the same cause. To outsiders, it might seem incredible, even now, but to us, good friends, the campaign was as natural as tackling a big community project.

The likelihood of defeat didn't come up again until six months later, when some of us were writing my acceptance speech to the San Francisco convention. With bittersweet humor, I told the staff that we were going to lose.

The Arizona Mafia were soon joined by others, none from our state—Bill Baroody, Ed McCabe, and speechwriter Karl Hess. They were part of the team for one reason: I trusted them.

Not long ago, nearly twenty-five years after the campaign, Denny Kitchel and I looked back on the role of the Arizona staff. He said, "Barry, I don't think the staff knew what we were doing. I blame myself a lot. I had no background, no expertise. A great deal of my performance was inadequate. We didn't play according to the rules because we didn't know the rules. But you know, I don't think the pros would have done much better."

Denny confessed he never understood why I had chosen him as the general director since he had virtually no understanding of a political campaign. He was my friend, and I trusted him. The pros never would have done it our way—putting the conservative cause before winning the nomination or the election. So who needed them? We weren't going to compromise. We were going to conduct a campaign such as America had never seen before—or would again.

We made a lot of mistakes. It was my decision to discuss the selling of the Tennessee Valley Authority in Knoxville and Social Security's financial crunch in Florida. We made other strategic and tactical errors from the shortsighted viewpoint of an election victory. I never blamed anyone. Nor did I ever believe the media were the major reason for my defeat, although in my opinion they were unfair to us at times. Denny accepted some blame: "I think the criticism of the Arizona Mafia was absolutely valid. Our ineptitude made us different from most campaigns. How much more ridiculous can you get than taking guys like Kitchel, Burch, Kleindienst, and others with virtually no background whatever? Then, you stick them in a campaign. But that's Goldwater, the real Barry. And that's what the country saw in the campaign."

There was never a hidden agenda in our campaign. The staff and I sat down as friends, and I gave them hell about overscheduling me, or they told me to stop the off-the-cuff remarks. We just sat down and chewed the fat. Motorcades and hoopla were a big headache, a necessary but tiresome activity. As for the Goldwater people in those limousines and shiny cars, we were simply a bunch of people who liked one another, believed in one another, were united in the same cause, and were willing to give up part of our lives in an unforgettable adventure.

Dick Kleindienst, a Tucson attorney who had been chairman of the Arizona GOP, had another view of the campaign. He called it "the screwiest experience of my life." He may not have been entirely wrong.

Dick and his wife, Marnie, were returning home from the 1964 Rose Bowl game in California. We had a state-wide police bulletin put out on his vehicle. An Arizona highway patrolman spotted their license number at a border inspection station and stopped them. He told Kleindienst to drive straight to my house. That's all Dick knew.

When he arrived, Kleindienst saw the mob scene. It was a little more than an hour before I would announce my candidacy. We went into a back bedroom with Kitchel and Burch. Dick's jaw dropped when we told him he was going to be the national director of field operations for the campaign. We all laughed when he said, "What the hell's that?"

We told him he had to get 665 delegates to vote for me on the first ballot.

"Barry, you've got to be crazy!" he replied, very reasonably.

"You're right, Dick. If I weren't nuts, I wouldn't be doing this!"

Kleindienst talked about the criticism we would receive from having so many Arizonans at the top of the staff. I shot back, "Get this straight. I'm not going to turn my life over to people I don't know and trust. The three of you have to agree to do this thing, or I'm not going through with it."

It was a wild, magnificent, screwy, splendid undertaking.

These words about my 1964 campaign are an examination of conscience in the twilight of my life when excuses are neither necessary nor particularly becoming to a tough old guy like me. The record speaks pretty much for itself. But I want to make it complete.

I didn't want to run for the presidency. That's God's truth. To my knowledge, no individual who has run the race has ever made such a statement. It's also true that I knew, and said privately from the start, that I would lose to President Johnson. Also, as best as I can determine, no presidential candidate has ever said that on the eve of his campaign. From my perspective, the race itself—explaining the conservative viewpoint—had greater historical value and meaning than winning. That was a very tough concept for me to handle. You don't go to war to lose. The first order of battle is victory. As we shall see, ours was a different victory.

Not long ago, in a chat about this book, George Reedy, press secretary to President Johnson, penetratingly described our campaign: "The Goldwater campaign was right out of the Old Testament—the blood of the sacrificial lamb—Barry and the true believers. I never believed Barry Goldwater wanted to become President. Instead, he was on a modern crusade—blood shed in what he and the conservatives believed was a sacred cause."

The New Hampshire primary was a lesson in how not to run a campaign. For more than three weeks, from dawn to dusk, I sloshed through the snow for as long as eighteen hours a day. We flew up and down the state in random leaps that made no sense, sometimes spending more time in planes and cars than campaigning. I often spoke to as few as a dozen people. I fell into bed most nights completely exhausted. There was no agenda of issues, the crux of our campaign. Just about everything we did was extemporaneous.

State Republicans were divided. Senator Norris Cotton and New Hampshire House Speaker Stuart Lamprey did not agree on how to run the race. Kleindienst, who was supposed to be out helping run the campaign, was busy trying to mediate the differences between our two most important supporters.

In Concord the campaign exploded. Responding to a reporter's question, I said that the Social Security system might be improved if we made changes in it, including making some contributions voluntary. The system was actuarially unsound. It had been sold to the American public as a kind of retirement insurance when its real purpose was only to prevent starvation. Every single statement I made was accurate. The next day, the Concord *Monitor* headlined: GOLDWATER SETS GOALS: END SOCIAL SECURITY.

The headline was a complete distortion of my views. To this day, my statement stands as accurate. Democrats and Republicans alike have made the point for me in recent years by declaring that the system was in danger of bankruptcy and that changes had to be made to salvage it. They also admit that Social Security is not a retirement fund. If someone wishes to provide for his or her retirement, he should do so privately. Many members of Congress have finally admitted publicly what they have long known. Private retirement plans wouldn't wreck the system. I did not say the Social Security system should be immediately junked, as Rockefeller, Scranton, and my Democratic opponents were to suggest. It had to be changed over time.

Other controversial issues also emerged in New Hampshire. I said the commander of NATO should have the discretion to use tactical nuclear weapons in the event of an enemy attack on Western Europe. The fact is, my statement represented official American policy under Presidents Eisenhower and Kennedy. Some reporters said I used the plural "commanders," which changed my entire meaning. None confirmed that with me before writing front page stories of their own version the following morning. Later, some did put the question of number to me, but it was too late.

Whose fault were these two incidents? Everybody's, including my own. Did I shoot from the hip? A more accurate way of putting it was that I should have used more precise language, qualifying what I said.

The media also were at fault. The financial problems of Social Security and the NATO policy on nuclear strike potential had already been established. Neither was a secret. My views were neither eccentric nor irresponsible. The conservative views of fiscal integrity and the like were rarely headlined in New Hampshire. The media had either dismissed or ignored my challenge to the New Deal and the failed welfare state.

Henry Cabot Lodge, the U.S. ambassador to Saigon, won the primary by some 12,000 votes over the second-place finisher, Barry Goldwater. Nelson Rockefeller was third.

A somber and wiser group of Arizonans returned to Washington. We had lost but were not defeated. We'd come back. We had some experience now, even if we still had a lot to learn. We would ask for help from more pros.

Rockefeller would be rough. His staff had reproduced the Concord Social Security headline. A "Stop Goldwater" movement was already under way among the other candidates. Each viewed the New Hampshire result the same way: Barry's bandwagon had lost a wheel.

One theme was shaping up among the media—fear. Fear of Goldwater. It was too early to calculate whether a deliberate campaign of fear was being orchestrated, but it was difficult to ignore the warnings.

I made two personal conclusions in New Hampshire. Pushing myself at people to shake hands for a vote just wasn't me—we'd do it only when it seemed natural—and the backbreaking daily schedules of the Granite State could not continue.

Candor, or "imprecise frankness," as one of our more erudite staffers corrected me, hurt us in New Hampshire. But it also helped us at the end. After coming in second, I concluded on national television, "I goofed."

We received thousands of letters, telegrams, and phone calls saying that this public admission had been refreshingly frank.

Clif White played a sweeping role in all of this. He and Bill Rusher had organized the Draft Goldwater Committee. White had traveled across the country for some two years, winning many delegates to the national convention for us. In San Francisco he, together with Nick Volcheff, an Arizonan, set up the most sophisticated communications system in convention history.

I probably would not have won the nomination without the work of White. It's a somewhat sad story, but one of the most important and gripping aspects of the campaign. The role of White, Rusher, Peter O'Donnell of Texas, and others was critical in elevating the conservative movement and ultimately moving the American people in a new political direction. To capture White and the breadth of what was taking place, I have to go back to before the Draft Goldwater Committee began.

White had worked in four Republican campaigns before 1964, starting with Tom Dewey in 1948, Ike's two campaigns in the fifties, and Nixon in 1960. White had been a city chairman, country chairman, and state executive committee director. He understood the complexities of how delegates were chosen from state to state. He was a grass roots guy, someone who hit the road and learned the hard way.

White and Bill Rusher were working out of New York when they organized the Draft Goldwater group. They had two aims: to broaden the base of the party and to change its structure along conservative philosophical lines. The White-Rusher goal was simple: to control the Republican nominating convention in 1964.

Without my knowledge, White began canvassing the country in 1962. There was no reason to advise me. I hadn't made up my mind to be a candidate and had distanced myself from both White and Rusher. Their operation was quietly being financed by conservatives. White worked with a secretary out of a small Manhattan office.

Not many Republicans paid attention, but White was adding to the twenty-two conservatives who had first met in Chicago to form the Draft Goldwater Committee. He eventually formed conservative cadres in all fifty states.

White's approach in the state of Washington was typical. First he made two visits to determine who the GOP conservatives were, made contact with them, and asked if they would organize a meeting of state conservatives; he'd return later to address them. The original meeting was planned for twenty-five people in a hotel room. Before the organizing was over, a large meeting room was rented, and the place overflowed. White always began his speech the same way: "We're going to take over the Republican Party and make it the conservative instrument of American politics."

He organized volunteers by precincts and often found that from one third to one half of the GOP precinct committeeperson posts were vacant. Conservatives filled these posts and contested those already occupied. They thus had an inside track on becoming delegates to the state, and eventually national, convention. White began a political file on each state. These meetings began in 1963 and continued in most states throughout most of 1964.

At this point, White approached Mort Frame, who was the GOP state chairman in Washington and Rockefeller's Western states campaign manager. He said, "I'm here to get delegates for Barry Goldwater. I hope we can work together. If not, we'll fight it out, and I'll defeat you."

The state chairman, of course, got a chuckle out of the brash challenge from this lone New York outsider. Frame was so busy electing Rocky in the Western states that the conservatives beat him in his home precinct by ten votes. Frame never even made it as a delegate to the county convention.

Why and how were Frame and many other old-line committeepersons beaten? They had gotten fat and lazy. When asked to call on a hundred people, many said they knew them already. The Goldwater volunteers hit the bricks. What they lacked in political experience, they made up for in shoe leather, phone calls, long hours, and dedication. They didn't know enough to quit.

Word on White's work filtered back to me. During a trip to San Francisco in 1962, I learned there was a Draft Goldwater headquarters near my hotel. So I walked down the street and paid a visit. Surprised, perhaps even stunned, they mobbed me. I was as astonished as they were. Two full years before the convention, here were these unpaid housewives, kids in their teens, the college crowd, and the proverbial little old ladies in tennis shoes licking envelopes and making phone calls. None had ever met Barry Goldwater. They didn't even know if he was going to run. Their enthusiasm touched me. Needless to say, we became friends—once they let me up from the floor.

Those were the beginnings of the first genuine draft in the history of presidential politics. Eventually more than 500,000 volunteers joined in what became a conservative crusade.

There was no secret to White's success. As he put it, "We didn't stack anything, as some candidates claimed at the convention. There was no lunatic fringe of fanatics. We beat 'em fair and square with work and people. Good people. Ordinary people. People who cared. They loved Barry Goldwater. They loved America. And they were proud to be called conservatives."

White wanted the campaign job of director of field operations, but I had named Kleindienst to the post. The two met in Kleindienst's room at the Mayflower Hotel.

Dick later described the scene to me: "Never in my life did I have a more sympathetic feeling for anyone in politics than I had for Clif that morning. Before me was a man who had worked long and hard, and he was literally crushed. Looking at me was a person of vast political experience, a national reputation, on the verge of tears. I told him that I had not asked for the job, but, as long as you had asked me, I was going to give it my best shot. I told Clif that I desperately needed his help and friendship."

Kleindienst offered White the job of codirector of field operations, and White accepted. However, this arrangement weakened Kleindienst's authority. Many of the party's longtime leaders, from senators to state chairmen, privately urged Kleindienst to step aside in the hunt for delegates in favor of White. The relationship between the two during the primaries was delicate.

In politics, there is always considerable jockeying for power, especially at the top. This networking covers a vast array of political and personal relationships, often conflicting and sometimes deadly. I wanted, above all, a campaign above reproach. Nothing would so violate the conservative cause as politics as usual. This was an extremely sensitive point with me. It was not so much that I could not trust Clif White in a top job. I just didn't know him well. He was an excellent professional, and both of us accepted that. He never tried to ingratiate himself with me. Clif never spoke one word of complaint or criticism about me, nor I about him.

To the credit of both White and Kleindienst, as events unfolded they worked effectively together. Yet White was dissatisfied with the way the campaign was run. He has since become one of the sharpest critics of our staff operation of those days. White made a tremendous contribution to our efforts in 1964 and deserves the opportunity to reflect on those events. He has never been franker than in a recent conversation:

"Do you want to know why I didn't walk out on the

campaign? Because every one of those little old ladies and others out there in the hinterlands, who had been bleeding and dying for two years for you, would have lost their voices near the top of the operation. Because Denny Kitchel and Dick Kleindienst didn't know them. I couldn't leave them voiceless."

White felt that Kitchel knew nothing of politics. He had no problem with my appointing Kitchel as my liaison with everyone else—none at all. White knew I had a right to a confidant in the campaign. The problem came when White saw Kitchel and others, because of their inexperience, as jeopardizing what he and others had worked so hard for. As White later put it to me, "The Arizona Mafia was inept."

White also told me I never had the fire in the belly to be President of the United States. He talked about my "humility" and added, "I believe you would go to your hotel room at night during the campaign and ask yourself, 'Would I make a good President? Do I really have the ability?' "

White is right. I did go to bed at night asking myself whether I had the ability to be President of our nation. That's the truth. Barry Goldwater never felt he had all the answers. He believed, however, that conservatives had a lot more than the liberals.

We appointed White to run our national convention apparatus.

As Lyndon Johnson began to move into his campaign, some political pros and the media dropped broad hints that the President would be facing conservative neophytes who didn't know what they were doing. The pros said we didn't know which end was up—as if they did. The message from the smart political money was that we should have learned how to play the game with the big boys. To tell voters what they wanted to hear—that American GIs would not fight the war in Vietnam; that we could have both guns and butter; that the NATO commander had no authority to use tactical nuclear weapons if the Russians attacked Western Europe because the President's finger alone was on the button; that the Tennessee Valley Authority was a vast benefit to the American taxpayer; that civil rights were a wide new social order that limited states' rights; that a Great Society would flow with milk and honey to our vast multitudes in a new era of federal abundance.

That was Lyndon Johnson's platform, packaged in the White House and on Madison Avenue by the President's minister-in-residence, Bill Moyers. Moyers portrayed himself as a poor preacher boy, but he was actually involved in the dirtiest work of the Johnson campaign.

We knew what we were doing, all right. We knew exactly where we were going—to defeat at the polls and victory in the party. The real tragedy is that Johnson, Moyers, and company also knew what they were doing, knew precisely where they were going, and still behaved with paranoia and cold deceit.

The battle for the nomination climaxed in California. The Golden State was bigger than life and more volatile than a Chinese firecracker factory. California, the largest political battleground in the country, would split the GOP wide open.

There was already a division between left and right factions in California. Senator William F. Knowland was on the right, with Governor Goodwin Knight leading the left. While these two Republicans struggled to defeat each other, the Democrats walloped both. Their division foreshadowed the events in San Francisco.

The primary was to take place on June 2. By mid-May, we had more than five hundred national delegates. If we could win in the Golden State, our total would soar to nearly six hundred. A total of 655 national delegate votes were needed to win the nomination. Since we were already certain of obtaining virtually all the delegates in four remaining Western states, the nomination would be locked up if we captured California.

The Who's Who of state GOP politics were for Rockefeller. Rocky also hired Spencer-Roberts and Associates, considered by many to be the top GOP political consulting firm in the state. The firm, in turn, hired other professional organizations. Rocky went all out. We estimated he spent $3.5 million in the primary—almost enough money to buy a house in California!

Our efforts in California were drowning in confusion. Kleindienst was sent there to see if he could make peace in the state party, organize our large volunteer groups into an effective force, and offer some direction to the campaign. After two weeks on the scene, Dick reported in mid-May that we'd lose by 200,000 votes if we didn't make drastic changes. I asked Dean Burch to meet me in Los Angeles, where we were campaigning.

Burch was waiting for me when we arrived. I was madder than a hornet. The schedule had been fouled up. We'd gotten stuck in an elevator for fifteen minutes, then in various traffic jams. Everything was late—not good for a guy with an obsession for being on time. To top it all off, Kleindienst's report that we were trailing Rockefeller had raised my temperature about twenty degrees.

I told Dean that everything was screwed up. We didn't seem to be doing anything right, from scheduling to getting television ads ready. He was, from that moment, in charge of the California campaign. Dean had understood me but seemed to hesitate, so I asked, "What do you need?"

"Money," he replied. "I didn't know I'd be staying. All I have are the clothes on my back—this seersucker jacket and pair of slacks—and only a few bucks. Knowing you, I guess you've got no dough."

Then I remembered a fellow in a reception receiving line in Texas—Dallas or Houston. He had put a bill in my hand and said, "Here's a Lyndon Johnson dollar for your campaign."

I reached into my pants pocket to see if it was still

there. Sure enough, it was—all folded up in a tiny square. I handed it to Dean. He unfolded the square. It was a new $1,000 bill. Burch set up shop, and we began our battle. If either one of us ever thought about whether using that money was illegal or not, neither has ever mentioned it. The fellow never gave me his name.

One of the first decisions we made was not to over-schedule ourselves—no working eighteen to twenty hours a day, as Bill Knowland had planned for me. We gave more set speeches, limiting our remarks, because Rocky was spoiling for a public fight to put more life into his campaign. We also heard that Spencer-Roberts was about to hit us with a blitz of TV commercials depicting me as a nuclear hawk. Most of our efforts went to organize an army of Goldwater volunteers throughout the state.

We were soon being hit from all sides. On May 24 and 25, two separate bombshells exploded. The first occurred during an interview on ABC with Howard K. Smith. We were discussing the possibility of the U.S. military cutting off communist supply lines in North Vietnam. That subject had come up at a recent meeting I and other members of the Senate Armed Services Committee had had at the Pentagon with the Joint Chiefs of Staff. They mentioned the possibility of using an atomic "device" or low-yield weapon—not a nuclear bomb or large-scale weapon —to defoliate forests hiding the Ho Chi Minh Trail. Our military leaders consider various options, and such distinctions, in contingency planning. In that sense, the Pentagon is no different from any corporation or other organization in the country. It would be a dereliction of duty if the military—or anyone else in a position of public responsibility—did not engage in planning.

Smith said he understood I favored interdicting communist supply routes from mainland China to South Vietnam. I replied, "Well, it's not as easy as it sounds because these aren't trails that are out in the open. . . . There have been several suggestions made. I don't think we would use any of them. But defoliation of the forests by low-yield atomic weapons could well be done. When you remove the foliage, you remove the cover . . ."

The Associated Press, United Press International, and other news media reported that I had advocated using nuclear weapons in Vietnam. Those reports were then and are now manifestly false. There was then and is today not the slightest room for doubt about what I was discussing—merely a possibility. Indeed, I said, *"I don't think we would ever use any of them"*—playing down even the *possibility.*

UPI later retracted its story, and the AP finally issued a correction. So far as I know, others ignored their error. Howard K. Smith said recently for the record, "Barry Goldwater never suggested or recommended the use of nuclear weapons in that broadcast. A precise reading of what he said never backed up those stories. I don't believe the reporters were trying to get him. The phrase 'nuclear weapons' may have triggered an effect. Use of the term was inflammatory. I think those reporters just thought they had latched on to something. But it wasn't there."

Smith interviewed me after the election and told me after the broadcast, "The media were not completely fair to you."

The record clearly shows that I've never advocated the use of nuclear weapons. I would not have used nuclear weapons in Vietnam. However, neither a President nor a candidate for the office should rule out the option of using nuclear weapons. He cannot offer an enemy—or a potential enemy—the security of knowing it can launch a war or other attacks without the possibility of the United States retaliating in kind, perhaps quickly and overwhelmingly. Peace is maintained through strength. I learned that at about the age of seven, had it reinforced as a pilot in the Air Force, and have maintained the belief for more than seventy years.

* * *

The second bombshell exploded the following day on the front page of the New York *Herald Tribune*. The newspaper had long been an organ of the Republican Eastern establishment. It sought to hold off any new ideas from Republicans west of the Alleghenies. The *Tribune* ran an article, signed by former President Eisenhower, describing the type of candidate Ike believed the Republicans should nominate. The article mentioned no names.

The newspaper ran an accompanying column by Roscoe Drummond which interpreted Ike's comments as anti-Goldwater. Eisenhower had been mousetrapped by his brother, Milton, and by friends who preferred Rockefeller but would accept Scranton. Ike later made it clear that he did not oppose me and endorsed no one for the nomination. He said, referring directly to the *Tribune* and others in the media, "You people tried to read Goldwater out of the party; I didn't."

Meantime, we sent the *Tribune* and Ike's associates a message. It was a photo which made the front pages around the world—Goldwater at California's Shasta College with an arrow in his back. Actually, it was stuck under my arm. We thought it humorous under the circumstances, and so did Ike.

At the same time as the TV interview and *Tribune* article, we noticed considerable political movement by Richard Nixon. Rocky had defeated me in the Oregon primary. We hadn't campaigned there because the nomination would be won or lost in California. Nixon was speaking out on the issues all across the country, clearly hoping to win wide conservative support and the nomination if I stumbled in California. We learned that Nixon and some of his political cronies had met secretly in New York's Waldorf-Astoria Hotel over the Memorial Day weekend. Here was a guy who had just lost the California governor's race and, blaming the media, had told them they wouldn't have Dick Nixon to kick around anymore. Now he was plotting behind closed doors to take over the convention and give all the current candidates the boot. Yet we had the power to block anyone's nomination. But Nixon had a trump card—he always expected me and others to be fair and square with him.

If I dropped out because of a loss in California, we wouldn't have supported Nixon. There wasn't a conservative in the country who had forgotten his sellout to Rockefeller in the 1960 campaign. Nixon had broken his word of honor to me by meeting Rocky privately in New York. He had agreed to a more liberal party platform as well as to having Henry Cabot Lodge on his ticket.

I leaned toward dropping out if defeated in California, but it was still a big if for two reasons: we wanted to preserve conservative unity then and in the future, and there was a large personal problem between Nixon and me. That problem became even larger when we learned of Nixon's secret meeting in Manhattan. I hadn't seen Nixon in four years. He had tried in various ways to make peace with me but never did. Nixon had lied to me.

If we failed completely, I planned to support Scranton. He was not a conservative, and it would have washed away years of work. The Pennsylvania governor had one thing going for him—he had not assailed the conservative movement. We could live with him and fight another day. It was a very painful consideration, but politics is often an extremely agonizing process.

We were the underdog in California, but Dean Burch was doing a tremendous job in reorganizing our campaign from top to bottom. We began an advertising blitz of our own. There was a large undecided vote, but Rocky was heavily favored as we entered the last week of the campaign.

Then, as someone later jokingly said to me, God entered the campaign. To be honest, I tried to keep Him out, as we shall see.

Rockefeller was to address the students at Loyola University, a Roman Catholic institution. Cardinal James F.

McIntyre of Los Angeles withdrew the university's invitation. McIntyre said he and the archdiocese didn't wish to leave the impression that the Catholic Church blessed the candidacy of anyone who had been divorced and later remarried. Soon afterward, a group of Protestant ministers issued a statement suggesting the New York governor should withdraw from the race. Then, three days before the primary, Happy Rockefeller gave birth to a son. That resurrected the divorce and remarriage issue.

We won the primary by about 59,000 votes of 2.1 million cast. It was a narrow victory, but, considering the all-out effort made by Rocky and our comeback from a disorganized start, we felt the victory was deserved. Indeed, if anyone won the California primary, it was the Goldwater volunteers, who performed herculean labor, especially in the last few weeks of the race.

Some have maintained that the resurgence of the divorce-remarriage issue harmed Rockefeller in California. That's quite possible but hard to prove. I was, however, certain of one thing. We had not, in any way, raised the issue. Our staff had been ordered never, under any circumstances, to mention Rockefeller's personal or family life. If anyone had, I would have fired that individual immediately. That was something that the media, and perhaps Rocky, never learned.

Rocky never seemed to be himself during the California campaign. He turned over too much of his campaign to the professionals, instead of just being himself. We never thought much of the Spencer-Roberts team. They ran a rotten, underhanded campaign against me in California. In a final act of desperation, knowing the vote would be close, Spencer-Roberts mailed to the state's 2 million registered Republicans a pamphlet entitled "Who Do You Want in the Room with the H Bomb?" It contained a series of quotes from me, taken out of context, trying to show I would blow up the world. The media described the attack as savage.

Later, when he was Vice President under Gerald Ford, Rocky and I flew home together from Taiwan after the funeral of Chiang Kai-shek. We talked politics most of the way. Neither of us brought up the "extremism" and "radical right" charges that had poisoned 1964. It was clearer than ever that Rocky had a banker's analytical mind. He wanted to talk about where the chips were in politics. It gnawed at Rockefeller that he hadn't gone all the way to the Oval Office, although he never directly referred to the White House or the presidency. He asked indirectly, delicately, why he hadn't hit the top. With typical Goldwater tact, I said, "It had nothing to do with anyone else. It had everything to do with you. You could have whipped my butt in 1964, but I went out and worked a helluva lot harder than you did over the years. As a result, a lot of people worked for me. You thought that, because you were a Rockefeller, you were owed the presidency. You weren't. It's one of the beauties of America."

Just two weeks after the California primary, the racial issue thundered across the political scene. Few events in the campaign created more headlines, some fair and many false, than my vote against the 1964 Civil Rights Bill.

I cast the lone Senate vote against the measure and was quickly branded a racist by various liberal and civil rights groups. They claimed I was appealing to the Southern "redneck" vote. Some asserted the GOP was now the "white man's party." However, no man, woman, or child who knew me—black or white, Indian or Hispanic, of any color or creed—has ever accused me of such views— never, not to this day.

During the Senate debate, I questioned the constitutionality of Titles II and VII of the proposal. These sections were devoted to fair employment and public accommodation practices. It's important to recall precisely what I said about parts of the bill on the Senate floor, referring to the Tenth Amendment, before voting: "I am unalterably opposed to discrimination of any sort. I believe that, though the problem is fundamentally one of the heart, some law can help; but not law that embodies features like these, provisions which fly in the face of the Constitution . . .

"If my vote is misconstrued, let it be, and let me suffer the consequences. My concern extends beyond any single group in our society. My concern is for the entire nation, for the freedom of all who live in it, and for all who were born in it . . ."

I had expressed these constitutional views in layman's language for more than a decade in the Senate. The debate went far beyond race. Rather, it referred to a central principle of conservatism, clear limits on the central power of Washington. States have all the rights not specifically reserved to the federal government by the Constitution. Supreme Court Justice John Marshall Harlan agreed with me. He said the racial controversy was "a clash of competing constitutional aims of high order: liberty and equality."

I believed then and still believe today that more can be accomplished for civil liberties at the local level than by faraway federal fiat.

I had voted for the Civil Rights Acts of 1957 and 1960. That was because they sought to end government discrimination against its citizens. Later, in 1963, I offered four amendments to the Youth Employment Act, which forbade discrimination because of race, color, creed, or national origin.

Never in my life had I ever advocated, suggested, or implied any form of racism. Nor, contrary to the repeated claim of various civil rights organizations, had I ever believed I was contributing to a "racial holocaust" by my vote. Indeed, I later promised, as the Republican Presidential nominee, to withdraw from the campaign if my presence caused racial unrest.

In organizing the Arizona Air National Guard in 1946, I acted alone to provide a desegregated unit. That was before President Truman's desegregation order and nearly two decades before the 1964 Civil Rights Bill. My friend Harry Rosenzweig and I were the leaders in desegregating the lunch counters of Phoenix more than a decade before the 1964 Civil Rights Bill. I had long supported the National Association for the Advancement of Colored People's campaign to test segregation laws in Phoenix.

The 1964 act was debated on the Senate floor for nearly 740 hours over 83 days. It filled almost 2,900 pages of the *Congressional Record.* During that entire time, the senator from Arizona made it abundantly clear that he wanted to vote for the measure. Being branded a "racist" and "segregationist" in national headlines was appalling enough, but some in the media went even further. They asserted that candidate Goldwater was motivated by a "Southern strategy," whereby the GOP would sweep the electoral votes among the Democrats' old solid South. That was demonstrably false. Jack Kennedy wouldn't be my opponent; a Southerner, Lyndon Johnson, would be. Was I out to out-Southern Johnson? Hardly. Apart from the constitutional and moral debate, it made no political sense for me, as a candidate for the Presidency, to be the only senator in the U.S. Congress to vote against the bill. Why risk losing the general election on one issue?

Civil rights was a political issue from the start. I became a little sick of the hypocrisy connected with it. Everyone told me that, as a candidate, I had to vote for every civil rights bill. Various people, black and white, wanted the 1964 Act passed for their own ends. This was not a moral crusade in America. This was hard-nosed politics based on self-interest.

I found Title VII of the bill, the so-called Mrs. Murphy clause, particularly repellent. Simply put, this said you couldn't refuse to rent your home to anybody. The fact is,

I would not rent my home to a lot of whites for many reasons. That aspect of the bill was unconstitutional, and still is, in my opinion.

Columnist James Reston, hardly a Goldwater supporter, wrote in the New York *Times* that the Senate speech I had given in defense of my vote was one of the most courageous addresses he had heard in the nation's capital. The final judgment is for history to make.

My approach is still legitimate, and the history of civil rights bears it out. Each separate twist and turn along the road toward equality has either had to be settled on constitutional grounds in the courts or at the local level in the hearts of individual Americans. We also have a long way to go before settling the larger issue—the civil liberties of every American as distinct from the civil rights of minorities. We're witnessing that today in work seniority and other disputes.

The media played a peculiar role in the racial issue. As a matter of record, I had supported civil rights proposals while Lyndon Johnson had voted against them or eased away from the issue during most of his Senate career. Yet much of the media saw me as a segregationist throughout the campaign, while Johnson's public record was virtually ignored.

More reflective of the actual record was the following passage in Theodore White's book *The Making of the President, 1964:* "It was Barry Goldwater who, on his own initiative, approached the President . . . and volunteered to eliminate entirely any appeal to passion of race in the fall campaign, to which the President agreed in private compact."

I would never appeal to race, not for any reason.

Despite the tribulations on the road to San Francisco, the convention, we still hoped, would be a happy triumph. Instead, it was a bloody Republican civil war. Nixon, Rocky, Scranton, and Romney united in a Stop Goldwater movement. They launched the most savage attack that I had witnessed in my political career.

In these quiet days, as I seek a peaceful close to my life, these reflections hurt. At times I close my eyes to the world around me because it behooves an old man to forgive others while seeking forgiveness for his own transgressions.

Yet the purpose of these reflections is truth, and what we may use of it to fashion a better society. The truth is that power often drives good people mad. It's now time to review such madness—and the powerful lessons learned at San Francisco—so Americans will not condemn themselves to such errors in the future.

Reversing the conservative image he had projected in the two previous months, Nixon attacked just about everything I had said and done since announcing my candidacy. He concluded, "Looking to the future of the party, it would be a tragedy if Senator Goldwater's views, as previously stated, were not challenged—and repudiated."

There were many battles at the convention, and they've been reported so extensively that few new and meaningful details can be added. What is pertinent today, and still difficult to understand, is why my opponents allowed their views and ambitions to degenerate into such personal attacks. Those accusations became a public indictment that was later to be used almost word for word against me by Lyndon Johnson and the Democrats. More important, however, was the fact that the many issues we conservatives had longed for decades to bring before the American people were ignored in favor of assaults on me: that I was a trigger-happy mad bomber, a racist, and a right-wing kook who should never be allowed to become President.

In my dozen years in the Senate, despite deep political differences with many of my peers, I had never once attacked a colleague personally. I was deeply hurt by the accusations of fellow Republicans, especially the harshness of their language.

* * *

The convention opened in an uproar after a series of major, unexpected developments involving "CBS News." These events culminated in a crucial broadcast by Daniel Schorr from Germany.

The first was the false Cronkite report that I would not be attending the Kennedy funeral because I'd be in Indiana giving a political speech.

Second, "CBS News" chief Fred Friendly and CBS commentator Eric Sevareid told me in 1963 that they wanted to produce an hour-long documentary on the conservative revolution in America. They even mentioned a title, *The Conservative Revival.*

Frankly, we didn't want to do it because "CBS News" had a liberal bias. Those fellows, however, appeared to be gentlemen and men of their word, and such a program could help the conservative cause greatly. So I agreed.

Sevareid interviewed me in my office for two and a half hours. Tony Smith was present. The interview went downhill shortly after the start, when Sevareid asked in these general terms: Senator, you don't have a college degree; do you regard this as an impediment to your ambition? I replied that I wasn't a Phi Beta Kappa but had extensive military, business, and political experience that rounded out my general knowledge.

The questions got meaner and nastier as we went along. They suggested I was an accomplice of the John Birch Society and similar groups. Tony stood up at one point and was about to ask if the interview should be halted. He was very angry. I shook my head and he sat down. I'd given them my word, and I would keep it. I expected them to do the same.

A CBS camera crew followed me around for a month or so and took what seemed to be several hundred thousand feet of film. One day CBS called our office to alert us that the long-awaited documentary was about to appear. It was to be called *Thunder on the Right* and would report on the John Birch Society, the Minutemen, and other far-right activists. The program turned out to be an attack on these groups, not a documentary on the conservative revival. The only part of my long interview with Sevareid that was used was a single answer on the John Birch Society. The selection and editing of the film attempted to link me directly with the group. After the narration blasted the Birchers, Barry Goldwater suddenly appeared saying the society was not violating the Constitution. Yet we had long opposed the views of the Birchers and similar groups. In view of their conduct, I would never again accept the word of Friendly or Sevareid.

CBS had called two strikes on me. We didn't want them to call a third. But they did in Schorr's broadcast from Munich: "It looks as though Senator Goldwater, if nominated, will be starting his campaign here in Bavaria, center of Germany's right wing.

"Goldwater has accepted an invitation to visit, immediately after the convention, Lieutenant General William Quinn, commander of the Seventh Army, at Berchtesgaden, Hitler's onetime stamping ground but now an American Army recreational area.

"In addition, I learned today, Goldwater has given his tentative agreement to speak next weekend at the annual roundtable of the Evangelical Academy at Tutzing, on Bavaria's Lake Starnberg, where Chancellor Adenauer spoke last year.

"It is now clear that Senator Goldwater's interview with *Der Spiegel,* with its hard line appealing to rightwing elements in Germany, was only the start of a move to link up with his opposite numbers in Germany, and this has added an element of confusion in German politics.

"The Bavarian Christian Social Party, led by ex–Defense Minister Franz-Josef Strauss, opened its annual convention here today preparing for a showdown with Chancellor Erhard over his so-called 'soft line' and refusal to unite with DeGaulle.

"Erhard, close to President Johnson, showed no interest in meeting Senator Goldwater during his recent trips to Washington. Now Goldwater plans to come to Munich, but not to Bonn to see Erhard.

"Thus, there are signs that the American and German right wings are joining up, and the election campaign is taking on a new dimension."

The CBS broadcast was false, and Schorr's was the most irresponsible reporting I've witnessed in my life. The New York *Times* followed with an untrue account of its own.

CBS violated the most elementary rule of reporting by not checking with me—the accused—on a series of very serious charges. The Schorr story did not name a single responsible individual or group as the source or sources for the allegations. Even if the network did not check with me, it had an indisputable journalistic obligation to show beyond Schorr's personal conjecture that the report was accurate.

CBS compounded its unfairness with a report whose critical timing could affect not only the GOP Presidential nomination but the outcome of the national election campaign as well.

Schorr now recalls that the story was requested by Av Westin, then the CBS Saturday evening news producer. Schorr says, "My recollection is that he [Westin] called, asking for something that would give a German angle on Goldwater for the weekend before the San Francisco convention."

That's quite a coincidence. CBS New York calls Schorr in Munich for a story on Goldwater at the GOP convention in San Francisco. Westin didn't respond to my requests for an interview to clarify this point.

Schorr now claims, "As it turned out, a man who worked for Goldwater had tentatively accepted an invitation [to address the seminar] in his name." Who was the member of my staff who gave that tentative acceptance? Schorr didn't name that person. Why?

Schorr's suggestion that the Evangelical Academy was a breeding ground of neo-Nazism with which I was somehow trying to link up was, to say the least, farfetched. To be precise, he didn't provide the slightest proof of any relationship. I knew nothing of the academy and would have said that to CBS if they had asked me about it.

The New York *Times,* in a story by Arthur J. Olsen from Germany, headlined similar allegations—that I had been in "frequent and friendly correspondence for some time" with academy officials and others on the right, that I had agreed to speak at the academy but later canceled the address, and that I had given an interview to "an extreme rightist weekly." The extreme right referred, of course, to the neo-Nazis. The *Times* story obviously had not been checked out. Schorr later admitted that the *Der Spiegel* interview had never occurred.

Schorr now says he was "guilty of sloppy writing, writing that could be construed to mean that there was some volition on Goldwater's part instead of saying what was true—that the German right wing was all excited about the idea of Goldwater. That's the one phase of the story which was the most lethal."

"The most lethal"? That was Schorr's precise expression. He had written earlier that his broadcast detonated a "megatonnage" in San Francisco.

Schorr recalls that "the Scranton people" transcribed his broadcast and distributed it under the door of every delegate.

Three aspects of the broadcast are critical: First, neither anyone on my staff nor I ever agreed—in any manner—that I would address any right-wing (neo-Nazi) group in West Germany; second, no plans were made by General Quinn or anyone else for me to visit Berchtesgaden, and, finally, my wife and I had only considered a European vacation after the convention, and it was by no means firm. That and all which followed in Schorr's report were untrue. It was a classic caper—not only guilt by association, but guilt by false association.

Robert Pierpoint was the "CBS News" correspondent covering me in San Francisco. He now says that Schorr's reporting was unfair, and that it was harmful to me and our campaign. He adds, "He also hurt 'CBS News' and hurt Dan Schorr."

The relations between Pierpoint and me prior to the Schorr broadcast were good. He recently told me what had followed:

"I woke up in San Francisco and here was Dan Schorr's broadcast under my hotel door. Apparently, it was under everyone's door. I think they were put there by the Scranton people.

"I was absolutely astounded, just as you and everyone else were. I read this thing and felt that somehow there must have been some kind of misunderstanding. To me, even though Senator Goldwater was a conservative, he was certainly no neo-Nazi or any other kind of cult figure."

Pierpoint contacted his office, saying he expected problems as a result of the report. He was barred from our briefing that day. I made the decision not against Bob, but to protest the CBS broadcast and the network's consistently questionable coverage. Pierpoint now says, "The Goldwater people, Kitchel and Burch in particular, told me to cool it. They realized the broadcast wasn't my fault, but everyone on Goldwater's staff was angry at CBS and Schorr."

Pierpoint now reveals he was summoned to a meeting with CBS board chairman William Paley and Friendly. He recalls: "They had one question: Was CBS going to be shut out from covering the Republican presidential nominee? I told them I didn't think so, but the senator was very angry. I also said I understood why he was angry. Paley and Friendly also were upset with Schorr's broadcast. I said I'd like to know where the hell Schorr's stuff came from? I just didn't think it was accurate or fair. They said they were looking into that." The two asked

Pierpoint to try to restore coverage for CBS. The meeting ended.

"To this day, I can't blame Barry Goldwater and his people," Pierpoint told me recently. "I'm not going to defend Schorr and really have trouble defending CBS for putting his report on the air. I don't think it should have been put on the air. I was the conduit, the correspondent covering Goldwater, and nobody ever contacted me about that story. You had better check a story like that. I don't blame the senator for being upset at the time. I don't blame him a bit."

Pierpoint was in an outer office when Dean Burch and I came out of a meeting. He said, "I'm sorry about what happened."

I replied, "Bob, it's not your fault. It's Schorr's and CBS's. None of this is personal on my part. But those fellows have to be taught a lesson."

Pierpoint was back covering the story that day.

Schorr never contacted General Quinn about any details of his report. He had to know the broadcast would put the Seventh Army commander in the political frying pan. The least he should have done was phone Quinn and ask whether, indeed, we were coming to Germany and under what circumstances.

Quinn recalls that General Johnny Johnson, the U.S. Army chief of staff and a classmate at West Point, had sent him a message which questioned the Seventh Army commander about the CBS report. Quinn replied that there had been no contact between us in more than a year. If the Goldwaters, who had been family friends for many years, were coming to Germany, it was news to him. He reported that no one had advised him or his Stuttgart headquarters of any such visit, official or otherwise.

Before the Schorr broadcast, I had mentioned to a Washington *Post* society writer, Betty Beale, at a reception that my wife and I might tour Europe, whether I won or lost the nomination. I had also mentioned that we might visit the Quinns in Germany. There were, however, no firm plans. It was a casual remark.

Quinn said that the White House had leaked two reports involving him. The first came to him from colleagues in the Pentagon. It said that Lyndon Johnson had passed the word that Quinn would never receive a fourth star as long as he, Johnson, was President. That effectively blocked Quinn, generally considered a candidate, from ever becoming U.S. Army chief of staff.

The second leak was to the New York *Herald Tribune,* the same GOP newspaper that had printed the Eisenhower article, which implied I was not Ike's choice as the Republican presidential nominee. The story, written by Douglas Kiker, said that Johnson had invited me to an intelligence briefing in the White House, but I had declined. The White House official indicated that the reason for my refusal was that I had been receiving such briefings from Quinn, former deputy director of the Defense Intelligence Agency.

The story was totally false. As I had told my staff, "I'm not going over to meet with that bastard Johnson. He'll just talk about his ranch, start pouring bourbon, and try to get me drunk. I'll leave, and the next day he'll say he told me everything."

The truth is, Quinn and I hadn't been in personal contact for more than a year. We hadn't even exchanged a postcard. Peggy and I were thinking about getting away to some place where no one would recognize us—where we could walk down a street, have dinner in a restaurant, or take a boat trip without public attention. We had talked about Europe—Switzerland, France, Spain, England, and Germany. But no firm plans were ever made. We eventually did decide to tour the continent, and did so the following spring.

Johnson's decision to wipe out any possibility that Quinn might become Army chief of staff was reported by respected senior officers. It was blatantly political and mean-spirited. Quinn had a very distinguished military record as the intelligence officer of Generals Patton and Patch's Seventh Army in World War II, the director of the Office of Strategic Services before it became the CIA, a front-line commander of the 17th Infantry Regiment, 7th Division, in Korea, and other top military posts. Despite personal pleas from former President Eisenhower, General Lyman Lemnitzer, the NATO commander, General Creighton Abrams, chairman of the Joint Chiefs of Staff, and others to hang tough, Quinn decided to retire from the Army. It was a bitter ending to a brilliant military career and a sad time for both families. Our friendship somehow survived the ordeal, and we're still friends today.

A letter to me from Bill Scranton landed like a bomb just before the convention opened. It was an act of political desperation. The letter's intemperateness was to affect not only my campaign against Johnson but the conservative movement to this day. It should be remembered, in reading the contents, that Bill had urged me to run for the nomination. The letter, addressed to "Senator Goldwater," said, in part: "Will the convention choose a candidate overwhelmingly favored by the Republican voters, or will it choose you . . . you are a minority candidate. . . . They [your organization] have bought, beaten, and compromised enough delegate support to make the result a foregone conclusion."

I read those words with total disbelief—that we had bought and beaten our delegates, who didn't represent Republican voters. The letter continued: "You have too often prescribed nuclear war as a solution to a troubled world.

"You have too often allowed the radical extremists to use you.

"You have too often stood for irresponsibility in the serious question of racial holocaust.

"You have too often read Taft and Eisenhower and Lincoln out of the Republican Party.

"Goldwaterism has come to stand for being afraid to condemn right-wing extremists . . ."

The letter continued on the same level and concluded with a challenge from Scranton that we debate before the entire convention.

My wife, Peggy, was dressing to attend the formal Republican Gala, a normally pleasant reception that preceded the convention opening. It was also a fund-raiser for the campaign.

Peggy was happy. Her face was radiant. She loved to meet people in a pleasant atmosphere. It would be a wonderful evening.

I looked at her, the sparkle in her eyes, the lightness in her step. How she had sacrificed, suffered for these fleeting hours. She had warned me so many, many times to stay away: "Barry, you'll be hurt. National politics is not you—and not for you."

I hid the letter from her.

Tom Dunlavey was standing watch in the hall outside our hotel suite. We'd met at the 1960 convention in Chicago. The redheaded Irishman had volunteered to be my driver. We had become friends and something more—fellow conservatives. Tom had accepted the letter from a member of the Scranton staff. I asked him if he was certain the young man was with Scranton. He was sure. I requested he call Kitchel, Burch, Baroody, and Karl Hess, our speechwriter, to a conference—quick. He rushed off.

Peggy was humming in the bedroom. She hummed when she was happy.

My mind couldn't focus. A surge of bitter disappointment welled up inside. ". . . Minority candidate . . . nuclear war . . . radical extremists . . . racial holocaust . . ." It was incomprehensible.

Kitchel and the others arrived. It was soon clear we were going to have a long meeting. Peggy and Naomi Kitchel had to go to the gala alone. I still remember the pain in Peggy's eyes when I told her. It was the lowest moment of the entire convention for us.

"Have a good time," I said to her, but the words rang hollow. Once again, at a time when we should have been together, politics pulled us apart. It was really sad.

As soon as we began the discussion, I told the group I didn't believe my old friend, Bill Scranton, had written the letter. He was a gentleman. This couldn't be true. We'd suffered a lot of adversity since the campaign had begun. This was among the lowest blows of all, especially on the eve of the convention. But this was not Scranton. Some other candidate had to be using him. He hadn't signed the letter. His name was only typewritten at the bottom.

We agreed that the contents were deliberately insulting, perhaps an attempt to provoke a rash response. We'd be conciliatory. Kitchel proposed that we send a copy of the letter immediately to every delegate. We'd say nothing. Let them decide. I agreed. We also returned the original letter to Scranton.

The contents had not been written or read by Scranton, although he had agreed to send a letter challenging my views and calling for a debate. It had been composed by his staff and sent without his seeing the wording.

Most of those in the room were aware that Scranton was my personal choice to become our vice presidential candidate. Several now interjected that the letter had finished him.

The truth is, it had not. It was necessary to see Bill, to speak with him, to find out what the hell had happened. What had I or anyone on our staff done to him? Was someone trying to use him?

Unfortunately, such a meeting became impossible. I never, however, changed my high opinion of Bill. You don't turn your back on someone until you know the facts. Somehow, we would work it out. He'd be on the ticket. The episode was, however, never clarified. When we later met to discuss the vice presidential nominee, the entire staff ruled Bill out. I agreed. I still believe Bill is a decent individual and have never inquired further about the incident.

Nevertheless, the letter did two things. It shocked and angered conservatives. Also, it handed the Democrats their campaign slogans and strategy on a platter—only Lyndon Johnson and Bill Moyers were to exceed the vulgar indecencies of Scranton's staff.

As the convention unfolded, Rockefeller led the attacks on so-called extremists as he dissected the party platform. He stood before the delegates and claimed that extremists had threatened to bomb his headquarters a hundred times or more, that he and his campaign workers had been frightened by threats, and a host of similar charges. The governor then said, "We repudiate the efforts of irresponsible extremist groups—such as the Communists, Ku Klux Klan, the John Birch Society, and others to discredit our party by their efforts to infiltrate positions of responsibility in the party or attach themselves to its candidates."

The attack on extremists was an attempt to include conservatives among the worst elements of American society. As the governor spoke, a chorus of boos began to swell from the audience. Rockefeller encouraged the crowd to attack him, frequently pausing to allow them more time. His address was interrupted twenty-two times in five minutes. It was as if each series of yells from the crowd had been written into a script.

The scene, carried on national television, brought into millions of homes and public places across the nation the almost barbaric atmosphere that had come to characterize the convention. I was appalled at the spectacle. We contacted White at our communications command post and requested that our delegates halt the booing. White and the regional directors assisting him in the trailer quickly contacted delegation leaders and returned to us with this report: Most of the booing was coming from spectators in the galleries. The majority of our delegates were sitting on their hands, ignoring Rocky. We were convinced then and throughout the convention that our opponents were trying to create an incident—a smoking pistol—to show that we were "extremists."

There was antagonism on our side, no question about it. If the old party leadership had tried to exclude the conservatives from power, the "true believers" on the right were not ready to make peace with the liberals. Some of our supporters did boo and shout at Rocky. Kleindienst had met with the Wyoming, Colorado, and Oklahoma delegations, among others, and they were in no mood for compromises of any kind with GOP liberals. Dick had to warn them, for example, that we would publicly repudiate them if they weren't more reasonable about who would be seated and voting on the convention floor. If there was little or no accommodation on the left, the same was true on the right. Republicans had alienated one another in the struggle for the party's soul.

My major difference with GOP liberals was simply this: I wanted more alternatives to what was going on in the country. That seemed a reasonable position. The harshness of their attacks on us, however, exploded the unity we so desperately needed to wage an effective campaign.

Conservatives were convinced that the party's more liberal elements were prepared to wreck the GOP's presidential chances in 1964 rather than turn over leadership to the conservatives. They recognized as well as we that this struggle would affect party direction for decades to come.

This was the feeling on both sides as the balloting for the Presidential nominee began in the Cow Palace on Wednesday night, July 15, after almost seven hours of nominating and seconding speeches. Senator Dirksen nominated me in a stirring address. He lifted up his rich baritone voice to the galleries and television cameras carrying it across the country. The Wizard of Ooze threw back his head, rolled his eyes, and talked of "the peddler's grandson."

It seemed fitting that South Carolina, which had offered my name as a candidate in 1960, would be the state to assure the nomination by topping the magic number of 655 in the roll call vote. The final tally was 883 out of 1,308 votes, still one of the largest such majorities in history.

The dramatic moment of nomination was, in many ways, an anticlimax. Several of us were watching television in my hotel suite. There were a few cheers. Somebody uncorked champagne. Kitchel and my brother, Bob, were the first to shake my hand. Bob and I phoned our mother. She was enjoying the hoopla but was very calm. Baroody, Ed McCabe, and Tony Smith also were there. Peggy was at the Cow Palace, enjoying the excitement of the crowd.

The celebration had a somber note. It was already clear that the possibility of my being elected President was now dead. Most of the party leadership had deserted us. I would have to go it alone. It was a deeply agonizing realization.

Going it alone was not quite accurate. I personally put in a phone call to Bill Miller, asking him to be our Vice Presidential candidate. The former Republican National Committee chairman accepted with the good humor that characterized him throughout the campaign. The upstate New Yorker, a fast-talking quipster with a biting wit, had driven Lyndon Johnson nuts in the past with his sharp tongue. We'd need a bit of such humor in the campaign to keep LBJ at bay. If Lyndon felt he could get away with his Texas-size promises, we would be buried—to use his favorite expression—in bullshit.

Miller was the most logical of the choices available after Kitchel, Baroody, and the rest of the staff had unanimously ruled out Scranton. Miller, with his experience as national committee chairman, could return the party to some semblance of unity.

Today, some people wonder whether Miller contributed as much to the ticket as we had anticipated. Bill did everything we asked of him. He maintained his good humor and enthusiasm throughout the campaign. Our personal relationship couldn't have been better. Bill was a good trooper, fought the good fight, and went home to Lockport, New York, with a smile and good grace, after which he renewed his law practice in nearby Buffalo.

Miller liked to joke about his obscurity after 1964—as he did in a famous American Express commercial—but he was far from being an anonymous American. Bill had been one of the prosecutors at the Nuremberg war crimes trials in Germany after World War II. He gave fourteen good years in public service. Bill died in Buffalo's Millard Fillmore Hospital in 1983 at the age of sixty-nine. It was an irony from which he would have gotten a great laugh. Fillmore, a U.S. President, is far more obscure than Bill, an unsuccessful vice presidential candidate.

My acceptance speech before the convention was already written. While putting it together, we received the latest poll from Opinion Research in Princeton, New Jersey. One of their representatives was flipping charts to show that President Johnson had an 80–20 percent lead over me. I said to Hess and others in the room, "Instead of writing an acceptance speech, we should be putting together a rejection speech and tell them all to go to hell." Everybody laughed, but it wasn't really funny. There was some truth in the remark, and I knew it. Hess wrote the first draft of the speech, but Kitchel and Baroody took it over. Neither was in a conciliatory mood. Kitchel recently recalled his feeling: "There was no use trying to conciliate with guys as adamant as the Rockefeller, Romney, and other groups. I think it would have been wrong to try to heal those wounds before taking on Lyndon Johnson in that speech. We wanted to get the party on a new track. I agreed a hundred percent with Barry attacking his critics and Johnson."

We went over every word carefully. The most important point we wanted to make was this: The conservative movement aimed to take the country in a new direction. It seemed politically illogical and personally contradictory for us to offer olive branches to Rocky and the others. If I walked out on that convention dais and embraced Rockefeller, conservatives in the Cow Palace and across the country would have thought it was some political ad paid for by the Democratic National Committee. We'd just been through a bloody war on a host of issues. The libs had called me just about every dirty name in politics. The address had to make clear that this was a historic break. That's exactly what we were doing, breaking with history—taking over the party from the Republican National Committee on down and setting a new course in GOP national politics. Frankly, I never expected our critics and the media would focus on the now famous phrase, "Extremism in the defense of liberty is no vice, and . . . moderation in the pursuit of justice is no virtue."

The reference came from Harry Jaffa, a professor of political science at Claremont Men's College in California. As was explained to me at the time, the words were first used by Marcus Tullius Cicero in the Roman Senate while speaking in defense of the state's rule and honor against Lucius Sergius Catilina, a patrician considered dangerous to Rome. The quotation was: "I must remind you—Lords, Senators—that extreme patriotism in defense of freedom is no crime, and let me respectfully remind you that pusillanimity in the pursuit of justice is no virtue in a Roman."

An immediate debate erupted in the media over what I was supposed to have meant by the phrase. Some critics claimed it was a counterattack on Rockefeller and other GOP liberals for branding some conservatives as extremists. Others asserted it was a call for conservatives to exercise extreme action in the national election campaign. The truth is, no reference was meant to either. Nor was there any sinister meaning in the word "extremism." All of us were merely saying there was nothing wrong in being strong in the defense of freedom and no particular good in being weak toward justice. If any single word has expressed my political philosophy since entering public life—and to this day—it is "freedom." I wanted freedom to be the theme of the speech and our entire campaign.

Perhaps I was carried away by the eloquence of the statement. Maybe the address should have quoted Cicero directly. However, I didn't think so then, nor do I now believe it would have made a great deal of difference. Dean Burch put it this way: "Barry Goldwater could have recited the Lord's Prayer or the Twenty-third Psalm as his acceptance speech. He still would have been attacked."

I've never personally met anyone who ever accused me of being Machiavellian. Yet that was precisely the accusation made against me in one editorial after another regarding the extremism statement—that I was somehow assailing the liberals in my own party and, at the same time, urging conservatives to radical, if not violent, action during the campaign. Both views are pure baloney.

Ben Bradlee and others who are certainly not conservatives have often said to me that Jack Kennedy, with his urbane charm and wit, would have gotten away with that statement. In fact, they argue, many editorial writers would have praised it.

Whether that's true or not, I still believe our acceptance speech, including the remark on extremism, was a good one. In fact, I set out to prove it twenty years later when asked to address the 1984 GOP national convention. Word got out that I was going to use the extremism quote. Some of my Republican colleagues on Capitol Hill said I'd be dredging up the acrimony of the past. One dear friend of mine, Paul Laxalt, implored me not to do it. I told Paul and others, "If you fellows give me any more trouble on this speech, I'm going back to Arizona. You can find yourself another speaker."

I gave the speech and the line on extremism, delivered tongue in cheek, drew a burst of laughter from the delegates. It was all in fun, and they understood it immediately.

A hundred or two hundred years from now, if a historian reads that speech, he will find an entirely new meaning in it. None of us is now in a position to guess what that will be. I haven't met any conservatives who believe in instant analysis.

The greatest of American spectacles was about to begin —the indescribable merry-go-round we call a presidential campaign. My longtime Democratic colleague, Senator Sam Nunn of Georgia, has described my campaign style in great good humor: "Barry Goldwater's motto has never changed: Ready! Fire! Aim!"

7

The Presidential Campaign

THE CAMPAIGN TOOK ON NEW DIMENSIONS AFTER MY acceptance speech—it became a drama of personal power. Three people were central—Clif White, Bill Baroody, and Ralph Cordiner—but no one more than White. He had worked nearly three years in the hope of becoming chairman of the Republican National Committee under a conservative banner. Clif deserved the honor, and I put his name on the table when Kitchel, Baroody, and other advisers met. The job would become much more significant because we had decided the campaign would be run by the chairman.

Baroody strongly opposed White. He viewed him as somehow standing in for those at *National Review*—Bill Buckley, Bill Rusher, Brent Bozell, and James Burnham. That was false. Baroody saw himself as the head of a new brain trust around me. He would gather the research, direct the speechwriters, and be our resident intellectual with a team of his own bright young assistants. Baroody was a classicist, almost an ancient Greek or Roman. He was also a man who enjoyed power.

Kleindienst had the highest praise for White's political savvy and organizational ability. But he warned that White was not a team player but rather an independent, single-minded individual who might go his own way.

Everyone in the room opposed White. Reluctantly, I said, "All right, let's take Dean Burch. Kitchel will remain campaign manager—do liaison work and travel a lot with me."

All present immediately agreed.

White deserved the post because his Draft Goldwater Committee had given us the political muscle to assure the nomination. When he wasn't appointed chairman, it caused dismay among Buckley, Rusher, and others whose intelligence and active help would have been very valuable in the campaign. They backed off after White was not chosen. Many other people across the country assumed Clif would get the job, and when he didn't, they were upset.

Not selecting White was a mistake. I should have insisted on him and tried to mediate any inside tug-of-war that would have followed. Buckley, Rusher, and others should have been aboard working with us. They would have brought back some Easterners to the fold, added some professionalism to our ranks, and perhaps accelerated the political change that was taking place.

Despite continued criticism of the Arizona Mafia, they actually became a minority among our top staff. Kleindienst left to return to Arizona politics. Kitchel, Burch, and Mrs. Emory Johnson, although in key posts, were surrounded by a score of others in major jobs who weren't from Arizona. In any event, we would have lost even if Abraham Lincoln had come back and campaigned with us.

As the new leadership of the national committee was being confirmed, a personal crisis was taking place. Most of us were unaware of it.

White, his wife, and his two children were scheduled to fly to Hawaii for a restful vacation. White was unable to pack. He simply lay down and stared blankly at his family and friends. The turn of events had almost broken him. The Whites flew home to New York. Clif remained motionless on his couch for about two and a half hours.

My father, Baron, and me in 1912. *(The Arizona Historical Foundation)*

Mom (Josephine Williams) arrives in Phoenix. *(The Arizona Historical Foundation)*

Bob, Carolyn, and me with Mom at a party in 1938. *(The Arizona Historical Foundation)*

Camping out on one of our annual treks to California in the late twenties. *(The Arizona Historical Foundation)*

With my kids at the end of World War II. Peggy is in my arms, and Joanne, Michael, and Barry Jr. surround me. *(The Arizona Historical Foundation)*

This is me alongside my P-47, *Peggy-G. (The Arizona Historical Foundation)*

At the 1960 Republican National Convention in Chicago.
(Republican National Committee)

With JFK. *(Courtesy of the JFK Library)*

With President Johnson, 1964. *(The Arizona Historical Foundation)*

President Nixon and me in happier times. *(Official White House Photograph)*

In the Oval Office with President Ford. *(Official White House Photograph)*

With President Reagan on the day they honored General Jimmy Doolittle. *(Official White House Photograph)*

The last formal portrait with Peggy. *(Herb and Dorothy McLaughlin)*

At West Point to receive the Thayer Award, September 1987.
(U.S. Army Photograph by Vincent Guariglia)

He couldn't believe what had happened. Numbly, he asked himself:

"What did I do wrong? What was it?

"I knew, deep down in my mind and heart, that I'd helped change the direction of American politics. I got a kick in the teeth for all that I had done, but we'd won. The conservatives had taken over the party, and that was truly joyous.

"Yet it really threw me. My wife wouldn't let anyone talk to me—or me speak with anybody else.

"I seriously considered not taking part in the campaign. That was ego talking. I was still a man of faith. I'd told so many people that the conservative cause was worth fighting for. What the hell, I got up off the couch and ran Citizens for Goldwater-Miller. I never had any regrets."

White now says he would have opposed some of Baroody's speech and other political decisions if he had been named national chairman. He maintains Baroody was a person who dealt less in political realities and more in philosophical theory. White and Baroody met before the research foundation leader passed away. They spoke of their disagreements. In the end, however, like most things in politics, all was forgiven and forgotten.

Another behind-the-scenes drama had been going on for months and would continue through the campaign. It illustrates once again the most volatile part of politics—people.

Baroody played a major role in our campaign. He was the chief of our so-called brain trust. Kitchel, his closest friend during the race, and Dean Burch now say that the *National Review* people were "squeezed out" of the campaign by Baroody.

Kitchel told me recently that Baroody was very jealous of his own prerogatives, that Baroody was an intricate man, a conniver. There was never any effort on Kitchel's part—and certainly not on mine—to keep Buckley or the others out of the campaign. Baroody wanted to hold control and keep them out. Kitchel now sees Bill as a Svengali.

Paul Wagner, our press secretary on the campaign, remembers Baroody as writing our ideological speeches with the help of others. Hess wrote the daily material. Wagner says, "I thought Baroody and his group wrote lousy speeches. They were exceptionally good as classical documents, but not as political speeches to the American people."

White and Baroody represent some of the unseen strains and stresses of the campaign.

Another man put an indelible stamp on our race. Ralph Cordiner, former chairman of the board of General Electric, became our finance chairman. Cordiner knew nothing about campaign financing, but he had a brilliant economic mind. Kitchel was sent to ask him if he'd take the job after the convention. Ralph accepted it on one condition—there would be no deficit financing. We'd run the campaign on a balanced budget and end it in the black. I agreed. That was a political mistake.

We were broke, as most campaigns are, as the race began in late August. Cordiner insisted that we cancel the television spots booked for the last ten days of the campaign, when we needed them most, until we had money to pay for them. Of course, when we received those funds, it was too late to obtain the commercial time. The networks refused us the time because they were afraid that the Johnson administration would get back at them if they created some for us. The President was notorious for his vindictiveness.

Cordiner and a fellow by the name of Frank Kovac made political fund-raising history. Kovac assembled massive mailing lists that sought funds from millions of grass roots Americans—the real conservative constituency, who were tired of Big Brother in all his forms. More than 1.5 million people contributed to our campaign through various mailing lists. We created a vast volunteer army of more than a half million people who solicited funds and gave their time to the campaign in other ways. The national political scene had never seen anything like it. Americans contributed more than $13 million to our campaign. We finished about $1 million in the black. Kovac, who was from Washington, D.C., seemed to come out of nowhere several months before the campaign began and disappeared once it was over. We always wondered what had happened to him. In his own way, he was a genius.

Cordiner and Kovac were to have a more profound effect on the Republican Party than they—or any of us—ever dreamed. We began to see this several years after the campaign ended, when Richard Viguerie and others leap-frogged the Democrats in the use of large mailing lists and other technical innovations.

White, Baroody, Cordiner—these names stand out in the campaign. But only one man runs for President. He alone must inspire and lead. He wins or loses the race.

Barry Goldwater was a free spirit, short on a grand election strategy and shorter on a surrounding court of establishment intellectuals. We were a bunch of Western-ers, outsiders, with the guts to challenge not only the entire Eastern establishment—Republican and Demo-cratic alike—but the vast federal apparatus, the great ma-jority of the country's academics, big business and big unions, and a man with an ego larger than his native state of Texas, Lyndon Johnson.

The hundred-day journey took us to more than a hun-dred cities and towns—nearly 100,000 miles. I addressed millions of my fellow citizens and ate more lousy cheese-burgers than I care to remember.

I was fired up when it began—a considerable change in outlook since the convention. I was chomping at the bit to address the American people. A new spirit also buoyed those around me. We'd make a fight of it.

No one would ever know my feeling about the inevita-bility of defeat. It would be the greatest adventure of my life, more exciting than flying, rafting down the Colorado, or climbing Navajo Mountain. We were going to give the Democrats, all those liberals, and Lyndon Johnson hell.

We kicked off our stumping from the steps of the Yavapai County Courthouse in Prescott. Conservatives were rising across the country. It was finally our hour. We were the new wagon trains—from West to East. And others would follow in the trails we blazed.

Two concerns began to nag at me—that neither the racial debate nor the Vietnam War should become issues in the campaign. No momentary political gain should be allowed to cause bloodshed at home or hinder the war effort in Asia. In late August, I phoned President Johnson and requested a private meeting of "mutual concern." Johnson agreed but quickly sent his White House scouts around Washington to "find out what Goldwater is up to." He never learned, since no one but me even knew that I wanted a meeting. Some White House aides guessed, however, that I might bring up civil rights. They were half right.

The meeting took place a few days before Labor Day. Johnson shook hands warmly. He put his hand on my shoulder. In the Senate, we called that the "half-Johnson." You were in a bit of trouble, but it wasn't serious. When he stretched his long arm completely around your back to the other shoulder, that was the "full-Johnson." It meant you weren't cooperating, and he was going to squeeze you on some project you needed back home until you voted for his latest pet bill. Then, there was "skinny-dip Johnson," who invited you to the White House pool and insisted you swim in the raw with him. Some fellows got embarrassed when Johnson began leading them around the basement without a towel. A few would agree to almost anything to keep their shorts on. Not me. I've been swimming in the nude since I was a kid, and I still do.

When Johnson negotiated, and it was clear he felt some deal would be proposed, his eyes began to narrow.

He was taking a bead on you, like he would on a squirrel. It was his intimidation routine. I began by saying that both of us had been around Washington a long time, that we were divided by philosophy and party, but that we shared a love of country.

"That's right, Barry," he said. "You and I are not like some people around the country. We're Americans first."

He appeared to refer to the antiwar protesters. It was a perfect opening, and I took it, telling the President that there was already too much division in the nation over the war. We should not contribute to it by making Vietnam an issue in the campaign.

Johnson took a deep breath and sighed in relief. He jumped into his Sam-Houston-at-the-Alamo defense with a do-or-die pitch about his difficulties in Vietnam. Finally, out of ammunition, he thanked me for the pledge. I interpreted that to mean he agreed.

I said the same about civil rights—that if we attacked each other, the country would be divided into different camps and we could witness bloodshed. The President solemnly nodded. He said events were moving too quickly, and we should try to calm the country. We shook hands. Both of us honored the spirit of that private pact throughout the campaign.

After I left the Oval Office, the White House issued a statement which didn't refer directly to our meeting but was an attempt to put a Johnson spin on it. The first half declassified a new plane to show that the President was strong on defense. Johnson evidently believed we might try to mousetrap him with a new charge that he wasn't offering enough help to the military. The second part said that Americans had the right to know where each candidate stood on every issue, including civil rights. The statement, which had been written before our agreement, indicated that Johnson planned to speak out on the subject. I don't know why he issued that part, because he maintained our overall agreement throughout the campaign.

On civil rights, perhaps it may now finally be clear that I didn't seek the so-called redneck vote in the campaign. We repudiated such organizations as the Ku Klux Klan and were forced to repeat that we were unalterably opposed to discrimination of any kind. I did agree with nine articles of the 1964 Civil Rights Act. Again and again, it was inferred that I was a racist. No criticism of my record was so false and demeaning, however, as that of Walter Lippmann in *Newsweek* of June 22, 1963, in which he said:

"In his extreme views on states' rights, (Goldwater) is in fact one who would dissolve the Federal union into a mere confederation of the states . . . he would nullify if he could the central purpose of the Civil War amendments, and would take from the children of the emancipated slaves the protection of the national union."

Never in the political arena, not in the darkest hours of the Presidential campaign, had any critic challenged my respect for the Constitution. The attack came from one of the most honored men in American journalism. He was wrong and untruthful and caused us unending criticism during the race. As the record clearly shows, I voted against the Civil Rights Act because it contained "no constitutional basis for the exercise of Federal regulatory authority" in the areas of employment and public accommodations.

Civil rights was a big problem for me in the campaign —no question about it. Looking back today, we took a bum rap on the issue from many in the media, some minorities, and others.

A discussion of the issues was crucial to conservatives. That was why I ran. It was the cornerstone of the years of political building that we saw ahead. We had to break the liberal monopoly on communication to the American people. As far as I was concerned, communicating the issues was the make-or-break point of the entire campaign.

In desperation, we finally challenged Johnson to a debate. He refused because he never was good with the heat on in public. I had had plenty of experience under fire. Johnson liked closed doors and, if possible, closed windows. And sometimes closed minds.

I never understood the media's judgment. They virtually ignored some of my proposals while reacting in a vituperative way to others. This didn't contribute to public understanding of our campaign as a whole. Let's look at the three issues that hurt me most—Social Security, the Tennessee Valley Authority, and nuclear weapons.

In 1964 about 21 million Americans were receiving Social Security. My opponents, from Rockefeller to Johnson, claimed that a voluntary plan, which we suggested, would bankrupt the system or require a big boost in payments by the 55 million Americans then paying into the plan.

At the same time, as many of us in Congress were aware, the Social Security trust fund of about $22 billion was in those days in the form of U.S. securities, not cash. The government had borrowed the money from the system and spent it in other ways. How would any employee like to be part of a pension fund that had spent their contributions for other purposes? When Social Security began, it had about thirty-five workers for each retiree. Today, it's three to one retiree. By the time the Yuppies retire, it will be two to one.

There were various projections that attempted to show that making the system voluntary would bankrupt it. These were given wide attention in the media. Instead, we were proposing that the worker be given a choice from the beginning, opting out of the system and never making a claim on it. We also stressed that any change-over to a voluntary system would have to be made over time so as not to disrupt the program.

My point was that the federal government was playing games with the money and that the system was financially overextended. That's precisely what has been made public in recent years and caused Congress to bail out the plan.

In 1977, some thirteen years after our warning, Congress passed the largest peacetime tax increase in U.S. history to give a massive financial transfusion to Social Security. The system was propped up again in 1983. The program faces massive problems in the future, as the ratio of workers to retirees is expected to fall to two to one about the year 2020.

Our explanation got little attention in the media. Nor did the fact that I had voted to increase Social Security benefits in 1956, 1958, and 1964. This isn't to make a blanket claim that the press was unfair. It's to call attention to problems inherent in daily news management and formats, not reporters. When we went to Tampa, Florida, and discussed Social Security again, the media once more exploded with headlines that we were threatening the system. The daily news business—newspapers, radio, and TV—is geared to quick, easy, black-or-white answers. That's the problem. It's easier to say that Goldwater is threatening Social Security in a few words than to explain in depth precisely what he's proposing. Daily newspapers excuse themselves by saying readers are bored with such detail. The answer to that is obvious. If being fair means reporting the entire story, then responsible newspapers as well as radio and television stations should change their formats. Instead, all of them are now compressing individual stories even more. There's an increasing danger of unfairness in such a policy.

The Tennessee Valley Authority was a big fat sacred New Deal cow. It was a mammoth, multimillion-dollar federal water- and power-dispensing development on the Tennessee River water that served Southeastern states. I told Joseph Alsop, the columnist, "I think we ought to sell TVA."

You would have thought I had just shot Santa Claus. Democrats and Republicans, senior citizens and school-

children—all wrote letters defending their empire. The
Tennessee Valley was Goldwater Country, but from a
conservative viewpoint the statement had to be made.
Otherwise, we'd be just an echo of the Democrats—and
some fellow Republicans.

My case against the TVA had already been made in
The Conscience of a Conservative. The book took issue
with large government developments which invaded the
private sector of the economy. The TVA was a sweeping
network of different business activities which were not
directly related to its three original purposes of generating electrical energy, navigation, and flood control. These
other activities included its fertilizer production program,
steam generating plants, and other enterprises.

The issue involved a clear conservative principle:
Washington shouldn't intrude in the private sector and
begin competing with companies and citizens who already support it through taxation. Government should
do for its citizens only what they cannot do for themselves—period. Private firms would not only put TVA on
the tax rolls but operate it more effectively than the bureaucrats could. Because of cheaper nuclear power, the
TVA is now close to bankruptcy.

Among our staff there was a lot of confusion on the
issue, with various statements being released at different
times. But I still believe that the utility should be sold—if
anyone would buy it. As a matter of fact, Democrats and
Republicans alike have since offered variations of my proposal for TVA and other large federal utilities. No one is
saying the entire TVA should be sold at once, but various
satellites could be put on the market over time. We now
have a fancy name for all this. It's discussed regularly on
the front pages of daily newspapers and is called privatization. President Reagan is selling more federal land in
the West to put it on the tax rolls. Democrats want to
market hydropower from Hoover Dam to the highest
bidder. There are numerous examples of all this today in

the name of fair market value pricing and the free market system.

If anything, the change in attitudes shows that conservatives have made some progress. I'm proud of my stand on TVA and would say it all again.

On nuclear weapons, one of the most disturbing aspects of the issue was never really discussed. Why was it that so many high government officials, military analysts, think tank types, and others could dissect the subject among themselves, but it was taboo for a candidate for the presidency to bring its sweeping dimensions before the American voter? We brought the whole question out in the open to debate it. Lyndon Johnson refused to discuss it publicly with me. Today the horrors of nuclear war are not only discussed on the front pages but featured in left-wing movies, television productions, and, above all, on the floor of the U.S. Congress.

Reflecting on the campaign now, perhaps the Vietnam War should also have become a matter of public debate. I suggested to and agreed with President Johnson not to make a partisan political issue out of it to avoid further division on the home front. In retrospect, had Johnson and I squared off on the issue, the President might have revealed his intention to escalate the conflict without a military plan or diplomatic policy to win it. We might have saved many American lives.

During 1964 I discussed the theoretical possibility that some day the American military might use tactical—not strategic—nuclear weapons. Tactical weapons are used against enemy military forces on the battlefield or directed at operations and supplies supporting those troops. Strategic nuclear weapons are used against enemy countries and their war-making capacity. In discussing the Ho Chi Minh Trail, I was talking about a theoretical option —the U.S. military had included in its wide-ranging contingency planning the possibility of using small tactical nuclear weapons there. "Small" meant causing a narrowly defined area of destruction.

The distinction between tactical and strategic weapons became even more significant when the potential use of nuclear weapons by NATO became an issue in the campaign. I had long been on record as favoring a "special safeguard"—that only one person apart from the President, the supreme commander of NATO, could approve the use of "conventional" nuclear weapons. Tactical weapons came to be called "conventional" as they became available in large numbers in NATO's defensive arsenal.

It became "nuclear madness" to discuss the subject. The possible use of any nuclear devices was talked about only in terms of doomsday, not limited destruction. Yet, in a New York *Times* article as early as October 7, 1958, General Earl E. Partridge, a former commander of NORAD (North American Air Defense) said that his command had been authorized to fire a nuclear weapon in combat. Partridge further said he could order the firing of nuclear weapons without the specific approval of the President.

Most Americans, with the exception of certain attentive readers of the *Times,* knew nothing of this. They were unaware that President Eisenhower had agreed that if Western Europe were attacked, the NATO commander could fire the weapons in certain defined circumstances.

Today, NATO's defense is based on the possible use of nuclear weapons. As a candidate, I had brought to the attention of the American people an issue of the gravest importance and was castigated for it. Never once did I advocate the use of such weapons.

Yet Lyndon Johnson, Bill Moyers, and others in the White House waged a campaign of fear against me in what came to be known as the "card" and "bomb" ads. The pair portrayed me as a destroyer of Social Security and a mad nuclear bomber in their campaign television commercials. I was depicted as a grotesque public monster. They converted my campaign slogan from "In your heart, you know he's right" to "In your guts, you know he's nuts."

Their "card" ad showed two hands—meant to be mine —tearing apart a Social Security card. That was what Barry Goldwater would do if he became President, the commercial threatened, so save the system and elect President Johnson. The ad was a repellent lie. Moyers knew it yet approved the ad, and it was shown throughout the campaign.

Moyers ordered two "bomb" commercials from the New York advertising firm of Doyle Dane Bernbach. He oversaw and approved their production. The first was a one-minute film which appeared during prime time on NBC. It showed a little girl in a sunny field of daisies. She begins plucking petals from a daisy. As she plucks the flower, a male voice in the background starts a countdown . . . ten . . . nine . . . eight . . . becoming constantly stronger. The screen suddenly explodes, and the child disappears in a mushroom cloud. The voice concludes by urging voters to elect President Johnson, saying, "These are the stakes: To make a world in which all of God's children can live, or go into the dark. We must either love each other, or we must die. Vote for President Johnson on November third. The stakes are too high for you to stay home."

There was no doubt as to the meaning: Barry Goldwater would blow up the world if he became President of the United States.

The White House exploded its second bomb about a week later, again on network television. Another little girl was licking an ice cream cone. A soft, motherly voice explained in the background that radioactive fallout had killed many children. A treaty had been signed to prevent such destruction. The gloomy voice said a man—Barry Goldwater—had voted against the Nuclear Test Ban Treaty. A Geiger counter rose to a crescendo as a male voice concluded, "Vote for President Johnson on November third . . . the stakes are too high for you to stay home."

The commercials completely misrepresented my position, which called for treaty guarantees and other safeguards for the United States. Dean Burch filed a protest about the commercials with the toothless Federal Campaign Practices Committee. The committee requested that the Democratic National Committee drop the ads, which Johnson and Moyers were forced to do. They later claimed the ads would have been canceled anyway.

Moyers, in a revealing interview with Merle Miller, who later wrote a biography of President Johnson, admitted he was responsible for the advertising campaign. Moyers pronounced the ads a "success." He said,

"Johnson called me not too long after [the daisy commercial], and said he'd been swamped with calls . . . I could tell the moment he answered the phone that he was having a wonderful time putting on an act. He said:

" 'What in the hell do you mean putting on that ad that just ran? I've been swamped with calls, and the Goldwater people are calling it a low blow,' and on and on and on—typical, wonderful, Lyndon Johnson fashion. His voice was chuckling all the time. He said, 'You'd better come over here and tell me what you're going to do about this.'

"So I went over at ten o'clock, and he said, 'Don't you think that was pretty tough?' I said, 'Mr. President, we were just reminding people that, at this time, it might be a good idea to have an experienced hand on the button.' I said I had only ordered that it be run once.

"I turned and went back to the elevator . . . and heard, 'Bill, Bill, just a minute!' He got up out of his chair and came down to the alcove with his back to the group [of dinner guests]. He said, 'You sure we ought to run it just once?' I said, 'Yes, Mr. President.' "

Why just once? Why not a dozen times? The answer is that if you stab a man in the back deeply enough once, you can murder him. Moyers, an individual who professes his religious righteousness publicly, apparently believes it's moral to do that. But it's apparently immoral if you get caught stabbing someone five or ten times.

Those bomb commercials were the start of dirty political ads on television. It was the beginning of what I call "electronic dirt." Moyers and the New York firm will long be remembered for helping to launch this ugly development in our political history.

Over the years, I've watched Moyers appear on "CBS News" and the Public Broadcasting Service. He has lectured us on truth, the public trust, a fairer and finer America. He portrays himself as an honorable, decent American. Every time I see him, I get sick to my stomach and want to throw up.

While writing this book, I tried to speak with Moyers about these ads, to allow him to discuss the commercials in his own words. He declined to return about a half dozen phone calls made by my researcher.

Moyers' successor as White House press secretary, George Reedy, did. He said he was "bored and sick" at Moyers' dirty tricks operation.

Reedy confirmed that Johnson and Moyers had had a "spy" inside our campaign organization who had fed them advance texts of my speeches, announcements, and scheduling information. He said, "I felt this espionage operation was silliness because we had the race won. However, some around the White House reveled in dirty tricks. I was out of step with them. That was one of the major reasons why LBJ and I drifted apart. I really like Barry Goldwater. He has always been a decent, honorable man."

Hal Pachios, deputy White House press secretary under Johnson, tells of an interesting sidelight. Johnson detested anti-LBJ or pro-Goldwater signs at his rallies. He ordered that they somehow be removed. Marvin Watson, an LBJ aide, had people sprinkle itching powder behind the necks of people holding those signs.

Vice President Hubert Humphrey, after assuming office, described the film depicting the child swallowed up in a mushroom cloud as "unfortunate." I asked him why he ever ran with Lyndon. A lot of us knew that he had been called to the White House by Johnson and had almost had to get on his knees to take a loyalty oath. I don't recall Humphrey's precise words, but he said something like this: You and I have been around a long time, Barry. We've seen it all. Sure, he's an SOB, but in politics, like everything else, you take the chance when it comes along. So I took it.

James "Scotty" Reston, columnist for the New York *Times,* says, "I wish the media had kicked the stuffing out of LBJ and the White House on the TV ads issue. I think the senator is absolutely right in saying the press was remiss in letting that garbage get out without nailing them. It was outrageous—no doubt about it. He's got a legitimate gripe."

The Washington *Post*'s Ben Bradlee now describes the two Moyers bomb ads as "a fucking outrage. I was outraged then."

David Broder, the veteran political reporter and columnist for the Washington *Post,* today describes the campaign this way:

"The Johnson White House involvement with some penetration of the Goldwater campaign and its attacks on Goldwater were highly irrational because they were so heavily favored to win. Also, the media's original perception of Goldwater was fundamentally false. He was not the crazy madman that some depicted. However, some substantial criticism was justified. He made some mistakes and misstatements that we reported as facts.

"The media have a tendency to characterize men and events and oversimplify them. We presented a scary picture of Goldwater. It was not the whole cloth of the man and politician. Our characterization of him as an extremist was a terrible distortion."

We tried to find out who was supplying information to the White House but failed. Paul Wagner, Lee Edwards, and others did their best to plug the leaks, but they continued. The penetration did some harm because Johnson was able to take various steps to neutralize what we were about to charge in a speech or make public in an announcement.

We were witnessing some of the reasons why I never wanted to run against LBJ from the beginning. They went to the very core of the man, his basic character.

When we first met in the Senate, Johnson enjoyed mentioning the fact that he had come to Congress as a $6,000-a-year, dirt-poor Texas schoolteacher. Later, he was to boast that he had become a multimillionaire. Johnson explained this new wealth with a knowing smile: His wife had inherited money.

It was common knowledge on Capitol Hill and around Washington that Johnson was involved in who got which radio and television licenses in the country and other deals. He and his family had received the only TV franchise in Austin, Texas. Johnson and his longtime administrative assistant, Bobby Baker, were widely regarded in Washington as two of the biggest wheeler-dealers of their time. Baker later went to prison for his activities.

The case against Johnson has been documented at length over the years. It serves no purpose to dredge up that background here except to indicate my misgivings about being in the same ring with him.

Johnson wanted a national party—a party of power, a machine that won, an apparatus that controlled. His opening sentence on almost any issue was, "Who's got the cards?"

Johnson's politics was intervention—by government, by power brokers in either party, by those who would form the strongest alliance on any issue. His ideology was three words: Let's do something.

A good example of this was his use of every federal department and agency to help guarantee a landslide victory. Government was his political action committee, his slush fund, his firepower, his troops. Above all else in the campaign, LBJ wanted his own massive mandate to govern. He was too big to live in anyone else's shadow. He would show Bobby Kennedy and the rest of that crowd, who joked about him behind his back, how the game was really played.

To Johnson, the Democratic Party was a place with a fence and four walls where you retreated to rest, heal your wounds, and to gather strength—and then rush out into the street for more combat. It wasn't a home of strong beliefs and principles. LBJ would build another house, another power base, another shifting alliance. This was done by trading principle and power through an exchange of promises. His politics was the promissory note.

Johnson ducked the issues throughout the campaign. The White House strategy was to put Goldwater on the defensive, to use the Rockefeller and other Republican charges against him. To keep him off balance so he wouldn't be able to attack the President's policies and the Johnson image of himself. Above all, to run a campaign of fear—to make the American people fear Barry Goldwater.

On the evening of October 7, the President's closest aide, Walter Jenkins, was arrested in the men's room of a YMCA a few blocks from the White House. Police had staked it out as a hangout for homosexuals. Jenkins was booked along with an Army veteran on charges of disorderly conduct.

We knew about the arrest within two days. LBJ also was told of the arrest but remained silent. I said nothing. The Chicago *Tribune* and Cincinnati *Enquirer* learned of the story on Monday but decided not to publish it. The Washington *Star* called the White House about the incident on Tuesday, and Jenkins immediately left his office. Abe Fortas and Clark Clifford, two intimates of Johnson, immediately called at the *Star* and asked the editors to kill the story. Reports of the affair were now all over Washington as Fortas and Clifford made the rounds of news offices to suppress the damaging disclosure. Finally, seven full days after the incident occurred, the story broke.

Baroody and a few others on the staff saw the incident as a political windfall. Jenkins had been arrested previously on a similar charge, yet he had continued to work as Johnson's top White House confidant. We had been hammering away at ethics in government—Bobby Baker, Billie Sol Estes, and other cronies who had profited from running LBJ's errands. Reporters pestered me for a reaction to the Jenkins story. I said nothing, nor was I going to make an issue of the incident. We would separate Barry Goldwater from Lyndon Johnson on this matter. I told no one what I was thinking except Kitchel. He was to pass the word to everyone on our staff to say nothing —no comment whatsoever.

Meantime, reacting to mounting questions from the media, Johnson asked the FBI to investigate the case on national security grounds. Jenkins had sat in on meetings of the National Security Council. There was a question as to whether he had ever been blackmailed. Jenkins had not.

Later, we discovered that the President's second move was to summon his pollster, Oliver Quayle, to a midnight meeting. Johnson, who kept every current political poll in the breast pocket of his suit coat, wanted a quick poll to determine the damage to his campaign. He said nothing publicly about the case, distancing himself from Jenkins as he had from Baker, Estes, and other sidekicks who found themselves in trouble.

Mrs. Johnson, on her own, publicly asked for compassion for Jenkins and his family. It was her finest hour— doing what her husband should have done immediately instead of stalling and having his pals try to suppress the story. Lady Bird Johnson was one of the finest women I've ever met. She was a gracious individual with a particularly wide knowledge of nature and the nation's natural treasures. Lady Bird came to Phoenix to dedicate

Camelback Mountain as a national preserve on one of her many trips across the country to protect the nation's natural beauty.

Meantime, the White House anxiously awaited what we were going to say about the matter. It drove them crazy when I refused comment. Here was the cowboy who shot from the hip, the Scrooge who would put the penniless on the street with no Social Security, the maniac who would blow us and our little children into the next kingdom in a nuclear Armageddon. If he would kill a million men and women, why wouldn't he destroy one individual? Why was the extremist pursuing moderation?

When the media clamor over the case had climbed to fever pitch, I said the only matter which concerned the campaign was the national security aspect. We never spoke of it again except to repeat the security factor in response to questions and pressure from the media. Our reply was always the same: The FBI was the competent agency to answer any such questions.

It was a sad time for Jenkins' wife and children, and I was not about to add to their private sorrow. In political terms, it would have made no difference if we had summoned a thousand angels in witness to our cause. This reality never got through to Johnson and Moyers—that winning, even by a landslide, isn't everything. Some things, like loyalty to friends or lasting principle, are more important. Any cause will go on if it's a good one. We're only players. It reminded me of the great Western writer Willa Cather, who spoke so profoundly of our relationship to the land around us: "We come and go, but the land is always here. And the people who love it and understand it are the people who own it—for a little while."

Being a man from the open range, Johnson should have understood that. He never did, and that was pitiful. He forgot his roots in reaching for more and more power. We conservatives wanted to return that power to the open range, to the ranchers, to the Big Sky country, and to the cities and streets of all America.

Some advisers wanted us to run a so-called morality film on TV to strike back at Johnson and Moyers and their garbage. The half-hour documentary was sponsored by an independent women's group. It attacked American moral decay by showing topless bathers, nudists, and pornographic books and portrayed LBJ as a reckless driver throwing beer cans out of a limousine. There were numerous claims he had done that. I killed it—because it was tasteless, and especially because it portrayed the presidency in a poor light. It was simply a cheap shot.

Two other attacks on me indicate how low the campaign had degenerated. C. L. Sulzberger wrote in the New York *Times:* "The possibility exists that, should he [Goldwater] enter the White House, there might not be a day after tomorrow."

Those words may well be one of the most unfair statements ever printed in the history of the New York *Times.* Sulzberger, as far as I can recall, had never spoken to me or interviewed me. What did he really know of Barry Goldwater? Of the men and women who would be his cabinet members and other advisers if Goldwater became President? What qualifications and what direct knowledge did Sulzberger have to suggest his apocalyptic vision? When the next history of the *Times* is written, those responsible may well reflect on Sulzberger's sources of prophetic revelation—and whether the Sulzberger statement that I might destroy mankind and the earth was fit to print.

A magazine called *Fact* published a sixty-four-page "psychological study" of the GOP presidential candidate which began with this question: "Do you think that Barry Goldwater is psychologically fit to serve as President of the United States?"

The editors claimed to have polled 12,356 psychiatrists across the country, saying they had received 1,846 replies. The respondents were not required to sign their names. The president and medical director of the American Psychiatric Association wrote in a joint letter: "By attaching the stigma of extreme political partisanship to the psychiatric profession as a whole in the heated climate of the current political campaign, *Fact* has in effect administered a low blow to all who would advance the treatment and care of the mentally ill of America."

Other medical and professional groups criticized the survey as unscientific and said any doctors who might have taken part in it were guilty of unethical behavior. It was obvious that *Fact* was involved in a hatchet job. Yet the New York *Times* published a full-page advertisement for the survey, and many newspapers published its results —all critical of the Republican presidential candidate. I later sued the magazine for libel and won a financial judgment.

Running for the presidency is really two different journeys. Sometimes it's like flying with no wings or engine. Your heart and mind soar like a glider. You ride the currents of public opinion—the cheers, the handshakes, the deafening roar in a big stadium. Then, after three months or so, you land quickly, quietly. The horizons disappear in the sunset. As suddenly as the opening words of your first campaign speech, it's all over. You hear your heart beating again. You're alone.

At other times, it's one helluva bumpy ride with all four engines pumping, clouds behind and a storm ahead. Your ear always catches that jeer among the cheers. For all the good handshakes, someone is shaking his fist at you. Your heart is beating so damn fast during some of those hectic twenty-hour days that you can hear it an hour after you've fallen asleep. And you're never alone. Somebody's just gotta talk to you. And you can't sleep.

Denny Kitchel used to sit down with me at 2 A.M., and we'd begin battling over the same old subject—the daily schedule. I was going from a 7 A.M. television interview to an 8 A.M. breakfast and speech to a 9 A.M. outdoor rally and speech in the center of downtown Billings, Montana, to a 10 A.M. flight to Cheyenne, Wyoming, with a noon rally and speech on the state Capitol grounds followed by a twelve-thirty lunch with leading townsfolk, with a news conference to follow. We were to take off for Denver at one-thirty with an airport rally and news conference before heading to Albuquerque for a 4 P.M. news conference, a 6 P.M. dinner speech, and an outdoor speech at the University of New Mexico at 8 P.M. A strategy session would begin at 9 P.M., followed by finance, advertising, and speechwriting conferences. As I told Kitchel a few dozen times, "You guys are killing me."

Sometimes, however, I skipped out on the staff's advice and Kitchel's fatherly requests. One such incident involved Herblock, the longtime cartoonist at the Washington *Post*. He depicted me as an upstart who had inherited his father's department store.

I could feel the arrow in my rear end. Without telling anyone, I phoned Phil Graham, who was then the publisher, and said, "I haven't seen any cartoons in the *Post* about the publisher marrying the boss's daughter." (Graham had married Katharine Meyer, whose father had owned the paper. She later became its publisher.)

I'm not ashamed to admit that I popped off in the campaign. I was not about to let conservatism die of sleep and boredom. Sure, I talked at times with my heart and guts. But if you look at the record, Barry Goldwater didn't take cheap, dirty shots at his opponents that were masked in the skilled surgical language of columnists like Walter Lippmann and Joseph Alsop.

A politician learns to take a lot of shots. As the years have passed, I've learned to live and often laugh with them. Sure, I sometimes still get mad. But that's when an issue is really serious or a person is not telling the truth. It has often been said, "You don't lie to Barry Goldwater."

I don't like liars—never have.

I like stand-up guys who'll say, "Yes, I said it. I'm sorry. I'll try not to let it happen again."

Political campaigning is often a nutty world. Bill Miller and I had some wonderful, wacky experiences. We had a Mata Hari aboard our whistle stop train. It was Dick Tuck's idea. Dick was a practical jokester at the Democratic National Committee whose idea of fun was to pull the elephant's tail. The gal's name was Moira O'Connor. A cute pixie, she worked as a volunteer for the DNC. Moira got on the train at Washington's Union Station posing as a reporter. At night, when everyone was asleep, she distributed the morning editions of *The Whistle Stop,* which, among other things, said I remained on Washington time—George Washington, that is. Vic Gold discovered O'Connor and put her off the train at Parkersburg, West Virginia. I didn't mind her at all. I hope she had bus fare.

Gold was a wonderful guy on the campaign. He really ran us ragged from 6 A.M. to midnight, urging bus drivers to go faster, pulling reporters out of bars to catch the plane, having our laundry catch up with all of us. Some wit in the press corps wrote a song about Vic to the tune of the old Wobbly song "Joe Hill." A few of its last lines tells the story:

> When we have run our worldly course,
> And done our mortal chores,
> Vic Gold will be our escort on
> The trip to unknown shores.
> His face a mask of outrage
> In the tones we know so well,
> Vic Gold will shout the devil down,
> And lead us all to hell.

One evening in Wichita Falls, Texas, I was winding up a serious speech on the meaning of freedom and was dead tired. The sun was slipping behind the Texas plains, making me even drowsier. I was almost asleep on my feet, ad-libbing the close of the address. If you can make sense out of what I said, be my guest: "There are no heights to which our people can't go. There is no limit to the heights, no limit to their expanse if we go as a free people. I say, as a great man once said, 'Let my people go.' Thank you."

I saw Kitchel and said, "You heard the speech. Let me go—to bed."

Bill Miller had a wild bunch of reporters with him. No campaign crew in history drank more booze, lost more laundry, or bet more money on card games. Bill won hundreds of dollars from them playing bridge. Miller had the quickest wit in Congress, as good as Senator Alan Simpson, the Wyoming Republican, is today. One of the newsmen, down on his luck, said to Bill, "I'll bet you a hundred bucks you guys lose the election—and give you five to one odds."

Bill shot back, "I may be a gambler, but I'm not crazy enough to bet on this election."

After almost every game, as the plane began descending to the next stop on the campaign, the newsmen sang Miller these words to the tune of "The Wiffenpoof Song":

> We are poor journalists
> Who have lost our shirts
> Bah . . . bah . . . bah.
> Little lost scribes
> Who lost till it hurts,
> Bah . . . bah . . . bah.
> Gentlemen, newsmen, off on a spree
> Doomed from here to November three;
> Bill, have mercy on such as we.
> Bah . . . bah . . . bah.

They formed a morals committee which used the cabin microphone to announce various escapades of the night before. It usually ended with a master list of reporters who'd had a merry eve.

Before flying back to Washington from Miller's home in Lockport on November 4, the day after the election, the reporters breakfasted on beer, champagne, toast, and eggs. Miller concluded the campaign on the cabin microphone with these words: "What we have said apparently was little noted by the electorate, and certainly will not be long remembered. But it is for us the living, not the dead drunk, to here resolve: that this government, of the birds, by the birds, and for the birds shall not continue on this earth."

On that solemn note, his vice presidential bid ended. When their plane landed in Washington, Miller, his staff, and the reporters drove to Bill's house, where the party continued.

One of our craziest episodes came in Bristol, Tennessee. We were flying in an American Airlines 727. We called it "Yai-Bi-Kin," which is Navajo for "House in the Sky." Ralph Long, the pilot, took off, turned, and roared back down toward the tower. I crawled on my hands and knees up to the cockpit to find out what was going on. Ralph told me he had just buzzed the tower to salute an old pal. I crawled back to my seat, giving everybody the thumbs-up. The incident eventually got up to C. R. Smith, the president of American Airlines. Smith wasn't going to do anything to the pilot, but he was getting heat from somewhere. I told him that if he changed pilots we were changing airlines. That quieted things down, and we crisscrossed the country, covering forty-five states.

I've never admitted this, but perhaps it's time to do so. I piloted our Boeing 727 at times because it relaxed me. The aircraft was new at the time, and I wanted to get a feel of it. After the election, when we returned to Washington, I landed it at Dulles Airport. We didn't come down like a paintbrush. One of the reporters caught sight of me in the cockpit, came up, and whispered, "Your third bounce was pretty good, but that first one was real exciting."

We had no U.S. Secret Service protection in 1964. Frankly, I didn't want it. The candidates began to be covered in 1968 after former Alabama Governor George Wallace was shot. A fellow by the name of Charlie Justice, an auto salesman we met in New Hampshire, just stayed by my side through the campaign. He was a big, burly fellow but never carried a gun. I'm about six feet tall and weigh 185 pounds, but Charlie looked like the Fort Knox Mint by comparison. We picked up a few more Charlies after I got splattered with an egg in New Jersey.

One time, a fellow flashed a sign at us with the chemical formula for Gold and Water. On the other side, it read, "In your guts, you know he's nuts." Charlie looked just once, and that guy disappeared like a puff of smoke.

The best speech of the campaign was delivered by Ronald Reagan on October 27, a half-hour television address. It was called "A Time for Choosing." Reagan had already delivered it in California. When our staff suggested I make a national fund-raising address like it, I didn't want to do it. The words just weren't me. I watched a film of Reagan delivering it and immediately phoned him and said, "That was an eloquent speech. You're more eloquent than I am. You do it."

He did. The speech got us a bundle in nationwide campaign contributions but, more important, launched Reagan as California's GOP gubernatorial candidate in 1966 and as a national political figure. Ron was a class act. After he won the governor's race, Reagan couldn't phone me because of a California phone strike. He and Nancy flew to Phoenix to see her parents. Reagan called me on landing and said, "I never would have made it if you fellows didn't help me."

There was no better place in the nation to study 1964 from the GOP grass roots level than the state of Texas, the home base of President Johnson. The Texas Republican Party was a virtual zero as the campaign began. Although Republican John Tower had been elected senator in a special 1961 election after Lyndon Johnson became Vice President, the victory had been seen as a political aberration for many reasons. One was the fact that Johnson had shown such disdain for the voters by running for two offices at the same time in 1960. His decision had left a bad taste in the mouths of most Texans. Johnson had had a special law enacted by the Texas legislature so he could do this. The decision was half ego and half cynical self-protection. It was also LBJ's way of saying the GOP had no one who could take his place in the Senate. The Republicans had also been beaten badly by John Connally and the Democrats in the 1962 governor's race. I campaigned long and hard for Tower in 1961, and he never forgot it. Neither did Texas conservatives.

Texas GOP morale was very low in 1964. Yet a new, youthful strength, the vigor of thousands of young volunteers, was sweeping the country. The Young Americans for Freedom (YAFs) had begun only a few years earlier with a hundred members. In 1964 they numbered over 100,000 members, and many more were joining them.

After I won the California primary, Lance Tarrance got a phone call at home from a Texas party leader. He thought he had been forgotten. Some young Texans in the state had already done volunteer work for me. The party now wanted to set up a Goldwater for President headquarters—with young enthusiasts. All were in their early twenties. Tarrance became the research director at our headquarters in Austin. Tad Smith of El Paso was our campaign director and graybeard. He was in his thirties.

As director of research, Tarrance soon saw we were getting many $50, $100, and sometimes $500 contributions from small businessmen in Dallas and Houston. Virtually all had less than fifty employees. The Democrats were receiving most of their contributions from the fat cats. We were getting almost no big money from the richest precinct in the state, River Oaks in Houston. The corporate types were going for the big government contracts of LBJ.

These developments reflected the great conviction of conservatives in 1964—that the party had to be reconstituted from top to bottom. The process was reinforcing the belief that we had to examine not only the party but its relationship to government, corporations, and anything that would threaten our bid to broaden the base of the GOP. We needed true believers, not just accommodaters like the elite who wanted to wheel and deal and narrow the party's agenda to their special interests.

This conviction arose before single-issue groups became so prevalent in the political picture.

We learned another lesson. Considerable Republican debt had been piled up by the Shivercrats—Alan Shivers, a popular governor, had bolted the Democrats to join the GOP in the 1950s over the Texas tidelands issue. It was not until my campaign of a decade later that the GOP climbed out of debt. These people could help us, but they weren't conservatives.

How did we free ourselves from such red ink? Most of our contributions came from little guys who believed in our principles. We had no big base among large corporations or the rich, nor did we aim for it. We had surplus contributions elsewhere. This helped the party stay on its feet in other states.

I lost Texas two to one. But new people had come into the party, new contributors, new ideas, new hopes. The same was true in other states.

As Texas research director, Tarrance was very much aware of these new contributors. So was Richard Viguerie of Houston. He went to Austin and copied down by hand the names of contributors listed in the secretary of state's office. Viguerie also obtained the lists made up by Tower and others. Then he went to Washington and obtained our national mailing lists. He developed additional names from what is now the Federal Election

Commission (by law, the names and addresses of all contributors must be filed). He then obtained more names on his own and has gone on to become the major originator and master of direct political mailings.

Direct computer mail, soliciting thousands of small contributions, began in Texas on the state level. With our Washington master lists, it later exploded across the country. Many of the things those Texas neophytes did in 1964 became the politics of the future.

It's essential to realize that this new GOP financial power came from the South, West, and Midwest. This money helped John Tower win a big upset victory over Waggoner Carr in the 1966 Senate race in Texas. The same is true in other races across parts of the West and South in later years.

I take no credit for the GOP's new financial base, although we wanted our campaign to wind up in the black. The real work was done by others, who saw the campaign as a way of demonstrating conservative financial integrity as well as individual initiative. We also received an avalanche of contributions in the final days of the campaign. None of this money was spent. It was a base on which the party could start to build.

Since 1964 there have been thousands of GOP meetings, conferences, and seminars in various parts of the country. And I have met thousands of people whose political lives began with the 1964 presidential race. At times it seems surprising to meet yet another person in public life who was part of that campaign. It's all the more interesting that so many have remained in politics.

Of all the GOP meetings and conferences that have occurred over the past twenty-five years, one stands out. It was held in Kansas City in 1965 at the request of Ohio's Ray Bliss, who had been named the new chairman of the Republican National Committee. The meeting was a national conference for those Republicans interested in targeting political groups and issues with computers.

Bliss, a very successful state chairman, was viewed by many as a conciliator. He would bridge the gap between the Rockefeller and Goldwater wings of the party. Ray believed the GOP was not targeting the vote right. Republicans had virtually given up the big cities; they were not concentrating on ethnic shifts as they should. Those attending were young and green.

Republican veterans were oriented toward the Washington debate on national issues. They were not computer-, not survey-, not staff-oriented. These people had already been old when they had worked under national committee chairman Leonard Hall in the fifties. They saw themselves as quality people—and many were—but they didn't have a broad-based view of the party. Meeting in Kansas City were such people as Tarrance, John Deardorf, now a political media and advertising leader, Pat Buchanan, Walt DeVries, who later wrote a number of incisive books on politics and became a political consultant and professor of political science, Billy Wilkins, executive director of the GOP in Mississippi, Jim Rock of Oregon, who later went on to the American Farm Bureau, Fred Currier of Market Opinion Research, and many others who later became leaders in the GOP.

They were smart and stimulating and were to become skilled in computer politics, surveys, and direct mail. Bliss expected twenty people to show up. Some 115 came, and they paid their own way. They hadn't forgotten or abandoned the experience of 1964. They had built on it.

The effort to move the party from the dominance of less than a dozen families and others in the East to hundreds of thousands of small businessmen and others in the South, West, and elsewhere was now really under way.

Bliss put a lot of money into computers, even established a computer division at the national committee. He saw the party's future in the Goldwater donors, an independent new financial base for the party. Bliss went on to the widespread use of computer solicitation letters rather than one-thousand-dollar-a-plate dinners and similar functions to raise money from wealthy families and large corporations.

These rich families and big firms owned the national committee and the party. They were the Rockefellers and others. We could dispense with the few and the powerful if we could find hundreds of thousands of small contributors through computers. And we did locate such support.

The national committee adopted an important research manual that Tarrance wrote for the party in Texas. It had been prepared for Tower's 1966 Senate race and was a computerized schedule for the candidate listing how many hours he should be in certain parts of Texas, what he should talk about at each stop, where the ticket-splitter counties were, and what we would do to divide the ticket our way.

In 1967 Bliss brought Tarrance to Washington to become the number two research person in the party. The Texan was still in his mid-twenties. Tarrance and I had never met, although he had heard me speak. One evening, my wife and I were having dinner at a seafood restaurant on Washington's Potomac River. Tarrance and his wife arrived. They had been in Washington only a few months.

Suddenly this young man was standing at our table and he said, "Senator, you don't know me. My name is Lance Tarrance. I worked as one of your volunteers in the sixty-four campaign.

"You brought in a lot of young people like myself to work for the party. We got the hell beat out of us. But I want you to know that some day, people are going to look back at sixty-four and say that we changed the Republican Party. I just had to tell you this."

I got a lump in my throat and didn't know what to say.

Many of us felt we would come back. There were simply too many of us, too many hopes, and too much faith to have us die in some political wilderness. We were lonely before Ronald Reagan came along.

The GOP was thus able to use modern technology to leapfrog a full decade beyond the Democrats, not only in fund-raising techniques but in just about every aspect of campaigning.

We gave and allowed youngsters more responsibility than any presidential campaign in history had. The reason was hardly profound. Many old-timers, who belonged to the liberal wing of the party, had simply deserted us.

It may seem like a platitude, but I believe every campaign, without exception, should have a good number of young people in it. The young have an immediacy about them, a "now" quality that helps to interpret and explain many issues, and they are geared to the latest technology much better than, say, someone ten or twenty years older. We older folks often do not grasp the immediate importance of the latest technological changes.

I can see it in my grandchildren. They can make a computer talk and, for all I know, sing. I just putter along. That compliment to the young comes from a fellow who has spent his entire life trying to keep up with the latest electronic and other technical advances.

In 1964 Ed Feulner was a rare bird. He supported our ticket on an Eastern campus and offers a much different view of our bid. It was considered downright treasonous to be for Goldwater at the University of Pennsylvania in Philadelphia. Feulner was a graduate student in its Wharton School and became politically energized for the first time in his life. He worked as a part-time volunteer for the Goldwater-Miller committee. He soon learned it was unpopular even to be a Republican. Nevertheless, *The Conscience of a Conservative* and Kirk's *The Conservative Mind* moved him to action.

In Pennsylvania, our situation was very bad. Senator Hugh Scott, the GOP Senate minority leader, didn't want to have anything to do with the Goldwater-Miller ticket. The Republican Party structure had frozen us out. So we left it to young eager beavers like Feulner to mobilize some kind of effort for the ticket.

Two things stand out about the Pennsylvania campaign: First, that Professor Robert Strausz-Hupe, director of the Foreign Policy Research Institute at the University of Pennsylvania and one of the foremost political scientists at the time—he later became a top U.S. ambassador—was booed and shunned by his colleagues at the university because he supported me. Some academic freedom in the Ivy League.

Second, on election day in November 1964 Feulner was assigned to watch some of the polls in Philadelphia. He and other volunteers used imitation radio antennae on the roofs of cars because they didn't have the money for two-way radios. The idea was to let those working for the Philadelphia Democratic machine think they were being reported for voting irregularities. But these leaders of brotherly love laughed and clobbered me. We never had a chance. The machine, second only to Chicago's, carried the city for Johnson by half a million votes. Feulner had never seen a political machine in action before. He became a lifelong conservative.

No candidate for national office could be nominated or elected in many states without the support of corrupt city political machines. Indeed, the Kennedy victory over Nixon in 1960 is still questionable, not only because of its closeness but, much more significantly, because of the role of Chicago's Daley machine in the waning hours of ballot counting in Cook County.

In 1964 we challenged the entire Republican establishment, not just the East. No one had ever really taken on the total apparatus, down to the county and district levels. These young conservatives broke their backs because they believed in an idea. They stayed up later, mailed more letters, made more phone calls, pounded more pavements, and got their candidate nominated.

Chuck Lichenstein, who has done considerable research on 1964, has made an interesting observation about our campaign. He says it paved the way not only for a new Republican Party, but ironically for Democratic candidates like George McGovern, Jimmy Carter, and Gary Hart. None was from a big state. None had a major power base. Neither did Arizona's Barry Goldwater.

Vic Gold once paid a tribute to me which I will always treasure: "I believe it was his role not to be President, although I still believe he would have made a good one. But Barry Goldwater's work was to be the conscience of the United States Senate and, in his time, for the country as well."

In many ways, I've been both a dissenter and, I hope, somewhat of a leader. My mission in politics has been to take the hard knocks, get up off the floor, and keep the conservative cause alive while others—much more gifted by God than I—had the talent, time, and opportunity to build the movement to where it is today.

If I've been a political conscience for Vic Gold or anyone else, I just want to say: "Hell, I hope I wasn't too much of a burden!"

Frankly, for years I expected to hear some distant wails of regret among those who took part in our campaign. We had been beaten badly. Yet, in traveling around the country since 1964 and hearing every conceivable reason for why we had lost by such a landslide, I haven't heard a single tale of grief or abiding anger.

It has been argued that the media played a major role in 1964, that they themselves became a series of campaign events. Indeed, some of my conservative colleagues maintain the media had rarely taken such a decisive role in American politics. Further, they insist, the full impact of media participation in public events was not adequately understood until they began to assume a questionable role in the Vietnam War.

It should serve a useful historical purpose to let some of those who covered the 1964 campaign look back and compare those times with the political atmosphere of today.

Arthur Krock, the New York *Times* columnist, said that I'd been attacked by the media "with a bitterness unexampled in recent history." Publisher John S. Knight, who had not backed me, said that I had received "shabby treatment from most of the news media." Even *Newsweek* finally admitted that some reporters were "less than neutral."

James J. Kilpatrick, the conservative columnist, believes many in the media were biased against us in 1964. He suggests some newspeople speak more moderately of us today because the conservative movement has risen to respectability and power in the country. Kilpatrick explains that the media are responding to public opinion to a large degree.

Ben Bradlee and I have refought 1964 a few times. We agree that both the media and I have changed. We don't agree on which has changed most.

We strongly agree that, if Jack Kennedy and I had faced one another in 1964, the campaign would have been much better. As Bradlee puts it, "The issues would have really hung out there to see. They never did with Johnson."

Bradlee says that five sources created bias against candidate Goldwater: myself, my staff, fellow Republicans, the Johnson White House, and the media. He argues that I shot from the hip, that our campaign leaders, particularly Denny Kitchel, were "hardasses" and inadequate to their jobs, and that some reporters portrayed me as "an unthoughtful guy giving simplistic solutions" instead of reporting the facts. He says that none or very little of this bias was personal—that none or few in the media disliked Goldwater personally.

Bradlee was tough on my campaign staff in the Clif White case, saying, "They broke his heart," when White didn't receive the RNC chairmanship. "He was the best guy around, a total pro, and understood the fabric of government better than any of them."

The Washington *Post* executive editor says, in retrospect, that the media and others misread me on the so-called extremism issue: "Barry Goldwater is not a zealot and never was a zealot. He's a traditional person, a traditional Jeffersonian, not a single-issue politician, not a neo-conservative. As a matter of fact, I never saw anything wrong with the extremism quote in his acceptance speech."

He believes our campaign would have been more successful if I had spoken more and our speechwriters less: "He was more in control of himself later, and particularly now. Barry has also changed. He's much less conscious of political necessity. He doesn't give a shit, for example, about giving some credit to Sam Nunn, Ted Kennedy, or Mo Udall."

Bradlee argues that conservatives become more liberal when they enter the White House—as witness Nixon's opening to China and ending the Vietnam War and Ronald Reagan's deficit spending. And liberals become more conservative—as witness various policies of the Carter administration as well as a movement toward the center by many liberals, including Senator Ted Kennedy. The *Post* executive editor adds, "Let's face it, to a large extent, the liberal ethic and liberal programs of the Great Society have failed."

Bradlee explains that journalists have also changed, that they are more responsible today. He says that Goldwater, the candidate, was ahead of his time, adding, "The thing I remember about Barry Goldwater then and today was his absolute, essential decency. It overwhelms you. He never returned the unkindness he received. A bunch of us have sat around at times and wondered why we didn't do justice to Goldwater's run for the presidency. Today, we love him."

Howard K. Smith says that one of the reasons the media now treat me better is that I'm no longer a threat to the liberal establishment. He also cites the biggest change: Barry Goldwater was known as a military man, yet he led the way in changing the Pentagon—in reorganizing the command structure and defense contracting. Goldwater has given tremendous weight to changing the powerful political action committees. He did the impossible in 1964 in getting a genuine conservative nominated, and an individual who happened to be half Jewish. Smith concluded, "Goldwater said to me during the presidential campaign, 'You're going to be surprised one day when you find out how much you agree with me.' He was right. He's voicing the views of many of us today."

Charles Mohr of the New York *Times,* Mary McGrory, and Bob Pierpoint strongly argue that the media were fair to me in 1964. They maintain that I shot from the hip at times and should have been much more careful about the preciseness of my language. They maintain I have mellowed over the past twenty-five years. All concede the obvious rise and new power of the conservative movement.

Mary wrote a sentence in the campaign which perhaps shows how much times have changed. It was published in the Washington *Star,* under a New Orleans dateline on September 19: "Often [Goldwater] sounds like the village anarchist as he calls for 'less and less government.' "

David Broder now looks back on our 1964 effort with long distance perspective. He says, "There's now no question but that Barry Goldwater contributed to enormous political change in the country. He changed the way we look at the American political world—the shift in the nation's political direction to the West—away from the East. Goldwater changed the country's political axis not only geographically but in terms of values and beliefs. He introduced modern conservative political thought to the national debate."

He adds, "Goldwater has never wavered, and many of his beliefs have been vindicated. His race also is of the greatest importance because, despite Goldwater's loss, his campaign saw the greatest recruiting in the past generation."

Broder, assessing the role of the media in 1964, now explains, "We failed to see, we missed the enormous significance—yes, unequivocally—of what he was saying and his political effects on the country and the Republican Party. There's a direct relationship between Goldwater of 1964 and Ronald Reagan of 1980 and today. We missed where American politics was headed. Have we learned from the Goldwater campaign? I think we go on making the same mistakes."

From a personal viewpoint, Broder concludes, "Barry Goldwater has made himself a monumental figure in American politics—beyond philosophy and ideology. He is an authentic American."

We flew to San Francisco for the last big campaign stop. There was a tremendous crowd. None of us could believe it. Somebody said it was a larger throng than had greeted General Douglas MacArthur when he came home from the Pacific. We were thrilled but exhausted. I just wanted to go home.

We flew to one final stop, a sentimental journey to the little town of Fredonia, about three hundred population, on the Arizona-Utah border. I'd always ended my campaigns there. It was sunset. About 1,800 folks from nearby farms and ranches stood in front of a one-room office building in the middle of town. The American flag cracked in the wind. These were my people, in their frayed cowboy hats and worn boots, with plain, open faces and children in their arms, and they stood straight and tall with looks of wonder at all the media lights and equipment. Some Navajo and Paiute Indians stood at the edge of the crowd wearing black hats and solemn expressions.

I talked about their mothers, fathers, and ancestors who had come to these hard plains and mountain country, the hard winters and the chilling snowdrifts and winds, to farm and raise cattle. They had asked nothing of the government. They made it on their own—with hard work and God's help.

Some Navajos shook my hand when the speech was over. We exchanged best wishes in Navajo. Some mothers smiled, and their kids tugged at my suit coat for autographs.

It was real, unpretentious, simple. I was home.

We took off for Phoenix. As our plane banked south, a sweeping rainbow of lights glowed in the dark sky to the west. Kitchel was awestruck by it and called the lights "a good omen."

We stopped at the Camelback Inn on arrival in Phoenix for a drink with the hundred or so reporters who had covered us. I was tired and aching all over. I couldn't eat the delicious-looking Mexican chili, enchiladas, tortillas, and tacos.

Several newsmen asked me for one last thought on the campaign. I was sipping a bourbon and finally began to relax a bit. There was one big disappointment, I told them, "We may not have spelled out the issues as well as we could. That was the point of it all—the point of the entire campaign. If only Jack Kennedy were here."

I put down the drink and repeated, "If Jack were here, we would have had a good campaign."

Those were my final words of the campaign. Peggy and I went home. As we drove north toward Camelback Mountain, she was very quiet. I looked at her and simply said, "Peg, we were ahead of our time."

We lost to the Johnson-Humphrey ticket, 43 million to 27 million votes, a Democratic landslide. The Goldwater-Miller ticket won six states—Arizona, Alabama, Georgia, Louisiana, Mississippi, and South Carolina.

Some of us believe the conservative movement has had broader and deeper national implications than any other movement of our times. The reasons are that it now reaches beyond single segments of the population into all classes of society, and it is involved in virtually every major issue facing the nation.

Conservatives now hail from all regions of the country, every social class, each and every creed and color, and all age groups. The new GOP was forged in the fires of the 1964 presidential campaign.

8

Vietnam: Past and Future

IT WAS PEACEFUL COMING HOME. THE WARS OF THE campaign and Washington seemed a world away. Peggy and I were always together—on a short vacation with friends in the Bahama Islands, off on camping trips to photograph more of the state, enjoying long hours with the family. Our two girls, Joanne and little Peggy, were married. Barry Jr. and Mike were working and still bachelors. Many old friends called at the house. My mother celebrated her ninetieth birthday. The sunny Arizona winter of 1965 seemed to make life serene, too soft for this old war-horse.

I opened a small office in Phoenix with a staff of one, Judy Rooney, who had worked with me in Washington. (She later married Earl Eisenhower, a nephew of the former President.) We were deluged with mail, especially requests for speeches. Slowly, I got back on the speaking circuit, but this time I was making money, more than ever in my life. The speeches covered the gamut of public issues, but audiences were primarily interested in two topics—where the Republican Party was going and how to win the War in Vietnam.

For the next four years, the war became one of the driving forces of my life. I regularly spoke with American troops in Vietnam through the MARS network that had been patched into the ham radio shack next to our home. I also toured our military bases on five visits to Vietnam, getting the views of many old friends and acquaintances —military commanders, pilots, and GIs in the field. I was still flying in the Air Force reserve. All we talked about was the war. But nowhere was the conflict of greater interest than on the nation's college campuses. I spoke at dozens of them and listened to the conflicting views of young people.

In the spring of 1965, I visited President Johnson in the White House. We discussed the war and my travels to Vietnam and around the United States. I told the President that when you go to war, the first decision you must make is to win it. There were too many political restrictions on our commanders, including bombing limitations and a ban on "hot pursuit" into enemy sanctuaries in Laos, Cambodia, and North Vietnam. We weren't trying to win the war. We were in a twilight zone, fighting a political conflict while using troops as pawns. Their mission was to defend themselves as best they could. It was a pleasant but pointed conversation. I concluded, "The way we're now fighting this war, there's no way we can win it."

It was clear from our conversation that Johnson was playing the war by ear. Neither he nor Defense Secretary McNamara had any definitive strategy or policy for victory. I told Johnson and old colleagues on Capitol Hill that we had two clear choices: Either win the war in a relatively short time, say within a year, or pull out all our troops and come home.

If the choice had been to win it, I would first have addressed the Congress and the American people and spelled out our choices—a short or long war, projected casualties and financial costs, the long-term effects on the American economy, and the need for national unity. As commander in chief, I would have stated precisely what I proposed to do. At the same time, I would have warned the North Vietnamese by dropping thousands of leaflets on Hanoi and the rest of the country. My address and these messages would have said clearly that either they halt the conflict or we would wipe out all their installations—the city of Hanoi, Haiphong harbor, factories, dikes, everything. I would have given them a week to think about it. If they did not respond, we would literally make a swamp of North Vietnam. We would drop 500-pound bombs and obliterate their infrastructure. Also, I would have sent our troops north and used our sea power to mine and blockade North Vietnamese ports.

I never discussed nor advocated the use of nuclear weapons with Johnson or anyone else in authority. I supported a total conventional air, ground, and sea war. That was not to be. Indeed, late in the conflict, it would not have been supported by most Americans. By then, millions saw little purpose to the war.

Some argue that in the course of the conflict we actually hit North Vietnam more heavily than all the bombs dropped in World War II. They add that our most sophisticated weaponry did not halt the march of men and supplies from the North to South Vietnam along the Ho Chi Minh Trail.

The trail was the wrong target. There was, in fact, no single supply route. The trail changed every few days. In our limited time frame, knocking it out was not the answer. There was too much territory to cover in Laos and Cambodia.

I know, because I flew over the trail as well as North Vietnamese supply depots and troop sanctuaries in Laos and Cambodia on visits to Vietnam between 1965 and the end of 1969. The official reason for my visits was to talk with MARS outfits to see if they had sufficient equipment to contact radio relay stations leading back to the United States. I later attempted to get them needed equipment through the Air Force so GIs could talk with their families through our stateside volunteer switching points. I was still a brigadier general in the Air Force reserve.

I've never wanted to talk about these missions because

some people might say, there goes Goldwater again, still trying to get into combat. Now that the war is over and I'm pretty much out of public life, a few thoughts about those flights might be informative.

In flying over the trail, we couldn't see a damn thing for the most part. Jet fighter pilots saw even less because of their high speeds and high altitudes over the thick jungle. On a few lucky occasions, they spotted supply convoys from the North.

My first flight over the trail and Communist staging areas in Laos and Cambodia was in 1965. It was about six months after the presidential campaign. I was fifty-six years old. The last was in 1969, when I was sixty and had returned to the Senate.

That first reconnaissance was in a slow-moving army twin-engine Beechcraft Bonanza which flew at about 2,500 feet. I wanted to have a close look at the thickness of the jungle and determine whether our pilots could see supplies moving. It was important to know if heavy bombing in the area was a realistic objective. No one should spout off on such a subject unless he knows what he's talking about.

I saw very little of the trail despite our low altitude and slow speed. The same was true for our small spotter planes. On some passes, the pilot and I saw indistinguishable movement beneath the jungle cover, but whatever it was had disappeared by the time we returned on a second pass. After a two-hour flight over the trail, during which we caught glimpses of narrow paths as well as some open stretches, I saw that hundreds of walkways crisscrossed one another over the long, wide terrain. It was a hidden and very dispersed target, not ideal for heavy bombing.

On other missions, I flew in T-39s. We went farther north, where I spotted North Vietnamese surface-to-air missiles and smaller antiaircraft support. Presumably we were flying over North Vietnam, although I no longer have the flight plans. We again flew over Laos and Cambodia, where the North Vietnamese had placed SAM and other antiaircraft firepower. U.S. pilots were not allowed to bomb these sites unless fired upon.

On several occasions, I flew Marine helicopters from Danang. We were never fired on, but these flights were tricky because we often flew lower than the hilltops on either side. It would have been easy for any sniper to open up on us. After one of these flights, the North Vietnamese fired a 120-millimeter rocket into our Danang billets. It exploded nearby and killed several Marines. I still have a piece of that shrapnel as a reminder of that day.

These flights convinced me that we should never have made the trail a prime target. Rather, we should have concentrated our firepower on the North's sources of waging war—harbors, cities, protective dikes, and similar areas.

My plan to win the war had two crucial aspects. It would have been launched in 1965, when we were a credible adversary, and carried out quickly. That would have convinced Hanoi that we meant business. To this day, I believe the North Vietnamese would have stopped the war if we had carried it to them by land, sea, and air over a three- to six-month period. This triple action would have forced the Communists to mass their troops and supplies. We could then have used our overwhelming firepower to full advantage. Our all-out air-sea-land attack would have been intolerable.

Some have claimed China would have entered the war. That was unlikely for three reasons: First, China is protected by massive mountains north of Vietnam. Also, while friendly with Ho, the Chinese never really trusted or respected the Vietnamese. This was clear from their contentious history and was later reflected in border fighting after we pulled out of Vietnam. Beijing also was beginning to move toward Washington as its confrontations with Moscow continued. None of this is hindsight. I spelled out the strategy at that time.

As our military tactics, strategy, and diplomacy shifted

with the winds of politics and public opinion, Hanoi saw we were not a serious, total adversary. The Communists, however, were fully committed to their cause. There is only one way to deal with a fierce enemy in war, and that is to kill him. There is no middle ground. America chose to fight a halfway war.

Johnson and McNamara lost the conflict in 1965, when they made two critical decisions. The first was to "squeeze" the enemy—also called a "measured response" —with more troops. This involved heavier bombing but restricted the targets. The second was to hide their escalation of the war from the American people.

This is not to blame them alone. President Kennedy had made the original commitment of nearly 17,000 soldiers to Vietnam, in effect giving them orders not to shoot back. At the same time, he was telling James Reston of the New York *Times* that this was his answer to Soviet Premier Nikita Khrushchev's challenge at the Vienna summit. He would make our might credible. If Kennedy wanted to be believed, he should have told North Vietnam that he would blow away its ability to fight unless Hanoi quit the war. But the President was only bluffing. In war, you threaten and mean it. You do not bluff.

General Maxwell Taylor, who later became ambassador to South Vietnam, was advising Kennedy. He argued that we should fight a war of counterinsurgency instead of carrying the battle to the North Vietnamese, who were the decisive threat. It's ironic that such a distinguished soldier helped politicize his longtime military colleagues in his diplomatic role. Taylor sided with McNamara, battling the Secretary's military critics.

My plan—as tough as it might seem to some—would have been more merciful to both sides. The war continued for another decade with 58,000 American dead, 303,000 wounded, and perhaps 1 million Vietnamese killed. Many more were injured on both sides. And none of this describes the civilian suffering.

As Johnson and McNamara upped the ante in Vietnam, an ironic twist from the presidential campaign came to haunt them. It was an anonymous quote on Johnson's claim that, if elected, Barry Goldwater would lead the nation into a massive war in Southeast Asia. The quote was: "I was told that, if I voted for Goldwater, we were going to war in Vietnam. I did, and damned if we didn't."

Vietnam divided the United States into political and moral camps. Much has been written and said about the two conflicts we were actually engaged in, the one at home and the other in Southeast Asia. Many misconceptions and errors still cloud our perspective about both. It's important to consider them because unless we change some of our thinking and attitudes, the United States may lose the next war.

We lacked an understanding of Vietnamese culture and history, especially its people's fierce desire for independence after long rule by the Chinese and French. Rather than weakening the Vietnamese view of themselves as one people, these occupations had strengthened their wish for unity.

After World War II the United States had agreed to France's reoccupation of Indochina in exchange for strong French support in resisting Soviet pressures in Europe. We were unable to know the importance of Indochina in the future of Asia. Ho Chi Minh's Viet Minh had wide popular support in their eight-year guerrilla war against the French, which ended at the 1954 Geneva Conference. Indochina then won limited independence. France's civilian population had played a major role in ending the conflict when it became disenchanted after the fall of Dien Bien Phu. A decade passed before the United States entered the no-man's-land that had existed between the French and Vietnamese. And it would be another decade before we left.

In my military tour of Asia during World War II, nothing made a greater impression on me than the cultural differences between Asians and Americans. Most of their personal, religious, and social values are very different from ours. They were not about to change these basic views just because they liked American cigarettes, clothes, or happy-go-lucky friendliness. Twenty years later, in Vietnam, it was transistor radios playing American music and Hollywood movies on new TV sets. Yet we could no more make an American out of a Vietnamese in Vietnam than they could make a Vietnamese of an American in Arizona.

The North Vietnamese, in their measurement of values, were prepared to lose what we viewed as an extraordinary mass of men and women. To them, these people were heroic martyrs.

Johnson and McNamara knew little of Asia and much less of Vietnam and its people. The President understood domestic politics, and McNamara was the Ford Motor Company embodiment of the modern technocrat. With these historical and personal backgrounds, the two took over the war in all its major aspects, including making decisions on daily military actions.

The pair became our generals and admirals by imposing official rules of engagement on the military. Details of these rules were classified "top secret" by the Johnson administration until I was able to get them declassified in 1985 with the help of Defense Secretary Caspar Weinberger.

These restrictions were divided into three categories. The first involved the border areas of countries neighboring Vietnam, the demilitarized zone, and air operations over North Vietnam. Under these rules, for example, if the North Vietnamese sent large concentrations of men and war materials down inside the Laotian border, U.S. embassy diplomats in Vientiane had to approve any American air strikes or other operations against them.

The second set of rules restricted our ground war, tactical air operations, and naval gunfire. The third included prohibitions against striking enemy locks, dams, dikes, hydroelectric plants, and fishing boats.

To ensure that these Johnson-McNamara restrictions were followed by our pilots, the U.S. Seventh Air Force was required to have all its strike air crews and forward air controllers (light-plane spotters) complete a written examination on the rules.

These are some examples of the restrictions: American pilots were not permitted to attack a North Vietnamese MIG sitting on a runway. It could be shot at only when it was flying and showed "hostile intentions." For most of the war, our pilots were not allowed, even when pursuing enemy aircraft that had shot at them, to attack North Vietnamese military air bases. In some areas, enemy supply trucks could escape attack merely by driving a few hundred yards off the road.

SAM missile sites and supporting radar systems could not be struck while they were under construction, only after they became operational and actually fired at U.S. aircraft. Until the end of 1971, air crews in South Vietnam had to refer to at least four different sources of operations orders to determine which rules they were fighting under. Seventh Air Force records show that the average time between identifying a target in Laos and receiving clearance to hit it was more than fifteen days.

In 1967 the Preparedness Investigating Subcommittee of the Senate Armed Services Committee issued a report that was sharply critical of the "Rules of Engagement." It said that the American air campaign had not achieved its objectives because of political limitations which prevented our air leaders from waging the war in a manner and on a timetable best calculated to achieve maximum results. The report cited McNamara specifically and the Administration in general. It said that they had discounted the "unanimous professional judgment of our military commanders and the Joint Chiefs, and substituted civilian judgment in the details of target selection and the timing of strikes."

The subcommittee enraged McNamara when it reported, "During the entire year of 1966, less than 1 percent of the total sorties flown against North Vietnam were against fixed targets on the JCS list." McNamara was angry because his secret controls and personal power had been publicly exposed. The subcommittee statement was the centerpiece of a detailed accounting which showed that targets chosen by our best military minds could not be hit without specific approval of the Secretary of Defense or other high civilian authority.

Most of the U.S. air war was limited to targets south of the vital Hanoi-Haiphong regions, to which the enemy could import and concentrate war materials in the knowledge that they were untouchable. The North Vietnamese sent these materials south and, at the same time, were allowed to build up an extremely sophisticated air defense system provided by the Soviet Union. Our military leaders were furious with Johnson and McNamara about this because their restrictions directly increased our casualties in the war.

This is not to argue that the commander in chief and the Defense Secretary should not have broad war powers. They clearly did. It is to question their military competence in making extensively detailed decisions about how to fight the war.

Some Johnson administration officials now suggest that our military leaders never conveyed the depths of their concerns about the rules of engagement to either McNamara or the President. However, it's abundantly clear from the Pentagon Papers and various declassified documents that the Joint Chiefs of Staff repeatedly argued against the political limitations forced on them. Time after time, they requested changes. At one point in early 1968, the Joint Chiefs showed Clark Clifford, who had replaced McNamara as Defense Secretary, photographic intelligence reports which clearly demonstrated that civilians had been removed from much of Hanoi and Haiphong and war materials had been stockpiled throughout almost half these cities.

Johnson rejected the JCS pleas on March 31, 1968. In

the same speech, in which he said he would not seek reelection, the President restricted air strikes on North Vietnam to a line south of the nineteenth parallel. On December 1, he ordered the total halt of bombing and of B-52 flights over North Vietnam.

During the last week of March 1972, North Vietnam launched a major offensive against South Vietnam. President Nixon quickly resumed and broadened air operations against North Vietnam to just below the Chinese buffer zone. These assaults concluded with twelve consecutive days of B-52 strikes in December 1972. Hanoi then began moving toward a genuine peace settlement.

How did we get into such a faraway fight in the first place?

Vietnam is about halfway around the world from Washington. It's as large as the major Western European nations, with nearly 130,000 square miles of land. And its population has been almost on a level with the same nations. Its ancient recorded history goes back to 111 B.C.

At the time President Eisenhower sent a few hundred military advisers there, it was difficult to determine whether the Viet Minh insurgents were operating under the global designs of world communism or were independent nationalists trying to liberate their country. However, the intention of Ho Chi Minh—to secure Communist domination of all Vietnam—was clear by mid-1965.

We entered Vietnam with considerable ignorance. Our goal—to halt the spread of communism—was clear, but most other considerations were confused. Our military leaders repeatedly warned us not to engage in a massive land war in Asia. These warnings were reinforced by indications from Hanoi that it would be willing to fight a long war. We were willing to accept the risks because of the danger that the Communists might overrun all of Asia. But in stepping into the faraway conflict, no one dreamed we would engage in such a struggle with our hands tied behind our backs.

One man assumed the role of managing the war and would lead us out of the jungle. Robert McNamara took over explaining the conflict to the Congress and often to the American people. He was the whiz-bang technocrat who wanted to win the war almost by himself.

Yet McNamara had alienated critical supporters in the Congress, the military, and, increasingly, among the public. In the face of this overwhelming division, it became questionable whether we could win the war over an extended period of time. That was the heart of my argument against a protracted war, a conflict that was even more in doubt because it was to be managed to an unprecedented degree by civilians.

My own belief in civilian control of the armed forces is unshakable. Also, not a single military officer expressed the slightest reservation about it during or after the war. But a critical question arose then and is still with us today: To what extent can a President and Secretary of Defense politicize a war? Put another way, to what degree may the limited competence of civilians be allowed to dominate professional military decisions? This is the precise path down which LBJ and McNamara led the nation—an ever widening, politicized conflict with no effective plan for military victory.

President Johnson was ultimately responsible for the war. Some claim McNamara's calculator so dazzled LBJ that he was blinded to reality. That is false. McNamara was telling Johnson what he wanted to hear—that he could have his Great Society and conduct a war, too. The eventual realization that he could not was what brought the President to his knees.

A few months before Jack Kennedy died, word leaked from the White House that McNamara had told Kennedy that if he received sufficient support, the Vietnam battle could be won by the end of 1965. Kennedy was skeptical. But Johnson fell for the idea of a drop-by-drop war of attrition that perfectly suited Hanoi's intention to wait out the Americans, as they had the French.

I said at the time that it wasn't going to work. Neither the Congress nor the American people would stand for a prolonged conflict. The military wished to avoid it. Johnson and McNamara recognized the dangers of an open-ended commitment, so they hid their escalation of the war in hopes of an early victory.

I began to distrust McNamara when, on becoming Secretary of Defense, he lied about U.S. missile strength. It was not so much his support of Jack Kennedy's false campaign line that the Soviets had surpassed our missile power. I was taken aback by the extent of McNamara's charade before Congress and the media.

The Central Intelligence Agency had proved beyond a reasonable doubt that there was no missile gap. Up stepped McNamara, the management expert. He proposed that the President could seem to end the politically manufactured disadvantage by having the United States more than double its missiles, to a total of 950, and still tell Moscow that we weren't launching an arms race. How? By limiting the throw weight, or destructive power, of the more numerous new missiles to that of the 450 already in place. The old missiles would presumably be destroyed. McNamara was willing to have this country spend billions of dollars on new missiles to cover up a Kennedy falsehood and fulfill a phony campaign promise. It was an incredibly deceitful performance.

McNamara was nothing if not nimble. He later argued that the United States should accept nuclear parity with the Soviet Union. The Secretary maintained that missile equality was good for America—that parity supported nuclear deterrence and the theory of mutually assured destruction. It was MAD all right. McNamara would deliberately abandon our policy of nuclear superiority, the greatest defense not only against a surprise Soviet nuclear strike but against the massive Russian army, which could launch a sneak assault with conventional weapons.

We later learned that McNamara and others had miscalculated and that the Russians had been building nuclear missiles much faster than we had recognized. Ironically, the Soviets actually took a missile lead on McNamara's own watch. The CIA reported that to President Nixon after he took office in 1969.

I considered McNamara one of the most unreliable and untrustworthy men in America and still do. He continues to posture as an expert on our military defense. Yet his record is one of repeated failure.

McNamara was a numbers cruncher, a systems analyst, logistics administrator, bean and body counter who knew little or nothing of the military or warfare. He also knew little about people, whether Vietnamese or American. He confounded Johnson with his glib certainty. The Secretary was the ultimate superachiever; he saw figures and functions but not the men fighting the war. He quantified Vietnam without ever understanding the meaning of its complex human equation.

McNamara even ordered his staff to compile a statistical digest on Southeast Asia that eventually became nearly two inches thick. Some data were updated daily, others weekly, and all monthly. He regularly spent hour after hour analyzing these numbers, as if they would somehow lead him and the nation out of the wilderness of Vietnam. Ultimately, more than 380 separate numerical tables filled the defense leader's three-ring binder. Each page was crammed with digits in small print. He memorized the small print but never understood the shooting war.

McNamara never comprehended either the trained officers under him or the determination of those faraway little men in the black pajamas. Nor did he fathom Hanoi's leadership, which took every advantage of Washington's hesitation to undertake a massive military assault. In the final analysis, McNamara knew the cost of everything but the value of little.

There are many reasons why we failed in Vietnam. But

we did not lose on the battlefield. We lost at home. It's critical to understand what happened if we are not to lose a future war. We must have a clearer definition of the roles and responsibilities of our political leaders, the military, the public, and the media. The same is true for a limited nuclear war.

The Vietnam War truly began for us on August 7, 1964, when the U.S. Congress passed the Tonkin Gulf Resolution after reported attacks on two U.S. destroyers, the U.S.S. *Maddox* and *C. Turner Joy,* by North Vietnamese patrol boats.

The so-called attack on the *Maddox* took place on August 2 and the one on the *Turner Joy* two days later. A week after the incident—two days after the Congress voted the resolution—Johnson and McNamara were still so confused as to what had actually occurred that the Defense Department had to send a special Navy team to the Far East in an attempt to reconstruct the events. I took a lot of flak for saying what was basically accurate: "With the great communications system which McNamara is always bragging about, they're waiting for an airmail letter to find out just what did happen."

Those were the hazy circumstances under which the Congress approved American involvement in Vietnam. It became the equivalent of a declaration of war. An actual declaration eventually became impossible as support for our effort faded. Presidents Johnson and Nixon used their authority as commander in chief to continue our participation.

In fact, the attack on the *Turner Joy* never took place. Our ship sonar operators had made a mistake. And based on the numerous contradictions in McNamara's testimony before Congress and the accounts of others, I still question whether the *Maddox* was shot at by the North Vietnamese. There was no doubt about one thing, though: McNamara misled Congress and the American people, particularly by not revealing the critical fact that the *Maddox* was on a secret mission. I later learned that the operation involved U-2 spy flights over North Vietnam, kidnapping North Vietnamese for intelligence interrogation, commando raids from the sea, and parachuting psychological warfare teams into North Vietnam. This was an example of Johnson-McNamara duplicity—to act and then hide it. In this case, the facts were not revealed to the Congress. We voted on the Tonkin Gulf Resolution with critical aspects of the situation withheld from us.

I couldn't believe that McNamara would stage a second big deception after his elaborate Bay of Pigs scenario. By 1964 many in Congress had deciphered his first series of lies. It seemed inconceivable that he would try again. So we supported the Tonkin Gulf Resolution with only two members opposing it—Oregon's Wayne Morse and Alaska's Ernest Gruening.

At the time, uneasy about the circumstances of the incident, I recalled an observation by Mark Twain: A lie can travel around the world before the truth gets out of bed.

That was their first and perhaps worst mistake—misleading the Congress and public. It was to take various forms on different occasions over the next several years, but the result was the same. Many members of Congress and more and more of the public became convinced that Johnson and McNamara were lying. This weakened their political and moral authority to conduct the war.

I had suggested to LBJ as early as 1965 that he fire McNamara. One of the reasons was the Secretary's repeated untruthfulness. But equally important—contrary to what many thought—was his professional incompetence, which flowed from his erratic behavior. An early example of this occurred on Christmas Eve of 1964, when McNamara summoned the vice chief of staff of the Army, General Creighton Abrams, and told him in approximately these words:

"I've just canceled the army aviation program. I'm impounding funds and there will not be one dollar in the budget I'm about to take to the Congress in January for one new army helicopter, one new army airplane, to train one new army pilot, or buy any spare parts—unless and until you undertake a study that gives me the answers to the following questions: Why do we need army aviation? How much do we need it? Why do you need helicopters instead of fixed-wing aircraft?" Similar questions followed. This incredible conversation was reported to me by some of those in the Pentagon called upon to answer McNamara's inquiry.

The questions, which came from McNamara's celebrated civilian systems analysis whiz kids, caused a major flap inside the Department of the Army. It quickly organized a special task force headed by Brigadier General Edward Mueller and Dr. Wilbur Payne, director of operations research, to answer the challenge.

In mid-1965, while his staff was still distilling the army study, McNamara flew to Vietnam on a five-day fact-finding mission. En route home, he fired off a series of cables from Hawaii: How soon could the Army ready two more airmobile divisions for deployment to Southeast Asia? How soon could the Army send other aviation units there? *How rapidly could the Pentagon increase helicopter production rates and in what stages?*

The messages made little or no sense to McNamara's own staff or the Army. Six months before, the whiz kid of all whiz kids had canceled the army aviation program. Helicopter production had been wiped out by his own edict. McNamara was now demanding that his staff and the Army tell him, within three days of his return to Washington, how to resurrect the corpse. On the fourth day, McNamara planned to brief the President so LBJ could quickly ask Congress for a supplemental appropriation.

Funds were needed because the Secretary of Defense planned to persuade Johnson to deploy new army airmobile forces in Vietnam. But how? He had halted production of the helicopters needed for their missions. A Pentagon review of army aviation was still under way.

Never mind. McNamara would equip them with helicopters that would, under new orders, crackle off assembly lines like popcorn. The Secretary wanted to know how quickly UH-1 Huey helicopter production could increase to 300, 500, and even 1,000 a month from his previous zero production order. He also pushed the panic button on new troops: How soon could the Army deploy eighteen airmobile companies equipped with UH-34 helicopters?

However, the UH-34, a piston-engine helicopter, was out of production. The Navy and Marine Corps were already short some 3,000 replacement engines for UH-34s they were then operating. These engines had not been produced for years. It would take years to restart the production lines. Newer, turbine-powered helicopters, such as the UH-1, could be built much more quickly. But McNamara had ordered that these lines come to a virtual standstill, with only a few choppers produced. Production lead times for critical components, such as transmissions, averaged twenty-four to thirty months. Knowing that he had canceled army aviation, McNamara turned to the old UH-34s. However, his computer memory had blown a fuse. The Navy and Marines, the last customers of the UH-34, were already into the transition of new turbine machines like the CH-46.

Ben Schemmer, a member of the Secretary's systems analysis staff and the army special study team, was disturbed by McNamara's contradictory demands. He asked Charles Hitch, an assistant defense secretary who was compiling responses to McNamara's frantic cables from Hawaii, "What are we trying to accomplish? Tell us the objective so we can sort out the conflicting priorities. Are we going to war?"

Hitch told Schemmer, in words repetitive of McNamara's response to such questions, that he was out of order. The Secretary of Defense asked the questions. The staff provided the answers.

That was McNamara's problem. He rarely answered questions—of the military, Congress, the public, or his own staff. He was accountable to only two men, the President and himself. Schemmer said, "He was escalating the war but keeping his actions even from his most trusted aides. I went home the evening after talking with Hitch about McNamara's contradictions and told my wife that we were going to war. She almost fainted."

McNamara's defenders argue that he had to shock the military with difficult questions to force them to justify their actions. Schemmer, who worked under the Defense Secretary for three years as director of land force weapons systems, denies that claim: "In this case, McNamara impounded funds authorized and appropriated by Congress. This effectively shut down engine, helicopter, and spare parts production. This went on at what contractors called a minimum sustaining rate. Some companies continued limited production on their own, believing their firms would be reimbursed later."

He also recalled, "Industry reps told Pentagon officials that nobody could be this goddamned nuts!"

Schemmer estimates that after McNamara's Christmas Eve edict to General Abrams, the rate of production of UH-1 Huey helicopters fell from about forty a month to five. Then, after McNamara's July 1965 tour of Vietnam, production climbed to 300 a month. However, this rate was throttled back at various times for different reasons, either to keep the war's cost down or when combat losses in Vietnam were lower than forecast. McNamara ordered surges in production when American losses rose or when even more aviation units were needed for deployment. Schemmer called this the "hot rod, cold douche routine."

McNamara overruled his deputy, Cyrus Vance, who had agreed with the Defense Secretary's own staff and the Army. They argued that a new attack helicopter—the AH-1 Cobra, developed by Bell Laboratories on company funds—should be rushed into production for Vietnam. McNamara sat on the recommendation for months. In another, later reversal, he was critical because the Cobras could not be produced fast enough. Production rates of other helicopters—CH-47s, OH-6s, and Marine Corps CH-46s and CH-53s—were whipsawed in similar ways.

Yet McNamara boasted to Johnson and Congress that he could manage the war "efficiently" while keeping the military at high readiness levels around the world. The Congress eventually—and rightly—challenged McNamara on this. LBJ also began to question the wisdom of his computer-brained secretary.

Under McNamara the army aviator training pipeline was so constricted that at the height of the war, pilots were being involuntarily returned to Vietnam for second and third combat tours. The intervals between tours also became increasingly shorter. From about mid-1965 to the beginning of 1971, more than 6,400 army aviators had to be returned involuntarily to Vietnam for second and third combat periods. We were short of pilots because from 1961 through 1965 McNamara had slashed eight separate Army requests to increase its pilot training program. Did McNamara know of these shortages? That some of these men were flying 150 hours of combat each month, a total never previously reached or believed possible? Schemmer, now editor of *The Armed Forces Journal International,* says he personally wrote more than a dozen memos to McNamara and Vance about it: "I had to fight to increase pilot production by fifty to a hundred people a year—every year—when we needed thousands of new pilots, not hundreds. This man suddenly wanted to build thousands of helicopters, like a popcorn machine, but wouldn't give us the money to train pilots. He told Congress the services were wasting money because they had more pilots than cockpit seats. The reality was, he had kids flying eighteen hours a day in Vietnam."

McNamara was saying to them, as he had to all the country's military: You're just a number.

McNamara's contradictory policies had all the bang of a whimper in mid-1965 when Lieutenant General Harry W. O. Kinnard was told at Fort Benning, Georgia, that he would shortly lead the 1st Cavalry Division to fight in Vietnam. The division's effectiveness depended on about 450 helicopters. Where did Kinnard get them? "A large part was stripped from another unit," he said.

Kinnard, widely considered a brilliant field commander, was told by his Pentagon superiors that President Johnson would declare a state of national emergency. Such an order would allow him to take all the men he had trained to Vietnam. Now retired and living in Virginia, Kinnard recalls the shock that hit him: "The President didn't declare a national emergency. So I had to eliminate thousands of men, including more than five hundred aviation specialists, because they were not eligible to be retained under a nonemergency. It made no sense to send us to Vietnam under those conditions. We took men with as little as a month's time to go in the Army because I was told we'd probably be fighting as soon as we got there. It was the stupidest thing you could imagine. I was being asked to train an entirely new division in a few months before going to war. That was an incomprehensible political decision."

The general and his available troops arrived at An Khe in north central Vietnam in September. Two months later, they were engaged in an all-out battle with three North Vietnamese regiments in the Ia Drang Valley. The fight was one of the fiercest and most significant battles of the war. It illustrates the kind of mess the contradictory Johnson policies caused for men in the field.

North Vietnam's top military commander, General Vo Nguyen Giap, planned and directed the enemy operation. He had become famous for organizing Hanoi's victory over the French at Dien Bien Phu. The enemy attack across the central highlands, which came from Cambodian sanctuaries, was an attempt to cut Vietnam in half. The North Vietnamese were to succeed in doing just that against South Vietnamese troops late in the conflict. The battle also marked the first major engagement of the war between regular North Vietnamese and American troops. American B-52 bombers were used for the first time in close support of U.S. troops in Vietnam.

The North Vietnamese were routed by the Americans in one of the best-planned operations of the war. The Communist forces suffered nearly 1,800 casualties in three days of fierce around-the-clock fighting. The enemy finally fled, some into Cambodia, while others crossed into the North.

Kinnard wanted to destroy all three North Vietnamese units completely to teach Hanoi a lesson. He asked permission to follow them into Cambodia and elsewhere. This was approved by General William Westmoreland, our commander in Vietnam, and, significantly, by Ambassador Henry Cabot Lodge. Kinnard says:

"It was disapproved in Washington—a decision that could not have been made by the military. So these people escaped. They were refitted, rearmed, and fighting again by March 1966.

"The objective should have been to totally eliminate the North Vietnamese as a threat. The way we elected to carry out the war was a disaster. The idea of permitting them a sanctuary, into which you can't go on the ground, was absurd. It's like telling a football team it can't cross the fifty-yard line."

Kinnard believes, as I do, that we should never have allowed the North Vietnamese to fight as guerrillas. But how could one get these hit-and-run troops to mass? As Kinnard puts it, "You go where he lives. The most stupid decision of the war was a political one, to restrict our fighting to South Vietnam. We could have whipped the North Vietnamese by going into their territory and heading for Hanoi. They'd have had to stand and fight. We could then have used our artillery, tanks, helicopters, planes, and other logistics en masse."

Kinnard remembers asking for B-52 strikes on certain

areas. He was told such approval had to come from Washington. LBJ and McNamara sat in the White House and not only blocked bombing runs but chose targets of their own. It would take a week or more to get a response. Kinnard and other generals rarely, if ever, knew what targets they would be hitting a week later.

The political decisions and objectives of Johnson and McNamara were inconsistent and contrary to our military goals. We were engaged in counterinsurgency, a war of attrition through a long process of search-and-destroy missions, to defeat the Communist guerrillas. However, beginning in 1966, Vietcong and North Vietnamese regiments and divisions moved their bases into Cambodia, Laos, and the North Vietnamese panhandle north of the demilitarized zone. We did not begin to attack these sanctuaries until 1970, when U.S. forces were being withdrawn. The U.S. embassy in Laos, claiming the war might be widened, opposed any serious American military operations against the Ho Chi Minh Trail.

Our counterinsurgency alone could not push Hanoi out of the war. The Communists simply retreated to sanctuaries from which they would strike again and again. It was obvious we had to hit border areas in nearby Cambodia and Laos because they were major sources of support for the war. Indeed, the North Vietnamese were able to put as many men in the field as we did because of the protection allowed them by Washington.

In 1965 Johnson and McNamara increased American troop strength in Vietnam from about 23,000 soldiers to more than 184,000. That total rose to 385,000 in 1966. The two were pouring troops into Vietnam beyond any projections. Their only plan was to send more men.

The Secretary's own words demonstrate how he eventually led Johnson to approve a total of more than 500,000 troops in Vietnam. In January 1962 McNamara told the President and the American people that the situation in Vietnam was "encouraging." In September 1963 it was "getting better and better." In March 1964 it had "significantly improved." By November 1965 we had "stopped losing the war." And in July 1966 he was "cautiously optimistic."

These were the years of decision, the most crucial of the conflict, during which McNamara told LBJ that the war could be fought both efficiently and on the cheap. Johnson believed him.

McNamara's concealing and disguising the cost of the war to the American people are well documented in government files, books, and other sources. They show he had various sets of figures for each annual budget, from high to low, while telling Congress and the public the outlay would be the lowest figure. Meantime, LBJ plunged ahead with his Great Society spending.

In previous wars, we projected costs into the future. McNamara's costs covered only one year ahead, as if the war would then end. He was well aware that this was untrue. LBJ resisted his own party's demands for tax increases. That would have been an open admission of the war's rising cost.

In November 1966 the Secretary of Defense finally admitted his charade and dropped his annual cutoff date on the end of the fighting. The media began to report what many economists had known all along: The cost of the war would immediately double.

We're still paying for Vietnam.

In all this, McNamara tried to protect himself—and Johnson—by writing draft memos to the President when, in fact, they were final recommendations and understandings between the two. A draft memo, if and when it surfaced, would allow them room to deny that any or all of a document was actual policy.

McNamara was shortly to turn against the war he himself had created because it was no longer cost-effective. Perhaps he also began to see that the numbers he had crunched and sent to Vietnam were really flesh and blood. Casualty rates had been rising steadily.

At Georgetown cocktail parties, McNamara began to confess doubts about the outcome of the war. It was too late. The character of the conflict had changed. We were committed. No honorable man can walk away from a war to which he has sent hundreds of thousands of men. The situation was all the worse because the President and Secretary of Defense continued to place limited trust and responsibility in our military leaders. And the brass privately wondered whether Johnson, McNamara, and their staffs had any comprehension of their own lack of military competence.

That professional capability was challenged on April 24, 1966. The New York *Times* carried a front page story by its veteran military affairs analyst, Hanson W. Baldwin. It said there was a bomb shortage in Vietnam and at various U.S. bases. The report explained that there were "current ordnance shortages" because available bomb components did not match. The number and intensity of U.S. aircraft missions had been sharply reduced because of various aviation ordnance shortages. The article noted, "The problem is believed to be largely one of distribution or shipment rather than overall shortages."

McNamara, the efficiency genius, was being reduced to a plumber trying to unclog his own pipeline. As Schemmer recalls, "Robert McNamara went ballistic over that story. He went into random trajectory—into the ionosphere like a crowbar without fins. Some of us from systems analysis—he had a team juggling the numbers—spent three days and nights in the Pentagon working on a response. Everything precious to McNamara's integrity had been challenged. This could never have happened under his management reforms at the Defense Department. This was impossible."

Baldwin and Schemmer say to this day that the *Times*' story was solid. It included the charge that the American stockpile of 750-pound bombs around the world was so low that supplies might be exhausted before production of new bombs later in the summer of 1966. Schemmer reported that Navy pilots were flying off our aircraft carriers with as few as one or two 500-pound bombs, when they could have carried loads of ten or twelve.

McNamara called a Pentagon news conference after conferring with his entourage of whiz kids. Schemmer recalls that a McNamara staffer told him, "We don't have a bomb shortage. We have a surplus of targets!"

The Secretary put on one of the most remarkable performances of his career before Pentagon reporters and later the Congress. He said that there was no bomb shortage ("That's baloney!") and, at the same time, that the military services had screwed up the distribution of bomb parts. Indeed, there was a surplus of targets! Of course, it was a maze of contradictions. But the perception of performance was what counted with McNamara —blow them away with statistics!

The Secretary quietly had the Air Force buy back more than 5,500 bombs sold earlier to a West German firm, as well as thousands of bombs shipped to our European allies. Under government agreements, Washington could recover surplus military bombs and weapons at cost. However, this was not the case with sales to private firms. So the German company resold the bombs to McNamara at a large profit. No wonder the Secretary of Defense was upset with Baldwin. The disclosure had tarnished his image as the ultimate manager and money saver. Baldwin, a highly respected military writer, now says:

"McNamara was not telling the truth. He took umbrage with anyone who disagreed or took issue with him. McNamara placed me on his blacklist. Cy Vance suggested I speak with him. When I attempted to do so, he refused to see me.

"Unfortunately, his loyalty was only up—not equally down to the Joint Chiefs of Staff and other military commanders. He was very disloyal to the people under him. I didn't trust him. It's too bad we then didn't have stronger Joint Chiefs of Staff."

Baldwin confirmed what many of us already knew about the Defense Secretary. He cited a McNamara trip to Fort Bragg, North Carolina, in the mid-1960s, during which the Secretary had viewed a parachute drop. After it was over, Baldwin recalls, McNamara told those present he had learned nothing. He'd known it all before he came.

That was precisely what McNamara did on all his trips to Vietnam. He had reached his conclusions and decisions before ever leaving Washington. A draft of what he would report to Johnson had already been typed. There would be minor adjustments. It was what the Pentagon whiz kids called "managed decision making."

The Secretary did not kindly view appeals or questions from the field—those fighting the war—about decisions in Washington. There was no more dramatic appeal from Vietnam than one which began in late 1965. It's an untold story—a horror. Schemmer and others were involved on the Washington end.

A general officer from the Joint Chiefs of Staff asked Schemmer's help in expediting the transfer of sixteen UH-34 helicopters from the U.S. Navy or Marines to the Vietnamese Air Force. The request carried the highest wartime priority of the U.S. commander in Vietnam, General Westmoreland, and the commander in chief of the Pacific fleet, Admiral Ulysses S. G. Sharp. The helicopters were needed for sensitive cross-border operations, missions LBJ and McNamara wanted to be able to deny knowing about.

Some involved inserting Vietnamese CAS (Controlled American Sources) agents into North Vietnam or extracting them. Others concerned intelligence missions into Laos, Cambodia, and Thailand. McNamara did not want to risk having to explain why an American helicopter might be shot down or a crew captured in these places. The helicopter shortage was so severe and McNamara's micromanagement of the war so pervasive that no one but the Secretary himself could approve the transfer of these sixteen obsolescent helicopters.

McNamara sat on the request. Week after week, month after month, McNamara's staff sent him memos explaining why the helicopters were urgently needed. There were critical military and moral reasons for these requests:

Cross-border operations had mounted, with increasing numbers of Vietnamese pilots shot down on these missions. The pilots as well as CAS agents were signaling frantically for extraction.

Yet McNamara returned one memo after another from his staff. All were, in effect, pleading for the lives of Vietnamese pilots and CAS agents who were in immediate, critical danger. The Secretary nitpicked the memos to death, often raising irrelevant questions which he scrawled in the margins. At one point McNamara objected to taking some helicopters from the naval reserve because Congress might interpret that as an indication that he was scratching to find resources for fighting the war. In other memos, McNamara vaguely asked for "more analysis." That was a commonplace reminder of what the new Pentagon was all about.

A straightforward operational problem had become a nightmare. For ten long months, McNamara overrode plea after plea to release the UH-34s. By then, the Vietnamese Air Force was clamoring for seventy-five helicopters to launch the perilous rescue missions. In his most incomprehensible move of the entire debacle, McNamara scribbled in the margin of one memo: "Why do we need a VNAF (Vietnamese Air Force)? I don't believe it's very effective?"

If American pilots were ruled out, who were to fly the rescue missions? Or were these courageous downed pilots and agents to die slowly twisting in the wind?

McNamara's conduct raised serious questions. The Vietnamese were volunteering to do just what Johnson had asked of them—more of the fighting. Why not accept their offer? Why refuse to help allies risking their lives behind enemy lines to free their brothers facing certain death? What was McNamara's problem?

The Secretary never answered these questions. He answered to himself. I have often asked myself if, in his tormented soul, McNamara ever faced the memory of the men he left behind to die. No man involved with the military—I don't care what nation he might be from—would leave troops in such a predicament.

Schemmer wrote a final brief, frantic memo urging transfer of the UH-34s to the South Vietnamese. McNamara returned it to Vance with this note in the margin: "Cy, get Schemmer off my back. RM."

Vance's senior military aide called Schemmer to the front office. He handed him the reply, which McNamara had initialed, and said, "The boss thought you might want to keep this, Ben. But don't show it to anyone."

Schemmer concluded at the time, "McNamara is very sick. It's time to leave the Pentagon. It's futile to play mental isometrics with an irrational man incapable of coming to grips with such a simple problem."

One of McNamara's aides, whom Schemmer won't name, called Ben into his office and said, "Yes, Ben, McNamara is sick. But that's why you should stay. That's why I'm staying. McNamara needs help. By now, not many people are willing to argue with him."

Schemmer left the Pentagon at the close of 1967. A few months later he learned that LBJ—as part of his halt to the bombing of North Vietnam—had forbidden any further missions to resupply CAS agents who were still operating up north. The Vietnamese Air Force, denied helicopters, was no longer in a position to offer help. Some agents had died or been captured and were believed shot. Others, who managed to survive for several more months, were told to "hang in there." They were advised there were "resupply problems which were being worked out." Eventually, forty-five CAS agents were quietly abandoned. Their radios fell silent. They were never heard from again.

A few months before Schemmer left the Pentagon, a young man about six feet six inches tall with curly orange hair and a large motorcycle belt buckle appeared at Schemmer's office from out of nowhere. Dolf Droge looked like a rock singer. He had just completed his third tour in Southeast Asia with the Agency for International Development. He came to tell someone how badly we were losing the war and how we could either win it or leave Vietnam. After being shifted to various offices, Droge was directed to Schemmer. Ben offered him fifteen minutes. The two talked all night.

Droge's offered nineteen ways to end the war. Schemmer put them in a ten-page paper to Vance. One stood out: We should bribe Ho Chi Minh to end the conflict, offer him aid to bring his country into the twentieth century. There were no political nuances, no moral imperatives, just an old-fashioned, outright bribe, whatever it would take to have Ho and his forces quit fighting while we pulled out of Vietnam. Droge's point was simple and direct: It would be a lot cheaper for the United States in blood and treasure to bribe Ho than continue a war with a no-win policy.

Vance told Schemmer to write a special paper on bribing Ho. He did. A few days later, Schemmer was told by his immediate superior to knock off the "peripheral stuff" and get back to work. Schemmer then resigned.

Later, after Vance became our chief negotiator at the Paris peace talks, he invited Schemmer to visit him in New York. In the midst of their conversation, Vance suddenly asked Schemmer, "Do you remember when you brought me that memo about bribing Ho Chi Minh?"

Schemmer did.

"Well," Vance said, "it almost worked."

Startled, Schemmer asked what he meant. Vance answered, in effect, "We tried. We almost had him ready to come over. Then Lyndon Johnson shared an indiscreet confidence with a foreign leader. The word leaked. It's dead."

Vance now says he doesn't recall the conversation. Schemmer does—vividly.

If McNamara was a poor leader and perhaps even unwell in the latter part of his seven years as Defense Secretary, why didn't the Pentagon's military leaders stand up to him and have a greater influence on events?

This has been the subject of an intense private debate among the nation's military. The answers are many and varied. Perhaps no one understands the issue better than Ambassador Edward Rowny, a retired Army lieutenant general who served under McNamara. Rowny headed the Army Concept Team, fifty officers and fifty scientists whom McNamara sent to Vietnam in 1961 with instructions to return in a year with a plan that would win the war. The group studied nearly twenty projects. Pacification and other programs were implemented. Rowny later became our representative at the Geneva disarmament talks with the Soviet Union.

Rowny explains, first, that most of our top military never understood McNamara. He intellectualized and computerized all issues, even the simplest human problems, and never talked a language they could understand. Nor did McNamara comprehend them—or war. He saw the answer to almost every problem in some form of quantitative analysis, especially cost-effectiveness. The answer was not strategic military conception and execution or leadership, not troop training or GI morale— rather, logistical numbers. Rowny recalls that McNamara was constantly massaging and manipulating data. McNamara did not lead the Department of Defense; he analyzed it.

For example, Rowny explains, McNamara transformed the selection of military officers into a programmatic systems analysis which didn't fit individual men or the services. Instead of thinking about strategy and the nature of war, the services became cost analysts. Effectiveness became cost management. Efficiency—how to plan and execute a war—is completely different in the military.

McNamara could never understand that morale was as important as materiel. He never comprehended why the chain of command was critical. He hadn't the slightest knowledge of military or service tradition. McNamara selected managers, not leaders. Some of his whiz kids couldn't lead a troop of Girl Scouts. Since McNamara's tenure at the Pentagon, a disproportionate number of administrative managers have been chosen for promotion over field leaders. The system badly needs balance. Rowny estimates that McNamara's leadership caused the military problems that still have not been solved. The services are top-heavy in administration.

Rowny and others point out that McNamara never visited U.S. troops on his tours of NATO bases in Western Europe or Vietnam. He expressed no interest in them whatsoever. He would fly into bases with his stacks of data, charts, and programs. The Secretary would meet with several leaders, then fly out.

Nor did he have any personal rapport with the Joint Chiefs of Staff. He recognized this and once obliquely asked a staff member how it might be arranged. The staffer replied, "Go and have a drink with them."

McNamara never raised the subject again.

Rowny recalls an elegant restaurant dinner in Paris with McNamara and Air Force General Lauris Norstad, then commander of NATO. They sat together sipping mineral water because McNamara frowned on them having a glass of wine. It was unreal to Rowny—the taut, stilted, almost tense conversation that was merely an antiseptic interlude between formal conferences.

Yet in White House and other meetings, McNamara became the killer shark, embarrassing Secretary of State Dean Rusk, other members of the cabinet, and presidential advisers. He used statistics as the critical measurement in political and military decisions. Rowny, who became a special adviser to President Reagan and Secretary of State George Shultz on arms control policies, now explains:

"For all these reasons, McNamara and the military leadership never got along. In the end, there was no one of stature in the military who stood up to him. They could have done so—not in public, because that was against tradition—but internally. They could have said, 'Either you support us or we quit.'

"Had they resigned and then protested his decisions, they would have been on better grounds. Instead, they were silent."

If the Pentagon brass would not protest, I did. In speeches across the nation, I described McNamara as a dishonest man wielding military power with little or no professional competence. There is nothing more dangerous in the world.

My relationship with the Secretary went from one public confrontation to another. Whether or not the Joint Chiefs and others fought McNamara was their business.

If the top military brass didn't resign, neither did McNamara. This is despite the fact, Paul Hendrickson of the Washington *Post* told us, that McNamara had admitted at a Georgetown dinner in January 1966—just after completing the most massive troop buildup of the war there—that the conflict could not be won militarily. McNamara was telling the American people one thing and the cocktail and dinner party crowd another.

Nor did anyone in the Johnson cabinet quit in protest over the way the war was being conducted. The President himself finally dismissed his Defense Secretary in a surprise announcement, saying McNamara was going to the World Bank.

McNamara answered my protests about his conduct of the war with personal pettiness. Air Force General Gabriel P. Disosway, now retired in Shreveport, Louisiana, recalls one incident. In 1967 Disosway, then assigned to the Pentagon, tried to get me some kind of medal on my retirement as a major general from the Air Force Reserve. He went to General John McConnell, the Air Force chief of staff, and said there was a precedent for such an award because he had personally pinned a medal on General Jack Foster when he had retired in San Antonio. McConnell then went to McNamara and asked about an award. The Defense Secretary told him, "No, we're not going to do anything for Goldwater. And I don't want a bunch of generals going out to Arizona to his retirement."

Disosway and other Air Force officers from around the country came anyway, and presented me with a plaque. I'll never forget the guts it took, because McNamara was notoriously vindictive.

McNamara blocked a retirement ceremony for me at Luke Air Force Base just outside Phoenix, so the Arizona Air National Guard held it at Sky Harbor International Airport. I said of McNamara over a loudspeaker in my farewell dinner speech:

"If that bastard thinks he's through with me, he's mistaken."

I was a dissenter. I wanted out of Vietnam as much as the antiwar protester did and said so. But I would leave in a different way. The antiwar crowd wanted to cut and run. I wanted to defeat the enemy, but, since we were unwilling to do that, I finally supported a negotiated settlement of the conflict. There was no choice left. The South Vietnamese could not fight on alone, although I backed aid to them after the peace treaty was signed. It was a last grasp at honor and an attempt to give some of them a chance to decide their future.

The antiwar movement had a profound effect on military thinking in Vietnam and still does. It's now clear that our military leaders do not wish to go to war again without the overwhelming support of the American people. They cannot fight one war on the battlefield and another behind their backs. This is not to criticize all those who questioned our involvement in Vietnam. Many decent people saw it as a mistake.

The United States has had dissenters in every war, but never to the extent of Vietnam. We must yet come to terms with such dissent. It is reasonable to ask how much opposition is acceptable in wartime. One of the most logical places to begin answering such a question is amnesty for draft dodgers. This still disturbs me and millions of Americans. It goes to the heart of fairness: Who is obliged to defend this country?

I happen to believe all Americans should defend their homeland in time of war or a major conflict, such as Korea or Vietnam. A citizen need not carry a gun if that is contrary to his religious beliefs or moral views. However, each has an obligation to serve as a noncombatant —medic, truck driver, cook.

Some Americans still attempt to justify their unwillingness to serve in any capacity by saying all war is immoral and they wish no involvement whatever in any conflict. We still face the mundane but crucial question of whether others should die so they themselves may enjoy freedom.

Many draft dodgers have long said that since they didn't agree with the War in Vietnam, they bore no responsibility for it. Most still maintain that view. That's like saying they will obey only those laws that accommodate their personal views. Others, who don't pay taxes or who disobey speed laws, are fined and sometimes jailed. Yet we have a precedent of offering amnesty to those who fled to other countries rather than fighting for their own. I propose that the country resolve that issue now.

It may startle the draft dodgers, but I'm not sure any war is moral. I am certain, however, that we are a nation of laws. Those who break them must pay a penalty.

I believe it's incumbent on the President and the Congress to make clear that this country will never again grant blanket amnesty to draft dodgers. It's important to distinguish between amnesty and a pardon. Amnesty is generally viewed as a grant of immunity from legal prosecution and punishment to entire classes of unnamed individuals who have been guilty of a crime. Pardon is viewed as a release from prosecution and punishment of a crime only for a specified individual in an unusual case.

There is real doubt in my mind as to whether President Carter had the power to grant such an amnesty. The Constitution may grant the President the right to offer a pardon, but not amnesty. The expression "amnesty" is not in the Constitution and was not even used until the Civil War. There is a strong legal argument that the power to grant amnesty may reside only with the Congress.

A national debate on amnesty is needed in a calm atmosphere, not during a time of crisis. It is relevant because all of us should be clear about our obligations to defend the United States and the consequences if we refuse. Those who hold that their religious and personal views come before their country and fellow citizens can have their say. But this is a democracy, and if they will not abide by the reasonable will of the majority, they can go to Canada, Sweden, and elsewhere now. They can leave today, and I will be at the pier to wish them bon voyage.

The Congress has an obligation to hold hearings and vote on this issue because every time this country comes close to an international confrontation, some Americans immediately say that this is not their fight and they will not defend the President's actions. If these wartime obligations and the consequences of not serving are made clear now, amnesty will cease to be an issue. I believe those who refuse to fight or serve as noncombatants should be imprisoned for ten to twenty years.

All the pronouncements and promises of Johnson and McNamara about the war exploded in their faces in early 1968 and drove the two apart. A series of events forced some critical decisions. On January 30, the Vietcong and North Vietnamese launched the Tet offensive. They mounted major military drives in most of South Vietnam's forty-four provincial capitals. The U.S. embassy in Saigon was attacked. The imperial city of Hue was captured by the Communists. On February 1 Richard Nixon announced as a GOP candidate for the presidency. On February 20 the Senate Foreign Relations Committee began hearings on the events that had led up to congressional approval of the Tonkin Gulf Resolution. On March 1 LBJ's longtime friend Clark Clifford replaced McNamara. And finally, on March 31, the President announced he was de-escalating the war and would not seek reelection.

American television news coverage of the Tet Offensive during February and March convinced Johnson and millions of Americans that the war could not be won. Yet, as our military leaders said at the time and Hanoi has since admitted, Tet was a military disaster for the Communist forces. The best troops of the Vietcong were virtually wiped out. North Vietnamese support troops were forced into battle much earlier than expected. They were also beaten into bloody, massive retreats. The Communists suffered more than 10,000 casualties in two months of fighting.

If the United States lost the war, as so many commentators remind us, the American media were defeated at Tet. There is no doubt about their failure, especially that of television news. The media's insistence on U.S. defeat and disaster throughout February and March was thoroughly misleading. Peter Braestrup, who covered the war for the Washington *Post*, and others have documented these inaccurate reports. Robert S. Elegant, one of the best and most experienced reporters covering Vietnam and the Far East, also wrote broad criticisms of his colleagues in the print media. As I and millions of other Americans watched this wretched posturing night after night on TV and in our newspapers and magazines, we became angrier.

One of the worst examples of inaccurate TV coverage came on NBC's "Huntley-Brinkley Report" within four hours of the first shot at the U.S. embassy in Saigon. "NBC News" reported, "The Vietcong seized part of the U.S. embassy in Saigon early Wednesday, Vietnam time. Snipers are in the buildings and on the rooftops near the embassy and are firing on American personnel inside the compound. Twenty suicide commandos are reported to be holding the first floor of the embassy. The attack on the embassy and other key installations in Saigon, at Tan Son Nhut Air Base, and Bien Hoa north of Saigon, came as the climax of the enemy's biggest and most highly coordinated offensive of the war. There was no report on allied casualties in Saigon, but they're believed to be high."

The networks continued this guessing and bird's-eye interpretation of what had happened even after the battle. They reported that the six-and-a-half-hour Vietcong occupation of the embassy grounds appeared to be the most embarrassing defeat the United States had suffered in Vietnam. It was suggested that General Westmoreland had lied in offering rosy projections about the war.

The truth is, the Vietcong never entered the chancery. They never even held the grounds. They had tried to but failed. The "snipers" firing on Americans on the embassy grounds actually were U.S. personnel firing into the compound at nineteen VC commandos. Our casualties in Saigon were not high, but the Communists' were.

To suggest that a relatively small group of terrorists fighting on our embassy grounds for six and a half hours was the most embarrassing U.S. defeat in Vietnam is absurd.

The Communist offensive throughout Vietnam was reported in the same doom-and-gloom scenario by the overwhelming majority of the broadcast media. The reasons are now clear:

• Most radio and TV reporters were unwilling to wait and evaluate their sketchy knowledge of widespread battles before pronouncing judgments about the overall conflict. Indeed, they were unable to do so because no network had the staff to cover what was actually occurring in many cities and towns throughout South Vietnam, especially the performance of the South Vietnamese army. The truth is, in their constant attempts to appear knowledgeable about events, many reporters pretended to know what was happening. As McNamara would have put it, they suffered from "an insufficient data base." These newsmen were a professional catastrophe, not only in Vietnam but in their faraway New York editing rooms.

• In order to lend significance to their narrow focus and scant knowledge of Tet events, TV reporters offered interpretive reporting that was carried by networks as "straight" news. This was invariably inaccurate. I used to get screaming mad at this "instant analysis" of the war. It was so manifestly dishonest. Like millions of Americans, I was outraged at the arrogant effrontery of reporters who didn't know what the hell they were talking about.

• Newsmen were generally skeptical of the war and pointedly suspicious of Johnson and McNamara. This compromised their objectivity during normal coverage and destroyed it during Tet.

• The three major television networks never fully set the record straight, even when they knew the facts had favored our side at Tet, which was then and is today professionally unforgivable.

• These failures magnified the most glaring weakness of television news—its presentation of increasingly shorter stories with only a short-range view of events.

This is not just Goldwater talking. It's Americans in every walk of life, reporters and editors themselves, and a wide array of government and military leaders.

My purpose is not to attack the media. To dispel that notion, this long and tough critic of the New York *Times* will say categorically that the best coverage of Tet was by one of its men, Charles Mohr. My real aim is rather to ask a question: Can we run the risk that the media may repeat Tet at some other place and time? I don't believe the American people can—or should—accept such a possibility. Nor do I consider it prudent to leave that important question to the media alone. All involved must have a voice.

The Congress, other national leaders, the military, our educational institutions, public policy groups, foundations, and those in the media must make a much more serious evaluation of this issue than we have done thus far.

There must, for example, be still more critical judgments on where the reporter's adversarial position ends and where his responsibility to society as a whole begins. If this is not more clearly defined, then all of society must make it more legally clear. The federal government in general and the military in particular must protect their integrity.

The responsibility of the media is one of the most crucial unanswered questions of Vietnam. There must be greater self-discipline and professional ethics than many reporters and editors exhibited during Tet. The outcome of the next war may depend on it. The media cannot shrug off this challenge. Our political leaders, the military, and others have taken their lumps over Vietnam. The media are not exempt from the same accountability. They cannot hide behind the First Amendment, as some try to do, amid the present scrutiny and criticism of their performance by millions of Americans.

I believe the military and the media must now calmly work out a statement of principles and conditions on news coverage during wartime or international conflict. This statement would commit the media to the safety and security needs of the military, while our commanders would guarantee independent reporting of their operations on a timely basis. Mission security and troop safety must be protected in time of conflict in ways which must be more clearly defined. This may include limiting the number of reporters accompanying troops on certain missions, voluntary reporting restraints, and censorship of or delays in the disclosure of information that might assist the enemy.

Under our system of government, the media should not be excluded, as they were during the invasion of Grenada. The government cannot become the extended, total source of military reporting. If secrecy is critical to a major operation, a small pool of reporters should accompany U.S. troops—at their own risk. No operation can be compromised to save them if they are not in condition to keep up with a military assault.

Discussions along these lines have taken place among military and media representatives. They should be firmed up and become a formal, written agreement.

I believe that if this is not done, we will see more court cases like those of Westmoreland against "CBS News" and Israeli General Ariel Sharon against *Time* magazine. In my opinion, everybody lost in those cases, especially the media. CBS was unwilling to concede what it daily demands of others—to tell the truth and admit a mistake. CBS's ethics in claiming Westmoreland suppressed critical intelligence on the enemy were questionable to say the least. There is no question about *Time*'s ethical concern, but it stonewalled the truth about Sharon's alleged role in the massacre of Palestinian refugees in Lebanon.

If the military and media do not have the foresight to agree on news coverage, it's likely the Congress and courts will do so. Such a confrontation will not be uplifting.

On a more basic level, more reporters and editors might voluntarily take a few fundamental courses in law, particularly the rights of individual citizens.

I don't think many Americans have fought more public battles with the media than myself. Yet I'll defend their freedom to my death. But I warn them. If they do not become more responsible and accountable, they are headed for a battle with society—and they may lose the rights to some of their present practices.

In the same sense of fairness and accountability, McNamara was offered the opportunity to answer questions and make whatever statements of reasonable length he wished to in this book in defense of his work at the Pentagon and World Bank. He declined to do so.

At a White House ceremony on February 28, 1968, his next-to-last day in office, McNamara received a citation from President Johnson. In response to the award for his seven years of service as Defense Secretary, McNamara said, "I had better respond on another occasion." His self-imposed silence on Vietnam fails the test of accountability for every public servant in a democracy.

On leaving the Pentagon, McNamara became president of the World Bank in Washington, where he remained for ten years. When he retired, total lending by the bank skyrocketed from $954 million to $12.3 billion —an almost thirteen-fold jump. Many of these loans came from the bank's soft loan affiliate, the International Development Association. McNamara's easy loan policies are a major reason why a trillion-dollar international debt now clouds the Third World and the future of poor countries. The vast debt also threatens the financial solvency of many Western banks.

Harold Graves, the public information director of the bank for twenty-four years, agrees that McNamara was responsible for many bad loans and shares the blame for much of today's Third World debt.

Frank O'Brien, the former chief public information officer of the International Finance Corporation under McNamara, says, "It seemed as though he was giving money away, as if trying to make up for something on his conscience."

McNamara is now trying to jump the traces of his past. He talks about the "fantastic proliferation" of nuclear weapons. Yet this is the same man who once boasted that we surpassed the Russians in nuclear weapons buildup. It was McNamara who convinced our questioning allies in Western Europe to accept NATO's strategy of nuclear flexibility. This says that the West is willing to engage in "deliberate escalation"—the first use of nuclear weapons—if Western Europe is in danger of being overrun by overwhelming enemy forces. He now contradicts and attacks his own policies as Defense Secretary.

McNamara is accountable for his tenure at the Pentagon and World Bank. Yet he refuses to defend or answer questions of the past but says we should listen to him about the future because he is an expert. That is an intellectually impossible posture. As public figures, we are accountable to society for our records, and, if necessary, we must take it on the chin and get up. I did. And so have many others. I am genuinely sorry for McNamara. He still does not understand that accountability is part of public service.

Westmoreland never walked away from accounting for his responsibilities. The general gave dedicated, honorable service to his country. He bore much of the blame and burden for Vietnam, not all of which were his. I believe that history will vindicate Westmoreland as an outstanding officer.

In 1969, at the age of sixty, I returned to the U.S. Senate for a third term after defeating Roy Elson, a longtime aide to Senator Hayden, by a wide margin. Richard Nixon became our thirty-seventh President. A few days before he left office, Lyndon Johnson invited me to the White House for a private drink. He said he should have taken my earlier advice and fired McNamara. He wasn't bitter but confused about Vietnam. Johnson still didn't understand why we had failed to win the war.

9

Nixon and Watergate

IF THE WAR IN VIETNAM TAUGHT THE AMERICAN people and their political leaders anything, it is that truth is their strongest weapon. The Watergate scandal taught the same simple but supreme lesson. Without truth there cannot be freedom or justice, wisdom or tolerance, courage or compassion. Truth is the foundation of a stable society. Its absence was the crux of Richard Nixon's failure.

Unfortunately, despite the positive contributions the former President made to his country, his lies will probably be remembered longer than his legitimate labors. He was the most dishonest individual I ever met in my life.

President Nixon lied to his wife, his family, his friends, longtime colleagues in the U.S. Congress, lifetime members of his own political party, the American people, and the world. The lies persisted for more than two years, from at least June 23, 1972, when he personally undertook an active role in covering up the Watergate burglary, to his resignation on August 8, 1974. No lie is intelligent, but his were colossal stupidity because they involved the presidency of the United States.

The Watergate break-in was little different from some of the illegal dirty tricks practiced by the two previous Democratic presidents, Kennedy and Johnson. Each used the excuse of national security to place hidden and, in my opinion, illegal wiretaps on reporters, authors, CIA officials, lawyers, congressional employees, and others, including Dr. Martin Luther King.

Nixon's masquerade was, however, a long and tortuous trail of deceit that plundered the generosity and goodwill of millions of Americans who wished desperately to believe that their President was not a liar. It was the manipulation and misuse of this vast American storehouse of bigheartedness that history will condemn.

Nothing in my public life has so baffled me as Nixon's failure to face Watergate from the time of the burglary and tell the entire truth.

I first met Nixon in 1953. He was the Vice President, and I was the new and very junior senator from Arizona. Nixon had a very fine wife and family. He was hardworking, a dedicated Republican. He had the reputation of being a loner—not normally something said about a politician—but was well known for some outstanding investigative work as a member of the House. He had doggedly pursued Alger Hiss, a former State Department official who was eventually convicted of perjury.

I didn't see much of Nixon until 1954, when I became chairman of the Republican Senatorial Campaign Committee. He would then occasionally invite me to his office to discuss politics, particularly the direction of the party. Nixon seemed outwardly friendly but inwardly remote. I didn't pay too much attention to this aloofness because I've always felt it takes time to get to know anyone.

One morning on Capitol Hill, while discussing the 1960 Republican National Convention, Nixon promised me that he would personally advocate a right-to-work plank in the party platform. I made a note of what he said and put it in my file. Then, without my knowledge, Nixon abandoned his right-to-work promise at a secret New York meeting with Nelson Rockefeller. This was in return for the governor's support for his presidential nomination. He not only reversed himself but agreed to call for its repeal under Section 14b of the Taft-Hartley Act. I was shocked that Nixon would betray his word without explanation. My shock was mixed—anger that I had not allowed for the pressure of a political deal and resentment that Nixon would act so brazenly. I wrote in my file, "The man is a two-fisted, four-square liar."

Another tip-off on Nixon's character came in January 1969, when I returned to the Senate after a four-year absence. The Nixon-Agnew ticket had captured the White House in 1968 by a narrow margin. As is customary, there were various galas around Washington. Governor Reagan of California was host at a ball in the Sheraton Hotel. When Nixon and his party arrived, they were ushered to the stage, where the President was introduced to the crowd by TV host Art Linkletter—not by Reagan, who was the host. I thought it strange but concluded that some signals had been crossed. Nixon certainly knew that Reagan and his wife, Nancy, were the hosts, but after his remarks he walked directly past their box without shaking hands or saying hello. I was then certain there had been no mix-up. It was deliberate. Why? Was it because Reagan had been elected governor of California just four years after Nixon had failed? Because Reagan was widely seen as doing a good job and was already being hailed as presidential timber? Or was Nixon already being isolated by his two closest aides, Bob Haldeman and John Ehrlichman? If a wall were being built around him, why would he permit it? I wrote in my file, "Mistakes like that do not just happen."

On February 15, 1969, several weeks after Nixon entered the Oval Office, I added to my private file, "I've tried for three days to get an appointment with President Nixon. I'm beginning to be afraid that a wall has been built around him. Nixon has told me on quite a few occasions that, if I wanted anything from him, all I had to do was ask."

On April 24, 1969, I had a pleasant lunch with Admiral Lewis Strauss, former head of the U.S. Atomic Energy Commission. Our chat got around to the President. Strauss told me that in June 1968 Nixon had asked him two favors—to visit former President Eisenhower at his Gettysburg farm and to talk with some of his old acquaintances at the AEC. The purpose of the Eisenhower trip was to have Ike endorse Nixon for the presidency as soon as possible, in case he died before doing so! Strauss, a good friend of the general, obtained Ike's endorsement for Nixon.

Nixon asked the retired admiral to determine if there had been any problems at the AEC under President Johnson that might be blamed on him if he were elected and did nothing about them. Strauss did investigate and told Nixon aides that the AEC could not account for certain fissionable materials. Some shortages were as high as a half ton. Officials didn't know where the material was. Nixon never thanked or communicated with Strauss after the admiral accomplished the missions.

Two weeks after Nixon became President, and for the next four years, I was constantly admonishing him to clean out the high-level Democratic political appointees from the Kennedy-Johnson era. All I ever got was promises.

On March 24, 1970, I wrote myself this private note: "All bureaus of government are still filled with holdovers from the Johnson-Kennedy administration. They are making the President's task an extremely difficult one.

"It was just a year ago this time that the President suggested we should visit at least twice a month, perhaps more often if needed. It has been since August of last year that I have even seen the President, let alone talked with him. He has drifted more and more away from availability. Whether he realizes it or not, a very effective shell has been constructed around him."

On December 18, 1971, I met with Vice President Agnew in his office. We talked and had lunch in the White House Executive Mess. He said something which amazed me: "I don't know the President any better today than I did when he first asked me to be his running mate. The President never telephones me. I receive messages through third parties."

Agnew believed Ehrlichman was blocking him from seeing Nixon, and he told me he would not run again if Ehrlichman remained in the White House.

Many notes on the President's isolation dotted my private files. Nevertheless, if a shell were being built around Nixon, it could not be done without his knowledge and approval. This was dangerous—for the President personally, for the Congress, for the American people. A President must feel the pulse of politics and people. I spoke privately with former President Eisenhower about him. Ike was cautious but finally said, "There was not a single thing he accomplished in our administration."

That rocked me. I began to study Richard Nixon more closely.

Nixon had his hands full with Vietnam. But he drastically reduced the number of American troops there and was well on the way to pulling out of the war. Henry Kissinger, the President's national security chief, was having secret meetings with the North Vietnamese in a bid to formally end the conflict. Antiwar protestors had become nightly celebrities on television news. Draft dodgers were dating the comely girls of Stockholm and enjoying excellent Italian pizza in Toronto.

On May 2, 1971, some of the professional peaceniks involved in the massive march on Washington shoved and shouted their way into the reception room of my office. They swore and slapped red paint on the walls before police towed them off to Robert F. Kennedy Stadium, where they smoked pot, drank cheap wine, and wondered, as the songs of the times asked, where Joe DiMaggio and all the flowers had gone.

Nixon was delaying or ignoring many domestic policy decisions, except for temporarily imposing wage and price controls, something he had insisted he would never do. All the time, virtually alone, he was secretly under-taking new thrusts in U.S. foreign policy, namely press-ing detente with the Soviet Union and China. In July 1971 Nixon announced he was going to Beijing.

Nothing Nixon did surprised me anymore. He had contradicted himself so often that I was beginning to ex-pect it. Kissinger had contacted me before the announce-ment of the China trip. He and Nixon wanted to avoid my criticizing the move since I had always been con-cerned about our relationship with Taiwan, a loyal friend. The visit was set. There was nothing I could say that would stop it. Kissinger claimed there would be no adverse effect on the Taipei government. I told him that if there were, we conservatives would abandon Nixon. I adopted a wait-and-see attitude.

The official Shanghai communiqué of Nixon's meeting with Chinese leader Mao Tse-tung and his foreign minis-ter, Chou En-lai, caused me genuine anxiety about our friends on Taiwan. The mainland Communists had de-clared that the islands were part of the People's Republic, the sole legal government of China. The statement had added that the liberation of Taiwan was China's internal affair. Nixon and Kissinger publicly denied that their ad-ministration was abandoning Taiwan.

I attended a White House briefing by Nixon, Kissinger, and Secretary of State William Rogers after their return. It was a long and detailed explanation which stressed that the normalization of relations between the two coun-tries was good and that no one should seek to dominate Asia.

I returned to my office very downhearted. I had always been loyal to my friends. Taiwan had always been a good friend of the United States. Its leaders were now forced to question our loyalty. Yet the President and his advisers had made some good points. The ultimate impact of the trip was still not clear in my mind. So I wrote down each point. At the end I had still not made up my mind about its true significance, since no one could be certain that no secret understandings had been made by Nixon. He had betrayed good friends in the past. Finally, tormented by my own reluctance to come to a conclusion about the communiqué, I wrote in my private file, "If I cannot believe my President, then I have lost all my faith in men, friends, and in my country's leadership."

I sent word to the White House that I had misgivings about the Shanghai communiqué, especially its effect on our future relations with Taiwan. Our office received a message that I would receive an answer. I never did. This later came to be known as the Haldeman-Ehrlichman sense of humor.

I wasn't planning to attend the 1972 GOP National Convention in Miami. My wife and I wanted to be together at our summer place in Newport Beach, California. I facetiously wrote to Bob Dole, chairman of the Republican National Committee, that it would take a White House invitation to get me there.

A week before the convention I got a call from the organizers, saying the White House wanted me to give a convention speech. They asked me to pay tribute to those who had passed away since the last conclave. The organizers furnished me with a list of forty people, mostly Democrats. The theme seemed inappropriate. I decided to give a different speech. The organizers, acting for the White House, kept demanding an advance copy of the remarks. I stalled them. The White House repeatedly changed the time of my address. Also, it had not been listed in any of the publicity or printed programs. This seemed odd until I realized that some of the White House types might be putting me on. Finally, Bill Timmons, a presidential aide, called and said my address was being put back from Monday evening to Tuesday. I was tired of the runaround and said I would deliver the talk Monday or not at all. I had learned that the President would be arriving in Miami on Tuesday evening, about the time they wanted me to speak. The convention would be pre-empted, of course, and the television networks would switch to the President's arrival.

That would be the White House answer—some joke on Goldwater, the guy who wouldn't buy the Shanghai communiqué. It was a put-down typical of the Haldeman-Ehrlichman operation.

A few hours before I was to deliver my speech, White House aide Fred LaRue came to me as I was being made up for television, never an uplifting experience in any case. He asked that I make two major changes—no criticism of draft dodgers or of former U.S. Attorney General Ramsey Clark, a left-wing Democrat. We had this discussion in a bathroom where a TV man was messing with my hair. Finally I turned to LaRue and said, "If you want me to make these changes, I'm leaving right now."

He gulped and left.

When I gave the speech on Monday, the Clark and draft-dodger remarks were greeted with more applause than any other part. Later I wrote in my file, "I have a little bit of honor left."

The episode caused me to reflect even more about the President and his White House crew. I had heard rumors about some crazy things happening over there, especially vendettas with cabinet members and others who wouldn't jump through their hoops, but I wanted to wait and view the situation more closely.

In 1972 Nixon won a landslide victory over Senator George McGovern. He was ecstatic about it for two reasons: First, he had been his own campaign manager, as in 1960 and 1968, confirming in his mind his own political astuteness. Second, this was not a narrow win, as in 1968, but an overwhelming mandate to govern.

About three weeks after the election, Nixon invited me to Camp David for a chat about the future. I told him he had his mandate to lead—47 million votes to McGovern's 29 million. He had received 520 votes in the electoral college to only seventeen for McGovern. Now, I insisted, he had to take full control of the federal government and boot out every single Democratic holdover.

Nixon insisted he would finally tackle the federal government—rid it of Democratic appointees in various posts and slash its size and cost. I suggested he transfer Democrats in civil service posts who were actively opposing his policies. Nixon talked of dropping Bill Rogers as Secretary of State but didn't mention Kissinger as a possible replacement. I discussed waste in the Pentagon—overlapping and duplication in our different air tactical commands, as well as lack of competition in procurement. Finally the President said he would force Vietnam into substantive peace talks. On leaving, I mentioned that I'd probably not run for reelection in 1974. It was about time to do something else. We talked about the possibility of my becoming ambassador to Mexico. Watergate, which had been gaining momentum, was never mentioned. I viewed the publicity about the burglary as a distraction from our real goals. The whole thing had to have been carried out by some crazy crew of political neophytes who had been swept up in the excitement of the campaign.

My talk with the President was quite positive. I was delighted that he was finally going to get a grip on the biggest problem in Washington—the enormous appetite of the federal bureaucracy for more power and money, particularly at the expense of state and local governments. This was at the top of the conservative agenda.

Despite my thoughts of leaving Washington, I looked forward to 1973 with as much excitement as my first year in the Senate two decades before. It was going to be a truly great Republican triumph as we got Washington off the backs and out of the pockets of the average American. I found it difficult not to smile on the Senate floor as the Democrats immediately began singing their favorite political hymn, "More." I was whistling "Less."

* * *

The War in Vietnam ended in January 1973. We never really fought the good fight, so it was just as well. The year would close with Agnew's resignation on October 23 and a national storm over Watergate.

It became obvious, as the months passed, that Nixon was preoccupied with Watergate. Discouraged that he had done little to fulfill his promises, I wrote him a letter on June 20, 1973. It read in part:

"I'm writing this letter on my little portable typewriter because I don't want anyone but you to read what I have to tell you. I am doing this, in my opinion, in the best interests of yourself, the office of the presidency and most importantly, the country and, to quite an extent, the Republican Party.

". . . what I am saying to you comes right from the heart. . . . You may be angry with me for saying these things, but I have never been one to hold back when I think words are needed, and I think they are needed at this particular point.

". . . you have not started to get acquainted with the Congress. Having a few leadership meetings, a few for state dinners is not getting down to the little fellow who has to go out in his district or state to keep the Republican Party going. . . . Some said in the press this morning that they had seen more of Brezhnev than they had seen of their own President. Frankly, I think that's a hell of a crack and you should take it seriously.

"You have to stop living alone. You have to tear down that wall you have built around you. You have to emerge from the cocoon that you have been in all the years I have known you. . . . No one whom I know feels close to you . . . you've got to become the warm-hearted Nixon and not the Cold Nixon, which you are now.

"The party is going to continue in a leaderless fashion, dependent only on senators, congressmen, and governors who are, more and more, assuming the leadership that seems vacated by you. Whether you like it or not, you are the leader of the party, and you have to act like it. I would be derelict in my obligation to my country and my party if I didn't tell you what is on my mind."

In the light of the leadership issue, the Agnew affair was all the more unsettling. I didn't know whether the Vice President was guilty of the charges of his accepting financial kickbacks while holding office in Maryland or not. However, I was positive of one thing: The White House itself was leaking some of the allegations against Agnew. This startled me. Some presidential aides and Agnew had never gotten along, but would the President allow his staff to undercut his own Vice President? If so, why?

Agnew asked that I meet him privately at his home shortly after Labor Day. He confirmed rumors that U.S. Attorney General Elliot Richardson was investigating him based on information provided by the Maryland attorney general. Agnew indicated that several Maryland businessmen who were being investigated by the Internal Revenue Service may have tried to implicate him in tax fraud in a plea-bargaining arrangement to help their cases. Then Agnew dropped a bombshell. He said Nixon had known about the investigation for a week, but neither he nor anyone else in the White House had discussed it with him. If the Vice President were in trouble, why wouldn't the President and his staff be concerned about his answers to the allegations? The conduct of the White House was purely and obviously political. They should have been concerned—unless someone wanted to use Agnew, perhaps even force him to leave his post, for some purpose. What could that purpose be?

Agnew said he had been advised that Richardson was about to ask that he be indicted by a grand jury. He asked whether I thought he should go to Representative Carl Albert, Speaker of the House, and ask for a hearing. There was a precedent for such an action. Vice President John C. Calhoun had asked for a House hearing in 1824 after he had been accused of taking bribes. I advised Agnew to see Albert but not tell the White House he was doing so. I left his home perplexed about the roles of both the Attorney General and the White House. Whether Agnew was innocent or guilty was not my immediate concern. It was, rather, the motives of Richardson and the White House. Surely they would give him the opportunity to defend himself—or would they?

Over the next several days, I began asking myself more probing questions about the matter and finally came to one which stopped me in my tracks: What if the White House is using Agnew to take the glare of Watergate publicity off the President and his staff and place it elsewhere? And if Agnew were to leave office in disgrace, could it not be argued that the Administration had been sufficiently punished by its critics—that enough was enough?

My questions increased when Agnew sought to see Nixon but the President sent word he was unavailable. Suddenly, General Alexander Haig, who had succeeded Haldeman as White House chief of staff, and Bryce Harlow, a presidential counselor, visited the Vice President and suggested he resign. In the meantime, leaks continued to pour out of both the White House and the Justice Department implying that Agnew may have misused campaign contributions while he was the county executive of Baltimore and governor of Maryland.

More questions arose with each day's headlines. Why was the Administration making such an obvious effort to blow its own man out of the water? At the same time, the White House was highly protective of the President and executive privilege. Why would Nixon not hear Agnew's side of the story when the White House was asking the media to be fair to him?

I knew that Nixon didn't particularly care for Agnew personally, but this was ridiculous. He had to have some feeling for the Vice President and his family because they were being destroyed by rumor. Some evidence indicated that Agnew may well have been involved in shady dealings, but he still deserved a hearing.

About a week after our first talk, Agnew called and asked me to meet with him again. He disclosed that Nixon had requested that he resign. I was not surprised. In fact, I was beginning to smell a rat. Agnew indicated that Nixon had stopped him from going to the Speaker of the House to ask for a hearing there. He never said how or why Nixon had done this. I concluded that the President had cut him loose among the wolves. However, I learned much later that Agnew had not told me the truth. He had, indeed, gone to the House and met with Speaker Albert and others. The Democratic leadership was not anxious to become part of a Republican dispute which was already in the courts.

I flew home to Phoenix tired and depressed. Even if the Vice President were guilty, Nixon's handling of the affair was indecent. Agnew had been tried and found guilty through leaks before he knew what the Attorney General's formal charges were.

The White House apparently had gotten word that Agnew and I had been talking. When I got home, there was a message that one of the President's lawyers, Fred Buzhardt, and Harlow had left Washington by plane just after I had and would soon be at our house. The two arrived shortly after I did. They said Richardson would drop the bribe charges if Agnew entered a plea of no contest to a single charge of failing to pay a certain amount of federal income tax.

This was shameful. The White House was threatening to allow Agnew's prosecution unless he handled the matter their way—resignation in disgrace. Why not allow him to be heard in the House? I was willing to give him the benefit of the doubt. Yet Nixon was not, although he was asking Congress and the American people to give him the benefit of any doubts they might have about Watergate.

I was sick of this dirty business, so I spoke to the pair

in plain, political terms. A lot of us in the GOP knew Nixon would have preferred Rockefeller or former Texas Governor John Connally as his running mate in 1972, but conservatives would not have tolerated that. Both were still unacceptable, and if Nixon tried to replace Agnew with one of the two, we would strongly oppose it. I warned them that the White House was threatening to divide the party by acting this way toward a conservative like Agnew. I was certain they carried that message back to Nixon.

The Vice President obeyed orders. He pleaded no contest to the charge of income tax violation, paid a fine, and resigned.

I don't profess to know the precise role Nixon and his staff may have played in the Agnew affair, but they were already maneuvering behind the scenes to move Michigan Representative Gerald Ford into the vice presidency. There is also no doubt about their long-standing enjoyment in putting Agnew down.

Later, when the President resigned and some of his staff sought pardons for their involvement in Watergate, I couldn't help but wonder if, in the darkness of their souls, their consciences didn't remind them of what they had done to Agnew.

Since the Agnew affair, a good number of people have said to me that I was wrong to offer Agnew any consolation—that he was a crook. Perhaps he was. But I do not lightly view abandoning anyone under fire. The Agnew case was a study in the contradictory character of Richard Nixon. He quickly deserted Agnew while asking me and millions of other Americans not to flee from him in his hours of trial and torment.

Haldeman and Ehrlichman had resigned earlier, on April 30. Dick Kleindienst, who had preceded Richardson, resigned as Attorney General about the same time. Richardson had moved from the post of Secretary of Defense to take charge of the Justice Department. Nixon's directions to him are worth recalling, since they offer another insight into the man in the Oval Office: "You must pursue this investigation even if it leads to the President. I'm innocent. You've got to believe I'm innocent. If you don't, don't take the job."

Richardson hired his old Harvard law professor, Archibald Cox, as special prosecutor. Cox later insisted that Nixon turn over to him certain conversations that he had secretly taped in the Oval Office. Nixon refused and in October 1973 told Richardson to get rid of Cox. When he wouldn't, Richardson was fired. His deputy, William Ruckelshaus, resigned. This was called the Saturday Night Massacre. Judge Robert Bork, next in line at Justice, fired Cox at Richardson's direct request. Richardson felt it essential to reestablish the continuity of office amid chaos. Leon Jaworski, a Texas lawyer, became the new special prosecutor. The President, still insisting that he knew nothing of the break-in or any activities connected to it, was stonewalling any attempt to investigate Watergate.

Charges against Nixon and the White House staff—that they were withholding evidence on the tapes—continued to mount. There was an 18½-minute gap in a tape of June 20, 1972—three days after the break-in and arrest of five men—in which Nixon and Haldeman had discussed the burglary. This could be destruction of evidence. Jaworski was attempting to determine what had happened. Word was filtering out that the special prosecutor might seek to charge the President with conspiracy to obstruct justice. Nixon would probably appeal any indictment in the U.S. Supreme Court. Some in Congress had introduced impeachment resolutions. Jerry Ford had replaced Agnew as Vice President. It was mind-boggling.

In April I had publicly asked the President to level with the American people on Watergate. Trying to move Nixon off his butt, I told *The Christian Science Monitor:* "The Watergate. The Watergate. It's beginning to be like

Teapot Dome. I mean there's a smell to it. Let's get rid of that smell."

In December, during another interview with the *Monitor,* I tried again to get Nixon to open up by saying the President was doing too little, too late about Watergate: "He chose to dibble and dabble and argue on very nebulous grounds like executive privilege and confidentiality when all the American people wanted to know was the truth."

I said Americans wanted to know how honest their President was, adding: "I hate to think of the old adage 'Would you buy a used car from Dick Nixon?'—but that's what people are asking around the country."

Within hours after giving the interview to the *Monitor,* I was invited to have dinner that very evening with the President and Mrs. Nixon. It was, to say the least, remarkable timing and turned out to be a most unusual experience.

Pat Nixon greeted me in the second-floor Yellow Oval Sitting Room of the family quarters. A comfortable Christmas fire crackled. I had a small glass of sherry. We chatted amiably.

Other guests arrived—Bryce Harlow and his wife, Betty; Pat Buchanan and his wife, Shelley; speechwriter Ray Price; Julie and David Eisenhower; Rosemary Woods, the President's longtime personal secretary; and Mary Brooks, an old friend of the Nixons, who was director of the U.S. Mint.

The President entered after we were assembled. He was quite amiable, even garrulous. He moved quickly among us, rapidly jumping from one topic to another. Then, unexpectedly, his mind seemed to halt abruptly and wander aimlessly away. Each time, after several such lapses, he would snap back to a new subject. I became concerned. I had never seen Nixon talk so much, yet so erratically—as if he were a tape with unexpected blank sections.

Pat Nixon eased us into the private family dining

room. It was the first time I had the pleasure of dining there, and I must say the setting was beautiful. I sat at one end of the table, the President at the other. Pat was on my right with Rosemary to the left.

Nixon asked me if I preferred a red wine. I said no. He broke out a very fine bottle of German white. The President told me he knew a great deal about wine. He said he had learned about it from so many formal and state dinners at the White House.

As soup was served, Nixon was preoccupied with whether he and Pat should take the train to Key Biscayne, Florida, for a brief Christmas rest. The question seemed odd, even bizarre, considering all that was happening in Washington. The President asked for my opinion. I told him the trip was fine. However, if he were caught on the train without good communications and something serious happened in the world, the country would never forgive him. I said, "Act like a President."

The words shot out with a sting I never intended. Perhaps it was my subconscious talking. I was upset about Nixon's obsession with Watergate and lack of leadership. What was so important about a trip to Florida? He didn't have his priorities straight. I bit my lips to say no more. But such gibberish coming from the President of the United States, when the mood of the country was approaching a crisis, worried me.

Nevertheless, Nixon returned to the clicking rails and the family's Florida train trip. He muttered concern about having the U.S. Secret Service properly instructed because all the bridges might not be protected. His words were disjointed. The whole conversation was without purpose.

The President turned to Harlow and Price, dangling a new series of questions. He discussed Congress with Harlow but soon dropped the subject and took up the State of the Union Address with Price. He never allowed either to respond. Julie and David interspersed their own observations. It was like the babble at a Georgetown cocktail party, not the warm, intimate conversation of family and friends at home.

Nixon continued his ceaseless, choppy chatter. I was becoming more and more uncomfortable. What's going on? I asked myself. Why is Nixon rambling all over the map? Hunching and quickly dropping his shoulders? Incessantly sputtering something, constantly switching subjects? Finally, searching for some reaction to the President's erratic behavior among his family and other guests, I asked myself the unthinkable: Is the President coming apart because of Watergate?

Suddenly Nixon was addressing me: "How do I stand, Barry?"

He did not, of course, mention Watergate. I watched the expressionless faces on both sides of the table. Everyone knew what he meant. Each face was frozen in a plastic smile, as if we were being photographed for posterity.

The table fell silent for the first time that evening. I said the obvious: "People are divided—those who want you to go and others who wish you'd stay. Among the latter, there's a particular group who believe a President should not resign."

It was a tip-off. I was telling him that some of us in Congress neither expected nor wanted a President of the United States to quit. It would humiliate the office in the eyes of the world and was too horrible for Americans to contemplate.

There was no reaction to my remarks—none whatever. I sat back, stunned and silent.

Nixon had brought up the subject himself. He was asking me about the presidency itself, its future with the Congress and the nation. We were witnessing one of the most tempestuous times in the long and distinguished history of that office. Here we were at his dinner table, and the President himself was seeking the thoughts of his guests.

Yet, silence. Not a single word from anyone.

Julie looked at her plate. Price and Buchanan seemed to be staring into the distance. Harlow gazed at me without expression. Rosemary Woods toyed with her salad. Nixon peered into the bottom of his wineglass.

I straightened in my chair. With questions written all over my face, I was pleading with them. With open hands, I was silently begging them. Yes, Mr. President, ladies and gentlemen, let's talk about this matter as family and friends in the spirit of Christmas. Let's open our hearts. Let us solve all this together and put it behind us —for the good of the nation.

Silence.

They all knew what my face was telling them. It was simple and straightforward. I wanted the President to go on television and tell the American people the truth—whatever that was. If it was bad, he could ask for their help and forgiveness. We can all be guilty of poor judgment, even the President of the United States. Millions of good and decent people would understand. He could say he had made a mistake and explicitly say he was sorry. He could stand tall again. The office of the presidency, he himself, his family—and the country—would not be dishonored.

Complete silence.

It seemed that for at least fifteen or twenty seconds, everyone had crawled into some hiding place inside themselves. There was not a single word or sound. I couldn't fathom them. Yet, in recalling that moment today, perhaps they were more realistic than I realized.

Finally the President spoke. His mind had rolled back to the family vacation, and he was riding the rails to Florida again. Perhaps, he said, Barry was right. They should not take the train but fly. There would be no problems. He soon switched to the nation's gasoline and energy problems. Nixon insisted there was no oil crisis. Full supplies would soon return. He asked Harlow to speak up, to offer his views on the energy issue. The longtime Washington lobbyist and astute observer of the national and international scene slowly began to speak. The President cut him off. He suddenly opened an attack on liberals in the media.

A very odd feeling gripped me. There was something dreadfully wrong at the table—this whole scene. Nixon was making no sense to me whatsoever.

I asked myself whether I was witnessing a slow-motion collapse of Nixon's mental balance. Was the public pressure finally starting to tear the President apart?

Nixon began discussing foreign policy. His wife, Pat, quickly jumped in. She criticized Kissinger for taking too much credit in such affairs. David and Julie joined in the accusation. The President ruefully admitted that Kissinger was grabbing a lot of headlines. However, he firmly insisted, all the initiatives to China and the Soviet Union had been made by the President. He was making the real decisions.

I pointed out that the situation was not unique. Secretaries of State sometimes received more publicity than Presidents. John Foster Dulles and Dean Acheson were no slouches. If the President and guests would come back with me to the Hopi Indian tribe in Arizona, they would find a similar example. It was a Hopi custom that the chief rarely if ever spoke publicly on important matters. A promising young brave always did so. If anything went wrong, it was the brave's fault. If things went right, the chief was praised.

Dinner ended on a somber, strained note with several stretches of silence—all except for the President. He jabbered incessantly, often incoherently, to the end.

We exchanged early Christmas greetings and departed in different directions into the chill Washington night. The White House seemed cold and bleak as I got in and started my car. I let the engine run and looked up at the tall white pillars. They were so stately, so solemn, so seemingly strong.

How could anyone in these surroundings ever become involved in such a petty escapade as Watergate? It was just crazy. It couldn't be true. Yet the subject had seemed to haunt the room and dinner table, an uninvited guest. I drove home and dictated these words for my files: "I have reason to suspect that all might not be well mentally in the White House. This is the only copy that will ever be made of this; it will be locked up in my safe and Judy is pledged to secrecy."

I phoned Harlow the following day and bluntly questioned him about the President's behavior. He said that Nixon had been drunk before and during dinner.

Later Price lamely claimed that Nixon had been "working" each person at the table. Among his other aims, Price said, the President was trying to keep him and Harlow from jumping ship. Their leaving the President at this particular time would have caused embarrassment to Nixon and further media speculation that the situation inside the White House was deteriorating. All of that may have been true, but the point was Nixon's unusual behavior.

To this day Pat Buchanan will not comment on the dinner.

The evening was a watershed for me. Nixon appeared to be cracking. The presidency was crumbling. I would not stand idly by if the situation worsened. Nixon had to come clean, one way or the other.

I sensed that in the end there would be a confrontation between us. Nixon himself had remarked that he feared only one man in Congress—Barry Goldwater. If no one in the Republican Party would stand up to Nixon, I would. He was not going to make the GOP take the rap for him. We had done no wrong. Nixon was not above his party, the Congress, or those who had elected him. Nor was he above the country, the American people.

In March 1974 Watergate secrets were splattered in headlines across the country. A secret grand jury report contained "evidence" against the President, and he was named as an unindicted coconspirator. The grand jury recommended that materials in its possession—testimony, other documents, and tapes—be given to the House Judiciary Committee. The public indictment named seven of the President's onetime aides, including Haldeman, Ehrlichman, Charles Colson, and Attorney General John Mitchell.

It was clear before the close of March that the Judiciary Committee's counsel, John Doar, believed he had a case of impeachment against the President. The committee and Jaworski demanded that the White House furnish them additional tapes. Nixon was fighting them through a twisting delaying action.

Haig and the President's attorneys, James St. Clair and Fred Buzhardt, were now on the hot seat. They knew that the President had deleted critical material from typewritten summaries of some of the recordings the grand jury had requested. They, too, could be indicted for concealing evidence.

A tape from March 22, 1973, was particularly damning. There was reference to a meeting the President had had a day earlier with John Dean, then his counsel, in which they discussed paying off Howard Hunt, one of those implicated in the burglary. Hunt apparently had been threatening to talk. On the tape, in a meeting with Dean, Haldeman, and Mitchell, the President said, "I don't give a shit what happens. I want you all to stonewall it. Let [the accused burglars] plead the Fifth Amendment, cover up, or anything else, if it'll save the plan. That's the whole point. . . . We're going to protect our people if we can."

Nixon had his way. Edited transcripts—with passages deleted by the President himself—were delivered to the Judiciary Committee and the leaders of both parties at the end of April.

The 200,000 words of transcripts, which also were given to the media, caused a national sensation. Nixon's clear indications of a cover-up, plus his foul language, caused an endless stream of interpretation by the media. Some Americans were confused. Others said Nixon was innocent of everything. Still more insisted he was guilty all the way, from approving the break-in to clamping a lid on the investigation of it.

It was now clear that millions of Americans believed Nixon had ordered his aides to cover up whatever they knew of the break-in. No precise proof—the so-called smoking gun—had been made public as yet. There were endless rumors about conversations on the tapes still held by the White House. The tapes had become the center of national speculation—even jokes—from the corner pub to corporate boardrooms to late night TV talk shows. The whole nation seemed mesmerized by an almost daily dose of Watergate speculation and revelations.

I was getting phone calls from just about everywhere—people who said they had shaken hands with me during the 1964 campaign; others we had met while touring Europe; military officers I knew; scores of people whom I had never met. I took only a few of the calls. Our staff was bombarded. They told me it was, at times, frightening. Some callers were almost hysterical, warning of a military coup with possible bloodshed in the streets.

More than anything else, people wanted a reassurance about the continuity of government. Many Americans believed a crisis of vast proportions was possible—that the country could be left without presidential leadership. They were asking sophisticated questions about impeachment, about whether the President might stand trial in the Senate, about whether he would resign.

The questions also became very personal—whether Nixon was crazy or so isolated by his staff that he didn't understand what was actually happening, whether his staff could be trusted.

While many of the questions were about Nixon, most involved the institutions of government—the Constitution, whether the scandal would affect future presidents or the dignity of the office, and the effect on the balance of power among the executive, legislative, and judicial branches of government.

The question most asked was whether I believed Nixon was honest. We were asked that question not only by the Iowa farmer and Arizona cotton grower but by many in the Washington news corps. They were driving me nuts—some even got hold of the unlisted number for our Washington apartment phone.

Many of the callers were extremely agitated—some weeping. Some were in their teens, others quite elderly. Ellen Thrasher was new on our staff and only twenty-three. She told me, "Here I am, just a receptionist, and people are trusting every word I tell them. It's kind of heady. They want me to say that the country is going to be all right. They want reassurance about the whole system of government. If the President leaves, I tell them, it will be done properly, legally. We're a nation of laws and traditions."

The essential question in the thousands of calls we received was whether our system of government could stand the immense public strain that was being placed on it—not what would happen to Richard Nixon. This was the only time in my life I heard people express serious doubts about the future of the country. As Nixon became more paranoid, so did much of the nation. We were losing belief in our institutions, in our ability to cope, in ourselves.

On July 12 the House Judiciary Committee released nearly four thousand pages of evidence. The contents contained one damning section after another, all pointing to a cover-up. For the first time, the White House admitted Nixon would not be surprised if the Judiciary Committee voted for articles of impeachment. However, he didn't believe the full House would do so. The President left for the Western White House at San Clemente, California, as the scandal blew wide open.

Nixon was wrong. The Senate majority and minority leaders—Mike Mansfield and Hugh Scott—met to prepare for a Senate trial if the House voted for articles of impeachment.

Reports circulated on Capitol Hill that Nixon was unstable—moody, depressed, subject to fits of temper. It reminded me of his erratic behavior at the December dinner.

In rapid succession, Judiciary Committee Counsel John Doar said that a case for impeachment had been made, and the U.S. Supreme Court ruled unanimously against Nixon's claim of general executive privilege for the tapes. The decision, including the votes of three Nixon appointees, ordered the President to turn over sixty-four tapes to Jaworski.

The smoking gun—the tape of June 23, 1972, in which Nixon's own words showed his direct involvement in the cover-up—was about to become the centerpiece of the affair. The conversation flatly contradicted just about everything Nixon had said for two years. The President himself called it to the attention of his attorneys in late July. He suggested they might have some problems with the contents. As they were to conclude, the tape "convicted" the President of lying and withholding evidence. Haig and the lawyers now faced the charge of a crime themselves—conspiracy to obstruct justice—if they failed to disclose the contents to Jaworski.

We were not yet aware of the June 23 tape, but a growing number of my Senate colleagues privately asked me to see the President and suggest he consider resigning. I didn't ask to do this, because I believed Nixon would refuse to see me.

Meantime, in the waning days of July, the House Judiciary Committee voted three articles of impeachment. Republicans joined the Democratic majority. For the first time, I began to lean toward impeachment. Nixon clearly had abused the power of the presidency, and government would be at a virtual standstill unless and until he left office.

Impeachment would demean the office and the nation. We would wash our dirty laundry in public, and our country would be the worse for it. The damage could last for decades. There had to be a better way than either impeachment or forcing a moody President into a corner, not knowing what he might do.

I discussed the situation with the two GOP minority leaders, Scott of the Senate and John Rhodes, a fellow Arizonan, who was the House minority leader. All of us were upset at Nixon, but we decided to wait rather than force a confrontation. But how long could we wait? We simply hoped that an opening would develop which would not make it appear that we were putting Nixon up against a wall. The issue was, however, bigger than we were. Time was running out. Both the House and Senate had now lined up against the President. The question now was not whether but when he would be formally impeached and disgraced.

On Monday morning, August 5, Dean Burch, my former aide and now a special assistant to the President, phoned me from the White House. We met in my office late in the afternoon. Burch's face was unusually white and taut. He appeared to be holding something back, and I said, "Okay, Dean, out with it."

He handed me two white legal-size pieces of paper that had been stapled together. I held the pages, knowing we were close to the end of the long drama, and asked, "What does he say?"

Burch replied, "The President says he hasn't been telling the truth."

The June 23 tape had finally surfaced. Nixon tacitly admitted that he had used the FBI and CIA to cover up aspects of the break-in. He also indirectly confessed discussing how to limit the exposure of his people's political involvement in Watergate.

Burch said that the White House would be releasing the statement within the hour. He left quietly.

I was deeply distressed, almost speechless. I had believed Richard Nixon. I had wanted to. Every man deserved a final say. Yet Nixon would offer no reasonable explanation. He was hiding behind a lot of analytical legalese on two pieces of paper that said, "I was aware of the advantage this course of action would have with respect to limiting possible public exposure of involvement by persons connected with the re-election."

It was the same old Nixon, confessing ambiguously, in enigmatic language, still refusing to accept accountability. It was, above all, an insincere statement, as duplicitous as the man himself.

Yes, I said to myself, it is the perfect statement for Nixon—indeterminate, eminently deniable. Others were at fault. He had only tried to help them. It was always the others—"persons connected with the re-election"—never Richard Nixon.

Haig was walking a tightrope inside the White House. The number of Republicans who would vote for Nixon's impeachment was increasing each day. The higher this total, the more steeled Nixon became against resigning. Yet there had to be a way to show the President that resignation was his best option. That was precisely what Haig was trying to do.

It was August 6. I told Dean Burch that my head count in the Senate showed that the President had no more than fifteen or sixteen senators with him, not enough to block a two-thirds vote for conviction. And he might have as few as a dozen.

The Senate Republican Policy Luncheon convened at noon. Vice President Ford, who had just come from a cabinet meeting in the White House, said that Nixon had told them he was not guilty of an indictable offense. However, Ford made it clear that Nixon had admitted that more disclosures were coming and that the President had been involved in some deception. That did it. I blew my top.

I said that Nixon's position was hopeless, even among Republicans in the House and Senate. The President might continue to find some legal points here and there which might delay the process, but that would only be temporary. He had lied to us, and we could be fooled only so many times. We were sick and tired of it. The best thing he could do for the country and the party was to get the hell out of the White House—the sooner the better. As far as I was concerned, he could get out that afternoon.

I was interrupted to take an urgent phone call from the White House. I excused myself. I didn't want any more double-talk from them. I'd hang up if they started that. No more excuses. The operator said General Haig was calling from the Oval Office. When Haig picked up the phone, I heard a second click. I guessed it was Nixon. Haig asked how many votes the President had in the Senate. I told him no more than a dozen. I added that it was all over. Nixon was finished. I snapped, "Al, Dick Nixon has lied to me for the very last time. And to a hell of a lot of others in the Senate and House. We're sick to death of it all."

When I returned, Ford had resumed answering hostile questions from other senators. Senator Cotton said we were getting nowhere talking to one another and that we should send a special Senate delegation to see Nixon in the White House. We could no longer just sit and be expected to support whatever move Nixon made.

The Vice President departed, but we continued to argue among ourselves. Some insisted we should be wary of appearing to prejudge the President. Others maintained that the head count had been taken and Nixon was finished. The party should not go down with him. A few said I was the only one blunt enough to get across to Nixon the feeling of most GOP senators. The meeting broke up in disagreement. It was quickly leaked to reporters that a rebellion against the President had occurred and that I had called for his resignation. I believe not one but several, including Hugh Scott, revealed to newsmen what had happened. They were pressuring Nixon.

Later, at a meeting of the GOP Senate leadership, it was decided that I should go to the White House alone. I spoke to my wife on the phone that evening. We had finally decided that I would make one more run for the Senate and then retire. Perhaps if I called for Nixon's resignation, I should not make the race. It would infuriate Republicans back home. They had backed Nixon through thick and thin. Peggy said, "No, Barry, they will respect your truthfulness and honor. You do what you think is right, but don't retire. It's just not the way to leave after so many years."

Burch invited me to lunch at his home with Haig the following day, Wednesday, August 7. The meeting was the general's idea. He wanted to speak with me before I saw the President late that afternoon. Haig said that Nixon wanted Scott and Rhodes there, too. The President wanted as broad a picture as possible on what the Republicans might do.

Haig described Nixon as a man dancing on the point of a pin. He was someone who could be set off in any one of several directions. It would be best not to demand or even suggest that he resign. Every time that had happened in the past, Nixon had reacted defiantly. The best thing to do would be to show him there was no way out except to quit or lose a long, bitter battle that would be good for no one—the country, Nixon, his family, or the party. Haig summed everything up succinctly: The President needs to know that there are no more alternatives, no more options.

About a half hour after I returned to the Capitol, Bob Clark reported on ABC radio and television news that I had said the President would resign. I was never more furious in my life. I had told him no such thing. Clark, a normally reliable newsman, finally phoned me, and I really gave him hell. He promised a retraction. ABC did retract its story, but NBC refused to withdraw a false report it had been broadcasting since the evening before —that I had sought entrance to the White House but had been refused.

I rushed to the floor of the Senate and requested thirty seconds to speak on a point of personal privilege. It was immediately granted. I blew my stack again, stating that both the ABC and NBC stories were completely false. I looked up at the packed press gallery and declared in a loud voice, "You are a rotten bunch!"

I never heard such spontaneous applause and cheers from visitors in the gallery. Even senators on the floor applauded.

Later, Scott and I met Rhodes at the White House. We waited in a nearby office before seeing Nixon. None of us was in a mood to talk. We knew what we had to do. All of us were aware of Nixon's moodiness, his habit of trying to conceal his real thoughts, the unpredictability of his character. The minutes seemed like hours. Finally the phone rang, and we were invited to the Oval Office. The White House had just issued a statement: The President had no intention of resigning.

Nixon put his feet up on the desk, leaned back in his swivel chair, and began reminiscing about the past. It was as if we were a foursome of old golfing partners sitting on the shady lawn of some nineteenth hole, listening to stories about games gone by, and sipping tall, cool drinks.

I didn't buy it—not one bit. I was sitting directly in front of Nixon with Scott and Rhodes at my side. I was looking at the public man, waiting for the private person to emerge.

Slowly his voice began to harden. Some of the men who had campaigned with him—fought the wars over the years—had turned against him. Yes, he remembered them well. His voice was becoming remote now, and the sound of the words was lengthening, as though he were alone listening to his own voice.

Suddenly, sharply, Nixon ended his soliloquy. He snapped at Rhodes that the situation—meaning impeachment—in the House was not good. Before Rhodes could answer, Nixon abruptly clumped his feet on the floor, wheeled his chair around, and faced Scott. Scott turned to me, saying I would be the spokesman for the group. For a split second, Nixon stopped. He had not planned it this way. Goldwater face to face. He stared at me, then said, "Okay, Barry, go ahead."

This was no time to mince words. I said, "Things are bad."

Nixon: "Less than a half dozen votes?" His voice dripped with sarcasm. His jaw automatically jutted out as his eyes narrowed.

"Ten at most," I said. "Maybe less. Some aren't firm."

The President asked Scott if he agreed. He did.

I could see that Nixon's blood pressure was rising. Now was the time to warn him without causing him to make some reckless, suicidal move. I said, "I took a nose count in the Senate today. You have four firm votes. The others are really undecided. I'm one of them."

I hit him as directly and as hard as I could. It didn't seem to hurt him. Nixon turned to Rhodes, who said the situation was about the same in the House.

For the first time since we had entered the room, the President paused. He looked at all three of us. I was on the verge of tears—of humiliation, not sorrow.

Nixon leaned over the desk toward Rhodes and asked, "Do I have any options?"

Haig was right. He would try to beat the rap until it was absolutely clear that the situation was hopeless. Rhodes replied, "I want to tell the people outside that we didn't discuss any options."

Nixon snapped his agreement, stressing, "It's my decision."

There was no modulation in Nixon's voice now. He spoke in a monotone. He was not interested in a pardon or amnesty. He would make the decision in the best interests of the country. It was going to be all right. He would make it so.

The President stood and thanked us for coming. We shook hands. Haig was waiting for us. We told him there had been no demands and no deals, but Nixon now knew beyond any doubt that one way or another his presidency was finished. None of us doubted the outcome. He would resign.

I told the waiting reporters that no decision had been made. The President would act in the best interests of the country. All three of us fudged on the overwhelming congressional count to impeach the President. I intensely disliked not laying it on the line but if I had said Nixon was certain to lose in both houses, there was no telling how he would have reacted.

My office was bedlam when I returned. It overflowed with reporters, and the phones were ringing off their hooks. I quickly slipped into my office and phoned Mrs. Katharine Graham, owner of the Washington *Post.* My opinion of the *Post* hadn't changed. We opposed one another. But now the country came first.

I told Mrs. Graham what had happened in the Oval Office—that Nixon was wobbling and could go off in any direction, depending on how the media, particularly the *Post,* handled the story. Could they play it cool for just one day, refrain from saying Nixon was finally finished, and let the President resign? If they threatened Nixon and got him mad, there was no telling what he would do. As things stood, I believed he would resign.

The *Post* was as circumspect as it could be the following morning, Thursday, August 8. Since 1953, when I entered the Senate, I have taken second place to no one in my criticism of the *Post.* And I'm well aware that the newspaper led every news organization across the country in uncovering the ungodly mess we call Watergate. However, that morning stands out in my mind as the *Post*'s finest hour. It may have spared the nation the agony of impeachment and a long, wrenching aftermath.

Mrs. Graham never mentioned the subject to me. I understand why. Newspapers call their own shots. There are times in the history of a nation, however, when the media should put their country above themselves. That hasn't happened with some in the past generation, but the *Post* did it on August 8. I will never forget their recognition of responsibility as long as I live.

President Nixon resigned that evening, effective at noon on Friday, August 9. Vice President Ford was sworn in as President at that hour in the East Room of the White House.

I watched Nixon's address on television with tears in my eyes. Despite his long record of political treachery, my heart ached for him and his family. It was, in the end, ironic that he had betrayed himself and become his own executioner.

I waited vainly for Nixon to say he was sorry and ask the forgiveness of the American people. Instead, he spoke of his preference to carry through to the finish although he had lost much of his base in Congress. The one phrase of consolation in those final words was "hastening the healing."

He did not mention, of course, that Bob Haldeman had used that very word, healing, in asking Nixon to pardon all his aides before leaving office. Instead, he flew away to exile in California.

To this day, Nixon has never asked the nation for forgiveness. Yet he was given a pardon by President Ford. I've never discussed this publicly, but it's time to do so. Ford called me just after granting the pardon but before announcing it. It was 4 A.M. when the phone rang at Newport Beach, California, where Peggy and I were on vacation. I said, "Mr. President, you have no right and no power to do that. Nixon has never been charged or convicted of anything. So what are you pardoning him of? It doesn't make sense."

Ford said, "The public has the right to know that, in the eyes of the President, Nixon is clear."

I was stunned by Ford's words. This was the same man

who had openly admitted that Nixon had deceived the Congress. That was most likely a criminal act—obstruction of justice. I replied, "He may be clear in your eyes, but he's not clear in mine."

It was a bad mistake by Ford. He should never have opened his mouth. Nixon had never been formally charged, although Jaworski and Judge Sirica were aware of a sealed grand jury indictment. Nixon had never been ordered to go to jail. He had, in effect, already turned down a pardon by refusing to ask the public for forgiveness. Ford saw the pardon as a holy act. I still do not understand how. To my knowledge, no one in a position of authority wanted to pursue the matter. So why the pardon? If Ford was trying to say Nixon was not guilty—and apparently he was—he knew that was false. The Congress had been certain to impeach Nixon. It's difficult to find more formal guilt.

Jerry Ford is a decent man, but the pardon never made sense to me and still doesn't. It hurt him politically and indeed may have been instrumental in his loss to Jimmy Carter in 1976.

I'll never forget Al Haig in this crisis. He put his butt on the line when many of the most powerful men in Washington went into hiding. Haig held the White House together in the last two weeks of the Nixon administration. He now recalls:

"The true story of Watergate was not then and has not yet been told. When it is, Barry Goldwater will be one of the good guys.

"During the months of July and August of 1974—before Nixon resigned—there was a growing impatience in the House and Senate with Watergate and the continued tenure of President Nixon. I and others around the President questioned whether he would receive due process of the law. There were certain legislators who were contemplating extraconstitutional solutions—anything from a sense-of-Senate resolution to certain direct demands. The chances of that kind of an unprecedented outcome were very high in the waning hours of the crisis.

"Barry Goldwater was, despite his disenchantment with Watergate and the President, an absolutely unflinching advocate of due process and that our constitutionally provided procedures be followed. He would tolerate no other approach to the problem. He was extremely influential. I think history and the American people owe Barry Goldwater a deep, deep debt of gratitude. I know I do personally."

I'm not going to discuss some of the final aspects of Watergate since I was not personally present at some crucial discussions. The full story has yet to be told. But I do wish to stress that the hysterical rumors about a military coup were completely unfounded. Al Haig and I know that. One day, those involved in some political moves may speak for themselves.

On January 23, 1975, I visited Nixon at his home in San Clemente. It was a sunny day. I flew from Phoenix to the Orange County airport, rented a car, and drove down the coast to the Nixon home. On approaching the gate, a Marine guard recognized me and waved me through. I pulled up in front of the house about 1 P.M.

The place was quite different from the last time I had been there. No helicopters or jeeps. No fleets of golf carts. No people walking around with papers in their hands, whispering. It was quiet, almost desolate.

I knew the young guard at the door. He motioned me to enter. There wasn't a sign of life anywhere—the rear patio, garden, the swimming pool. Finally I spotted the former President stretched out on a beach chair in a corner of the back patio, snoozing. I called to him, and he quickly awakened. Nixon greeted me warmly and put his arm around my shoulders, and we walked into the living room.

Pat's touch was everywhere. The onetime broken-down adobe home was now tastefully furnished in bright, cheery colors. We sat and immediately began talking politics. He asked how Jerry Ford was doing. I said Jerry had to quit listening to members of the House, who had never made an important decision in their lives, and forget compromising. We talked about the country's oil problems, the makeup of the Congress, and CIA surveillance of American citizens.

We went to lunch and continued the discussion. Without ever mentioning the word, we finally turned to Watergate. Yes, Nixon said, mistakes had been made. They were all his. Although he didn't know all these things were happening, it was his fault for waiting too long before acting. It was the old Nixon song, but I decided not to say anything in response. We talked about leaks in the National Security Council. Both of us knew who had been doing the leaking—a Navy man—but it had to be handled carefully. Nixon was talking about his health. He said that news stories speculating that he was losing his will to live were "bullshit."

Like any other person, Nixon said he wanted to live. He asked if I thought he should go ahead with a book. There had been criticism of his plans and the fact he would make money from it. I said, "Yes, by all means, write it. Tell the truth. Tell everything."

I had said it. Those few words were worth the trip. The truth—finally—the truth.

At 3 P.M., it was time for me to leave. Nixon was sorry to see me go. He walked me outside. Referring to the book, I said, "Perhaps you could do something about clearing your name, although that might be beyond doing."

He said nothing. I repeated, "Tell the truth."

Nixon stood there in the sun. Alone. His face was expressionless.

In April 1987 the former President temporarily blocked the scheduled public release of about 5 percent of 1.5 million pages of his private presidential papers. The National Archives had released a small part of the papers a year earlier. The batch Nixon stopped contained documents relating to the Watergate scandal.

Over his objections, some 250,000 pages of the papers were finally released by the archives about a month later.

10

Spies, Secrets, and National Security

INTELLIGENCE IS A NATION'S MOST ADVANCED weapon against attack. Such secret activity is also its most practical and powerful substitute for war. Yet no country in the world has made public more details of its secret military and other government intelligence activities than the United States. Never have these disclosures been greater than in the past dozen years: the Church and Pike committee hearings in 1975, the 1987 Iran-Contra testimony, and Bob Woodward's book *Veil: The Secret Wars of the CIA 1981–1987*. Until Senator Frank Church and Representative Otis Pike, Democrats of Idaho and Ohio, no officials had ever compromised America's secrets for political advantage. Today, that is becoming common practice among an alarming number of politicians.

Church, who chaired a Senate inquiry into the activities of the Central Intelligence Agency, made no secret of the fact that he hoped to become the Democratic presidential nominee in 1976. I have never more severely questioned the conduct of a U.S. senator than I have Church's display of ambition during those televised hearings. For a year, as a member of that committee, I watched his brazen bid for national power at the expense of undermining our national security.

Church waved a poison dart gun as part of a sensationalized opening day of public hearings. The gun was supposedly part of a CIA arsenal to assassinate foreign leaders. Church engaged in other dramatics, such as CIA shrimp toxin, for the benefit of a daily minute or so on the national TV networks. He launched a broad, biased attack on the CIA, describing it as a "rogue elephant." We were supposedly still in the process of evaluating testimony and other evidence.

Church was joined by Pike, chairman of the House Select Committee on Intelligence, who directed a special House group investigating the CIA. Pike was so partisan that even the media, hungry for the names of American "assassins," recognized that, in tearing the CIA apart, he was trying to build a platform for his own political ambition. The two men, who spoke of restoring decency to America after the Watergate scandal, eventually became political losers.

One of the few things that both William Colby, then director of the CIA, and Richard Helms, a former director, agreed on at the time was that Church and Pike were putting on a political melodrama. Colby and Helms had sharply opposing views about congressional oversight of the CIA.

More than a decade afterward, Helms told me the two committees had damaged the American intelligence community severely. He found very little in Senator Church's efforts that aimed to improve the quality of U.S. intelligence—how we either collected or organized it. Helms explained that the dart guns had never even been made in the agency and that he never knew what purpose or connection the shrimp toxin had had with the CIA. He concluded, "Church and Pike were on fishing trips. They just muddied the waters about the major issue at the time: whether what the CIA did was secret and would remain secret."

Church was eventually defeated in a bid for reelection to the Senate. Pike's ambitions finally dissolved in his swollen pride. He disappeared from the scene and was never missed.

I thought that Congress and the nation had learned something from the Church-Pike fiasco about the need to keep our national secrets. Instead, Congress made the Iran-Contra hearings another public spectacle in which our intelligence activities—sources and methods of operation—and certain classified information were paraded on television like a Mickey Mouse cartoon. Also, any foreign intelligence service reading Woodward's book could gain considerable information from it.

In my four years as Intelligence Committee chairman, we had a total of 260 meetings, hearings, and briefings. More than 90 percent of these were held behind closed doors. The result was little partisan debate or bickering but plenty of results. The committee produced seventy-one pieces of legislation and reports for the Senate, more than it had during the preceding years under Senator Birch Bayh or during the subsequent tenure of Senator David Durenberger. Senators are at their best in private.

The Iran-Contra hearings were a step-by-step, textbook demonstration of U.S. covert operations. The basic methods of U.S. intelligence operations—from planning to personnel and financial payments—were clearly diagrammed for the world. The disclosure of what appeared to be simple facts betrayed real secrets to professional foreign spies. As the hearings ended, I dejectedly closed my eyes, leaned back on my memories of three decades in the Senate, and asked, "Do we have any clothes on at all? Is the country now completely naked?"

Woodward's book covered very sensitive material as well. It has caused and will continue to cause this country real problems by compromising certain American agents and activities, disclosing particular techniques in collecting intelligence, and harming our intelligence relations with other nations. For obvious reasons, I am not going to go into specifics.

We are not naked—yet. America does have secrets, big

secrets, but they are few. Those who say sarcastically that U.S. intelligence has become an open book are not far from the truth. That era, which began with Church and Pike, continues today. Some members of Congress and others still place their own interests above those of their fellow countrymen.

Some of the Church-Pike probing had a basis. The hearings publicized assassination plots against Fidel Castro and Patrice Lumumba. The CIA had been involved in contingency planning, but not actually in carrying out attempts on the lives of the two. Other improper activities, mostly invasions of privacy, had also been conducted by the agency.

I found, however, few redeeming qualities in the sensationalized manner in which these matters were aired. It had long—indeed, for decades—been established that the United States had been engaged in "dirty tricks." By definition, that is the intelligence business. It is one of the world's dirtiest professions, blackened by lies, bribery, deceit, even murder.

The real question is the intention of this country in engaging in such conduct. If the intent is to keep us from national harm—from threats of economic injury or war —then the CIA performs a needed and, in my mind, just mission. We have a right and duty to protect ourselves. It is folly to suggest that 535 members of Congress will agree on what is moral or even ethical. Nor will the American people. That is why we place our lives and fortunes, to a limited extent, in the hands of trusted public officials. In this case, the Constitution gives the President the power to advance our foreign policy goals.

Under Article II, Section 2, the Constitution makes the President the commander in chief of our armed forces. It also gives him the power, on the advice and consent of the Senate, to agree to treaties and appoint ambassadors. The President makes foreign policy.

I am not suggesting that the CIA was justified in plotting the Castro and Lumumba murders. The law now prohibits that. U.S. espionage must reflect American values. We're not running the KGB. However, it's a good thing never to say never about many things. We could witness the coming of another Hitler or worse. I believe that killing a new Hitler would be morally and politically justified, and I would not rule out such a possibility.

There is a much more pertinent point in all this. I believe that private contrition—limiting access to the most sensitive negative aspects of spying to specific members of government—is much more reasonable than public confession, airing it on television and elsewhere for all the world to witness.

It has been my experience that unpublicized hearings and cooperation contribute to better policy. Our officials who handle these matters privately face ultimate accountability. I maintain that there is a more appropriate time and forum than TV or other media to make policy on our most sensitive intelligence matters.

The purpose of congressional oversight of intelligence activities is not to embarrass this country around the world. Neither should it jeopardize the CIA's ability to function abroad. Its purpose is to deal with the security interests of more than 240 million Americans in a world that does not necessarily share our interests or beliefs. I voted against the establishment of the Senate Intelligence Oversight Committee in 1976 for reasons that I will make clear.

Those who presided over the 1987 Iran-Contra hearings were well aware of the problems created by the Church and Pike committees. There were other compelling reasons to hold closed door sessions. A public prosecutor had been appointed to investigate, indict, and punish anyone guilty of criminal acts.

Members already knew most of the facts from private testimony before their committee as well as from the Senate Intelligence Committee's previous investigation. They granted limited immunity to Lieutenant Colonel Oliver North and Rear Admiral John Poindexter, the two most critical witnesses, to learn more. Yet they felt obliged to parade them in public. For what purpose? Certainly not to find the truth. That could better have been accomplished in private. The truth is, the Democrats thought they could damage the President. They were right. The Democrats also believed they would cover themselves with political laurels. They were wrong.

North became a new American hero as some members sat idly watching from the stage the committee had created for itself. Americans were hungry for North's faith in and loyalty to his country. Some committee members and others called him a liar. His truthfulness was never the issue. It was his moral intent. And that purpose was to save the lives of American hostages and prevent the Soviet Union and Cuba from gaining a base in Nicaragua. I don't know if North will prove to be a lasting hero. There are many questions still to be answered. But I regard his testimony as moral, uplifting, and heroic.

I won't easily forget North's calm as congressmen stammered questions from idiot sheets prepared by their staffs. It was clear that the majority had chosen theater over the tedious toil of the much more deliberate, detailed questioning that is characteristic of private sessions. I was at first disappointed at and ultimately disgusted with the public posturing of many of my former colleagues. That was particularly true of Texas Representative Jack Brooks, whose asinine performance as a political prosecutor made his Democratic donkey look good by comparison.

I believe such hearings should be held behind closed doors. That still does not solve a big problem. There is no guarantee that members of Congress and their staffs would keep the secrets of such private sessions. The fact that so much information was leaked before the hearings is proof of that.

So this country is faced with a dilemma worthy of a spy novel—only it's for real. We are a nation that cannot keep its secrets. Under the auspices of congressional inquiry and investigative reporting, we tell the world the most minute details of crucial intelligence activities. Even when such undertakings are discussed in congressional and executive branch privacy, their outlines are often leaked to the media in a matter of days. This cannot continue. It can only lead to catastrophic consequences.

These conclusions come from eighteen years of involvement in intelligence activities in the Senate, beginning in 1969, when I became a member of the Armed Services Committee. Later, I was a member of the Church committee and then was vice chairman of the Senate Select Committee on Intelligence from 1977 until the end of 1980. I served as chairman of the Intelligence Committee from 1981 through 1984. During my last two years in the Senate, I was chairman of the Armed Services Committee, where intelligence was an integral part of our activity.

The CIA and NSC work for the President, not for Congress. For that reason, during my early tenure in the Senate, only a few members of Congress knew intelligence secrets—Senator Richard B. Russell of the Senate Armed Services Committee, Representative Carl Vinson of the House Armed Services Committee, and Representative Clarence Cannon of the House Appropriations Committee. Russell held most of the information inside this informal oversight group because the CIA was the President's agency and Congress was limited to authorizing budgets without compromising secrecy. Russell believed in parliamentary procedure and prudence. Contrary to what his latter-day critics claim, he was not a man who sought power. The Georgian trusted the directors of these agencies to tell the truth to him, his colleagues, and the President. They did.

It is not true that Congress was ignorant about what intelligence activities were being funded in those years. These three members knew where every dime went on each operation or program. I know that firsthand. It is pure baloney to suggest that the trio ignored dirty tricks.

As fiscal conservatives, they followed the flow of funding, which led them directly to the operations being undertaken. They unquestionably did respond to legitimate queries from colleagues. Russell's prudence and deep patriotism caused him and the others to be concerned about leaks which could expose American lives and operations to danger.

Some members of the Iran-Contra committee were clearly concerned about what they were portraying to the country. Just as clearly, millions of Americans, including myself, saw them trying to further their careers at the President's expense. There is a time and place for politics. There is also a time and place—taught us by Russell, Representative George Mahon of Texas, longtime chairman of the House Appropriations Committee, and others —to be, in the nation's best interests, truly bipartisan.

I cannot help but reflect on the stark contrast between Senator Daniel Inouye and Russell, the masterful constitutionalist. I was astonished that the characteristically fair-minded Hawaii Democrat allowed the questioning to degenerate to the level of that of a criminal trial.

There are few if any rules in such a hearing—members live by their own interpretation of proper procedure—so Inouye had to allow members wide latitude. There's a difference, however, between a congressional inquiry and a political lynching. One man prevented such a hanging. Oliver North confronted the committee on the critical issue of constitutional separation of powers and beat members at their own game.

I believe the committee lost sight of the objective—to arrive at a meaningful understanding of the separation of authority between the executive and legislative branches. Members glossed over the critical fact that only the President can initiate and carry out foreign policy. The hearings became a strong-arm grab by Congress for more influence in foreign affairs.

The real objective of the hearings was raw political power, both personal and party. It was a bold new move by Congress to usurp the authority of, if not control, the presidency. It clearly aimed to take from the President some of the power to make foreign policy and the authority to gather intelligence.

Why does Congress want to control intelligence? Because classified reports from around the world are very significant in the making of foreign policy. If Congress can dominate our clandestine services—knowing and approving every operation and making the entire intelligence community serve it as well as the White House—members will have gone a long way toward not only influencing and regulating foreign policy but initiating it.

In my view, that would so politicize our international interests that we would be babbling incoherently around the world. The free world can never put its safety and trust in the inconsistent politics of 535 members of the U.S. Congress.

Democrats in Congress are embarked on a revolution to rewrite the Constitution in partisan power terms. It is one of the most dangerous developments in our public life. Inouye and others looked to the most obvious means to bolster their push for power.

So the committee chose a public roasting. But North, Poindexter, Reagan, and others openly challenged their maneuver to curb long-established presidential authority.

This is what the real fight is about. Congress wants preeminence over the executive branch. America is witnessing a classic internal power struggle, a revolution going to the constitutional foundation of the Republic.

These are strong words, but Congress has launched a powerful attack. That is why some basic understanding of American intelligence is important. This apparatus is now at the center of a battle at the highest levels of our national leadership.

The opening salvos, fired by Church, Pike, and other liberals as they savagely attacked the CIA in 1975 and 1976, were only the beginning. The Democrats then leaked the final House report to *The Village Voice*. They also leaked excerpts of the final Senate reports to the media. They broke the very pledge the committees said Congress could and would keep. And such leaking has persisted ever since.

In April 1976 I wrote a critical minority report for the Senate Select Committee on Intelligence Operations, saying the Church hearings had been "sensationalized." No one in government had adopted the assassination of foreign leaders as intelligence policy. Church and the Democrats had issued a special report which largely implied that. By listing various assassination plots, they lent credence to their claim that the CIA had become a bunch of killers. In many instances their proposed reforms brushed aside government cases in the courts that would have allowed the CIA and FBI to undertake certain counterintelligence activities. I refer in particular to activities to help block hostile foreign intelligence. I also disagreed with their recommendations that would effectively have paralyzed FBI efforts to deal with mob violence.

The climax of the hearings came in a bitter confrontation between William Colby, then director of the CIA, and former director Richard Helms. I recall their testimony well, but, for the purposes of these recollections, both men recently gave me their accounts of what happened then and the importance of events since. All of us agree that those were traumatic times for U.S. intelligence.

Colby was the principal player in this drama, which really began in 1974 with published reports that the CIA had conducted illegal activities inside the United States during the 1950s and 1960s. The agency had no such jurisdiction. It was President Ford, vacationing in Vail, Colorado, who publicly confirmed that the agency had been involved in assassinations abroad.

Ford then created the Rockefeller Commission to undertake a private investigation of the charges. After the Vice President's group was formed, Congress quickly established committees to look into the same allegations.

Colby decided that he would beat Ford and Congress to the punch. He disclosed the agency's "skeletons" to Ford himself. These secret files revealed details of illegal CIA activities during the 1950s and 1960s. This included a revelation that was a sure public shocker—that the CIA had plotted the assassinations of Fidel Castro and Marxist leader Patrice Lumumba of the Belgian Congo. Colby also confirmed that the agency had operated unlawfully within the United States, opening private mail, investigating reporters who had published leaked information that had been classified, engaging in electronic eavesdropping, and other invasions of privacy.

Colby's strategy was brilliant. He would go public with the revelations, appealing to fair-minded members of Congress and the American people to understand the shadowy world in which the CIA operated. He knew the Rockefeller Commission report, which would go to the President, could not long remain confidential. Colby and the agency would be seen as coming clean. He would be sacrificing his career, but it was dead anyway.

In the course of carrying out this strategy, Colby not only turned the other cheek to his attackers in Congress but went one crucial step further: He joined them. Colby mentally abandoned the agency to which he had given his entire career and was still directing—indeed, had risked his life for—for a mess of questionable motives.

Step by step, like a man confessing the sins of a lifetime, Colby began to disavow what he saw as sins of the Silent Service. In doing so, he dismantled its tradition of secrecy. Colby thought that Congress should be allowed into the innermost chambers of intelligence. This would protect our elected representatives from future embarrassments like assassination plots. The agency would also be protected. If Congress knew, both operations and bureaucratic asses would be covered.

Colby had found the CIA a new place in the cold—a calculated distance between the White House and Congress. This would isolate the agency from presidents like

Nixon, who had pushed the CIA into illegal domestic activities. But presidents Kennedy and Johnson had operated similarly with federal agencies.

The CIA chief apparently thought he had seen the handwriting on the wall when Congress passed the Hughes-Ryan Amendment in 1974. That statute forbade the agency from engaging in covert operations without informing eight different congressional committees. This meant that more than 160 members, plus staff members, would know of any secret operation. With a total of some 200 people in the know, leaks were as certain as sunrise.

I never understood how a circumspect man like Colby could cave in to so many big mouths in Congress. Members themselves openly admitted the Hill could not keep a secret, even to protect the lives of Americans engaged in dangerous secret missions. I made my disagreement with Colby and my disapproval of Congress's encroachment on these covert activities crystal clear. The CIA took another route: The agency simply didn't undertake missions that could be blown by Congress. That meant it put important covert operations in cold storage. The result was an absurd shackling of the CIA.

In fairness to Colby, the times had targeted him and the agency. Congress was marching on the White House to capture presidential territory because Nixon had left the office weakened. In the minds of some Democrats, the Oval Office was almost defenseless. Ford was trying to distance himself from the CIA and certain other agencies because Nixon had made improper use of them.

If one man is responsible for the increasing congressional challenge to the prerogatives and power of the presidency, it is Nixon. His ironic legacy was to destroy the protective gates of the White House itself.

Colby argued that the separation of powers gave Congress the right to be much more aware of intelligence actions. He also implicitly maintained that the American people had a right to know more of what their government was doing.

However, Colby never adequately addressed the constitutional question regarding congressional invasion of presidential power. Nor did he deal with the major problem of leaks. Neither Colby nor Congress answered other important questions: How many in Congress should be trusted with the nation's top secrets? Who in the White House and other parts of the executive branch, including the CIA, should share which secrets?

If America had not yet come to terms with spying, at least one man had—Helms. He maintained that the country should keep its secrets. Helms thus contradicted Colby's conclusion before the Church committee and other investigations. Helms would batten down the agency's hatches, letting it be known that extensive public disclosure could neutralize the agency's effectiveness and endanger its people.

Colby's premise that the CIA could deal its secrets to Congress in exchange for its protection was unacceptable to Helms. He had had just as much personal conflict over that crucial question as Colby but had come to a completely different conclusion. Although he was no Boy Scout, Helms was just as principled as Colby. His moral strength came from his fierce loyalty to the agency, its mission, and its people.

Helms and I were of the old school. If intelligence was to be effective, it had to be secret. On July 26, 1777, George Washington wrote to Col. Elias Dayton, "For upon Secrecy, Success depends in most Enterprises of the kind, and for want of it, they are generally defeated, however well planned and promising a favorable issue."

By virtue of his office and the power granted him by the Constitution, the President, as commander in chief, is the source and protector of this trust. He should consult with Congress and, indeed, trust certain members with the nation's most important secrets. But that trust, to be assured, must be restricted to a handful of members of both parties. A bipartisan foreign policy could thus be developed and continuously maintained. If internal conflict about a serious national security development were to arise, those trusted elected officials could consult with other appropriate Americans in and out of government.

Instead, Colby was in a mood to give Congress its way. I was not then and am not today. Colby was a compromiser, as the national mood then seemed to demand. The director thus broke the agency's code of silence and publicly damned its traditions in the process.

Colby says he acted on behalf of the separation of powers. I question whether that is an accurate description of his actions. I don't believe he had the right or duty to pose as a mediator while actually running interference for Congress in the dispute over who was to manage our intelligence activities. Colby has shifted ground a bit on congressional oversight. He recently told me, "I would be happy to see the present two congressional committees involved in oversight of the CIA boiled down to one—a joint committee of the Senate and House. To as few people as possible. I believe it would be a mistake to go back to the old days of Senator Russell. But I think it's very useful for Barry Goldwater to say, 'Now, wait a minute. Let's not go too far.' "

Helms has a much more direct approach: "You can't keep secrets with the present system. The whole ship of state leaks. Leaks are one of the five most critical problems before the nation. It's not important who leaks— Congress, the administration or anyone else. The real issue is that the officials charged with this trust must work out a system of checks and balances whereby they are actually accountable for the confidence placed in them."

One way to discourage leaks would be to force leakers to resign from the intelligence committees. This occurred, in effect, in the case of the Democratic senator from Vermont, Patrick Leahy. His colleagues were furious with him, and he resigned in the face of probable committee action after it was disclosed that he had leaked secret intelligence committee material to "NBC News." Leahy had voted with his colleagues not to release the information. So it was a real double cross. If an offense is sufficiently serious, I believe Congress should remove the violators from office, and, in some cases, jail them. If the President is not above the law, as so many legislators remind us, neither are members of Congress.

Helms is pessimistic. He told me that nothing would be done about the leaks until the United States suffers a disaster, something that shakes the Republic to its foundations:

"You don't have fellows like Senator Russell and Representative George Mahon in Congress anymore, men who were confident of who and what they were. They didn't feel they had to make political hay out of our secrets or a lot of other things that came down the political road. It's a rat race up on Capitol Hill today. Everybody is competing with everybody else. The senior men don't stand out as primarily interested in the Republic. Hell, no. These fellows think about what's good for them. When the country is mentioned, it's in terms of interest groups—real estate operators, investment bankers, a P A C, or some other group.

"Patriotism has slipped. Look at the number of American spies we are turning up—and for paltry sums of money in some cases. A minimum sense of patriotism would have prevented that. Take a hard look at what is happening in this country. Be my guest."

Colby, Helms, and I clearly agree on one point: The most important basic problems facing U.S. intelligence agencies today are not the Soviet KGB or other enemies abroad. They are the leaks and the American media's recurrent publication and airing of top military and other highly classified material that allows our national security to be compromised. Congress alone is not to be blamed. The executive branch is also guilty.

Colby was outraged when, in 1986, a detailed description of how this country had built the new American Stealth bomber appeared in print. The disclosure was the start of a major struggle that is now arising over specific media revelations that many of us see as compromising the national interest. There is an epidemic of leaks in Washington, as Woodward himself admits in his book.

The arrogance with which many in the media defend their position favoring disclosure has not diminished. They insist that the media have the right under the First Amendment to publish even top secret projects. The claim that they are somehow the major inheritors of our most basic freedoms is inherently false. The situation calls out for some of us to knock some constitutional sense into them. The media have effectively become the fourth branch of government, yet there is no provision for outside checks and balances on them. This has not worked, and it never will.

It's clear that the media's First Amendment chorus rings more hollowly across the country with each passing year. Millions of Americans are waiting for an opportunity to take the media on.

The issue may well become the fiercest fight in the history of media-government relations. We will see whether the media's uncompromising but tired defense—that it's the government's responsibility to protect secrets and the media's duty to reveal them—is correct. The government is now burdened with virtually all the responsibilities while the media enjoy most of the rights.

If it's our duty to protect those secrets, let's be a great deal tougher about it. A 1950 federal law makes it illegal to publish classified material on communication intelligence and provides criminal penalties for anyone who does so. The law is not being invoked for several reasons. The major one is that the same government leaders and others who would bring such charges are the ones doing the leaking. Some have formed arrangements with newsmen to obtain favorable treatment. Others are concerned that if they get tough on the law, the media will attack them.

I favor using that law as a starting point and changing it to penalize those who leak to the media as well. The law would be toughened to ensure that those peddling classified information would pay an increasingly higher price.

The business and sport of Washington is talking, night and day. The nation's capital is the Hoover Dam of leaks. I have long said there are more leaks in Washington than in Anheuser-Busch's biggest men's room. If any spy wants to know what is going on, all he has to do is frequent the bars around Capitol Hill and elsewhere and he will go home loaded with inside information. No law will entirely end the leaks.

I am not blaming the media for all the leaks. I do not, for example, blame Woodward or the Washington *Post* for the disclosures on the CIA. It appears painfully obvious that some people both in and out of government spilled their guts. Our first and foremost aim must be to stop the leaks within government. The only way I know how to do that is by law, with severe penalties.

Stopping the leaks means changing the character of Washington. Yet we are obliged as a nation and a people to try to do it. If we are to institute stiff prison and other penalties, the media and most liberals will begin a knockdown fight. Good. Let's go to it. The American people should know more about leaks.

No self-respecting conservative could pass up such a glorious showdown. I will be there swinging at the leakers in government and the media with everything I have left in my weary old bones. With my new artificial right knee, I'm more mobile for a fight, and my trusty cane is also ready!

This battle originated in the past. My recollection of events during the mid-1970s summarizes the first big struggle in Congress over the direction of U.S. intelligence. To me, Colby's attitude was just one example of the sad direction we had taken. Watergate and Vietnam had been used as crosses for a national crucifixion. To me, they were more like two thieves who had robbed the national treasury.

The country was filled with self-seekers and weak sisters—like so many street people and draft dodgers—who masqueraded under the banner of righteous dissent. We heard a new language—values, life-style, pop culture, counterculture, charismatic communication—the speech of a new and selfish generation.

Old-fashioned virtue, distinctions between right and wrong, were being ridiculed. For many, breaking the law had become their new Bill of Rights. Jane Fonda had gone to Hanoi to propagandize with the Communists and had become a liberal heroine. I believe she was a political whore.

Jimmy Doolittle and a lot of other guys with real guts were my heroes. I didn't believe God was dead. I still put my faith in country—and in the CIA, when the chips were down.

Jimmy Carter arrived in 1977 to let us know that we were being reborn under a messenger of God in the White House. He made it clear that Satan—"thieves and crooks" was the Oval Office expression—lived at the CIA's seven-story headquarters in Langley, Virginia. Carter appointed Admiral Stansfield Turner to cut the devil's fangs. That became Turner's First Commandment.

If Carter handed Turner the knife, Vice President Walter Mondale twisted it. Mondale detested the CIA. That was evident to me as I watched him in Intelligence Committee work. Mondale pushed Turner behind the scenes into what eventually became a massacre of some of the agency's best and brightest people.

Another wrecking crew was Ambassador Andrew Young and his "Manson family" at the United Nations in New York. Young had no use for the FBI and such agencies. That was because former FBI director J. Edgar Hoover had investigated Young, Dr. Martin Luther King, and other black leaders of the civil rights movement. Young's hatred had become pathological. CIA agents called his staff the "Manson family," referring to the drug-crazed California mass killers, because they believed their behavior at the United Nations was crazy. Our U.N. delegation often contradicted and sniped at U.S. policy while enjoying diplomatic life on Uncle Sam's payroll. They portrayed the CIA, for example, as bad guys who violated human rights. As a CIA agent once put it to me, "Young's people were leftovers from the hippie generation. They were what some of us called 'looney tunes.' "

Turner became the most distrusted CIA director in my thirty years in the Senate. I never met a man in the agency who felt he could rely on him. In the guise of ridding the CIA of deadwood and upgrading the agency's technical intelligence, Turner established his rotten reputation by cutting the throat of the CIA's clandestine service. Some 200 longtime covert operators' jobs were abolished. More than 600 others engaged in espionage activities were shoved out on the street. These were not "rogue elephants" of the Church era or break-in artists of Nixon's time. Turner was getting rid of the intellectual cadre, the brains of the CIA. These were people with insight into our enemies' strategy and capabilities. Turner castrated the clandestine service.

The White House word to me and others on Capitol Hill was that the agency had gotten too fat during the Vietnam War. It was necessary to cut back.

I didn't believe a word of it because Turner had already begun attempting to micromanage—politicize professional findings is a more accurate description—the assessment process among the agency's analytical corps. This told me a lot about Turner, because these professionals represented the highest cadre of government official in Washington. Their level of education exceeded that of any other department or agency. That included the State Department, which has always falsely claimed to be our elite. Even the superelite at State fall short of the academic credentials of these analysts. Also, these CIA professionals were appointed after objective criteria exams, while many of State's employees are simply members of the Foreign Service old boy network.

Turner was distrusted not only because he was a "political" director but because he did not accept the methods and men of the CIA. He not only substituted technological for human intelligence but instituted regular polygraph tests to determine the honesty of his people. The admiral had lost faith in them as human beings, and they lost confidence in him as their director. Many middle management officers no longer saw the agency as an elite breed. In all the turmoil created by Carter, Mondale, and Turner, they came to view it as just another bureaucratic colony at the mercy of those in power. Hundreds resigned.

President Carter and Turner also severely questioned CIA ethics and its secrecy. They were undermining the major reason for the existence of the agency. The CIA was built on this simple but enormously strong foundation: Intelligence can help us avoid major conflict. That is the major reason why I have been such a loyal supporter of the CIA.

No one can tell us how many American lives the agency may have saved. Certainly hundreds of thousands of young Americans did not have to go to war because the CIA was able to provide critical, timely information to our leaders about the intentions of our enemies. I know firsthand that the CIA has done extraordinary work during my many years of being associated with U.S. intelligence work. Its story—its own defense—can never be adequately explained for obvious reasons.

Let me try to show with a single example how the Carter administration failed the CIA. On November 4, 1979, the Ayatollah Khomeini's militants occupied the U.S. embassy in Teheran and seized sixty-nine hostages. That number was later reduced to fifty-three when they released some women and blacks. These diplomats were held for 444 days. Not a single American CIA operative was then on the scene in Iran to help Carter and Washington in their struggle to free the hostages. It was an ironic, incredible intelligence disaster. I believe, in significant measure, that wiping out the clandestine service cost Carter the presidency.

There was another irony to all this. Billy Carter, the President's opportunistic brother, flew to Libya to consort with Moammar Khadaffy as an honored guest of his poisonous regime. I don't pretend to know much about the Libyan government "loans" to Billy, but they looked more like gifts to many people—or, to put it more bluntly, bribes. I do know that Senator Birch Bayh, an Indiana Democrat who was charged with investigating Billygate in the Senate, got cold feet and iced the inquiry. He got a lot of hot letters from angry constituents and was subsequently upset in a bid for reelection.

Let's face it, Democrats do not investigate Democrats. They investigate Ronald Reagan, Judge Robert Bork, and Oliver North. They don't investigate House Speaker Jim Wright and his deep involvement in the Texas savings and loan scandal, nor how many times Delaware Senator Joseph Biden has lied about his life.

When Ronald Reagan became President in 1981 and the Republicans took over control of the Senate, I became chairman of the Senate Select Committee on Intelligence. One of the first things I did was write a letter to its members. It said, in part, "I believe the committee has to be non-political. This is the reason I haven't moved in and fired all the Democrats and replaced them with Republicans. . . . I want to repeat that Democrat or Republican doesn't make a darn bit of difference. . . . Some staff will be replaced but not on a partisan, political basis. I have always believed that our major job is to oversee the intelligence community and to do everything in our power to improve that community, but I don't intend to make a political community of it for one moment. I will not tolerate politics on the part of staff members, and I would implore members of the committee themselves not to take advantage of an eager press to make political brownie points out of the work of the committee. . . ."

I met with Senator Pat Moynihan and told the New York Democrat that I meant what I said in the letter. Although he was vice chairman of the committee, I considered him an equal. My secrets would be his secrets and vice versa. He would preside over the committee when I was not present. I told him that the country came first and our parties second—or even third if things got real hot. Pat is a very partisan guy, but the big Irishman loved the idea. It was kind of mystical to him. "Bipartisan" did not have the ring of poetry, but I could see that Pat was humming it, trying the word out, to see if the syllables had any decent lilt.

He rose with a roguish smile. We were marching in step like McNamara's Band. There was a certain irony in the thought. Yes, Moynihan said with a rise in his deep voice, there was a clear, statesmanlike ring to it all. It would do nicely, indeed.

Of course, I mentioned as casually as an old Arizona desert rat could that CIA director William Casey would at times give the committee highly sensitive information. That would be kept between the chairman and vice chairman—alone. There would be no leaks. I paused. Pat smiled just enough to let me see he agreed. I told him that before any highly classified material would be passed on to all members, both of us would have to agree there was some urgent and compelling reason for them to know. Moynihan nodded solemnly. He was liking things better every moment and had to repress a smile. In the four years we worked together, we never passed along the most sensitive information to the rest of the committee. This compartmentalization worked well.

Moynihan couldn't resist trying to putter at some politics on occasion, and he relished being acting chairman when I was away. Once or twice I hadn't even left town but had only gone to Walter Reed Hospital for checkups. Right away Pat was on the phone to Committee Staff Director Robert "Rob" Simmons. He told Rob that he had taken charge and began issuing a stream of instructions.

I was told by committee staffers that Pat and his minority staff sat around his office some evenings, plotting how to outflank Goldwater on certain issues. I found, nevertheless, that Moynihan was rather reliable, once he abandoned partisanship.

On one occasion, Pat was—as Irish Catholics like him often put it—the very rock of St. Peter himself. His hour came after a dramatic announcement on the Senate floor.

In April 1984 Senator Biden said the CIA had been directly involved in the mining of Nicaraguan harbors. I understood that the Contras—not the agency—had mined three harbors, the Atlantic port of El Bluff and the Pacific ports of Corinto and Puerto Sandino. I stood on the floor and said that, as Senate Intelligence Committee chairman, I had no knowledge of any such CIA activity and therefore did not believe the charge to be true.

Although the document was not marked classified, I began reading from a secret report on the matter. Contrary to Woodward's assertion, staff director Rob Simmons did not rush on the floor and rip it from my hands. He told Maine Senator Bill Cohen what was happening. Cohen quietly advised me to halt the speech. I did immediately. And for the first and only time in my three decades in the Senate, I had the record expunged so as not to disclose any secrets.

I returned to my office and met Simmons. He insisted that neither Bill Casey nor his deputy, John J. McMahon, had ever made such a disclosure to us.

I was uneasy. Casey had never been comfortable with Congress. He distrusted some members and disliked dealing with them. I had known Bill a very long time, and in all those years, that's the way he played the game much of the time. He would withhold facts when it was in his interest. Putting it bluntly, if Bill believed in something, he often did what he damn well pleased.

The reason Casey disliked and distrusted Congress was that he saw us as meddling in intelligence. For the most part, I agreed with him. He knew that. There were just too damn many leakers on Capitol Hill. However, he was not above the law which required congressional oversight. My own hope and aim was to change the law to allow less congressional intrusion. Casey just said to hell with Congress. He would find a way around us. I phoned him on various occasions and raised the roof with him. Bill would mumble and stumble around, but I knew he was going to march his own way.

Members of the Intelligence Committee used to laugh when Casey was scheduled to testify before us. While waiting for Bill to arrive, I would often do an imitation of him. I called Casey "Flappy" because both his mouth and arms flapped when he wanted to make a point. He would be like a kid blowing bubbles real fast or imitating a repeater water pistol. His mouth would spray in all directions. It was a mistake, however, to sell him short. That was his game, mumble and spray. Much of the time, I never knew what the hell he was talking about. Neither did anyone else on the committee. That was just the way Bill wanted it. Yet many of us admired him for his bedrock devotion to this country.

I had pushed Reagan hard to make Admiral Bobby Inman, former deputy director of the CIA, head of the agency. He had more than twenty years' experience in various aspects of intelligence. He was the first to learn that Billy Carter was playing footsie with Libya. Here was a government official who went directly to the FBI with his information, not to President Carter. Inman was a professional first and everything else second. He was one of the most brilliant men I had ever met in government. I told Reagan that. The President then said to me, "I don't care what you say, Barry. Bill Casey is going to head the CIA."

Reagan was adamant about Casey. He had a fierce loyalty to him. Bill felt the same way about the President. Woodward's claim that Casey told him that the President was lazy is beyond my comprehension. It's contrary to everything I know about Casey. Casey never knocked the President to anyone, and he certainly wouldn't do it to a reporter.

It would also have been highly uncharacteristic of Casey to admit to any newsman—Woodward claims it was to him—that he knew about the diversion of Iranian funds to the Contras.

It's also very hard for me to believe that Woodward got into Bill's room at Georgetown Hospital. If Mrs. Casey says that she or her daughter was in the room twenty-four hours a day during the entire time of Bill's illness, I believe them. I am also convinced that CIA security was good. Also, I was once a patient at the hospital, and my doctor ordered that no one could see me. No one got in.

Woodward has never personally told me a lie, and I respect his professional ability. But I believe it was impossible for anyone to have entered Casey's hospital room without the CIA and/or his wife or daughter knowing it.

If Woodward really did get in to interview Casey, this presents even greater problems. Was it right to put this pressure on a dying man? And can the testimony of a man as sick as Casey be relied upon? This is just not good reporting in any case—even if we accept the unlikely idea that Woodward actually talked with Casey as the CIA chief lay dying. If Mrs. Casey has no witness to categorically dispute Woodward's claim of an interview, neither has Woodward clearly confirmed it. In such circumstances, Woodward had a duty to prove that the interview took place and Casey's responses were sufficiently reasonable to be made public. He has not done that.

In any event, Reagan wouldn't listen to me on Casey. Bill was his man.

Inman always understood what Casey was up to. I said

to Bobby one day during a casual conversation, "I notice you often pull up your black socks when Casey is speaking with me or testifying before Congress. Why's that, Bobby?"

Inman looked at me as if I had just picked his pocket. Slowly, gauging how to phrase a delicate answer, he finally replied, "Well, I guess that's a habit of mine. Whenever Casey is not telling the truth or is getting something screwed up, I pull up my socks."

"Thanks, Bobby," I said, "that info may help me some day."

In any event, I wanted Simmons to find out what Casey was up to in the Nicaraguan mining affair. I told Rob to go over to the CIA and talk with Casey and McMahon as well as see whoever else was necessary to get the truth—and do it fast.

A few days later—it was a Friday afternoon—Rob returned to my office. I was alone, sitting at my desk, brooding. I was still trying to unravel the Nicaraguan mess. Only one small light was on. The fading afternoon light flickered through the window blinds. Rob sat down and faced me. His face was somber. He said, "The CIA was directly involved in the mining. Casey withheld the information from us. The President personally gave the go-ahead to start the mining in the fall of 1983. Casey and McMahon admitted it. They claim they told us."

I swallowed hard several times, but a lump kept popping up in my throat. I couldn't speak. I was devastated.

"Casey said he mentioned it in two hearings," Simmons continued. "I checked the record. In each case, Casey buried it in a single sentence near the end of more than fifty pages of testimony. He mentioned that mines had been laid at three Nicaraguan ports. But the reference was in the context of Contra activities and later Contra funding. There was nothing to indicate the CIA had laid the mines."

I lifted my hand, signaling him to stop for a moment, because a wave of bitterness began to surge through my mind. I started searching back three years. As chairman of Senate Intelligence, I had worked long and hard to restore the CIA. When the President and Casey wanted much more funding for the agency, I had been the one who put out the fires of opposition in the Senate and elsewhere. I had helped reduce the impact of the Hughes-Ryan amendment, which required that the CIA brief eight committees of the House and Senate on its covert actions. In a heated controversy, I had led the fight to reduce the eight committees to two. In exchange for the reduction, the Administration had agreed to keep the two committees fully informed in a timely manner about any "significant" covert operations. There was no question but that mining Nicaraguan harbors was "significant."

The Intelligence Oversight Act of 1980 had been signed by President Carter. It was one of his last acts in the Oval Office, and—to give him credit—it restored to the CIA the ability to conduct effective covert action. The act was clearly known to Casey, since he had discussed it in detail with our committee, and the law had to be known to President Reagan.

I had pulled Casey's nuts out of the fire on several occasions. One case had involved a public uproar about a Contra manual that appeared to support assassination. It hadn't been written by CIA personnel, nor did it have any Administration sanction. Casey ducked the publicity. Instead, the Administration asked that I go on television and defend it and the Contras. Casey even had some of his top people fly to my home in Phoenix to brief me while he laid low.

Contrary to Woodward's claim, I defended the ninety-page manual and the CIA. I explained that only a few passages had been singled out of the booklet, which had been written for men fighting a war. No one in the Administration or the CIA had written the text. The Contra cause was being wholly and wrongfully characterized in terms of assassination. The manual actually emphasized educating the Nicaraguan peasants about the Sandinista regime's Marxist goals.

On another occasion, when Casey needed help to protect the identities of our secret agents, I had fought to relieve the CIA from some provisions of the Freedom of Information Act. With those recollections still fresh, I turned to Simmons and said, "I feel like such a fool."

The President and Casey had known about the mining for more than six months. Yet their fellow Republican, the chairman of the Senate Intelligence Committee, had not been informed. Instead, he had learned it on the floor of the Senate from a Democrat. Not only Biden but Senator Leahy, another Democrat, knew of the CIA mining. Now I was being held up to ridicule as perhaps a liar and certainly uninformed by my own Administration. Finally, I said to Simmons, "I feel betrayed."

Simmons, a gentleman who bided his time and place, shot back, "The President and Casey didn't tell you because they knew you would try to talk them out of it. You would have said it was crazy and might even have publicly opposed them."

Such mining was tantamount to an act of war. International law is very clear on the point. Nicaragua is a coastal nation dependent on its harbors for food and other necessities of life. The purpose of covert action is to augment a clear and understood policy, not to put us in the doghouse.

After a weekend of reflection, I returned to the office on April 9 and sent this letter to Casey:

"All this past weekend, I've been trying to figure out how I can most easily tell you my feelings about the discovery of the President having approved mining some of the harbors of Central America.

"It gets down to one little, simple phrase: I am pissed off!

"I understand that you had briefed the House on this matter. Now, during the important debate we had last week and the week before on whether we would increase funds for the Nicaragua program, we were doing all right until a member of the committee charged that the President had approved the mining. I strongly denied that because I had never heard of it. I found out the next day that the CIA had, with the written approval of the President, engaged in such mining and the approval came in February!

"Bill, this is no way to run a railroad, and I find myself in a hell of a quandary. I am forced to apologize to members of the Intelligence Committee because I did not know the facts on this. At the same time, my counterpart in the House did know.

"The President has asked us to back his foreign policy. Bill, how can we back his foreign policy when we don't know what the hell he is doing? Lebanon, yes, we all knew that he sent troops over there. But mine the harbors in Nicaragua? This is an act violating international law. It is an act of war. For the life of me, I don't see how we are going to explain it.

"My guess is that the House is going to defeat this supplemental [request for Contra funds], and we will not be in any position to put up much of an argument after we were not given the information we were entitled to receive: particularly, if my memory serves me correctly, when you briefed us on Central America just a couple of weeks ago. And the order was signed just before that.

"I don't like this. I don't like it one bit from the President or from you. I don't think we need a lot of lengthy explanations. The deed has been done and in the future, if anything like this happens, I am going to raise one hell of a lot of fuss about it in public."

Someone leaked the letter to the Washington *Post,* where it appeared in full on April 11. The following day, Casey openly lied about the matter in the *CIA Employee Bulletin.* He claimed that press reports saying the agency had not briefed Congress on covert action programs in Central America were not true. The last line of the *Bulletin,* which he signed in his own handwriting and later apologized for, was outrageously false: "The agency has not only complied with the letter of the law in our briefings, but with the spirit of the law as well."

I was really steaming about Casey's disregard for the facts when Robert McFarlane, the President's assistant for national security affairs, bombed me at the U.S. Naval Academy in Annapolis. In a speech that was splashed across the front page of the Washington *Times,* McFarlane said that "every important detail" of the mining of Nicaraguan harbors had been "shared in full by the proper oversight committees." He told a large audience at a Navy foreign affairs conference that he could not account for why I didn't know of the CIA-led harbor minings.

I had flown to Taiwan just before the McFarlane speech. Pat Moynihan took charge of the Intelligence Committee. Pat went on ABC television and resigned as vice chairman of the committee to protest Casey's *Employee Bulletin* statement and McFarlane's address. He later described it to me with his inimitable flair: "When I read the newspaper account of McFarlane's speech, I said: 'Sonofabitch, he's calling Barry Goldwater a liar. It's not true. I'm acting head of this committee now. I'm going to tell the facts to David Brinkley on ABC. I'm not going to let this stand.' "

So Pat went on television and, putting up his political dukes, boomed that he would have no choice but to resign as vice chairman of the committee unless Casey and McFarlane retracted their statements. It was a bravissimo performance.

On April 25 Casey sent me a handwritten letter on CIA stationery. I still have it. The first sentence reads: "I'm as sorry as I can be about the misunderstandings and failure in communication which have developed to impair an activity which I thought we were handling well together."

It was about as close as Casey could come to an apology in an official letter. The following day, at a committee meeting, he apologized profusely for not keeping us properly informed.

We had heard nothing from McFarlane, so after the Casey retreat I wrote him a letter challenging his statements at Annapolis. On May 9, writing on White House stationery marked CONFIDENTIAL in red stencil, McFarlane replied that, at the time he had given the speech, "I had been advised that the material had been adequately addressed. I so stated this in my remarks." That is a bureaucrat in top form.

McFarlane well knew his statements would make us look like jackasses. Under the moral pressure of my note to him, he finally wrote us an antiseptic response that could have been read six different ways over a two-minute breakfast. By marking it CONFIDENTIAL, he implicitly asked us to remain silent. Moynihan told me that McFarlane had later confided to him, "I fear that what I was told was either disingenuous or outright wrong."

He apparently believed Casey had misled him.

My disagreements with Bill still flared up from time to time. Trouble seemed to dog Casey everywhere. On several occasions, allegations about past financial irregularities swept him into the headlines, compromising his authority at the CIA. Since he never appeared to be able to put these charges behind him and controversy seemed to be his middle name, I finally blew my stack and called for his resignation. I was simply tired of all the fights he was getting into, almost every week.

Then, just as suddenly, he would become the white knight. I remember distinctly the time Casey signed an agreement that he would inform the Senate and House Intelligence Committees promptly on any future significant covert operations. He met with Moynihan and me after the Nicaraguan mining flap. I could tell Bill didn't want to sign it because he kept looking into the distance and wouldn't touch his pen. Here was an old wild horse who didn't want to be broken. I could see the pain in his eyes, the fear of what was happening to him. When he finally signed, he immediately dropped the pen as if it had been poisoned. He shook his head and tried to smile at the same time. Bill wasn't happy, but he could take his medicine.

Despite our disagreements, I liked Casey. There was, contrary to what some claim, never a feud between us. Nor did we have any differences going back to his 1966 race for Congress, when he was defeated in the GOP primary by a Goldwaterite. I never even knew the man who ran against him. I liked Bill because we were cut from the same cloth—stubborn, bullheaded men who knew what we wanted and fought for it. Actually, when both of us were calm, we got along like partners in a million-dollar deal. At the end, I don't believe Casey had a better friend on the Hill than me.

To show what an upside-down, inside-out town Washington is from one season to another, the CIA eventually presented Moynihan and me with fine tributes and the Agency Seal Medallion. It meant, in effect, that they were handing us back our white hats.

It's important to recall the details of the mining incident because it's an example of the President's knowledge and approval of a very questionable operation. Also, it exposes attempts by Casey and McFarlane to protect the Administration and their own involvement by trying to shift the responsibility to Congress. More significant, the incident shows that the seeds for the Iran-Contra fiasco had been sown long before the affair occurred.

It is not easy to achieve the proper balance of governmental authority, as the events surrounding our public division over Nicaragua show. To put the debate in its rawest form, most Republicans support President Reagan's policy, which rests on the expressed purpose of denying the Soviet Union, Cuba, and other Communist governments another base in the Western hemisphere. The GOP aims to remove the threat of an inflexibly Communist Sandinista regime. Most Democrats claim the President's policies risk war. They maintain we should seek to end our differences with the Sandinistas by negotiation.

Today our two major political parties still have little confidence in one another's policies. The Democrats have decided that the most effective way for them to halt President Reagan's help to the Contras is to challenge and limit it. That is the real struggle. The Democrats, who control both houses, want to substitute the judgment of Congress for that of the President. To do that, they have to tip the balance of power. Though the liberals will not admit it, they effectively want to change the Constitution.

I believe that Reagan made serious errors in mining the harbors of Nicaragua and selling arms to the Iranian terrorists, even to obtain the release of American hostages. But these are not sufficient reasons to limit or change the President's constitutional authority or responsibility. On a practical level, without Reagan's support of the Contras, there would never have been Sandinista concessions to a regional peace plan.

The real issue is how to establish the understanding and trust that is essential if both the executive and legislative branches of government are to fulfill their distinct duties under the Constitution's separation of powers.

Edward Boland, a distinctly partisan House Democrat from Massachusetts, is at the center of this constitutional conflict. As chairman of the House Intelligence Committee, he was the author of the Boland amendments. The original legislation was passed in December 1982 and has been rewritten five times since then. It forbids the CIA and the Defense Department to fund military equipment, training, advice, or other support directed at overthrowing the Sandinista regime. The term "overthrowing" was never defined. That is important, since other Contra actions were thereby permitted. People have said to me: "How can you pick on gentlemanly Ed Boland and constantly refer to him as a partisan Democrat? He's no more partisan than you are. He always puts the country first."

Well now, let's see about that. During the same year in which Congress first approved the Boland measure, I was deeply involved in trying to obtain funding for a sophisticated new technology that could help us enormously in detecting significant military movements behind the Iron Curtain. However, Republican House colleagues told me Boland would not allow the plan out of his committee for floor approval. This was despite the fact that they had told him the new system would represent a major breakthrough in intelligence collection. I and others worked hard and the money was approved by the Senate, but Boland sat on his hands. We met in conference.

I made a short speech in the closed door session, saying that the new system would revolutionize U.S. intelligence collection for at least a decade. Boland spoke for about twenty minutes. He attacked the program, saying it would have big cost overruns, and strongly suggested that some technical problems, still to be worked out, could not be overcome. I was taken aback at his argument because of the enormous military advantage to the Western allies with such a breakthrough. It might even prevent war.

I explained that cost overruns could amount to perhaps $200 million at most. Such overruns were hardly new, but the amount was a pittance compared to the program's vast potential. Indeed, it would greatly bolster the defense of Western Europe at a time when Russian and other Communist troops greatly outnumbered those of the Western allies. As far as problems were concerned, every new technological system faces such barriers. There was nothing new or unusual about that. Every member of both parties finally agreed to support the plan—except Boland. He was adamant.

I quietly played my trump card. I told Boland I was going to take a walk and see Senator John Tower about getting the money. He didn't understand what I meant. I advised him that, as chairman of the Senate Armed Services Committee, Tower could have the funds appropriated as part of military spending. Boland squinted but said nothing. I rose from my seat. He quickly protested, saying I was undercutting the authority of the Intelligence Committees. I replied that it didn't bother me a whit. I was concerned about the security of the country. Boland asked me to sit down. The debate continued for another ten minutes. Boland finally said he could not agree to the funding. I got up, and Boland began sputtering something about where was I going. I muttered, "I'm going to see Tower" and walked out. Boland turned to Rob Simmons, our staff director, and asked, "Is he really going to see Tower?"

Simmons answered, "I assume so. He doesn't bluff."

"But he's undercutting us!" Boland stammered.

Simmons responded, "I really don't think he cares."

I walked over to see Tower, who was holding a committee meeting. I went in, sat down, and waited for the conference to break up so I could speak with him privately. About ten minutes later, Simmons slipped in a back door and crept up to a seat next to me. He said, "Boland backed off. They've all accepted your position."

I didn't say anything, just smiled. The program was saved, and it's still going on. The Russians are much the worse off for it.

I know that Ed Boland is a good American. But his amendments represent strict Democratic Party positions. Ed lived too long with Tip O'Neill, who was so partisan he thought U.S. taxes were part of the Democrats' party treasury.

The various changes in the Boland amendment are reflected in major modifications of aid to the Contras from its 1982 passage to the present. The Democrats want the country to believe that Reagan and the Administration violated the Hill's budget mandate. That's nonsense. Even a cursory reading of the public record shows that Congress flip-flopped on aid to the Contras, first approving military and intelligence support, then reversing itself. Even when aid to the Contras had been approved,

Congress constantly changed the amounts and conditions under which the money could be used.

The Democrats wanted to keep the Contras alive with a minimum of funds but increase appropriations when it appeared the freedom fighters might collapse. The American people and the Contras themselves have watched one funding crisis after another. If any one characteristic describes congressional policy regarding the Soviet-Cuban presence in Nicaragua, it is a lack of continuity. Ambivalence has long been the centerpiece of the Democratic majority's view of Nicaragua and all of Central America. The result is that Congress has copped out on its limited responsibilities and thus put pressure on the Reagan administration to go it alone in Central America.

This created the rise of North, Poindexter, and others involved in the transfer of Iranian funds to the Contras. Casey saw no way to deal with Congress's contradictions other than to go around them. Bill thus went directly to Poindexter and then North to launch new ways to keep the Contras alive.

I don't think the subsequent Iran-Contra hearings accomplished a damn thing except to harm Reagan's presidency. I've tried to look at them objectively. I believe the President did know of the diversion of Iranian funds to the Contras. If he knew about the sale of weapons to an enemy country and various ways in which Americans were aiding the Contras, Reagan knew about the transfer of funds. He had to know. The White House explanation makes him out to be either a liar or incompetent. There's evidence that some of the President's top aides were incompetent. They were supposed to have their fingers on every button, but some of them, like Don Regan, the former White House chief of staff, clearly didn't.

I warned the President when he mentioned to me privately in January 1986 that he wanted to "get closer to the moderate forces in Iran." I said, "Mr. President, there are no moderate forces in Iran. They're all dead or have fled the country."

Unfortunately, I believe that the Iran-Contra crisis cost Ronald Reagan the chance to be among the greatest presidents of this century. History will judge him much more harshly because of that unfortunate episode. The selling of arms to terrorist Iran unquestionably did the President irreparable harm. He will never regain his former stature. Now I think history will give him a passing grade—in some instances, such as domestic politics, an outstanding mark—but not the credit he deserves overall.

Reagan hurt himself by some of his top staff choices. Chief of staff Regan, as well as Poindexter and others, were among the worst I've seen in Washington. The President was not well served.

The biggest loser in the Iran-Contra mess has been Congress. The reason is that it was so hypocritical in its questioning of North and others while never accepting any blame for its own funding contradictions and other failures.

The immediate reason for the Iran arms deal was to get CIA Station Chief William Buckley out of captivity. Soon after Buckley's capture by Mideast terrorists, Casey came privately to Senate Intelligence and begged us to help him with funds to free Buckley. He made it clear that the Administration would go to extraordinary lengths to free the veteran CIA chief because he had considerable intelligence background on Mideast terrorism and our efforts to halt it. Buckley was tortured to death to pry those secrets from him. Stung by Buckley's death, the President and Casey kept the deal alive to secure the release of other hostages. The Iran moderates were only a secondary consideration.

Senate Intelligence lost nine senior committee members at the end of 1984. The members' tenure was limited to eight years of consecutive service. I moved to Senate Armed Services, and the new bunch, led by Durenberger and Leahy, was unable to keep up with the fast-moving Casey. Bill was a terrifically hard worker, and they simply fell behind him. That is one of the major reasons why the whole Iran-Contra affair got out of hand. Casey was involved in so many activities that Durenberger and Leahy were unable to hop and skip with his many leaps and bounds. He also avoided the two because of what some in the intelligence community viewed as Durenberger's lack of personal stability and Leahy's weakness for leaking. These critical aspects were never brought out at the Iran-Contra hearings because they reflected negatively on the committee. The Democrats wanted to bash the President, never revealing why Casey felt he had to outrun and outfox them. Casey never revealed publicly his mistrust of Durenberger and Leahy.

In reflecting on the Nicaraguan mining episode and the Iran-Contra affair, I believe this country needs to accomplish two major goals:

(1) Define the precise responsibilities of the President and Congress in foreign policy and intelligence. This will require going to the U.S. Supreme Court.

(2) Spell out and agree on the extent of secrecy in covert operations. This would include severe penalties, including removal from office and/or sentencing to prison, for anyone in Congress or the executive branch who breaks the new law.

The aim is to create an atmosphere of clear understanding and genuine trust between the two branches.

If we do not accomplish these aims, more of the same policy problems and errors on both sides are inevitable. As it stands, in my opinion, we are headed for a national catastrophe.

The American people do indeed have a right to know what their government is doing, but the government also has a legitimate need and right to guard state secrets. The Democrats have to stop their self-righteous posturing, especially their insistence on full disclosure of covert operations to Congress. They seem to believe that any operation is questionable or even evil unless it is blessed by the full membership of the two committees. The implication is that no one can be trusted but Congress, yet Congress has repeatedly violated that confidence.

I was not surprised when Senator Leahy leaked secret Senate Intelligence Committee material to "NBC News." His reputation as a leaker was already well established. In October 1985 Leahy requested a special private briefing from the CIA involving the hijackers of the *Achille Lauro*. It was a short-notice request, but the CIA complied because Leahy was committee vice chairman.

The reason soon became apparent. Leahy rode out to CIA headquarters in a CBS silver stretch limousine. It waited for him, and, after the briefing, Leahy was immediately driven to the CBS Bureau in Washington, where he appeared on network news. Leahy revealed that, despite a statement by President Hosni Mubarak that the hijackers had left Egypt, U.S. intelligence knew they were still being detained there. By leaking that information, Leahy disclosed that we had penetrated the highest levels of the Egyptian government. The disclosure substantiated what I and others who had been associated with the committee already knew—that not all its members could be trusted.

Leahy was an especially egregious case. The New Englander flagrantly used his place on the committee to help himself get reelected. It was a despicable performance, especially since we had agreed as a body not to use the committee for political purposes. Nor were the Republicans blameless. Durenberger also had a reputation as a blabbermouth and had been investigated for other leaks. Also on the GOP side, an aide to Wyoming Senator Malcolm Wallop was disciplined in connection with a leak. Any member of the Intelligence Committees, plus dozens of their staffers, can blow a secret operation for any political or other reason.

Other major congressional leaks included our knowledge of a 1984 New Delhi plan to strike at Pakistan's nuclear facility, China's transfer to Pakistan of vital atomic bomb technology, a secret CIA plan to undermine the Khadaffy regime in Libya, and revelations by the House which gave the Russians and others detailed knowledge about deployment and other problems with our new MX strategic nuclear weapons.

House Democrats used classified information from secret CIA briefings to gain public support for their views about Nicaragua. Incidentally, they never informed Republican colleagues of what they were about to do. The Democrats disclosed that the agency had concluded that the Contras could not defeat the Sandinistas. Only the use of American troops could affect the military outcome.

The CIA was right in saying the Contras couldn't win. That conclusion was based, however, on the vacillating and limited backing Congress was willing to give the freedom fighters. I and others strongly believed—and do today—that the Contras can be victorious if we support them with sufficient military hardware and other backing.

I am not suggesting the use of any U.S. troops in that support. Nevertheless, if Nicaragua or any other Central American nation were clearly dominated by Cuba or the Soviet Union as a base exporting revolution, I would send American troops there to deny communism further subversive footholds in the hemisphere. We cannot risk more Cubas at our back door.

Former CIA director Turner has admitted that President Carter delayed notifying Congress about three secret CIA operations in Iran. Carter wanted to restrict information about the initiatives because he didn't trust members to keep them quiet.

Even Ed Boland, as House Intelligence chairman, accused his Democratic colleagues in 1985 of "regularly and recklessly commenting on intelligence matters."

In all these horror stories, I know of no one in Congress with more contempt for his colleagues and the concept of trust than Representative Stephen Solarz, a Brooklyn Democrat. His rush to publicize himself beyond Flatbush was exceeded only by his speed to disclose confidential information that might hurt the GOP. Solarz descended to one of his neighborhood sewers in December 1986 after Bill Casey testified on behalf of the CIA for more than five hours before a closed door session of the House Foreign Affairs Committee. No sooner had the session ended than Solarz appeared before waiting television cameras. He announced that, based on Casey's testimony, it was now "absolutely clear" that a "higher authority" had approved the diversion of Iran arms-sale profits to Nicaraguan Contras. That authority was "almost certainly" President Reagan.

Contrary to Solarz, only two things were "absolutely clear"—that he had betrayed the confidence of the CIA director and his colleagues and that his judgment was, to say the least, premature. Other committee members, including Democrats, agreed there had been nothing in Casey's testimony to support Solarz' conclusion about the President. Members of both houses and parties were outraged by his contemptible conduct.

Not only did Solarz violate confidentiality in speaking, but he or another member of the committee may have leaked extensive parts of Casey's testimony to the Washington *Post.* The *Post* ran excerpts of Casey's remarks in the next day's editions. This was the same Solarz who regularly lectured the Administration on the morality of its foreign policy. He has a strange notion of ethics and honor.

The Solarz incident came during my final days in the Senate. It was a real downer because some of us had long tried to instill a sense of bipartisanship in the conduct of our intelligence and foreign policy. The episode is an example of how much the caliber of congressmen has degenerated over the past three decades.

Some claim there is an inherent contradiction between secrecy and democracy. Yet England has managed to be a free and democratic country for centuries while keeping its national secrets. The free world certainly believed it necessary to maintain secrets during World War II to preserve the democratic values for which it was fighting.

I have never understood how Congress and the executive branch can expect foreign governments, our own agents, our military, and others to trust the CIA and other intelligence agencies when we have so many leaks. Corrective action must be taken.

The present two intelligence committees and their staffs should be combined into one. In 1984 I spoke in the Senate against such a joint committee. I then disagreed with the claim that Congress could not keep a secret. However, the astonishing rise in leaks over the last four years has caused me to change my mind. Leaks are now so pervasive that we will be forced to reduce the numbers of those who know any classified information.

A total of only four members—two in the House and two in the Senate—should be fully briefed by the President, his national security chief, and/or the CIA director. I would not include the majority and minority leaders. The entire joint committee should be made aware of top secrets only for the most urgent and compelling reasons. The executive branch leadership must severely limit access to such secrets among itself.

The United States is only part of the intelligence scene in Washington. The Soviet Union and other Communist regimes have attempted to penetrate the Senate and House Intelligence Committees as well as other sensitive government bodies with spies and bugs. The case of David H. Barnett, a former CIA agent who began spying for the Russians in the mid-1970s, is one example. He tried to obtain a position on the Senate and House Intelligence Committees but failed. Barnett was finally convicted of espionage and imprisoned. There are other instances in which the Soviets tried to infiltrate the committees and intelligence community. So have friendly powers, such as Israel.

Both the Senate and House now have secure meeting

places—one in the Hart building and another on the House side of the Capitol itself—where we can discuss highly sensitive material without fear of Soviet or other electronic penetration.

As Senate intelligence chairman, I insisted on the secure room in the Hart building and on hiring our own reporter to provide verbatim transcripts of our meetings, hearings, and briefings. The reason was that I had learned two things: Certain Senate reporters had been selling such transcripts to the KGB, and the KGB had recruited a member of Senator Lowell Weicker's staff in 1983. On discovering the fact, Weicker fired the individual.

Regarding my own responsibilities, I either placed any sensitive documents in a safe every night or burned them. Woodward's report on counterintelligence problems in my office while I was intelligence chairman is grossly inaccurate. My office was not swept twice a week for bugs. It was swept only when I held discussions on sensitive committee matters there. That usually occurred when the pain in my knees became so great that it was extremely difficult for me to walk. Woodward also was wrong in saying that a microphone had been found in my desk with a wire or recording device which we were unable to trace. I built a microphone and recording device into my desk myself. I recorded important conversations, always asking the permission of whomever was present, so that I would have a clear and full record of what was said. There was no possibility, as Woodward suggested, that I could have allowed secrets to slip into the hands of either the KGB or another foreign spy service.

I met with Woodward in my office only once regarding his book. Most of the material he wrote about me and my work was not gotten through me. His inaccuracies are clear evidence of that.

The Soviets are still making extraordinary efforts to penetrate Congress, the CIA, the Pentagon, the White House, and other sources of top secrets in Washington,

New York, and California. They have already begun to establish their new embassy, located on Washington's second-highest peak, as one of the world's most sophisticated electronic spy centers. The Soviets have been tapping Washington phone lines for more than a decade. They also have maintained electronic and other spy operations in New York and California. These include Moscow's diplomatic facilities in Riverdale, New York, and Glen Cove, Long Island, as well as their high-ground consulate in San Francisco. The latter eavesdrops on high-technology centers in the Silicon Valley as well as U.S. military facilities on the West Coast. Soviet satellites, spy planes that fly along the East Coast and elsewhere, submarines, and ships off both U.S. coasts complete a sweeping network of efficient electronic spying.

In Washington, D.C., the Soviets have constructed a $70 million city-within-a-city—even their own school and gym—in a sweeping complex of eight buildings that has become the Communist capital of the United States. Two structures are eight and nine stories tall. The new citadel rises atop Mount Alto, about 350 feet above the city, near the intersection of Wisconsin and Massachusetts avenues, where Georgetown and Glover Park crest. It has a clear electronic line of sight to the Capitol, White House, Pentagon, and various federal buildings that are centers for U.S. intelligence, finance, and commerce. The compound also has a partial electronic sight of the CIA in Langley, Virginia.

Electronic spying equipment, already installed on its rooftops, can zero in on communications from the West German, British, and French embassies. The Russians are also positioned to tap into key microwave relay towers that serve telephone and other transmission communications on the East Coast. They now listen to supposedly private conversations among our military and defense contractors, as well as to discussions of big agriculture and other business deals that could affect them.

Their computers start tape recorders when certain words or expressions are used among hundreds of thousands of phone calls. The ten-acre site, surrounded by high prison-like walls and steel wire fence that stretch about a half mile around the complex, has become a fortress.

Before leaving the Senate in 1986, I flew over the compound in a helicopter to find how badly we were getting snookered. The roofs of the two tallest buildings were porcupines of antennae. I could barely see the roofs. Laser beam listening devices had already been installed. They were partially concealed by large, wooden enclosures—we called them "doghouses." The Russians were already using lasers against the windowpanes of the White House, Capitol Hill, and the Pentagon to pick up conversations inside as well as electronic emanations. The equipment has been in operation for some time.

In return, we are "tempest-proofing"—a technical term meaning we are shielding our office equipment with devices to prevent the escape and interception by the Russians of electromagnetic emanations from the White House and elsewhere.

Washington quipsters have managed to come up with some grim humor about the place. The tallest building, a 165-unit structure used as apartments and offices by hundreds of Russians, some of whom have lived there since 1980, has a large underground parking garage. They call it Russia's "Washington bomb shelter."

Washington and Moscow have spent billions of dollars in attempting to intercept each other's communications. U.S. ground stations have been built around the world to track Soviet communications. The Russians have long operated satellites, ships, and other means of spying on us. This includes their most sophisticated collection facility outside the Soviet Union at Lourdes, near Havana. Some two thousand Soviet technicians work around the clock at the electronic eavesdropping facility established more than twenty years ago.

Both the United States and Russia consider monitoring

telemetry—electronic data transmitted by missiles and reentry vehicles in tests—vital to their security. As missiles are launched, they are tracked by satellites, ground stations, aircraft, and ships with electronic equipment. This monitoring is particularly critical to the United States because the Soviets have played all kinds of games to avoid compliance with arms control agreements. Certain verification is absolutely crucial to us.

In return for the gleaming new Soviet diplomatic listening post in Washington, the Russians traded us swampland on the Moscow River and a highly bugged new embassy. It was our own damn fault—specifically, that of Nixon and Kissinger, as well as Carter and Secretary of State Cyrus Vance. I learned from the CIA and others that Nixon and Kissinger were originally responsible. They offered the land swap to Moscow as part of a package deal to get the Kremlin to agree to the Salt I arms accord. Carter and Vance signed off on actual construction approval as part of another pact to obtain Soviet agreement on Salt II.

The land deal was actually cut in 1969 and signed by Jacob Beam, then our ambassador to Moscow. A building agreement was signed in 1972 by Walter Stoessel, then our ambassador to the Kremlin. Obviously, neither could sign without presidential and secretarial approval. Nixon, Kissinger, Carter, and Vance should all hang their heads in shame. Their sellout in the name of détente is a national disgrace.

All of them knew that they were putting us in a fix. The National Security Agency, which conducts American electronic surveillance, warned as early as 1966 that the Mount Alto site would allow the Soviets to intercept sensitive American communications. Secretary of State Dean Rusk confirmed that view at the time to Assistant Attorney General Nicholas Katzenbach.

CIA and FBI officials kicked and screamed behind the scenes as Carter and Vance moved to hand Mount Alto to the Soviets. As Soviet Embassy spokesman Boris

Malakhov put it, "We did not capture the site. We were given it."

Carter and Vance not only accepted the Moscow swamp as the site of our embassy but even killed CIA and other intelligence community insistence that American workers—specifically Navy Seabees—be used to build the place. Vance personally confirmed that Soviets —not Americans—would construct our new Moscow embassy. This decision, pushed by the State Department, was made in the name of showing our good faith in détente. It ranks with the stupidest of my time in Washington.

The new ten-acre U.S. embassy compound in Moscow, originally scheduled for completion in 1983, is a house of construction horrors. The roof atop the nine-story central structure leaked so badly at one time that rain and snow created puddles down to the fourth floor. More seepage dripped down elevator shafts to the basement. Chunks of concrete, plaster, and other parts of that and other buildings in the complex simply fell down and collapsed in piles of rubbish. The building was one big electronic bug, not a normal structure.

In 1983 Russian workers walked off the construction site for several weeks to protest our use of an X-ray machine to detect structural flaws. They called it a health hazard. The Soviets were really more concerned, however, about the use of such machines to detect their implanting of bugs in walls and elsewhere.

The Russian "construction crew"—actually trained electronics experts—had accomplished their bugging mission well. Hundreds of sophisticated listening devices now riddle the walls, columns, beams, and floors of the structure. When it was discovered that the crew was not following certain construction plans—and we told them so—they walked off the job in a huff. Then we discovered that one steel girder was fitted to act as a large antenna.

The State Department, which is rarely intimidated by facts and warnings when its own order and authority are involved, had reported for years that all was well at the construction site. It finally faced reality and marched the Russian workers off the grounds several years ago, belatedly halting construction.

The General Accounting Office reports that State's Foreign Buildings Office has screwed up a good number of our foreign embassies—in Hong Kong and New Delhi, among others. Lousy workmanship compounded by cost overruns mark the FBO's reputation. But it has never botched anything quite as badly as the Moscow swamp construction project.

Needless to say, our new Moscow tomb has not been occupied, and there is already a big cost overrun. The original structure was to cost $89 million, but that total now runs at $200 million and is still rising. It could cost another $50 million to debug the central embassy structure—such as it is—or we could spend several hundred million dollars more and start from scratch. We could debug part of the chancery and hope it would be a complete job. Also, we might build a separate building for secret conversations and work. But this would be patchwork.

I believe our new Moscow embassy should be completely torn down. So should the new Soviet complex in Washington. The entire agreement should be scrapped because this is an incredible ripoff.

The State Department is concerned about our reopening the embassy matter. State argues that such a discussion might upset the Soviets. To hell with the Russians. This is business, not high tea. The department expresses these arguments behind closed doors and in confidential memoranda. They don't want to do anything that "might jeopardize relations." Our relations have been in jeopardy since at least 1945.

I also agree with Bobby Inman, who has called for replacing or renovating more than half of our 262 embassies and consulates around the world because they are vulnerable to spies and terrorists. Congress has approved the first appropriations in a $4.4 billion program to protect these missions.

It is of more than casual interest to me and others that not a single State Department official connected with the new Moscow embassy fiasco has been disciplined. On the contrary, several officers involved in overseeing Soviet construction have been promoted. Not only that, they have been given performance bonuses of $10,000 or more.

Instead, the Marine Corps has taken the rap, and Sergeant Clayton Lonetree has been convicted of espionage. The Navajo Indian was sentenced to thirty years in prison. He is the first Marine to be found guilty on such a charge in the 212-year history of the corps.

I would remove the Marines from guarding our embassies for two reasons: They are rarely, if ever, allowed to carry loaded weapons on duty. The Leathernecks cannot defend the embassy without getting permission from the ambassador, often a laborious and difficult process.

These men are also targets, particularly of Communist regimes, for two reasons: Marines are a symbol of U.S. power, and their guard jobs are boring, certainly not what they were trained to do. It goes without saying that the Reds want to embarrass America's fighting elite. Let's put the Marines back on their regular ship and shore assignments where they belong.

I recommend we hire senior, perhaps retired, military officers for such work. With wives and families, they will not easily be tempted. This system is working well in China, which refuses to allow Marine guards at our embassy in Beijing. That is because Marines protected foreign legations during the Boxer Rebellion.

I weep not for Lonetree, who certainly compromised himself, but for the corps, because it has largely become the fall guy for the striped pants crowd at State. That is true not only in Moscow but in Eastern bloc capitals and other embassies around the world.

Ambassador Arthur A. Hartman dodged blame for the

Marine episode, although it was clearly his responsibility. The Marines were not alone at the embassy. If some of them fell for the traps of professional Russian spies, it was essential for the ambassador and his security chief to have airtight backup systems that would allow no one to compromise U.S. security within the embassy itself. Obviously, they failed.

Hartman also opposed new and tougher security measures at the chancery three years before the Marine security breach took place. He argued along the classic department line: Changes might harm Soviet-American relations.

The FBI gave the White House, the State Department, and the National Security Council a devastating critique of embassy security under Hartman after one of its counterintelligence agents ran a sweep of mission offices in 1983. The report said that security was so lax that Soviet intelligence could have penetrated the embassy's three secure floors by avoiding guards and alarm systems. Even earlier, in 1977, the NSC had repeatedly warned the White House and State about slipshod security under Hartman.

Under Hartman, a nightclub called "Sam's" operated within the complex. Large numbers of people, including Russians, moved in and out of the compound in the late evening. Identification was rarely verified. There was no systematic supervision of guards on duty, not even random checks by the regional security officer. Nor were there any unscheduled inspections of so-called secure areas during the night. Members of Congress, who conducted an investigation of such procedures, reported, "The technical [monitoring and detection] system did not take advantage of available security technology. The system's lack of coverage of the entire complex was appalling."

Our intelligence sources report that at least six Russians working secretly for the United States within the Soviet Union were arrested and executed between late

1985 and the close of 1986. They said the leaks had come from our mission. Experts estimate the disclosures set back American intelligence efforts in the Soviet Union a full decade.

Two other independent studies of our Moscow security pointed out problems at the mission. These ranged from the ease of outside access to the vulnerability of young, single Marines. Hartman maintained that the primary purpose of the embassy was not keeping secrets but "penetrating closed Soviet society." That is a stupid comment from a career diplomat.

When it was pointed out to Hartman that his chauffeur in Moscow was a KGB agent and that there were other such plants on our embassy staff, he said, "No big deal. Everybody who has ever been to Moscow knows things like that." The former ambassador then blithely told the staff of the Senate Intelligence Committee, "I want the Soviets to know what we're thinking in Moscow."

An ambassador might adopt that attitude in some South Sea island nation where the biggest problem is fishing rights, but certainly not in Moscow. We clearly must practice special rules of engagement with the Russians.

Some of my Senate colleagues thought I was too critical of State's general performance in Moscow and elsewhere. That is a fair question. Consider some examples.

In 1985 it was announced that embassy typewriters there had been bugged with electronic devices. Sensors placed in these typewriters as well as embassy walls signaled to KGB listening posts outside what was being typed. Neither Hartman nor the department, however, broadcast the fact that it had shipped the typewriters to Moscow by ordinary commercial carrier, unaccompanied by security personnel, and that the Russians had planted the devices as easily as a child playing spy.

Nor did State report an earlier ominous incident. In 1978 department officials sent embassy typewriters from Antwerp, Belgium, to Moscow via a Soviet shipping firm.

Fortunately, security officers learned of the mistake and had the typewriters shipped back to the United States before they could be placed in service. Yet in the ensuing years, our Moscow embassy sent its typewriters to a friendly little repair shop around the corner, where the KGB systematically bugged them.

Foreign service officers do not repair typewriters. They do not wash windows. And they most certainly do not carry out the trash. More than 35,000 foreign nationals working in our embassies and the homes of Americans abroad accomplish those cumbersome tasks. The Japanese, West Germans, British, French, and Italians use much less foreign help than Americans do—from one half to as little as 15 percent of our total. Not one American works at the Soviet embassy in Washington or for their chancery at the United Nations. The United States employs some 120,000 foreigners on U.S. military installations around the world. This is not to suggest that our embassies and other installations do not need foreign assistance. They do. But not on such a lavish scale. Today's foreign spies do not have to work out of a murky back alley. They just walk in the front gates of U.S. embassies and other installations and get a job.

If lax protection of our secrets in Moscow seems a nightmare, consider an example of State Department security at its headquarters in Washington. The file cabinets of foreign service officers and others are regularly sent for refurbishing to Lorton prison, about forty miles downstate in Virginia. The maximum security institution houses District of Columbia inmates under a special agreement. Lorton prisoners discovered classified documents in some of the drawers. One even wrote to the Washington *Post* about it. Some at Foggy Bottom didn't think the foul-up was so funny. State vowed it would never happen again. It did, of course.

Some 260 Soviets, including members of the KGB, were employed at our Moscow conclave. These were drivers, maids, cleaners, translators, and others. The

Kremlin withdrew them in 1986, also kicking ten U.S. diplomats out of the Soviet Union, in retaliation for Washington's booting out eighty Soviet spies from the United States.

Hartman and State opposed our expelling the eighty Soviet spies. The NSC and CIA learned that the ambassador had fought the expulsions in blistering cables with extremely intemperate language. Yet it's generally agreed that our expulsion order broke the back of Soviet KGB and GRU espionage leadership here.

After the Soviets withdrew their people from working at our Moscow mission, Hartman drew up what I call "Operation Maid." He developed a plan that would have placed more support personnel in Moscow at the expense of intelligence and other key functions. Both the NSC and CIA strongly opposed him. The nation is fortunate that Hartman is no longer our ambassador to Moscow or anywhere else.

State is now recruiting Americans to serve as typists, telephone operators, translators, security monitors, and other such positions. Meantime, American diplomats and their wives are washing windows and carrying out trash in Moscow. The foreign service cadre is unhappy about the situation. Ladies and gentlemen, welcome to the rest of the world.

The United States and Soviet Union have restricted one another to 251 diplomatic personnel in each country. The official Communist presence here is, however, much larger. There are about 475 Soviets and some 1,250 nationals from Communist bloc countries at the United Nations in New York. In all, about 4,250 Communist diplomats, commercial officials, and other representatives reside in the United States. About 2,100 are from the Soviet Union and other Warsaw Pact countries.

Between one third and one half of those at the United Nations and elsewhere engage in some kind of espionage or intelligence work. The State Department has long avoided a congressional oversight directive that would force the Soviet and Eastern bloc delegations to reduce the size of their U.N. staffs.

The United States and other Western nations are paying most of the Russians' U.N. salaries. The Soviets are forced to kick back much of their salary to Moscow on the premise that they would not be paid as much there. That amounts to about $20 million a year. It's also clear that the Soviets, Cuba, and other Communist nations have widely infiltrated the United Nations. They use it not only to spy on us and others, but to spout Marxist propaganda to the world under U.N. auspices. It is also used to recruit Red agents here and among the diplomatic staffs of other nations.

The Communists also send literally tens of thousands of tourists, commercial representatives, students, and others to this country. At least one quarter of these are spies.

Pat Moynihan is leading the charge on Capitol Hill to do something about all this. I've long encouraged and salute his efforts. Pat is now concentrating on Mount Alto as a symbol of State's general don't-rock-the-boat attitude in dealing with the Soviets and other foreign governments. Moynihan hopes to neutralize the Soviet interception operations there and at other points by placing all domestic common carrier communications satellite links in special codes. That is only part of the solution. The federal government is burying much of its telephone cable in Washington to protect private conversations. We are also buying as many as 500,000 new scrambler phones that do much to block intercepts. The Defense Department has installed fiber optics and other means of protecting Pentagon communications. We greatly need to strengthen our telephone and other security in the defense industry.

The Soviets are, nevertheless, still skirting American law on a massive scale in New York, Washington, and San Francisco. Today the KGB invades more Americans' privacy than the FBI ever did. Even at the height of its most important investigations, the FBI never tapped phones to the extent the KGB now does every day. If an American were engaged in such invasion of privacy, he would be jailed for years. We are, in effect, under an electronic spy siege in our own national capital.

For a decade, I and others failed to rally enough of our colleagues in Congress to support Moynihan in his effort to get Congress to approve a Foreign Surveillance Protection Act. It would have given the President the power to expel foreign diplomats involved in electronic spying.

The Russians have been engaged in electronic attacks on our Moscow embassy since the early 1950s. The State Department has consistently underplayed the situation. State has argued that protesting will only harm "good diplomatic relations." The Soviets can only conclude that they should continue. We obviously spy electronically in the Soviet Union. But that is minor compared to what the Russians are doing here.

I am hopeful that Moynihan and other senators, like Ernest "Fritz" Hollings, the eloquent South Carolinian, will lead Congress to scrap the embassy agreement. Moynihan is now weakening for various reasons—he has been sold some false information—but I beg him not to give up the fight. There will be a hullabaloo about the United States' not keeping its accords. So what! That has been largely a Moscow monopoly for a half century. The critical fact is that the pact has not yet been consummated. The slate should be wiped clean soon because the Soviets have plans to greatly expand their Mount Alto facilities.

I also believe we should make another drastic reduction in the number of diplomats from the Soviet Union and other Communist governments in the United States. George F. Kennan, our former ambassador to Moscow and a veteran Soviet expert, has long advocated such cuts. The mutual reduction in personnel will not only help eliminate spying by all the governments involved but perhaps moderate tensions as well.

In 1986 the Reagan administration and Congress cut the number of the Soviet mission to the United Nations from 275 to 170. We also slashed our annual contribution to the U.N. budget by 25 percent. Both should be cut again. The number of Russian personnel at the United Nations should be reduced to a total of seventy-five, and we should cut another 25 percent from our part of the U.N. budget.

We have the legal power to do both. The U.S. government has, since its signing in 1946, expressed reservations about the U.N. Headquarters Agreement. Specifically, we have stated that our national security provides independent authority to limit the admission and restrict the movement of foreign missions.

The State Department could have advanced a much more vigorous case for greater reduction of Soviets at the United Nations. It said the Russians were engaged in espionage but failed to point out that they are secretly eavesdropping on our telephone and other communications systems.

Moscow and the Eastern bloc have some 1,200 spies here. We have many fewer behind the Iron Curtain. Also, we are open societies while they are closed. In addition, the Russians have had considerable success in recruiting Americans to spy for them. A significant number have been volunteers, but the Russians have had the manpower to handle all of them. Some recent cases indicate how active the Soviets and other foreign espionage units have been in this country:

• John Walker and Jerry Whitworth passed cryptographic material to the Russians, enabling them to decipher the most secret U.S. naval communications from the 1960s through 1985. Vitaly Yurchenko, the KGB double defector, disclosed that the Russians had read more than 1 million coded messages as a result. The information gathered allowed the Soviets to reduce the American lead in antisubmarine warfare.

• From 1979 to 1981 James Harper passed to Polish

intelligence a wide array of information on the survivability of our Minuteman Missile System. Harper also provided them with considerable data on U.S. defenses against ballistic missile attack. Army experts rated the loss "beyond calculation." In 1980 a team of twenty KGB agents flew to Warsaw, where Harper delivered about a hundred pounds of classified reports.

• Edward Lee Howard, a onetime CIA case officer, defected to Moscow when we discovered he was selling U.S. intelligence secrets to the Soviets. Howard had given the Russians information on sensitive CIA operations in the Soviet Union and other critical espionage data. He may have been responsible for the capture and execution of some of our top agents inside Russia.

• Larry Wu-tai Chin worked secretly for about forty years as a "plant" of mainland China within the CIA. He provided Beijing with American intelligence on China throughout that time.

• Jonathan Jay Pollard, a civilian intelligence analyst with the Naval Investigative Service, illegally passed highly classified documents to Israeli intelligence. These were extremely sensitive reports on the Mideast. The highest officials of the Israeli government were involved in this spying on the United States, although they concocted a "plausible denial" scheme from the beginning.

A dozen other Americans have been arrested as spies for the Soviets and other foreign governments in the past decade. During this time, the Soviets have acquired more than three hundred different types of U.S. and other Western computer hardware and software. This has allowed them to develop the technical ability to penetrate some American automated systems. The Russians are now engaged in an all-out effort to crack our supercomputers.

Some of these cases, especially Walker's twenty years of spying, reflect adversely on the ability of our intelligence agencies themselves to keep the nation's secrets. Were it not for Walker's wife and daughter, he might still be in business. So our counterintelligence operations are not what they should be.

I have long criticized the State Department. Yet State and the intelligence agencies can complement one another. If U.S. foreign policy is to be successful, both must work more closely together. The aim of each is the same: to protect the people and interests of the United States.

I have not found our intelligence services to be "rogue elephants." Rather, they have been dedicated in their service to the President and the executive branch. Indeed, they serve the legislative branch as well, responding to thousands of requests for information as well as participating in the budget process.

Unfortunately, I can't express the same unqualified support for State. I don't believe there has been a President since Eisenhower who has trusted the foreign service to carry out his expressed policies. Ike had some confidence in the department for two reasons—the Dulles brothers. John Foster ran State while Alan directed the CIA. Too many State officials have long had their own policy agenda. That has been influenced by their aristocratic self-importance: The old boys at State know best.

I don't believe that some of the most important career officers at the department are convinced the President should always decide foreign policy. This has been reflected over the years in battles among State, the Defense Department, and the NSC. That fight is really over whether State is preeminent in foreign policy. Control—"psychic pay," as it's called among upper-echelon careerists in Washington—is everything in the bureaucracy.

Congress is now trying to redefine its foreign policy role for the same reason—control. As the various power players are now positioned in Washington, confrontation in foreign policy is inevitable. If we can eliminate this conflict, the result will be better foreign policy.

State now has a split personality. Its veterans recall the grandeur of the old days when, because of the education and wealth of many officers, they contributed much more to the U.S. role in the changing global scene than is true today. The department is now, however, plagued with institutional weaknesses.

State's onetime closely held power has been separated into different functions at the department. Some of these have even left the confines of Foggy Bottom for the White House and other government departments.

In the 1940s State lost its sole control of reporting economic and political intelligence to the Office of Strategic Services and later to the CIA.

The United States Information Agency, USAID, and the Peace Corps also took a bite out of State's bureaucratic hide. These are still part of a "country team," but State does not have sole control of their activities.

Rapid communications have also reduced State's power. Fifty years ago, slow diplomatic pouches conveyed Washington's wishes to faraway embassies. Today, messages can flash around the world in seconds. Secure voice transmissions allow instantaneous communications. Ambassadors no longer run embassies. They are easily and often told what to do by Foggy Bottom, the NSC, or presidential aides. All major decisions are made in Washington.

The making of foreign policy has now been largely delegated. Some might not agree with that, especially after Kissinger, but that's a fact of life at State today. The result is that the nation's last great vestige of an American aristocracy has become just like any other hangout for bureaucrats.

Budgets are now crises. Policy making by committee is routine. Overall global policy is set by the White House and others. State has become provincial and has adopted "good relations" abroad to survive better at home.

The department's old personality, its grand ways and manner, return when officers are posted overseas. Aristocrats rise above Foggy Bottom into international prominence. They are going to set some policy, because they are "experts"—and to hell with Washington.

Hartman and others wanted more power over appointments abroad, not interference from the passing political crowd at the White House and elsewhere. Why should the President appoint an ambassador of his choosing when a career man is available at State? Their argument has some merit. But the pendulum has swung against the foreign service because of its past arrogance and Washington's current shakeout in foreign policy power.

For State's own good, there should be a massive shakeup at the department. It's no longer an elite organization. The department could do even more to reform itself along distinct professional lines instead of personal connections. Career paths must be much better defined with more professional incentives built into the organization. Only then will it work more effectively with the intelligence community and begin to restore its lost respect.

The country cannot afford another Hartman opposing the CIA and using the Marine Corps as a scapegoat. We must join our Big Three—State, Defense, and the CIA—to institute an effective strategy and program to combat international terrorism.

The main thrust of our present policy is to hit back at terrorists who strike U.S. citizens abroad. The American bombing raid on Libya was an example of this. We also support freedom fighters who oppose Soviet-supported regimes, primarily in Central America and Afghanistan.

However, Washington has no cohesive, comprehensive policy that combines the special competences of the CIA, our military intelligence, and State to battle the terrorists. Different elements work together on an ad hoc basis, for example, in our air attack on Libya. The targets and justification for the assault were worked out in a team effort. We have yet to integrate our resources into a unified, effective force. Short of war, we have no comprehensive strategy—much less a top-level strike command—to meet political violence face to face.

It is generally agreed that the most effective way to eliminate terrorism without going to war is to hit the leaders of countries sponsoring it. With the exception of our air attack on Libya, we and other nations have been unwilling to do that. We could also kill these leaders in covert actions. Democracies argue that they would be adopting the ruthlessness of dictatorships if they employed such methods and argue against them on moral grounds. Israel is the exception. The Israelis have clearly warned foreign leaders about terrorism. Their response to terrorists is to kill them. Israeli leaders realize they are at war.

We have yet to convince terrorists that they will pay a price for the murder and kidnapping of Americans. We have to take a tougher stand. That cannot be accomplished, however, without an effective strategy and strike force that integrate State, the CIA, and military intelligence.

National leaders and governments, including the Soviet Union, sponsor this violence. The Russians openly arm and train only one terrorist group, the Palestine Liberation Organization. However, to conceal their ties to other terrorists, the Kremlin uses its Communist cohorts —the Eastern bloc (particularly Czechoslovakia, Bulgaria, and East Germany), North Korea, Cuba, Nicaragua, and South Yemen. All furnish training and arms to terrorists. They work underground with such groups as Italy's Red Brigades, West Germany's RAF, and El Salvador's FMLN. Iran, Syria, and Libya sponsor, train, and arm other terrorists.

Groups supported by Communist states never make a major move without Moscow's instigation or approval. If the Bulgarians handle a group of Red Brigades—which they do regularly—Sofia checks with the Kremlin before approving a big operation.

The Soviet aim is to sow conflict and confusion in the West and to demonstrate its weaknesses to the rest of the world without waging a direct and open war. Nearly three hundred Americans have been killed in terrorist incidents abroad since 1968. The Russians have not been targets because we do not sponsor such terror. Moscow has introduced secret warfare into intelligence. The two are joined into a terrorist network. Terrorism has become part of a new undeclared war against the West. As Moscow sees it, the weak can wage war against the strong without fear of massive retaliation.

Soviet diplomats, military, and intelligence have been deliberately integrated into a unique new Kremlin strike force. Sweet talk, savage terror, and spying are spreading despite *glasnost* and promises of internal reform. That seeming contradiction is a well-planned Russian policy.

The United States must let Gorbachev know that the Russians will pay a price for this. We cannot make such a warning credible, however, unless we are prepared to carry out a unified strategy.

It also would be helpful if the media, especially American TV news, put into practice policies that more clearly recognize this crucial fact: Most terrorist acts are aimed not merely at the victims but at much wider audiences. The terrorists, in effect, write and narrate much of their story. No one is asking the U.S. media to act as if these horrors didn't happen. But it is quite another thing to play into terrorist hands by broadcasting and printing forced confessions and other terrorist propaganda. It's claimed the American public doesn't swallow this. If such tapings are false, then why broadcast them?

There must be international cooperation to halt terrorism. These murders and kidnappings probably will never be wiped out entirely. But they can be limited and the perpetrators punished.

The United States has a long way to go before we have an effective antiterrorist organization of our own, but it can be done. The battle against such violence will be long and bloody. Our first line of defense against terrorism and war is the CIA and other intelligence agencies.

11

Duty–Honor– Country

AT 5:40 P.M., IN THE FALLING DARKNESS OF MONDAY, February 3, 1986, a military van pulled slowly away from the Russell Senate Office Building and headed across the Potomac River to the Pentagon. In it were Jim Locher and Rick Finn, two staff members of the Senate Committee on the Armed Services, and myself. Jeff Smith, another staffer, had driven to Dulles International Airport to meet Senator Sam Nunn, the ranking Democrat on the committee, who was returning from California. We were to meet with the chairman and other members of the Joint Chiefs of Staff at 6 P.M. This was a hastily arranged, and not ordinary Pentagon meeting. The subject was a legislative proposal that would launch the most sweeping reorganization of U.S. military leadership in three decades.

Admiral William J. Crowe, Jr., chairman of the Joint Chiefs, had phoned the committee office that morning about details of the meeting. Crowe indicated that he and the Service Chiefs believed other members of the Armed Services Committee should attend the conference. I had received calls from three Republican senators, John Warner of Virginia, Jeremiah Denton of Alabama, and Phil Gramm of Texas. The three, who were among the strongest opponents of military reorganization, said they understood that committee members were invited to the meeting. I told them flatly that they had not been asked by me. On the other side, the Joint Chiefs saw no reason for our staff members to be present. I replied that the staffers would accompany Senator Nunn and myself.

It was obvious that those opposing military reform were trying to maneuver us into an early, full-blown confrontation—and Nunn and I would have fewer troops. If I had agreed on other senators' attending, Sam and I would have had to debate the five chiefs as well as return the fire of opposing colleagues. Without our staff, we would have been denied their support in interpreting the minute details of the plan's provisions. The chiefs were certain to have some staff. In fact, they did.

We met in Admiral Crowe's reception office. Crowe led the five of us to the Tank, a top-security meeting room. Despite its flags and paintings, the Tank is not impressive when empty. The room comes to life only when members of the JCS—silver stars on their epaulets, gold braid on their sleeves, and rows of colored ribbons emblazoning their immaculate uniforms—are present. The four service chiefs and four Joint Staff officers awaited us. The chiefs were: General Charles A. Gabriel, chief of staff of the Air Force, General John A. Wickham, Jr., Army chief of staff, Admiral James D. Watkins, chief of Naval Operations, and General P. X. Kelley, commandant of the Marine Corps.

The Tank is a plain setting, not at all what one might expect as the conference room for the nation's military leaders. No communications equipment is present, not even a phone. The room, about thirty by twenty-seven feet, is dominated by a large rectangular wooden table at the center. The chiefs sit around this table. The seating arrangement is established by tradition, with the chairman and each service chief having a designated position. Six small tables and chairs, where key Joint Staff officers may sit, are to the rear of the chairman. Behind this arrangement are five flags: one flag, with battle ribbons, for each service and the chairman's four-star flag at the center. The American flag stands alone in a corner. Additional chairs line the walls. Every chair in the room is identical, standard government issue—wooden with mahogany-colored simulated leather seats and backs. A lectern stands near a projection screen for briefings.

The carpet and drapes in the chamber are gold. No outside light enters. The walls are decorated with military art. Two paintings of the Army in Vietnam—moving infantry and firing artillery—are framed behind the chairman. A large print of a Norman Rockwell painting depicting the American soldier at six different times from 1776 to 1918 streams across one wall. Other paintings include an Allied military Mass in St. Peter's Basilica at the Vatican during World War II, a Navy warship with a Chinese junk nearby, a modern Air Force fighter aircraft, and a futuristic Air Force aircraft of the twenty-first century.

The original Tank was located in another building. Its entrance was down a flight of stairs and through an archway. At the first meeting there, on February 9, 1942, the walk reminded officers of entering a tank. The nickname stuck. In recent years, because of the color of carpeting and drapes in the current meeting place, it has also been referred to as the Gold Room.

The Tank reflects the military brass—somewhat austere and plain, yet proud and colorful in their own way.

Apart from certain religious groups, the U.S. military may be the most tradition-minded, conservative institution in America. It is certainly the most conservative institution of government. Our meeting concerned changes that would cut to the core of their professional lives and hallowed traditions.

The military is incomprehensible to many outsiders. Its seemingly archaic rules guide the most modern technology in the world. It is as old as the republic, yet as young as the latest probe into outer space.

It is critical to understand this background as Nunn and I faced these men. We proposed to transform inviolate military organizational command. Our reorganization sought to pin down a precise chain of command and the specific roles of officers in it. The chain itself was not to be altered, but it was to be much more accountable. These distinguished men were now facing the military mind's worst nightmare: the uncertainty of change.

Admiral Crowe occupied the seat at the center of the table, opposite Sam and me. General Gabriel was to his right. The three other chiefs were seated on either side of us. Crowe opened with a five-minute general statement. He expressed concern that the proposed legislation would subject the service chiefs, in performing their duties as JCS members, to the direction and control of their respective civilian service secretaries, such as the Secretary of the Navy or Army. He also wished to retain the "corporate character" of the JCS. That meant only one thing —continued watered-down decisions by committee.

For decades, the JCS has been unwilling to present anything less than a united front to civilian authority. Nearly every JCS action has been unanimous. Interservice jealousies, mostly over funding and the scope of their military missions, have caused each branch to protect its own flanks. It became painfully evident that the services' first loyalty was to themselves. Unanimity was therefore forged only by compromises to which each service could agree. This resulted in delayed, compromised counsel to the President, Defense Secretary, and others. Tough issues were avoided. Clear, forceful solutions were, for the most part, doomed. The system was actually a disservice to the country and the services themselves.

Crowe, of course, expressed none of this. With McNamara and his whiz kids in mind, he took aim at civilian authority's invading the chiefs' turf. He also knew that Sam and I were generally sympathetic to such a view. Gabriel joined Crowe in questioning the effects of such a measure on the chiefs' ability to perform overall planning and other missions.

Generals Wickham and Kelley and Admiral Watkins launched a direct, frontal attack on the bill. In sharp terms, Wickham argued that the measure would destroy the independent judgment and professional integrity of the JCS by placing each chief under the civilian secretary of his military department. Watkins and Kelley expanded on this theme in very emotional terms. Nunn and I were prepared for opposition but not this rancor.

I respect every one of these men. Each is a dedicated military leader who rose to the pinnacle of his profession because of his bravery, intelligence, and hard work. Yet, as tension and emotion mounted in the room, it was clear that calm had to be restored. I tried to do so.

I reminded the chiefs of my long efforts to strengthen the military. Neither I nor Senator Nunn was attempting to place them, in conducting their JCS duties, under a civilian service secretary. In cautious but clear language, I tried to tell them that a confrontational approach would not work with us. My conciliatory remarks had no impact. None at all. The chiefs, pressing a unified front, intensified their attack.

Midway through the meeting, it was clear that of all the sweeping changes our measure would bring to the military, the most important thing to the JCS was their turf—power. They were nervous about being dominated by civilians who were not their professional equals. They made no mention of their organization and command system, which was clearly flawed and dangerous for everyone.

All of us—Nunn and I as well as our staff—were taken aback at their sharp attack. Wickham, Watkins, and Kelley had completely misinterpreted the meaning and intention of our plan. All had become so emotional about defense reorganization that they were prepared to conclude the worst. Moreover, the principle for which they were arguing—professional military advice, independent of civilian restraint—was one they could convincingly defend because it would appeal to Nunn and me. The Joint Chiefs would, in fact, lose power, but not to civilians. They would lose it to the JCS chairman and specified commanders. All we had to do was rework a sentence or two of the bill's language to make their independence more precise.

I then asked Locher to review the history of the bill. He explained that we had never intended the JCS to be placed under departmental secretaries. Quite the contrary, we sought to improve the quality and enhance the role of professional military advice, not make it subject to the control of any secretaries in performing their JCS duties. I promised that further clarification would be written into the bill.

The crux of our plan was still on the table, and the chiefs had not said a word about it. Our central aim was to have U.S. air, sea, and ground forces fight as a team through a series of organizational and command changes within the services. These changes were crucial for the President, the Defense Secretary, the nation, and the military itself.

Wickham, Watkins, and Kelley joined forces again to open a second front. They opposed the increased authority which the bill would give to commanders leading troops into combat. The three argued that these leaders would be diverted from actual combat, becoming bogged down in allocating their material resources and other time-consuming administrative tasks, including contracting. At this point, Nunn joined the debate. He explained in detail that these claims were simply not accurate. In all, the JCS raised nine issues. Nunn and I answered all of them. But the chiefs' message was clear: They didn't believe in reorganization, and they were telling us to go to hell.

When the meeting ended, Crowe, Wickham, and Gabriel shook hands with Nunn and me. The others did not. They saw themselves as protecting their organizations.

The politics of the military makes Republicans and Democrats look like Boy Scouts. Watkins and Kelley were hardass about the meeting, but I admire that. They were standing up for what they believed was right. Kelley is retired now, but that bull-neck is probably still upset. Nevertheless, Sam and I saw him and Watkins then and now as great officers and patriots.

Crowe escorted all of us back to his office. He graciously gave up his quarters so we could hold a private meeting. We quickly agreed that effective cooperation with the chiefs was now out of the question. None of us had expected the emotion, particularly the open bitterness, expressed in the Tank. Nor had we anticipated the discussion to frame itself around the simple issue of turf. When united, the uniformed military is a formidable foe. Our hard work might not survive such attacks. Locher questioned whether we wanted to regroup and reconsider our alternatives. The staff turned to us for instructions on our first Senate markup meeting—spelling out precise provisions and language in the bill—scheduled for nine o'clock the following morning. Sam and I looked at each other. Our answer was clear and certain: Proceed as planned.

When the committee began the markup session on Tuesday, February 4, seven unrequested, highly critical letters arrived—one from each service chief as well as others from the Secretaries of the Army, Navy, and Air Force. Two requested letters, from Defense Secretary Caspar Weinberger and Chairman Crowe, were critical but, unlike the others, constructive in tone.

Senators opposed to reform spent most of the morning reading excerpts from the letters. All, except that of General Gabriel, were strongly worded. The battle was now out in the open. It was obvious that the entire might of the services and their allies in Congress would be spent in defeating our plan.

This is how members of the Armed Services Committee lined up as we began the markup. For reorganization:

Strom Thurmond, South Carolina; William Cohen, Maine; Gary Hart, Colorado; James Exon, Nebraska; Carl Levin, Michigan; Edward Kennedy, Massachusetts; Jeff Bingaman, New Mexico; Alan Dixon, Illinois; Sam Nunn; and myself. Those against were: John Warner, Virginia; Pete Wilson, California; Jeremiah Denton, Alabama; Phil Gramm, Texas; John Stennis, Mississippi; and John Glenn, Ohio. Three senators were leaning against: Gordon Humphrey, New Hampshire; Dan Quayle, Indiana; and John East, North Carolina. Ten members supported the plan, while nine were against or leaning that way. The committee was thus split almost down the middle.

Warner, a former Secretary of the Navy, was the most vocal opponent of the measure. He was forcefully backed by John Lehman, Secretary of the Navy, who did everything he could to torpedo the plan. From the time of John Paul Jones, the Navy has always considered itself autonomous, a separate, elite body of officers and men with a distinct mission and tradition. Its leaders have consistently maintained that no naval vessel or unit should ever be placed under the command of an Army or Air Force officer. Since World War II, the Navy has led the opposition to unifying the armed services. It has always been joined by its ground-assault arm, the Marine Corps, giving it at least two votes of five on the JCS, or a majority of three votes when an admiral became the chairman. No commandant of the Marine Corps has yet served as JCS chairman.

Historically, Congress also has been a foe of centralized leadership of the military and its branches. Individual members have always had close relationships with individual services and their senior officers. This was to attract military bases and spending contracts to their states and congressional districts. This combined congressional-military log rolling continued under a system in which smaller military agencies and groups handled such contracts. For example, congressmen wanted the semiautonomous Bureau of Naval Ships to determine how its own funds were to be spent. Greater centralization of resource decisions and contracting—part of our plan—limited these "favorite son" agreements, although they still don't entirely preclude them.

Thus, when the reorganization effort began in February 1982, only a handful in Congress supported reform. When Nunn and I began to make our move, I wouldn't have bet more than a sawbuck on our chances of success. History and tradition were against us. Yet I had made up my mind that I would not retire from the Senate without giving reorganization my best shot.

When the United States became a world power at the turn of the century, the Army, Navy, and Marine Corps were fiercely independent—even the Marines, who served as part of the Navy. They had separate missions and proud traditions.

The development of the airplane began to blur the distinction between land and sea warfare. Military aircraft covered both areas. All three branches fought one another for air power funds and mission authority. Brigadier General Billy Mitchell saw aircraft as all-purpose weapons—for the Army. The Navy built carriers from which to launch attack aircraft in World War II. The Marines had their own fighter-bombers to give their ground troops close air support.

It was obvious that no single service branch could fight World War II, yet an Army-Navy battle for control of military aviation continued throughout the conflict. President Roosevelt created the JCS, a command structure borrowed from the British, in order to have a board of directors assist him in fighting the war. He also established a joint command system. This was a series of multiservice commands, defined by geographic boundaries which the military services carved up among themselves. Each service fought to have its officers dominate these commands. It was, at best, an uneasy system that heightened interservice rivalry. At worst, it became a wide-open political dogfight.

The nation's modern defense structure was established in the National Security Act of 1947. This legislation, after a fierce political battle, was a compromise between friends and foes of the unification of our military establishment. It created the Office of the Secretary of Defense, but gave the secretary no department to direct. It formalized the JCS, but joint military policy never developed. Each service chief was committed to strengthening his own branch, and God help him if another service took away any of his funding or missions. He would answer to fellow officers. The U.S. Air Force was created, decentralizing our air strength to some extent but not halting the race for more aviation power among the services. The act also established the Central Intelligence Agency and the National Security Council.

Congress amended the act three times in an attempt to strengthen our national security. Most of the changes bolstered the civilian Office of the Secretary of Defense. The military structure was for the most part ignored.

When McNamara became secretary, he used the latest amendments to expand his authority. At the same time, McNamara made it clear that he and his whiz kids were in command—that the JCS and the country's other military leaders were being downgraded in the Pentagon power structure. He ignored the problem of separatism among the services because a divided JCS was a weak JCS.

The secretaries who followed McNamara—Clark Clifford, Mel Laird, Elliot Richardson, James Schlesinger, Donald Rumsfeld, and Harold Brown—had different priorities. Clifford, Laird, and Richardson were caught up in Vietnam and its aftermath. Schlesinger, Rumsfeld, and Brown were involved in new military technology and weapons systems. They also tried to provide the Department of Defense with a new, post-Vietnam direction.

When President Reagan was elected, I became chairman of the Senate Select Committee on Intelligence. It was not until his second term, in 1985, that I headed the Senate Committee on the Armed Services. It was then that Nunn and I quietly decided it was time to undertake the most sweeping reform of the Pentagon's uniformed leadership since the National Security Act of 1947.

There were many reasons why we believed the time was right. One personal, compelling reason was what I had learned in World War II. Others resulted from the aborted Iranian hostage rescue mission in April 1980, the terrorist bombing and killing of 241 Marines in Beirut in October 1983, and problems in the planning and execution of our invasion of Grenada. Serious organizational errors during World War II were also part of our thinking. We were also concerned with sweeping national criticism of multibillion-dollar cost overruns on defense contracts as well as widespread fraud in defense spending.

Nunn and I spoke frankly to each other at the start of our struggle. I wanted to establish two things—equality and trust. Although I was committee chairman, he would know everything I knew at the time I learned it. Our staff would be bipartisan, a unit reporting to both of us. I was in a hurry. In two years I would retire from the Senate. Nunn could have slowed our movement, hoping the Democrats would take over control of the Senate as a result of the 1986 elections, which they did. His party could then take credit for straightening out the Pentagon —a political coup going into the 1988 presidential election year. But Nunn didn't. He said full speed ahead. Sam had succeeded Richard Russell in the Senate. The Georgian was in the Russell tradition by birth and temperament. Nunn is one of the most selfless men in the Senate, almost unique amid the present crowd of glory hogs. He chose to become an expert in national defense and has succeeded Senator Henry "Scoop" Jackson of Washington, who was long the congressional Democratic leader in that field. In going into this battle, I placed absolute trust in Nunn. He never disappointed me, not once. With Sam, I'd take on the devil in hell.

Representative William Nichols, an Alabama Democrat, and Representative Les Aspin, a Wisconsin Democrat, spent years in this effort. They deserve no less credit for the eventual passage of the act.

We were mindful of President Eisenhower's statement of April 3, 1958, in which he unequivocally declared that there was a greater need for more effective coordination of our armed forces: "We must free ourselves of emotional attachments to service systems of an era that is no more."

That statement, coming from the former allied military commander in Europe during World War II, sent shocks through the Pentagon. But the JCS adopted the bureaucratic answer: Wait.

Ike's views were important, but military problems were more critical to our case. We began to study various examples to prove our point. There was no more noteworthy lesson of a military foul-up in our lifetime than the Japanese attack on Pearl Harbor. The extent of that surprise is still being debated by historians. We concluded that there had been many reasons for the disaster, but that our command structure had been a crucial one.

Two separate chains of command—Army and Navy—reported to different leaders in Washington. No one below President Roosevelt had authority over both. And no one, apart from the President, had access to all available intelligence. Yet we had considerable information indicating that a Japanese attack—the exact location and time were uncertain—was imminent. A timely analysis of the combined data could have placed our military on alert at Pearl and elsewhere. Our land and sea commands in Hawaii were divided. There was little cooperation and no coordinated plan of defense between Admiral H. E. Kimmel, commander of the Pacific Fleet, and Lieutenant General Walter C. Short, commander of our ground troops on the island. This was a crucial failure. Unfortunately, that message never got to our political or military leaders in Washington throughout World War II.

In 1944, for the same reason—lack of unified command—the United States almost lost one of the greatest naval battles in history, at the Leyte Gulf in the Philippines. The Japanese committed virtually all of their remaining three naval forces to the fight. U.S. naval forces were split into two fleets, the Third and Seventh. The two U.S. forces reported to different superiors—the Third Fleet to Admiral Chester Nimitz in Hawaii and the Seventh Fleet to General Douglas MacArthur, who had landed on the island of Leyte as a jump-off point to recapture Manila. The fleet's only common superior was the JCS in Washington. It was an absurd situation.

A series of confusing messages caused Admiral William "Bull" Halsey to leave the area with the Third Fleet. Without communicating with Admiral Thomas C. Kinkaid's Seventh Fleet, he moved to attack Japanese carrier forces, actually a decoy, more than 350 miles away. This left the Seventh Fleet vulnerable to the main Japanese thrust. Halsey ignored desperate messages from Kinkaid to return. The communications breakdown left an armada of MacArthur's troops—132,000 men and 200,000 tons of supplies—exposed on their way to reconquer the Philippines. An extraordinarily courageous fight by the Seventh Fleet, coupled with several major Japanese blunders, allowed the United States to win the battle. Halsey returned only when he received a now famous message from Nimitz. Nimitz asked:

"Where is Task Force 34? Whole world wants to know."

On arrival, Halsey learned he had missed the biggest naval battle of the war, with 1,130 Americans dead and 913 wounded. Nevertheless, Halsey was a fine commander and a very brave man. The main reason for the mix-up: No supreme commander was present.

* * *

We also studied the Iran hostage rescue mission and found it plagued with planning, training, and organizational problems. In late April 1980 U.S. military forces launched Operation Eagle Claw to rescue the fifty-three Americans who had been captured at the U.S. embassy in Teheran. They had been held captive by the Ayatollah Khomeini's militants since November 1979. The mission ended tragically with eight American servicemen killed and was aborted in the Iranian desert. Just about everything went wrong. Much of the free world, while saddened by the episode, concluded that the operation had been a military disaster. So did millions of Americans. The JCS commissioned retired Admiral James L. Holloway III and a Special Operations Review Group to investigate the Iran operation. Military experts agreed the Holloway Report criticized the mission in understated and indirect language. It should have fixed responsibility much more specifically on the mission's chain-of-command failures.

I spent considerable time finding the answers, including long talks with Colonel Charlie A. Beckwith, commander of our ground assault force in Iran. The mission was complex and explanations about the outcome are involved, sometimes even contradictory. But these conclusions are certain:

It was an ad hoc, improvised operation from start to finish. That was because all four services wanted a piece of the action. The plan was compartmentalized into a complex series of ground and air movements. These movements, for all practical purposes, were not coordinated. There was confusion not only over the training of helicopter pilots but who they would be. Marine pilots were finally chosen to join Navy airmen in flying Navy helicopters from the aircraft carrier U.S.S. *Nimitz* into Iran. But as everyone knew before the mission began, Air Force pilots were far better suited for the grueling six-hour flight because of their low-altitude, long-range training and experience. The Marines were trained for short-range assaults. This difference became even more critical during the actual mission, when a long and powerful sandstorm developed.

There was no centralized command responsibility, and therefore coordination at the joint training site in the desert near Yuma, Arizona, was poor. Few face-to-face meetings of the different units took place. The 130 Army Green Berets, Rangers, drivers, and some fifty pilots simply didn't know one another. They were belatedly forced into a temporary unit to satisfy the public relations image of all four services. In reality, the mission failed before it ever got off the ground.

Beckwith, commander of a special Army antiterrorist unit called Delta Force, told me what had happened from beginning to end. At 4:30 A.M. on November 4, 1979, the day that Iranian militants overran the embassy, he was called by the Pentagon while on maneuvers in Georgia. Beckwith was told his unit, the nation's primary strike force against terrorism, was on alert because Americans had been taken hostage in Iran. Beckwith moved Delta Force back to its base at Fort Bragg, North Carolina, to pick up equipment and personal belongings. He soon moved Delta Force out of that base in the event its movements were being watched. A week later, he was summoned to the Special Operations Office of the JCS in Washington. Charlie described the scene:

"I walked into this room and all these senior officers, including generals, were sitting there wringing their hands. [Zbigniew] Brzezinski, of the National Security Council, had just left. He'd asked 'em what they were prepared to do to get the hostages out. Now they were looking for answers. They asked me lots of questions. I told 'em none of the questions—including one about parachuting onto the embassy grounds—had any merit because they didn't have any hard information about the situation in Teheran. Still the questions flew. I told 'em this was all ridiculous. I had to have some facts. Then I'd frame a plan. I asked 'em to go to the CIA and get some answers."

Beckwith said that a man in a three-piece suit then laid a hand on his shoulder and asked him to step outside. The individual, who didn't wish to be identified publicly, said that no agents had been left behind. He claimed that not a single American in the embassy at the time of the takeover spoke Farsi (although that was later disputed). In terms of intelligence, we were naked. The hostages were completely on their own.

Charlie said that that first encounter typified the next five and a half months of planning and training. But it was only on the ground at the "Desert One" rendezvous point in the Iranian wasteland that Beckwith truly began to understand how fouled up the mission was.

Six giant C-130 transport planes loaded with men, equipment, and helicopter fuel had taken off from an Egyptian air base earlier in the day for the island of Masirah, part of Oman. They refueled and flew to "Desert One," a secret landing area about 265 miles from Teheran. Eight Sea Stallion helicopters left the *Nimitz* in the Arabian Sea to join Beckwith and his men at the rendezvous point.

While flying to "Desert One," one chopper went down in the desert during a sandstorm. The pilot was picked up. A second chopper pilot lost his way in the dust and returned to the *Nimitz*. The others finally arrived, but late. During that agonizing period, Beckwith could not communicate with the helicopters. But the White House, which was monitoring the mission, was pouring messages to the desert command. President Carter himself was on the horn. Who was really commanding the mission? Those on the ground in Iran? In Egypt? The President of the United States?

The first two helicopter pilots to land described their flight across the desert as the worst dust storm they had ever seen. Beckwith said they seemed "shattered." The mission was already an hour and fifteen minutes behind schedule. Beckwith wanted to fly on to "Desert Two," a remote mountain hideaway only fifty miles from Teheran. The landing area was to be the jump-off point for the final assault on the twenty-seven-acre compound the following night. Charlie said that the skipper of the chopper pilots refused to speak with him. They had had words earlier. Beckwith insisted they take off since the "shattered" pilots were recovering their mental bearings. Some of the pilots complained, however, that the mission should not proceed. The Marines, Navy, and special forces weren't talking the same language. They weren't a fighting unit. They seemed to Charlie more like passing strangers on the Iranian desert. Beckwith used strong language and at one point almost pulled his pistol. He called the hesitant helicopter pilots gutless. It was a bizarre scene. Beckwith recalls, "We finally began loading the men and equipment aboard. When we got to the third helicopter, the pilot told me with a smirk on his face that he couldn't fly. Something was wrong with his hydraulic system. I called him a son of a bitch."

Beckwith now had only five working choppers. He needed six for the mission. He sat down, buried his face in his hands, and knew the mission was over. As the evacuation began, an airborne helicopter, maneuvering so another could be fueled, crashed into one of the large transport planes. The ammunition and fuel on the aircraft exploded and burst into flames, killing eight men. The operation had been exposed. In the confusion and haste to escape in the C-130s, the five helicopters were left behind. So were weapons, communications equipment, secret documents, and maps. Beckwith now says, "I wanted guys who had flown by the seat of their pants. Pilots who didn't give a rat's ass if they got promoted or not—or got a medal—but who knew and cared about each other. Guys who were a team and would pick up and carry their helicopters to Teheran if necessary. We didn't have that team. We got the four services reaching up on a shelf and giving us different outfits. I believe it would have been a different story in Iran—and a different outcome in Vietnam—if the four services had fought under a unified command."

As in Vietnam, Beckwith pointed out, he personally knew of three officers on the JCS who were spending all their time writing "Rules of Engagement" for him in Iran. He was not to do this or that, especially endanger civilians. Charlie recalls, "That was ridiculous. It was crazy. They never told me what they could do to help me. We might have had to shoot our way out of the embassy. Finally, I got my orders from Jimmy Carter. The President simply said I should use whatever force necessary to save the lives of the hostages. I didn't need any more rules."

Beckwith now despises the term "ad hoc." He says he would never return to Iran or go on another mission with a group based on "those two dirty words." He explains the only way he would undertake such a mission today would be with "a bunch of guys who had worked together, slept together, drank together, and were prepared to give their lives together."

Charlie expressed deep interest in the National Defense Authorization Act for fiscal 1987. It established Special Operations Forces as a unified command. We were not prepared to offer the establishment of a separate unified command for such forces in the reorganization legislation, so it was introduced by Senators Nunn and Cohen in late 1987. Beckwith warns, "We have to be careful to choose the very best men to lead these unified field commands. They can't be a dumping ground like some of the officers shoved into the ranks of the JCS staff. I'm sick and tired of seeing commanders sent into special forces to get their ticket punched—just one more step up the ladder—instead of people who've fought up from the mud of special operations. We need commanders who know their asses from third base. Men who care about us, want to be one of us. Like the Israelis. Our special forces people are just as good as theirs. In fact, I think we could kick the crap out of them. The difference is leadership. Their leaders came up through the mud."

Nunn, Cohen, and I shared Beckwith's concern. Special forces must be insulated, but not isolated, from the large services—with their own budgets, force structure, maintenance, training, and recruitment. If the United States wants the best, it must make special operations the best. It must fight low-intensity conflicts like terrorism and guerrilla attacks with a high-intensity program and people.

These forces and equipment must be tested. They must train and work together as a fighting unit, creating the necessary teamwork and trust. The real authority for carrying out missions against unorthodox threats must be in the field, in the unit, not in the Pentagon. There cannot be a long string of military and political decision points that now move from one Pentagon desk to another, from one service to another, and finally from one point to another halfway around the world.

The terrorist killing of the Marines disturbed me greatly. From the beginning, I had opposed their being sent to Lebanon. It was a stupid decision for several reasons, including the central military fact that Marines are trained as assault forces, not troops who hunker down indefinitely in foxholes while getting shot at. There was also no clearly defined enemy. The truth is that those Marines were political pawns with no military mission.

Even politically, the mission was ridiculous. The Marines were to show the flag. To impress whom and for what? That we are tough and will go to war? It's all right to fly the flag at times, but that doesn't mean we should put American forces at risk under "Rules of Engagement" that unnecessarily expose them or actually tie their hands. For all practical purposes, the Marines were simply to sit out in the middle of a field and not assault those who were sniping at them. The Marine commander calling the shots was not a leatherneck on the ground in

Lebanon but an Army general sitting behind a desk in Stuttgart, West Germany. The command responsibility was that of General Bernard Rogers, NATO commander, now retired. He was isolated from Lebanon by multiple layers of command. The fault was in the Pentagon command structure. The cumbersome chain of command imposed on the general by the JCS and services precluded effective control. I'm still outraged by the whole military mess.

Command problems during the U.S. invasion of Grenada finally backed both Nunn and me against a wall. We had to come out fighting. Although hailed as a military success, Grenada was a minefield of errors.

On October 25, 1983, elements of the Army, Navy, Air Force, and Marine Corps assaulted the Caribbean island. They were to rescue American medical students, restore democracy, and expel Cuban forces. The JCS deny they insisted that all four services get a piece of the action. Whether they did or not is immaterial. That is what happened, despite the lessons of failure in the Iranian operation three and a half years earlier.

The Grenada operation did have a single commander, Vice Admiral Joseph Metcalf, but he was at sea on the U.S.S. *Guam.* There was no unified commander on Grenada itself. The Army was assigned to capture the southern half of the island, including the medical students and the capital, St. Georges, while the Marines took the northern half. No one had been designated to coordinate the two forces. These are some of the problems that resulted from the lack of organization:

Most Army and Navy units could not communicate with one another. Nor could they coordinate with Metcalf, the overall commander. Communication between the two was, in fact, poor to almost nonexistent. There were similar problems between the Army and Marine forces. The reason was that all four services continue to purchase independent, incompatible communications equipment.

The first Army assault waves were unable to speak with Navy ships offshore to request and coordinate naval gunfire. One Army officer reportedly was so frustrated in trying to communicate with the offshore ships that he went to a civilian phone on the island and used his AT&T credit card to call buddies at Fort Bragg so they could get to the Navy and coordinate fire support. The JCS pooh-poohed the story, but some troops privately insist it's true. An official government report shows that some early communications between ground troops and the Navy were conducted by American ham radio operators. Officers of the 82nd Airborne Division actually flew to the flagship *Guam* several times to coordinate naval gun-fire. These and other attempts failed.

Navy messages were delayed or failed to reach Army troops on the ground. One delay almost compromised the reason for the invasion. American medical students at a second campus—military intelligence was aware of only one—phoned parents and friends in the United States to tell them that more than two hundred of them were sur-rounded by hostile troops and needed urgent rescue. American Rangers were finally rushed to save them. Such intelligence and other failures caused good friends of the military to ask many probing questions. It was later learned that Army and Navy officers had failed to attend each other's planning sessions.

Organizational foul-ups caused serious logistical prob-lems. The 82nd Airborne Division was one example. A battalion commander reported that he had been forced to deploy his men on Grenada with nothing except their rucksacks. The battalion had no vehicles and no long-range communications gear. The Rangers arrived with-out any heavy antiarmor weapons. TOW missiles didn't come ashore until the third day the Rangers were on the ground. All this equipment was needed in the event of a major battle. Most of the delays were caused by air trans-port scheduling. Military aircraft spent more time cir-cling Grenada's Point Salines airfield than flying from the

United States. One commander said they were "stacked up to the ionosphere." Some were forced to return to Puerto Rico and other locations to refuel.

Army helicopters carrying wounded were turned back from landing on the U.S.S. *Independence,* a Navy carrier, because their pilots had not been officially qualified to land by the Navy. Finally, when they were allowed to touch down and unload the wounded, a Navy commander was ordered not to refuel them because funding compensation had not yet been worked out in Washington.

It took three days for seven thousand American troops to defeat fifty Cuban soldiers and a few hundred lightly armed construction workers. Eighteen American troops were killed and 116 wounded. If the Cubans had deployed a significant number of men on the island, the foul-ups would have been magnified. The "corporate character" of the JCS and its service politics in the Grenada operation demonstrated beyond any doubt some terrible weaknesses in our ability to carry out a unified military action. And it highlighted the fact that the U.S. military system was consistently producing only moderate to minimum results.

We were told by the JCS that errors had indeed been made in the Grenada operation, but that they were being fixed. That was what we had been told about our problems in Iran, Beirut, and elsewhere. I wanted the system to reform itself, but it was not doing so. In fact, it was resisting reform. The JCS and others in the military left me no choice. No soldier or sailor lives because a commander tried. The commander must do more than try. He must succeed. In warfare, there are no excuses—only the living or the dead, only victory or defeat. The rest is just rhetoric, unless, as in the case of Vietnam, the politicians take charge of the war.

Nunn and I concluded that so long as the JCS continued with a weak joint system—a single-service rather than a joint perspective—our divided planning and structuring of the armed forces could lead the nation into terrible trouble in the future.

Lines of communication remained mostly inside each service, and there was no flow of information in and out of all branches. So long as this persisted, military mission capabilities would overlap. Costly weapons systems would be duplicated. The JCS would never address the critical issue of creating truly unified commands. Each would continue to fight his brother service for high-tech, high-cost weapons systems and bicker over pieces of the action. We were facing a long and costly civil war at the apex of our military power. Greatly disturbed by what had happened in Grenada, many of us in Congress, independent military analysts, and others refocused on reform of the JCS.

During our study, one appraisal of our military leadership resurfaced more than any other. It was a February 1982 statement by none other than the then incumbent JCS chairman, General David Jones. The Air Force leader had issued an unprecedented 6,500-word critique of the nation's military command structure and its problems. At the time it had swept across the Pentagon and official Washington like a flamethrower, scorching the seats of pants all over town. Defense Secretary Weinberger was furious. He and others at the Pentagon had tried to talk Jones out of issuing the statement. All of them had failed. Four months before retirement, Jones had, as the military say so eloquently, kicked ass. However, his observations had been gathering dust because most of the Pentagon brass defended the system. Now I and others dusted them off.

Jones zeroed in on the basic JCS problem: "By law, if we cannot reach unanimous agreement on an issue, we must inform the Secretary of Defense. We are understandably reluctant to forward disagreements, so we invest much time and effort trying to accommodate differing views of the chiefs."

Jones declared that the military should abolish its current system in which each service has a virtual veto on every issue at every stage of a routine staffing process. In other words, dump command by committee.

He added, "We need to spend more time on our war fighting capabilities and less on an intramural scramble for resources."

Jones called for cross-service experience among our military—Navy men working alongside Army and Air Force officers on common missions while retaining their service identity. He called for more JCS time and effort on strategic planning and for strengthening the role of unified commanders in the field with interservice acceptance of one on-the-scene commander. Jones also asked for a vice chairman to help the JCS chairman become a more effective and timely adviser to the President.

The chairman's statement raised a very sensitive question which tormented all the chiefs: Had their indecisiveness and inaction allowed Secretary McNamara to ride roughshod over them?

Ultimately, Jones was warning his colleagues that unless they put their own system in order, change would be forced on them. The veteran fighter and bomber pilot was right on target.

General Edward C. Meyer, Army Chief of Staff, followed Jones's attack with criticism of his own. Since Meyer was still active, his remarks had even more force. He warned his fellow chiefs that, on joint military issues, the nation's civilian leaders were increasingly turning to other sources for advice. Meyer was referring, in part, to the rise of defense intellectuals who were operating in both the military and political camps. He said the command structure had serious organizational, conceptual, and functional flaws. He insisted that if these were not corrected and the chiefs didn't react more quickly to the fast-paced times, their ability to affect events would be seriously diminished. The rest of the JCS opposed Meyer.

Meantime, some of us in the Congress were waiting for an opening. It came in January 1985, when I was appointed chairman of the Senate Armed Services Committee and Nunn became the ranking minority member. We introduced our defense reorganization measure. The JCS, Navy Secretary Lehman, John Warner, and other senators said, "No way!" Warner argued, "Today we have the finest Navy in the world—bar none. We are more capable of fulfilling our national security objectives than at any time during the past forty years."

He declared that President Reagan was satisfied with the performance of the JCS. Warner warned that our open concerns might affect the military budget and the morale of our fighting forces. He conceded, however, that substantial changes were needed in military procurement. Warner said that only a few minor changes were needed in the JCS and command structure.

Lehman came out smoking. He fired off blistering letters to me and the others involved. The secretary described our proposal as "whiz-kid theories" that would make his post and that of other civilian service secretaries "ceremonial." Lehman concluded, "The draft [bill] would make a hash of our defense structure."

It was clear that Lehman would, if the battle came to it, go down with all guns blazing. First he tried to muscle me politically. The secretary and his legislative crew were involved in some eighty written and forty oral amendments offered by members of the committee to our bill. He dangled political plums at Congress, proposing to expand the number of the Navy's home ports. This, of course, would mean jobs and other federal income in certain states and congressional districts. Numerous names, including Seattle and Staten Island, were floated. He talked of a $100 million program to establish these new ports. It would have cost billions. Five members of our committee were up for reelection. Lehman was addressing them especially.

Lehman hoped that the old fox Goldwater would become a pussycat. I passed the word to the military and among the committee that if that's the way Lehman wanted it, I too would play hardball. I put the defense budget, including all military promotions, on hold. I told them that just about everything connected with the military would be halted until we voted on reorganization. Weinberger and the JCS got the message. Lehman did not.

The Navy Secretary set up a crisis management center in Room 5C800 of the Pentagon to oppose reform. I phoned the office myself, and personnel there confirmed they were staffing the Navy's fight against reorganization. I was given the names of these Navy and Marine officers, who were attached to the Navy's legislative affairs office. The Navy denied that such an office existed. Lehman, meantime, was steaming around Capitol Hill, lobbying lawmakers to scuttle Goldwater and Nunn. One individual who objected to Lehman's plans caught my attention —his mother. She happened to have been a Goldwater supporter in 1964 and later. Hearing that her son and I were battling, she wrote him, "Dear John: I don't know what the dispute is, but you're wrong."

What was our precise proposal?

The bill stressed, in accord with constitutional principles, the civilian supremacy of the President as commander in chief. It spelled out the role of the Secretary of Defense: "The Secretary has sole and ultimate power within the Department of Defense on any matter on which the Secretary chooses to act."

It greatly strengthened the JCS chairman in setting policies, drafting military strategies, and shaping Pentagon budgets. Many functions were removed from the four independent services and reassigned to the chairman alone. He, not the JCS, would advise the President and Secretary. The entire joint staff—hundreds of officers previously under the JCS—would answer to the chairman alone. The realignment created, in effect, a powerful partnership between the chairman and the Secretary.

A four-star officer would become deputy, reporting to

the chairman. He would become acting head in the absence of the chairman. The two would act as a team with the vice chairman to coordinate programs and, if the chairman ordered, even direct the staff.

Our bill retained ten basic commands, the most important being the Atlantic Command, European Command, Pacific Command, Strategic Air Command, and Military Airlift Command. It added statutory provisions that considerably strengthened these commands and their commanders.

Field commanders would have much greater control over resources to accomplish their missions with far less direction in the hands of service bureaucrats in Washington. They would also have much greater control over their men. Navy and Marine officers would, for example, work entirely for their field commander, not their service chiefs and others at the Pentagon.

As we wrote the bill, this simple conviction moved all of us forward: For far too long, our generals in the field have been without armies and our admirals without fleets.

By direct order of the Congress, a career specialty would be created for officers on joint duty assignment. Joint duty simply means an Army, Navy, or other officer serving an assignment outside of his military department, such as on the Joint Staff or a unified command staff. In the past, the military generally viewed such assignments as just this side of Siberia.

Under the new system, future assignments and promotions would depend, to a significant extent, on joint duty. Whenever a military board considered a joint duty officer for promotion, it would be required to have a joint duty member. Procedures would be established to monitor the careers of joint duty officers. A record of joint duty would be needed for consideration for flag rank. All these top posts, unless a waiver were granted, would be reserved for officers with significant joint duty experience.

The ad hoc plan developed for Iran and the mismatched planning affecting the Grenada invasion would be eliminated. The planning for all such contingencies or emergencies would specify resource levels, sufficient and proper equipment. Policy assumptions and military operational planning would no longer be disconnected, as they were for the Marines in Beirut.

We walked through a minefield in the area of service roles and missions. Is the Air Force, for example, providing adequate close air support for Army ground forces? Why can't the Air Force and Navy provide sufficient airlift and sealift? Should the Air Force be assigned greater responsibilities in helping the Navy to execute its sea control mission? Does the Marine Corps need its own air force? Questions like these may well provide the flashpoint for the next interservice battle.

The plan was written to produce results. The chairman and vice chairman of the JCS must now produce, in consultation with the services, useful and timely advice to the President and Defense Secretary. The JCS staff can no longer be a dumping ground for inept officers.

More than ever before, the commanders in chief in the field will decide how to carry the war to the enemy. Our separate ground, sea, and air warfare by individual services is gone forever. The unified commander reports to the President and Defense Secretary. His subordinate commanders report directly to him and then to their respective service chiefs. No longer will the Army determine how much ammunition is stored and the Air Force decide where to put it for eventual use by the Navy.

The brass must get off their ass. In 1945, as World War II ended, we had more than 12 million men and women on active duty. Of those, about 17,000 had the rank of 0–6 and above. These included 101 three-star generals and admirals. A few years ago, we had somewhat more than 2 million service personnel—about 10 million less than at the end of World War II. Yet we have nearly the same number of high-ranking officers today—almost 15,500 men and women. There were nearly 120 three-star generals and admirals—more than in 1945! As Sam Nunn put it, "Apparently, it takes more admirals and generals to wage peace than run a war."

Unification of the four services by itself means nothing. We need a product line organization. The product line means the mission to be carried out. We must truly integrate these missions, bringing the best of all available talent into an operation, regardless of uniform. Our committee focused on six major military missions of the Defense Department: nuclear deterrence, maritime superiority, general power projection superiority, defense of NATO Europe, defense of East Asia, and defense of Southeast Asia.

During this time of changeover, we are still organized around functional inputs geared to individual services. Under reorganization, the objective is the mission, not the service. We have too many wasted resources in some areas and critical gaps in others. The military must begin to cross service lines and learn the difference between loyalty to one's branch and accomplishing a mission in the most efficient and effective ways possible. This is not being done on a high policy level today.

The Defense Department spends as much time on its annual budget as it does planning to defend the country. It is a race involving next year's dollars rather than long-term military efficiency. Similarly, the JCS takes care of the needs of its individual services and calls that strategic planning. They have become more like business managers than military officers.

All of this can be summed up in a single sentence. We have failed to coordinate the efficient use of resources with clear military strategy. With large federal deficits and growing reluctance in Congress to accept higher defense outlays, it's obvious that defense spending must be more effective and efficient. Like all other national problems, this one will not be solved by throwing money at it. The services simply must have joint hardware programs when possible, and a new two-year budget cycle should lessen much of the incoherent scrambling for funds.

There is an inherent budgetary conflict between the generals and admirals in Washington on the one hand, and commanders in the field on the other. The Pentagon favors investment in big hardware, research and development, and military construction. Commanders in Europe and the Pacific are much more concerned about their state of readiness—what is needed most if they have to go into action tomorrow. There is a multibillion-dollar question: Do we have a balance between these two concerns? If our plan means anything, it gives field commanders a greater voice in the budget process to mandate that balance.

The act establishes a new under secretary of defense for acquisition. He is the Pentagon's top procurement official. Almost 18,000 workers, some 10 percent of the staff, are being cut from the Pentagon. The number of Defense Department reports to Congress is being reduced by about 265, or two thirds.

Considerable savings may be made through joint purchases and other means. Obviously, we acted in response to multibillion-dollar cost overruns on military weapons programs and in answer to charges of waste and corruption among defense contractors. It was also an attempt to come to grips with large hardware requests, such as a multiyear appropriation for $130 billion to build two new military aircraft and a helicopter. The $659 ashtrays, $640 toilet seats, and $436 hammers only added insult to injury. Single-source contracting would come under greater scrutiny.

The $300-billion-a-year defense budget represents about 30 percent of our annual U.S. expenditures. Ten percent of America's work force is employed in defense. As one of the few controllable budget items, it will always be a target for reduction.

The buildup of our defenses under President Reagan was unparalleled in peacetime. He added about $400 billion in real Pentagon growth. There's now a debate as to whether we got our money's worth. I believe we did for the simple reason that the Soviet Union has steadily become a more formidable foe.

Those who assume that Nunn and I turned on the military and tried to challenge its power and trample on its traditions have not understood our intent or motivation. One of the central reasons for our reorganization act was to renew the military's financial and functional integrity. Both of us are committed to the constitutional principle of civilian control of the military and to curbing harmful interservice politics. Nothing is more sacred in public life to either of us than the defense of the nation's freedom. To suggest that our words or actions are an indictment of military performance misses the point entirely.

On May 7, 1986, the Senate passed the reorganization act by a vote of 95 to 0. The House approved it by a vote of 406 to 4. Seldom in its history has Congress spoken so clearly. I did too: "It's the only goddamn thing I've done in the Senate that's worth a damn. I can go home happy, sit on my hill, and shoot jackrabbits."

Sam was much more subdued. He thought it was a pretty good day.

The Presidential Packard Commission, headed by industrialist David Packard, a former deputy secretary of the Defense Department, did much of the spadework for all of us. Contrary to some published reports, Cap Weinberger and the President did not try to cut us off at the pass. They supported us once we made our objectives clear. Both also knew they could not defeat the measure.

Another reason we were successful was the absence of major media attention. If TV news in particular had been able to make this into a dramatic, personal confrontation between the JCS and us, we might have failed. However, Nunn and I tried to keep the battle low-key and objective. Most in the media did not understand the subject well. It was very complex and therefore a story which the evening TV news could not easily tell. So they ignored us for the most part. To a large degree, the media—especially television—missed one of the most momentous stories of the past decade on Capitol Hill. We are still grateful for it.

We can now reveal that hundreds of military officers privately helped us in off-the-record and other briefings. Some risked their careers to do so. We also ran scared much of the time. The Pentagon loomed out there, and it is extremely powerful. It can do many things, including influencing the President. We proceeded, but usually holding our breath.

We interviewed about five hundred people in doing our research for the plan. The majority of the military men with whom we spoke, both active and retired, were highly supportive. Contrary to letters, statements, and other claims of our opponents, most active military saw the need for change. I believe the JCS now does as well. Our plan is now the law of the land, and public opinion is behind it. The JCS now clearly understands that the roles and missions of the services—unchanged since 1948—have been transformed by tremendous technological change; and, especially important, a hound dog is watching.

That watchful dog is Sam Nunn. He will hound everybody involved and not let go. I know Sam. Unless he is elected President and has too many other duties or his life is somehow shortened, Nunn will eventually corner those who stray from the law. He won't bite but will surely bark. Sam will long outlast those now in the JCS and will probably be in the Senate for at least another thirty years. Nunn is only turning fifty, and there's really no way he can be whupped.

Nunn and I talked long and hard about the outcome. We're convinced the legislative fight is largely over. Some adjustments to the law will be needed. Sam and others must monitor the details closely. They will have to hold further hearings and go out into the field to monitor various commands.

Implementation is only beginning. The statutory authority is strong and clear. It's as carefully written a piece of legislation as either of us has ever seen in the Senate. After the measure was approved by Congress, the two major concerns of the military were how the flow of officers to and from joint assignments will work and the precise role of the vice chairman, especially his power in presiding for the chairman. We believe both will stand up well over time. On a practical, day-to-day basis, it's up to Admiral Crowe to make the legislation work. Crowe is an intelligent, reasonable man. He must now prove he's also courageous and can rise above traditional parochial interests. If Crowe and the JCS try to drag their feet, they may win the next Grenada, but perhaps not more crucial battles.

Neither Sam Nunn nor I ever said the act is perfect. There will be some disappointments and problems. Nevertheless, we believe it can be fine-tuned and fully implemented in three to five years. We expect to see future opposition from some of the services, depending on whose ox is being gored during the changeover. There's no doubt about that. But the big, furious fight is over. Nunn, a modest man, gave me too damn much credit in saying, "This law would never have been passed without Barry Goldwater. He was the point man, the guy with the guts. He never minded standing alone."

The truth is, I never stood alone. Nunn was always by my side. He took all the flak I did. We were a team, creating close bipartisan cooperation between a chairman and the ranking minority member to an unprecedented degree. I hope our experience will serve as a model for Republicans and Democrats in foreign policy, intelligence, and other areas.

At 10 A.M. on December 10, 1986, an Air Force staff car picked me up at Walter Reed Army Medical Center. I had been at the hospital for treatment of a skin virus. It had rained in Washington the previous day, and the weather was damp as the driver headed across the Potomac River.

When we arrived at the east entrance of the Pentagon, the rain had stopped but the wind was sharp and chill. Secretary Weinberger opened the car door. I looked out, and the sun was trying to peek through the clouds. My right knee hurt, but with the help of my cane I got out of the car and stood straight.

Admiral Crowe joined us, and with the Secretary and the chairman of the JCS on either side, I walked down a ramp to the parade ground. The four service chiefs fell in behind us. We were escorted to our seats by young officers from each service. The seating was divided into four sections behind us. The two to the left were for members of Congress and retired military officers, including members of the Armed Services Committee and staff, my personal staff, and my son, Barry, Jr. The two sections to the right were filled with service chiefs, other active military personnel, and Defense Department personnel.

We sat and faced the parade ground. The Marine band had already played several marches. The band stood on the field with the Army, Navy, Air Force, and Marine Drill teams. A ceremonial color guard also stood at attention nearby.

The ceremony began with the four service artillery groups firing a sequential seventeen-gun salute across the river toward the Capitol. The smoke quickly disappeared in the stiff breeze. The guard presented the colors, and the Marine band slowly eased into the national anthem.

As we stood at attention with our hands over our hearts and the military saluting, a dull roar slowly rose into thunder behind us. It seemed a new storm might be kicking up. But it was not the weather. Four F-15 fighter planes were now streaking toward our backs. They swept in low and fast, dipping their wings slightly as they passed over us. The quartet peeled off high and left to avoid the skyscrapers in nearby Rosslyn. A tiny silver drop trickled down my right cheek.

Secretary Weinberger stood and read the citation for the Department of Defense Medal for Distinguished Public Service. He said that Barry Goldwater was a man of courage, conscience, and patriotism. He suddenly called out, "Extremism in the praise of Barry Goldwater is no vice because it's true." He said I had taught the country three lessons:

• Do not become involved in a war unless you intend to win.

• Government regulation of our lives becomes regimentation of liberty.

• Despite all her faults and shortcomings, it's perfectly all right to love America.

I stood and faced halfway toward the two hundred guests. Weinberger pinned the Department of Defense Distinguished Service Medal on my lapel. The secretaries of the four services then pinned their distinguished civilian service medals on me. John Lehman was next to last. The Navy Secretary wore a big smile. He showed real class. Tears were now streaming down my face. The Marine band played "America the Beautiful."

Admiral Crowe then spoke. He said I had helped resurrect the American spirit after Vietnam and the national doubt of the 1970s.

I didn't know what to say. I mentioned my mother and Sandy Patch. I recalled putting on a military uniform for the first time more than sixty years before at Staunton Military Academy. The most important words I'd ever learned tumbled out—that each and every American owes a debt of service to the country, whether in the military, politics, or community service.

I looked out over the officers and troops and began to cry, choking out, "Never in my life have I known such a high quality of enlisted men and officers as we have now."

I couldn't continue. Fortunately, the noise of air traffic from National Airport drowned out some of my words. I said, "I love those damn things, but I wish they'd quit for a while."

I reminded the gathering of our responsibility to uphold and defend the Constitution and closed with these words:

"I admire you. I respect you. And I salute you."

12

The Last Race

IT WAS ABOUT NINE O'CLOCK IN THE EVENING WHEN we rang the doorbell to young Peggy's home in Newport Beach, California. I was wearing a red-and-white nightshirt, red knee socks, and red tennis shoes, and had a red-and-white nightcap on my head. My wife, Peggy, always the lady, wore a dark cocktail dress.

"Haaaapy New Year!" we chorused when our younger daughter opened the door. Her husband and their three sons, hearing our voices, soon rushed to greet us. The grandchildren shouted, "It's Grandpa and Grandma!"

I wore a different costume each year to get our reunion off to a merry start. For about a decade, the entire family had gathered each New Year's at young Peggy's home to celebrate my birthday and that of Joanne, our eldest child. Our two sons, Barry Jr. and Michael, with his wife, Connie, completed the crew.

These reunions were always boisterous—poking fun at one another, laughing and shouting, singing, hugging, and devouring mountains of food. But this year, our get-together had a second, more serious purpose. We had gathered to make a very important family decision—whether I would run for a fifth term in the Senate.

I had made a solemn promise in writing to my wife more than a year before that I would not return to Washington. The four children were well aware of that pledge. After our many years of separation, Peggy and I would finally be together. We would be alone, away from the crowds, to share one another more closely. I would be seventy-one years old on New Year's Day. It was time for us to enjoy some of the freedom I had always talked about—to catch some last glimpses of faraway places before we were too old to travel, laugh and cry at the antics of our ten grandchildren, and watch the twilight fade across the Arizona desert.

None of us was certain what decision would be made in the morning. Peggy did not want me to run again. She had never liked politics. Her health was not good. She wanted me near her.

Each of our children is quite different. It was almost impossible to know how they would vote. Joanne and Barry are very independent and strong-willed. Both had children but were divorced. Young Peggy was happily married and devoted to her mother. She also ran a food business. Michael had a wonderful wife and children and a good job in the construction industry. We were a family, but a very diverse clan. Together, we were the third, fourth, and fifth generations of Arizona Goldwaters.

As casually as possible, I watched each of the children individually. I reflected on our marriage, how Peggy and I had done as parents. Whether each child, now an adult, had reached his or her potential, who and what we were as a family. The answers would be reflected in tomorrow's fateful decision.

My wife was always pleased when the family was together. Every laugh from our children and grandchildren brought a smile to her face. I was pleased she was so happy. In looking at her, my mind wandered back through the years. There was much to remember.

Peggy had brought up the children virtually alone for many years. Joanne had been born in 1936, and the others soon followed. Just five years after Joanne's birth, I left, except for infrequent liberty, for four and a half

years of military service during World War II. Little
Peggy was born while I was in India during the war.
Even after I came home, the hours at the store were long,
and local politics took more time away from the family.

I had tried to make up for this by taking Peggy and the
children on camping, rafting, and photography trips. But
Peg and I were happiest alone—or maybe only with another couple that had been close to us over the years. Our
fifteenth wedding anniversary, September 22, 1949, perhaps tells more about Peggy than almost any other time
or place in our marriage. We rode mules to the top of
Navajo Mountain on the Indian reservation in northern
Arizona. There was a winding trail to the 11,000-foot
peak. It took us about six hours to reach the summit.
Two longtime friends, Toni and Bert Holloway, and a
cowboy called "Whitey" climbed with us.

Darkness was falling by the time we reached the top. It
was cold. Peggy was exhausted but said nothing. I got a
fire going and cooked steaks. We began drinking the first
of four bottles of champagne that I had brought along in
celebration of our anniversary. I told Indian tales, including one about the mountain being the home of the Navajo
war god. We sang a few old songs. The wind whistled
across the mountaintop as we chewed on the steaks. I
surprised everyone with a big chocolate cake. I had
packed it in a tin box. We ate it, our teeth chattering as
the wind whipped more sharply, and night covered us.

Peg slipped into her bedroll—not a whimper—and
slept on the ground. It got down to freezing during the
night. As the temperature plunged, I kicked myself for
bringing her up the mountain. Yet she never complained.

That was Peggy all her life—soft, sweet, private. She
healed quietly from life's injuries. The separation of war
and politics left scars on her soul, but she said nothing.
After many years, I began to understand how deep these
wounds were. Now, in 1980, the ache of that same loneli-
ness caused me to wake nights and wonder whether it
was all worth it—whether I should go home to her in

Arizona or plow ahead in Washington to help strengthen the conservative movement.

I tried to guess what Peggy would say in front of the children tomorrow. My best was behind me now. A younger man could do the job in the Senate just as well. I had been ill a lot in the last several years—hip operations, heart bypass, painfully bad knees—and missed many votes. Despite that, Arizona Republicans had told me privately, if I didn't run, the state party would collapse. It wasn't sufficiently unified. Well, I thought to myself, if they haven't got their act together by now, they deserve to lose.

Peggy was smiling at me. It was a young smile, shedding the years and the pain. I saw her in some of the snapshots I had taken of her through the years. There she was, standing in front of the Royal Palms Apartments in downtown Phoenix, where we'd made our first home—a small two-bedroom place which we rented for $50 a month. Peggy had talked of designing clothes for Goldwaters. She had studied designing at Washington's Mount Vernon Junior College, a finishing school. Eventually our two daughters would go there. We would become a twosome at the store. It never happened. Yet not a whimper from her.

Suddenly we were rafting on the Salmon River up in Idaho. She got soaking wet from the spray. This roughing it, Peggy said, was for the birds. Next year, she laughed, we'd vacation in a California beach house. Instead we went to Monument Valley on the Navajo Indian Reservation, where we slept in bedrolls in a shed for storing wool. But not a word of distress from her.

We eventually rented a summer place at the Balboa Bay Club in Newport Beach. We bought a fifty-four-foot Hatteras, and I spent most of my time up to my elbows in grease and grime, working on the boat's engine. Peggy made some good friends, but I never really liked the place, and said so.

Later, Peggy got a big laugh on me in London, shopping with her friend, Dorothy Yardley. She bought me a nightshirt that had "Newport" scrawled across the front. Peg thought the reminder was very funny. For that reason, I wore it often.

She had a terrific sense of humor. That was one of her inner strengths. Peggy always laughed in recalling an incident in Portugal in the late 1960s. The two of us had taken a trolley from Lisbon out to the beach community of Estoril. We were walking down a narrow old road when a towheaded youngster of about twelve darted across the street toward us.

"Aren't you Senator Goldwater?" he asked. I nodded yes.

"Don't you remember me?" he inquired again.

"Well—" I stammered.

"Of course," he blurted. "How could you forget? I'm the kid who was riding with you on a plane going to Houston. I came out of the rest room and couldn't get my zipper up. You zipped up my pants!"

With that introduction, we met his mother. The four of us had an interesting chat about the ways and wonders of travel. She directed us to a fine restaurant that we would have missed. I told Peg over lunch, "As I've always said, if you pull your pants up, you stay out of trouble. If you pull 'em down, only God knows what'll happen!"

We went on to Paris and met Colonel James H. "Trapper" Drum, and his wife, Betty, two old and very dear friends. I quietly told Trapper that we had to give the girls the slip for a while. He made up an excuse, and we were off. Trapper, now retired from the Army, was very mystified about it all. I guess he thought we were sneaking away to one of those famous Paris girlie shows. I said, "Hell no, Trapper, I want to get a tattoo."

He seemed shocked but knew that I had a tattoo on my left hand. I had received it as a member of the Smoki People in Prescott, Arizona. The Smokis, formed in 1921, are a "tribe" of non-Indian business and professional men living in Prescott who recreate age-old Indian dances and ceremonials to help pay for the town's spectacular Fourth of July celebration. Their tattoo consists of dots on the outer side of the small finger of the left hand. I wanted to place an arc above the dots.

We had to ditch some reporters who were following us. Finally, we got the name and address of a tattoo artist in Montmartre. With a good taxi driver and a healthy tip, we dodged them.

The artist, who insisted on being addressed as "professor," showed us a wide array of his work. These photos included a full-rigged ship which the professor claimed to have placed on the chest of the King of Denmark. He showed us many other notable works, including some interesting but unmentionable tattoos on ladies. When I mentioned that all I wanted was a simple arc on one small finger, the professor ballooned up to his full height and looked down on me as if I were a Left Bank maggot. This was well below his artistic standards. This was Paris, the art capital of the world. Didn't we know where we were?

His French pique finally simmered down when Trapper pulled out a roll of francs. The professor sighed, "Okay," but scowled during most of the work. A drunken Frenchman roared into the shop in the middle of the arc. The professor slowly got up, screwed up his face, and pitched the drunk bodily across the street. Trapper paid, I meekly thanked the professor, and we hopped a taxi back to our hotel. I made it up to him by buying dinner for everyone. For years I've had to answer questions about that tattoo at the most unusual times and places. Trapper still thinks we should have gone to the girlie show.

The annual highlight of Peggy's social year in Arizona arrived during the last week of January. The Grand Canyon Hiking, Singing and Loving Club, which we had founded in 1948 with three other couples, set out to do just that. The eight of us, longtime friends, drove our cars up to the canyon. We rented cabins at Bright Angel Lodge and later moved to nearby Thunderbird Lodge at the south rim for three days of merriment and relaxation. Eventually we had to hire a bus because more than thirty couples had joined the group. We rode up from Phoenix, with me as tour guide.

Everybody was required to take over the bus mike and tell at least one joke. Some were pretty risqué. Peg often turned off her hearing aid, which she had begun to wear in the late 1960s, but she thoroughly enjoyed watching everyone else laugh.

Ollie Carey was the life of the party every year. Peggy loved Ollie, yet no two people were more different. Ollie was the wife of Harry Carey, the late actor. A big woman, Ollie could cuss the toughest truck driver on the road under the table. And, I think, drink him there, too.

Peggy and I met her at a drive-in cafe in La Jolla, California, late one night in July 1948. We were having hamburgers and Cokes when I heard this tough, coarse voice holler at me, "Hey there! You with the big silver-turquoise belt buckle! Wanna sell it?"

I saw this old gal in baggy pants and a worn shirt and hollered back, "Who the hell are you?"

"Ollie Carey!" she boomed. "Wife of Harry, the actor. I been up to see some friends of mine—Greg Peck, Mel Ferrer, and Dorothy McGuire—at rehearsal. They're over at the La Jolla summer theater. Who the hell are you?"

"I'm Barry Goldwater."

"Well, goddamn, Barry. Lemme sit down with you and the missus. I hope she is!"

Peggy introduced herself to Ollie, who tried to take my belt off. She said she wanted it for her son. I told her to get the hell away from me. She was laughing and poking me in the ribs.

Ollie told me she was a Democrat, but I forgave her. On each of these Grand Canyon visits, Ollie and I became gin rummy opponents. I beat the pants off her. The only things we ever agreed on were the beauty of sunrise over the canyon and Mexican food. We loved both.

Ollie is over ninety now. She was born in New York on January 31, 1896. I like her because she's older than I am and is a truly eloquent cusser. She lives in northern California on a farm outside Carpinteria. Ollie says she wants to live to be ninety-nine. Why ninety-nine? She hates round numbers!

Our eighteenth trip to the canyon in 1966 was a memorable one. Peggy and I had gone to bed at 10 P.M. About 2:30 in the morning, I heard somebody blowing taps over and over again outside on the rim of the canyon. It was driving me nuts, so I got up and staggered downstairs half asleep. I wandered outside and found my friend, Bill Bailey, still blowing taps. Bill was about half lit and wouldn't let go of the notes, so I pushed him back inside.

Fred Boynton, who couldn't read a note of music, was still pounding out whorehouse piano. Ollie was spread-eagled on the floor, passed out with a stale cigarette butt between her lips. A few other couples staggered around singing.

I was standing in the middle of the room in my nightshirt. I've worn one all my life. The last celebrators were laughing at a United States senator who apparently looked to them like Rip Van Winkle. I finally hollered, "All right, you've finished the hiking and singing. Now, go to bed and make love!"

I went to bed, asking myself whether Peggy and I should admit that these crazy people were our best friends!

It was the last time we went to the canyon because of the rarefied air. We used up six bottles of oxygen on that trip. We moved down to Sedona and lower flights of fancy.

These were wonderful, relaxing excursions. Once, on getting off the bus, somebody handed me a poster which I later hung in my Senate office: "STRESS: That confusion created when one's mind overrides the body's basic desire to choke the living shit out of some asshole who desperately needs it."

Peggy never accepted the bad language, nor many of the awful jokes. But I rarely saw her happier than when we were renewing our long relationship with these close friends. She thrived on the excitement and the good-natured kidding. But when these trips were over, she returned home and closed out strangers who would intrude on the sanctity of her family privacy.

Reflecting on this today, I remember her interview with "CBS News" after the 1964 convention. As Bob Pierpoint interviewed her, the camera roamed through our hilltop home. Watching the program later, Peggy cringed as it entered our bedroom. She didn't like it at all. She said it was dreadful. They were invading our privacy. The camera panned to our Indian and other Western art, into our two sitting rooms and library. It was intruding into thirty sacred years of marriage. She wanted to shout.

Pierpoint asked Peggy about us. She said the wife of a politician led a lonely life. Her husband was swallowed up by strangers. She said softly, "You get used to it, but you never accept it."

Peggy was uncharacteristically blunt. She described many newspaper cartoons of me as cruel. She said they bothered her. Peg detested any form of harshness. Asked why I ran, she said, "He couldn't let them down."

Besides husband and family, Peggy's major interest was Planned Parenthood. She was a charter member and onetime president of the Arizona group. She didn't believe people should bring children into the world unless they could properly care for them. If they could afford it, however, she believed in large families.

I recalled Peggy when the Reagan administration eliminated federal funding of Planned Parenthood because of its massive involvement with abortions. I am against abortion in principle and do not believe the government should intrude in the private lives of its citizens. But Peggy probably would have seen the cutoff as a mistake insofar as the poor were concerned.

When I returned to the Senate in 1969, Peggy came

less and less to Washington. She liked to attend White House receptions and Air Force balls. She enjoyed formal night life. I hated it, and even when we went out, I insisted on getting to bed early. Peggy talked easily with strangers, even though she was very shy. I have never been good at small talk and saw most of these parties as a waste of time.

Peggy surprised all of us by keeping a faithful diary of these social events. She even recalled what people wore. But she never liked Washington. Perhaps it was the constant political gossip. Peggy was the most gracious, generous woman I ever met. She despised gossip and the Washington rumor mill.

One of the reasons she didn't return to Washington was her worsened hearing. I still don't accept that, but my children, staff, and others insist it was a major factor. Dean Burch and Ellen Thrasher have described receptions at which Peggy seemed embarrassed because she couldn't hear properly.

The problem began in 1953. The family went to Nassau in the Bahamas for Christmas. Peggy woke up and couldn't hear well. We tried warm oil and every family remedy we could think of and finally saw a doctor. He said it was temporary. It was not.

After the presidential campaign, we were in New York. Peggy slipped on some ice on a sidewalk. After that accident her hearing steadily deteriorated. We saw different medical specialists. The problem was finally diagnosed as Ménière's syndrome. It's a malfunctioning of the semicircular canal of the inner ear which causes dizziness and a buzzing in the ear. At times, she appeared to lose her balance. The children and I had to raise our voices for her to hear. She began lip-reading lessons.

Beginning in 1979, Peggy rarely came to Washington. A longtime smoker, she had developed emphysema. The doctors scared the hell out of her, and she finally quit smoking that year.

Peggy's general health, her desire for privacy, and the

fact that politics had become a kind of mistress to me caused her to withdraw to our hilltop. She was convinced I was coming home at the end of 1980.

Tomorrow she would cast her vote on that decision.

Joanne sat across from me, sipping a glass of wine. She would be forty-four years old tomorrow. We were very much alike—stubborn and hardheaded.

Before I died, we'd both agreed, we'd sit down and resolve whatever it was that separated us. We hadn't been able to do so. She was boisterous and independent, I thought too much so. And I didn't care for many of her friends, who seemed like a fast crowd.

Joanne said I demanded too much of her. It was never that. I didn't accept her rebellious nature.

Joanne often complained that I didn't show her enough love, personally or publicly. Yet she'd always say, "Daddy, I know you love me absolutely—more than anything."

I did, from the day she was born. No father ever took his children on more outdoor trips when home. And when away, through all the years, I wrote Joanne and the other children hundreds of letters. They have saved most of them. One was written to them in June 1943, when I was stationed in India. They had broken a large limb from an old tree at our summer place in La Jolla, and I lectured them:

> I was walking down the street today, and saw a very pretty garden in a beautiful front yard. Daddy walked over to that garden, and sat down by a long row of sweet-looking flowers.
>
> Well, a bird suddenly landed by the flowers. He was tired. The bird had flown all the way from La Jolla, thousands of miles away. When the bird got his breath, he started to talk to the flowers and I couldn't help but hear what he said:
>
> "Say, fellows, you've heard me talk about that pretty patio in La Jolla with the big tree in the middle of it,

which shades all of your cousins. Well, last week, someone broke a limb off that tree, and you ought to see your
cousins now. They are all wrinkled and old-looking, and
they don't smile anymore."

With that, all the flowers started to cry. Their colors
ran and they drooped. Even the old tree above me sighed
and moaned at the plight of those poor California flowers . . .

Daddy wants you to know that God placed everything
on this earth for a purpose. He put the ground there for
us to walk on, and the flowers to grow in. He put trees in
the ground to shade us, the grass and the flowers. He put
rain in the sky to water the trees and the flowers so they
would all grow and be pretty—and we could be happy
looking at them.

When we break a tree down, or walk on the flowers, or
hurt little birds, we are doing things that will make people unhappy—just like the crying flowers made Daddy
unhappy.

Everything in this world has been put there by God for
some good reason. . . . Remember that we love everything that grows. We will not break up the lives of trees—
or flowers, or men, or anything. Of course, except those
things that are bad. I'll tell you about them one day. Give
Mommy a big kiss for Daddy.

Love,

Daddy

I wrote to them of starving children in war-torn countries and how lucky they were. On July 10, 1944, I wrote
to Joanne:

I want you to try your best at everything. If your best
won't win, don't squawk about it. I don't ever want to
hear you make an excuse for being beaten, other than
your opponent was better.

Love,

Daddy

She now wants to throw her arms around me. I want that, too. But she's not a kid anymore. She's an adult. I want important talks the old-style way—a sit-down at home with mutual understanding and respect, dignity, not chumminess at some public gathering. That's Joanne's word—chummy. Love is not being chummy. Love is honesty, truth, and generosity of spirit.

Joanne and I chatted, and I wanted to hug her. I had no idea how she would vote tomorrow.

Barry Jr. was speaking with his mother. He had as strong a personality as Joanne. He often talked of taking the clothes off emperors and showing the real stuff of men. Barry considered himself a leader in the tell-it-like-it-is generation. He had long told me that I spent too much time on politics and my hobbies and not enough on him. He said I wasn't home to help him with schoolwork, nor to advise him in untangling some of his problems and aims. Yet I had often said and written him: "Always be who and what you really are. Never be false. Be honest, God-fearing, dedicated to your fellow man. Whatever you do in life, give it a full day, a full week, a full year's work."

I never tried to influence Barry to enter politics or walk any particular path. That was his choice. He saw my reluctance to do that as forcing him to deal with his problems alone.

Barry said he had never understood his mother. She was obviously loving and had tremendous feeling about her family. But she wouldn't open up, he complained, and tell him her most sensitive inner feelings. He and Joanne demanded that we let it all hang out with them. They wanted to explore the innermost, most delicate aspects of human behavior. Peggy was too shy for that. And while we explained the facts of life to our children, neither of us had any interest in discussing every part of the human anatomy or conduct. Nor did either of us feel such chumminess had many redeeming qualities. Joanne and Barry saw us as loving parents but unable—if we would not share our innermost secrets and discuss some of theirs—to express our affection for them.

Barry served on Capitol Hill as a California congressman for fourteen years. He did a good job. His name came up in connection with a drug investigation. The year-long study finally exonerated him, but the ordeal for the family, especially his mother, was devastating. He ran for the Senate and lost. Barry is now back in California, working in financial management. He seems much happier being out of politics. Of all our children, his views on my retiring from the Senate were the least predictable.

I've thought long and hard about my relationships with Joanne and Barry. Both are stubborn and headstrong, just like their father. Both are outspoken. Yet none of that explains the distance that had increased between us over the years. It has taken me a long time to figure out why, and I'm still not entirely certain. But it's clear that the values of their generation and mine are very different. The greatest difference between us is our attitudes toward money or material things. I have always viewed money as a necessity, no more and no less. The two of them see owning money as an accomplishment in itself, an end. I've not given them all the money they wanted—although they have received a lot from Peggy and me—simply because I feel it should be earned. I've never believed our giving them money was a sign of our love. All that I possess, the four children will eventually have. But I'm fed up with money talk.

Young Peggy saw her parents in a different light: "When people saw them together, they knew my parents were very much in love. But in the house they were very private with their love."

When young Peggy was about twelve years old, she was very mature for her age. One day she experimented with peroxide and bleached her hair a bright orange. When her mother saw it, she banished young Peggy to her room and later admonished her, "How dare you! Who do you think you are, Marilyn Monroe?"

My wife shared her feelings more with young Peggy than any of the other children. She confided in her about the increasing loss of her hearing and explained why she wouldn't return to Washington: "I can't be just a drone there. When someone speaks to me, I just can't pick out many of the words. It's very frustrating."

Young Peggy, reflecting on her brother's leaving Congress, said perceptively, "Perhaps it's a good thing. He's always lived in Dad's shadow. One thing about Dad: He always knew who and what he was. He never had an identity crisis. His problem was that he was hyperactive. He just couldn't sit still."

I was certain one thing would happen the following day. Young Peggy would lead the discussion.

Michael was somewhat shy, like his mother. He and Barry Jr. had graduated from Staunton Military Academy. Neither had chosen a military career. Barry went on to graduate from Arizona State University in Tempe, while Mike was graduated from the University of Arizona at Tucson.

Mike and I shared a secret about tomorrow's meeting. On the previous July 21, I had written him a letter. I told him the question of whether to run for a fifth term was "driving me up the wall" and making me "a little bit crazy." The letter spelled out the pressures—from Republicans across the country, from the military, and from friends everywhere.

The dilemma was summed up in a few sentences: "I promised your mother not to run, and have a very clear idea about the sanctity of promises. The question I have in my mind is whether she would be mentally or physically able to stand another six years of my being in Washington, and she hating it. But, if I give up this job of being a senator, I can't stay at home day after day. I'd fly to the moon. At the same time, I don't believe any man is absolutely essential to the future of this country. If I felt that way, I'd get myself a cross, and nail myself to it."

Mike responded to my letter. He wrote one that I

might have penned. It was blunt: "You got yourself into this mess; now get yourself out."

Mike also hit me where many colleagues in the Senate did: "Don't discount your lawmaking ability and seniority."

He emphasized that the fate of Arizona's GOP should not enter into my decision. "Your allegiance is to the country first, the state second. You said that in 1964."

Then, Mike came to the nitty-gritty—Mom. This is a summary of the final part of his letter, much of it word for word:

There's not a more loved person I can think of than Mom. Her charm, wit, and intelligence are renowned. I like to think a little of them has sunk into each of your thickheaded children. God knows, she tried to impart them to you. She is sick and tired of politics, but I don't think that is the problem. She is very lonely a lot of the time because you can be inconsiderate about her hearing problem. She is alone in a crowd. She doesn't want her family and friends to have to speak loudly. Instead, she hears yelling and fighting. You have to take the time to understand the reasons for her not wanting you to run again—not what she says but why she says it. Only then will you make your being in politics easier for her.

Mike concluded: "I see it [whether to run] as a choice between living and dying. Make your peace with Mom however you can. She's a lot stronger physically and mentally than you think she is. You'll be no good to anyone if you're dead. Not to God; not to country; not to state; not to your children; not to mother, and especially not to your loving son."

It was time to go to bed. I decided not to do my New Year's Eve dance. It was too reflective an evening. I usually put on a silly grin, different nightcaps and hats, and did a hop, skip, and jump to the laughter of our grandchildren. For a finale, I would bend over, flip up my nightshirt, and show my bare bottom. The grandchildren always cheered wildly and called for an encore. Instead, subdued and thoughtful, I quietly slipped away to bed.

After a big breakfast, I lounged in the living room reading the morning newspaper. Young Peggy suddenly appeared and said, "Dad, we'd like to see you in my bedroom."

She took my hand, led me to her bedroom, and closed the door, saying we wanted a place away from the grandchildren. My wife and our children were waiting. Some sat on the bed. Others were gathered on chairs around it. Young Peggy opened, "Happy birthday, Dad!"

The others chorused the same as my wife kissed me. We repeated the same to Joanne. Then the room became quiet.

After a pause, young Peggy said, "Dad, we want you to know that whatever you and Mom decide, we're behind you. We've decided not to interfere. It's your decision—the two of you—yours alone."

Peggy's last word strung out like an echo—alone, alone.

No one spoke. I didn't know what to say. It was still.

Finally my wife turned, looked at me, and said, "I won't hold you to your promise, Barry. Whatever you decide is all right with me. I want you to be happy."

Tears welled up in my eyes. My wife began to cry. Soon everyone was weeping. Joanne put her hand on my wrist. Barry cried on my shoulder. Mike was shaking his head as tears streamed down his face. Young Peggy wiped her cheeks with a handkerchief. My wife finally said, "It's all right, Barry. I understand. I love you."

It was done. She knew that in my heart of hearts I wanted to run. That I could not come home and die. Washington was too much a part of me. Arizona was my home, but the Senate had become my life. I couldn't give it up. Not because I didn't love my wife and children. Not because I loved Arizona less. But because the Senate and Washington had become me. Yes, Washington had changed me, chipped at me, and marked me. I was one of them—not the young Arizonan who had arrived on the Senate floor so long ago. It was only now—in the fears and tears of my family—that all of us saw it so clearly. Peggy had recognized it better than I. It was she—not I or the children—who made the decision. She was reconciled to who and what I was and, because she surrendered so much, accepted me more than I ever understood. I was more than a husband, more than a father. I was a man—a political animal. I could not climb down from Capitol Hill. She saw it all. There was too much adventure up there for me, too much personal freedom. I had become old in the Senate, yet not old enough to descend from my mountain to the desert of Arizona.

Young Peggy stood, still wiping her cheeks, and said, "But there's one condition, Dad."

I looked at her silently, too emotionally drained to speak. She said, "You must give Mom your quality time. Not time, but quality time. You must come home more weekends. And you must stay for not just two days but three or four. You have to promise us that."

Barry Jr., Joanne, and Mike chorused their agreement. I nodded and took my wife's hand. Young Peggy opened the bedroom door, and we walked together into her living room, perhaps more of a family at that moment than we had ever been in our lives.

From the beginning, the 1980 campaign did not go well. I almost did not survive it, physically or politically. The physical aspect has never been disclosed. On June 19 I awoke a few minutes after midnight. My right hip was paining severely. I was in bed at our Washington apartment. Two days earlier, I had had the wires removed from the artificial hip that had been inserted there in 1976. The wires had been causing me recurrent pain, and it was decided they should go. I reached down to the hip, and my hand came up wet. I turned on the bedside lamp. The hand was covered with blood.

I tried to pull back the bed covers and see how much

blood had been lost. I felt dizzy and weak. I lay back and took a long series of deep breaths. The pain intensified. I wiped the blood on my right hand across the sheet. Pushing on my left side, I tried to get up. Somehow I would make it to the elevator, take it down to the garage, hold on to the basement wall, get to my car, and drive to a hospital. I was thinking it out, step by step. My mind was very calm. I had had some much rougher plane flights. I tried again to raise myself. It was no use. I didn't have the strength.

I looked at my wristwatch on the bedstand. It was already nearly 1 A.M. I didn't want to awaken anyone. I'd sweat it out.

My mind seemed to fade in and out. Peggy was talking to me. But she wasn't there. I seemed to hear voices, but no one was in the dark room with me. It was now nearly 2:30 A.M. The pain would not relent. The only way to relieve it was to take deep breaths, hold them, and blow the air out slowly. I reached down to the hip again. The blood had spread across the sheet and mattress. I pulled up my hand. It was covered in red. The clock showed a few minutes after 4 A.M. My hip was now throbbing, like a dull but heavy hammer. It was much more intense. I passed out.

At 5 A.M., my alarm clock rang. The room, my hands, the clock—all were unsteady. I struggled to reach the bedside phone. Then I passed out again.

Someone was pounding on the front door of the apartment. It sounded as though they were crashing against it. I could hear voices, but I was semidelirious. It was Earl Eisenhower, Judy's husband. He had smashed open the door and had had to slice through the inside chain with a heavy cutter borrowed from the downstairs night clerk.

I could see Judy and Earl standing above me. Somehow, in my delirium, I had phoned them. They were talking, but I couldn't understand or answer. They saw the blood on the sheets and soon discovered my hip was a bloody mess.

I saw the two ambulance men arrive. They lifted me onto the stretcher. A fierce argument broke out between Judy and one of the drivers. They began shouting at one another. I finally got the general drift. The ambulance would take me only to the District of Columbia–Maryland line. It was not allowed to cross and carry me to Malcolm Grow Hospital at Andrews Air Force Base in Maryland. Someone would have to arrange for a Maryland ambulance to meet them at the line. Judy was screaming. She shouted at the driver that he would be held responsible, because of the delay, if I died. I passed out again wondering what the neighbors would say about all the commotion.

I woke up in the middle of being given a blood transfusion in Malcolm Grow Hospital. I never discovered how much blood I had lost but later learned that the Washington ambulance service had made the entire trip. Peggy flew out from Arizona, although I asked Judy not to tell her what had happened. I had developed a staphylococcus infection after the hip wires had been removed. The gauze packing, which filled a ten-inch cut along my right side and was stuffed inside to the bone, had also broken loose. The doctors said I was lucky to be alive.

I was hospitalized and laid up in our Washington apartment for all of July and most of August. Hobbled by painful knees, two aching arthritic hips, and other physical ailments, I had become weak. On returning to Arizona to face the Senate race, I couldn't get keyed up for it. Steve Shadegg, my campaign manager, told me that I was far ahead and would easily win. He was dead wrong.

Fewer than 900,000 votes were expected to be cast. About 400,000 new voters had moved into Arizona since my last race in 1974. A good number of them, when asked whether they would vote for Goldwater, had replied, "Goldwater? Who the hell is that?"

Our television publicity was dull and defensive. My Democratic opponent, Bill Schulz, a multimillionaire real estate developer, was running commercials which showed me old, tired, and ill. Jay Taylor, a Tucson advertising executive whom we had used in the past but who had not been rehired by Shadegg, described our TV ads in this way: "One showed Barry Goldwater sitting in a parlor, talking with a group of elderly ladies with blue hairdos, discussing Social Security. Schulz was right. He looked old, weak, and sick."

Our billboards were no better. It was a ho-hum, complacent campaign because I had won in a walk in 1974 against Scottsdale newspaper publisher Jonathan Marshall. Shadegg had underestimated Schulz, who ran the most professional campaign ever waged against me. I was still trying to regain my normal strength.

Schulz had some of the slickest TV ads any of us had ever seen. He worked hard and was well organized. He emphasized three issues: I wasn't giving full horsepower to my job in the Senate; I was out of contact with the people of the state; and the United States was paying a disproportionately large amount of the free world's defense costs while Japan and Western Europe were having to pay less. Schulz hit hard on pro-choice regarding abortion. He also took on the military-industrial complex. The suggestion was that I was too close to the military, perhaps even to defense contractors.

It became apparent in early October that the race would be very tight. New Arizonans under thirty-five years of age responded very favorably to Schulz. From May to October, there was a big shift to Schulz. More than 20 percent of the voters switched to him.

My hip was still healing, but the doctors warned me to go easy on campaigning. Go easy, hell, I was in a real fight. I phoned Dick Wirthlin, who was Ronald Reagan's pollster, despite the fact that he was heavily engaged in the presidential campaign. Wirthlin had always done my polling, and, in fact, I had introduced him to Reagan. As a personal favor, I asked him to conduct a statewide poll between October 10 and 13. He did it, and the poll showed that Schulz had surged ahead of me by two percentage points—46 to 44 percent, with 10 percent undecided. Wirthlin phoned me and said, "Barry, you're in trouble."

Wirthlin said bluntly that Shadegg, my longtime campaign manager, was blowing the election. He had not identified me sufficiently with the state—the land, the desert, the people. He stressed that our TV ads were dreadful.

The Senate Republican Campaign Committee also saw what was happening and asked pollster Lance Tarrance to find out what was wrong. The committee was concerned because the GOP hoped to win control of the Senate, and each seat was important. Tarrance agreed with Wirthlin—we were in deep trouble. He said that one of the main reasons was that we had not kept up with the latest election technology that would have identified me more with the people and places of Arizona while projecting a better future for the state with me, an old hand, in Washington. New ads should stress my knowledge of the state and my experience and clout in handling its problems in Washington.

We completely revamped the campaign with less than three weeks to go. Ron Crawford, a longtime Washington friend and political strategist, and Judy Eisenhower, my administrative assistant, rushed to Arizona and took charge of the campaign. They immediately called in Jay Taylor, who had worked with us in the past but who, for some reason, had not been engaged by Shadegg this time. Working all night, Taylor came up with an entirely new radio-TV campaign by morning. He hired helicopters and had me in the desert within another twenty-four hours. I was talking Arizona problems and how an experienced hand like Goldwater was needed in the Senate to solve them. We dumped all the old commercials. In the closing weeks we spent nearly $370,000, most of it on new TV clips showing candidate Goldwater wearing a cowboy hat and talking to Indians beside a pickup truck.

I reestablished my long ties to Arizona, something my opponent lacked.

All this represented increased professional packaging. In this case, the package was me, and I didn't like it one bit. Yet the commercials were real—not baloney—since I had given my life to the state. Arizona and I were a couple of old mules still hanging around with a lot of new neon lights and buildings changing the landscape. Since I was physically unable to campaign twenty hours a day as I had in the past, the commercials traveled where I couldn't. Still, I was determined to campaign as much as I could, no matter what the physical consequences were.

Crawford and Judy, backed by Wirthlin and Tarrance, were concerned about an ironic twist—that I might lose while the man I had helped get started in politics, Ronald Reagan, would probably capture the White House. If I were defeated, the GOP might lose its first chance since 1954 to become the majority in the Senate. I had to win.

Old-time Democrats, blue-collar workers, high school graduates, those living in outlying areas, and many younger newcomers to the state hung in with Schulz. Republicans, senior citizens, the retired, Phoenix area residents, college graduates, and white collar workers favored me, but I had lost support among them.

Ralph Watkins, Jr., an Arizona native, longtime business leader, and strong Democrat, suddenly stood up when Schulz attacked my voting record. The Democratic candidate, who had never held public office, stressed my absences from the Senate but never mentioned that I had spent two months in the hospital after hip surgery. Hammering away with the slogan "Energy for the '80s," Schulz was convinced he could win by portraying me as too old and weak. Watkins and others viewed that as a personal attack and founded "Democrats for Goldwater." Their help put timely new fire into our campaign.

In the last three weeks of the race, I threw myself into a tough schedule. It was a painful, last-ditch fight, but I'd go down swinging. Schulz and I raced for the wire with everything we had. My schedule was packed. And every day, a nurse or Judy packed the gauze in my side. I just closed my eyes and gritted my teeth between every plane stop. The pain was almost paralyzing me. I told myself I would win or die trying. We said nothing of the pain and physical problems to the media because my normal strength would eventually return. But the campaign was killing. All I had to do was hang tough for three weeks. Hell, I told myself, Big Mike and Uncle Morris hung tough most of their lives.

Schulz spent nearly $2 million, including about $1.7 million of his own money, on the campaign. We spent more than a million, including national GOP funding.

After voting on election day, Peggy and I went home, and I collapsed in bed. I was exhausted and worried. Peggy was serene. Either way, one of us would win. The vote was nip-and-tuck. When I went to bed that night, Schulz was ahead by 12,000 votes. However, 30,000 absentee ballots were yet to be counted. The tally went on all night. Amid the first streaks of dawn, Tom Dunlavey of our Phoenix office rang our front doorbell and pounded on the door. I rose as the racket grew louder and opened the door. He shouted, "You did it! We won!"

But only by a whisker. Of the 874,238 votes cast, the margin of victory was only 9,399 votes.

Schulz felt he had lost because he had criticized me in what some had viewed as a personal attack. He said, "There's something emotionally powerful about Barry. People admire him. You can't take him on personally. It was a mistake to challenge him that way. I didn't mean it to be personal. In the end, I also have to say that Ronald Reagan's big win helped Barry. It was kind of providential because Barry had helped him."

That evening, over dinner, I turned to Peggy and said, "Peg, that was my last campaign, and I'll sign this promise in blood."

She smiled and said, "One day, Barry, we'll retire from all this. It'll be so wonderful. Just the two of us."

More and more, I could see that Peggy's health was slowly but steadily deteriorating. Her emphysema and arthritis were getting worse. Her heart started giving her trouble. She wasn't getting enough exercise. Her back and bones pained, and the doctor was giving her cortisone. She stayed home and became almost a hermit.

We had never in our lives had a serious argument, but I got upset at her inactivity. I tried to get her to take walks and swim in the pool. She wouldn't. She just wanted to talk with me.

I talked a lot with her—that she had been the perfect wife and mother. How much she had meant to me. These were very open, frank moments. I told Peg of my regrets about not being a better father. She had had to carry so much of the load. God, Barry Goldwater was far from perfect.

We also talked about Newport Beach, of all places. Of our summers there and different boats we had once owned. We would get another boat and cruise up to Alaska during the very first summer of our retirement. Then we'd motor down to Panama and the Caribbean. We'd live on the boat, just the two of us. Peggy would smile. She loved to talk about plans for these trips.

In the fall of 1985 her health slipped dramatically. Peggy was in a coma and unable to speak for the last two weeks of her life. The doctors finally told us they had no hope that she would ever come out of the coma. I asked for their advice, and they told me it was time to withdraw the artificial life supports. Our children nodded in agreement. About five o'clock on the morning of December 11, 1985, Peggy died in her hospital bed as she had lived— quietly, softly, without complaint.

The four children and I kissed her.

For months I wandered between disbelief and recrimination, bewilderment and depression. The grief of separation after fifty-one years of marriage rose and fell in long, slow waves that rolled across my mind every day. At times Peggy would rise, visibly present in my memory. I phoned her four or five times every day for months after returning to Washington. The phone would ring and ring. Then, her memory would fall away and my face would collapse into my hands. The healing process has been slow and painful.

I recently found among her papers a note I wrote to Peggy on September 22, 1951, our seventeenth wedding anniversary. It reads, in part:

> I arose this morning while you still slept to see the sun come up. It's a symbol not only of warmth and light for the world, but as full as your love and constant companionship have been for me. Through times of deepest darkness, your love has lighted the path for me. In nights of cold lonesomeness, the warmth of your affection has been my blanket. . . .
> The gratefulness I feel in my heart can never be shown by material things. The happiness that has been mine for these years cannot be expressed by words or even by a caress, kiss, or hand that feels hopefully for yours.
> The thrill and pride that is mine, given me by you in our children, cannot be sufficiently shown by any action or thought on my part. The only one in the universe who fully knows the things that dwell in my heart is God. I have thanked Him from a thousand canyon bottoms, from beneath a million trees, from the heights of His heavens in the cathedral of His clouds.
> As I grow older in the warmth of your love, I will pray that, one day, I will meet Him face to face so that I might shake His hand and thank Him for giving me you.
>
> I love you,
>
> Barry

Yet politics pulled us apart. I don't know what the good Lord is going to say to me about that when we meet. But now that my political life is over and Peggy is not here to share our dreams of retirement, the sunset over the desert seems to fade more quickly and I find myself alone. The crowds and cheers are gone. The children and grandchildren come to see me once in a while. They lift my spirit but do not fill it. It will not rise to fulfillment until Peggy and I are together again.

My greatest triumphs in the Senate—as chairman of the Senate Intelligence and Armed Services committees —followed the 1980 victory. These were not my conquests. The laurels belonged in great part to Peggy. The Defense Reorganization Act should not bear my name. It could just as well be the Peggy Goldwater Act. She neither claimed nor wished for public accolades. In reality, Peggy spent her life so that I might be a public figure. Her personal heights were hidden, but they were actually a lot higher than mine. I still have a long climb before I reach her.

13

The Future

THE MODERN REPUBLICAN PARTY CAN NOW BE viewed from the vantage point of three generations.

The first emerged in the 1950s—small, searching for its own identity, swimming against waves of expanding government power.

The second generation grew almost unnoticed as counterculture movements raged through the 1960s and 1970s. These new young Republicans with a more established and respected conservative philosophy and sense of identity swelled in number. They cut a clear direction of their own despite the angry mood of those explosive years.

The third sprang up in the 1980s with the election of President Reagan. It was a massive outpouring of millions of articulate young people. They seized the ideological offensive from the liberals and began a strong effort to change the direction of the country.

These changes have been enormous—from relatively few Republicans to many, from stale old principles to the philosophical and political offensive, from long-suffering conservative defeat to the vitality of victory with new ideas and movement for the nation.

Other transformations also took place within the party. The term conservative took on a broader meaning. Traditionalists like me emphasized individual freedom, the superiority of free enterprise, limited government, and stronger national defense. We stressed custom, rule of law, religious principles, and basic belief in the constitutional process.

The newer party included neoconservatives, new right conservatives, and libertarians. Neoconservatives had become disenchanted with the Democratic Party, especially with policies they felt had led to a breakdown of law and order. The neoconservatives emphasized institutional stability and shared with us a more traditional view of the nation than did the new left. Irving Kristol defined neoconservatives as "liberals who have been mugged by reality."

New right conservatives have identified themselves mostly with the moral aspects of social issues. These include support of voluntary school prayer, a pro-life agenda opposing abortion, various options in education (e.g., tuition tax credits through a voucher system), and opposition to such policies as job quotas, busing, and the tolerance or promotion of pornography.

Libertarians stress freedom, especially in economic enterprise, with as few government constraints as possible. The free market and individual beliefs are supreme. Drugs, pornography, and even national defense are completely open questions.

These views reflect change in the party and define its factions. The clearest such differences pit traditionalist values against those of the libertarians. There is a dramatic contrast between the socially liberal young professionals who are attracted to Reagan's economic policies on the one hand, and, on the other hand, the often affluent but religiously oriented social conservatives who are in step with his traditional values. These differences could become very divisive.

There are also divisions among traditionalists, especially among some old-timers like myself and the Moral Majority. I once said that the Reverend Jerry Falwell

needed a swift kick in the ass. That's shorthand for my
reservations about various Moral Majority preachings
and practices, including their emphasis on money. Although Falwell is no longer the formal leader of the
Moral Majority, he is still the real force behind it.

Falwell, Jim and Tammy Faye Bakker, Pat Robertson,
Oral Roberts, Jimmy Swaggart, and other TV evangelists
are not the only or necessarily the best representatives of
the moral America in which most of us believe. Some of
these checkbook clergy are too busy collecting money,
Rolls-Royces, and private jets. Their lives are clothed in
the materialist ethic.

Worse, some have mocked God. Oral Roberts suggested that the Almighty would "call him home" unless
listeners contributed millions of dollars by his deadline.
There is talk of raising people from the dead, miraculous
cures, and other larger-than-life powers. Such antics border on blasphemy.

The greatest threats to the present harmonious but
hands-off relationship between church and state are the
political preachers—both conservative and liberal—and
the far-left National Council of Churches—the Jerry
Falwells and Jesse Jacksons. Also the council members
who support the radical left here and Communist causes
around the world.

I am concerned about clergy engaged in a heavy-
handed, continuing attempt to use political means to obtain moral ends—and vice versa. It is one of the most
dangerous trends in this country. They are attempting to
institutionalize politics in their churches. Ironically, they
may ultimately bring their own empires crashing down
by dividing their congregations along political lines. This
may not happen today but will certainly occur in the
future.

There are already signs of this in the Catholic Church.
The war-and-peace and economic pastorals issued by the
National Conference of Catholic Bishops spite the consti-

tutional spirit of our government and people by merging religion and politics.

In historical terms, I believe we will eventually see that too much prominence and influence have been attributed to the party's New Right—Richard Viguerie, Paul Weyrich, Morton Blackwell, the Dolans, and others. Don't get me wrong. I like each of them, and despite our differences we have a lot in common. Every one of them got into politics during my campaign for the presidency, and they have been a driving force among conservatives ever since.

We began walking separate roads, however, when the New Right began pushing special social agendas involving legitimate legal, religious, and other differences. I support much of what they say, but not at the risk of compromising constitutional rights. Nor do I believe Republicans should splinter into a wrecking crew of special interests as the Democrats have done. And that is where these narrow but gifted men have been leading us.

For years, the New Right preached little or no spirit of compromise—political give-and-take. Viguerie, Weyrich, and others failed to appreciate that politics is the ordinary stuff of daily living, while the spiritual life represents eternal values and goals. Public business—that's all politics is—is often making the best of a mixed bargain. Instead, the New Right stresses the politics of absolute moral right and wrong. And, of course, they are convinced of their absolute rightness.

James Madison, the father of our Constitution, once wrote, "If men were angels, no government would be necessary." But men are not angels, and government is necessary. We settle our daily battles by reason and law, not on the basis of narrow interests or individual religious beliefs. Madison said the great paradox of representative government is this: How does a nation control its factions without violating people's basic freedoms?

Our Constitution seeks to allow freedom for everyone,

not merely those professing certain moral or religious views of ultimate right.

We don't have to look back centuries to see such dangers. Look at the carnage in the name of religious righteousness in Iran. The long and bloody division of Northern Ireland. The Christian-Moslem and Moslem-Moslem "holy war" in Lebanon.

The Moral Majority and most in the New Right oppose abortion. I oppose abortion. Yet in a pluralistic society the issue is not ours to decide alone. If abortion is both a political and moral issue, as the Moral Majority indicates in pursuing both levels of activity, then it has already lost the political battle and perhaps the national religious fight as well. There is too wide and complex a range of opinion for us to reach a national consensus on issues of morality. The truth is—and no one in the country appears to have the courage to say it—that the American people want it both ways on abortion. Most people are privately horrified by it, but they are either victims of peer pressure or favor it only in limited circumstances.

The Moral Majority has no more right to dictate its moral and political beliefs to the country than does any other group, political or religious. The same is true of pro-choice abortion and other groups. They are free to persuade us because this land is blessed with liberty, but not to assign religious or political absolutes—complete right or wrong.

My wife believed that each woman had the moral and legal right to choose for herself whether she was capable of continuing her pregnancy and then raising the child. I disagreed with her. That's as it is, and must be, in a free and pluralistic America.

If pro- and antiabortion groups each accept the other's right to disagree with them, legally, morally, or both— and some do in certain cases that are carefully spelled out —then the question can be resolved by the usual democratic means. But if either side insists on legislating morality in absolute terms, then the challenge to democratic society is too great. It's simply unworkable. For a democracy to function, there has to be give-and-take, some room for compromise.

The great danger in the new conservative movement is that, instead of broadening its base, the movement may tear itself and the GOP apart. Its real challenge in the years ahead is to broaden the Republican base and accommodate many new aims without weakening the party's foundations and pulling the whole house down.

There is a note of hope. Weyrich and some of the others are becoming more interested in taxes, labor policy, and other fundamentally political issues. They are working at the state level. Hooray!

Some observers already see cracks in the solidity of the new GOP and conservative cause. It's often summed up in a simple question: After Reagan, what?

Ronald Reagan is not the Republican Party any more than he is the conservative revolution. I always got angry at people who attributed such powers to me. In fact, I still get mad at people who say I was Reagan's political godfather or his prophet opening up the wilderness for him. Both of us are and have been our own men. We are merely symbols of a deeper political movement.

I don't believe that either Reagan or I started a conservative revolution because for most of our history the majority of Americans have considered themselves conservatives. They have often not voted that way because they were offered no clear choice. I began to tap, and Reagan reached to the bottom of, a deep reservoir that already existed. He came along at the right time and in just the right circumstances to lead a real surge in conservative thought and action.

Nor do I accept the idea that his presidency represents a permanent political realignment. Politics runs in cycles. The Democrats will come back strong about the year 2000 or shortly thereafter. But it will be a new Democratic Party largely because of Reagan. The nation's agenda has now been pulled to the right.

Contrary to what many indicate, it's not difficult to answer the question: After Reagan, what? The question must be put in perspective. What Reagan did was pull the trigger. He had the ammunition—clear and compelling evidence that much of the spending of the Great Society and earlier liberal programs had failed miserably. Most Americans also became convinced that government was beginning to get completely out of control, harming our overall economic and social well-being.

Reagan also has a gift of eloquence and generosity of spirit that demonstrates the concerns and compassion of Republicans and others. We had long been hurt by the charge of being driven by cold, calculated economic policies which favored the rich. That was not true. Republicans simply believed—and still do—that the private sector, not the government, is the driving force behind national economic growth and jobs.

The Democrats had perpetuated the myth of salvation-by-government for too long. Americans by the millions suddenly discovered one of the biggest political lies of the last half century—that Big Brother in Washington knew best. And Reagan had the firepower—a Republican Party with intellectual respect, numbers, and a mastery of political technology.

I got a good laugh out of Tip O'Neill's good-old-boy definition of the Democratic Party's contribution to America. O'Neill concluded his memoirs by boasting of his longtime support for higher taxes: "It's those taxes that made possible the tremendous progress we've seen."

I hope every Republican candidate for the next twenty-five years will quote Tip. It's the best proof I've seen in recent times that the Democrats will never learn.

He also repeats the pious platitude of onetime Boston mayor James Michael Curley, one of the biggest political crooks this country has ever seen: "Every American family deserves the opportunity to earn an income, own a home, educate their children, and afford medical care."

Federal, state, and local governments have never created a single job in this country. Nor does one American owe his home, education, or medical care to government. The fiscal advances and overwhelming advantages of this country have come from private enterprise. Government has never earned a dime. Tip, Curley, and the rest of their crowd would like us to believe government is a holy calling and they are its anointed. Instead, the Democrats have been this century's bagmen. Now they are fifty years behind the times.

One of the major challenges to Republicans is that our party, which has become larger, now has more disparate elements in it than at any time in the last twenty years. We don't have to become more centrist, but it's certain the GOP has to accommodate and balance a wider variety of opinions and political options.

We must become more a party of inclusion—not exclusion—especially among blue-collar workers and Hispanics. I am not excluding blacks, but GOP opportunities there are unfortunately limited. Blacks seem rockbound to the Democrats. That will change as they gain more insight into the fact that their disadvantaged place in society was partly caused by the Big Brother syndrome of the Democrats. When blacks understand that, they will seek out more educational and economic opportunity, which is the basis for uplifting their lives. That will take more time, and the Republican Party must be patient while this change takes place.

Yet the GOP will be weakened if it adopts the exclusionary views of the religious right. This will scare off moderates and others of the country's swing vote. The scandals among the TV evangelists, who are closely identified with the Moral Majority, have caused considerable disillusionment among a good number of the faithful. Some of these will no longer follow the political lead of fundamentalist preachers nor contribute to their causes. The more the Republicans embrace the fundamentalists or some of their self-anointed leaders, the more voters will be lost to the GOP.

The West and South—the Sunbelt—have lifted the GOP to victory in four of the past five presidential elections. Despite Democratic claims that this support is weakening, I find little or no evidence of that. On the contrary, more people in the West and South are becoming middle-class, urban technocrats and breaking away from their traditional agricultural base and historic bias. That's a mouthful, but, in simple language, the more educated and upwardly mobile tend to vote Republican.

It should be remembered that the West and South helped me lead the drive to overthrow the Eastern wing that controlled the GOP presidential nominating process. The urban middle class was just being born in those regions when I ran for the White House. Both regions were beginning to lose their agricultural orientation and becoming urban. That middle class has now become suburban. This internal economic and social explosion has been augmented by migration to the two regions from the Northeast and Midwest. These newcomers and many native Southerners—fewer in the West—have deserted the Democratic Party in droves and will not easily return. The Southern GOP no longer consists of a small number of upper-middle-class voters but has become a genuinely broad-based political movement. About as many Westerners and Southerners now call themselves Republicans as describe themselves as Democrats.

Both parties today are searching for a balance between the general good and special interests. The Democrats, badly shaken by Reagan's landslide victory over Walter Mondale, have been trying to project an almost completely different image ever since. They are paying the Republicans the sincerest form of flattery—imitation. The Democratic presidential candidates began appealing as early as mid-1987 to moral concerns and family values. At the same time, the Democratic Policy Commission placed "strengthening the family" as its highest priority. That came straight out of the New Right agenda of a decade ago.

No one should be deceived. The New Right is critical to the GOP victory coalition. Whether or not it includes 75 million evangelical Christians, as some claim, is not the central consideration. The real question is whether the New Right will defeat the party by splitting off and neutralizing part of its vote.

Who and what are in the GOP coalition? There are actually about a dozen different such coalitions, both formal and informal. The most basic Reagan coalition is composed of traditional Republicans, an increasing national strength in the West and South, a strong appeal to fundamentalist Protestants and many Catholics, big inroads among blue-collar workers, and a magnetic appeal to voters under thirty-five years of age.

The others represent a range of issues and interest groups—from privatization (moving the private sector into services now monopolized by the government, such as selling public housing to take it off government rolls), to education (choice through tuition tax credits), to the Strategic Defense Initiative (Star Wars) in defense and foreign policy, to expanding Individual Retirement Accounts (making Social Security a smaller component of retirement benefits). The list is long and complex. Conservative Democrats agree with much of this.

The particular groups range across a broad spectrum of interests, from youth leadership to congressional watchdogs.

The GOP now flows with many ideas from such think tanks as the Heritage Foundation and the American Enterprise Institute which are pushing it to the forefront of national change.

Reagan will be missed. I will miss him. We fought for the conservative cause and were good friends to boot. Reagan also will be missed by Republicans because he was able to keep the party united. I am not certain that unity will prevail.

I have been critical of the President, especially his Iranian arms sale. It was the biggest mistake of his presidency to have traded with the most notorious terrorist gang in the world.

But whatever mistakes he may have made, Reagan has managed to do something that no one in the nation has accomplished since Teddy Roosevelt. He has projected a Republican populism—indeed, a conservative populism.

He is a man of populist words and style. His themes of family, hard work, patriotism, and opportunity are in marked contrast to the Democrats' adoption of gay rights and other permissive behavior, new welfare schemes, affirmative action, and whatever greater "entitlements" the government may create.

Reagan represents the spirit of the modern Republican Party, which is about 75 percent conservative and 25 percent moderate to liberal. He's a social and national defense conservative. There is, however, a big difference between Reagan and other Republican leaders of this century. He's not a man who is tied to the economic status quo. Reagan is an economic progressive, an advocate of change. This is true not only in terms of broad supply side economics but also in various other aspects of the economy that relate to growth and job creation.

The Democrats would have us believe they will reverse the Reagan era. That's not likely. For openers, no administration can launch a new free-spending New Deal or Great Society because of the enormous federal budget deficits. Nor can any President stop Reagan's increased defense spending without jeopardizing big weapons systems, sharply curtailing the military's combat effectiveness, and wiping out tens of thousands of jobs. Amid such a sea of red ink, it would not be easy for the Democrats to justify big new spending. Their only weapon would be huge tax increases, which would make such an administration highly unpopular. The massive deficits cannot be brought under control in a short span, so their promises would have to be realistic.

When historians judge Reagan's eight years as President, they will probably decide that he left his greatest mark on the nation's judiciary—from overhauling the federal bench at the district and circuit levels to the U.S. Supreme Court. Reagan has now appointed more than half of the country's federal judges, most of them conservatives. His appointment of more conservatives to the Supreme Court will influence the nation's social and other directions into the next century.

In the two years since I left the Senate, I have mulled over my previous assessments of the eight Presidents during my tenure on Capitol Hill. Truman was unquestionably the finest President in terms of pure decision-making leadership. Eisenhower, contrary to many political pundits then and now, was our best all-around chief executive. He was helped by choosing extremely able men to be around him, but that does not diminish his own excellence.

Finally, and this is a tough call, I believe Reagan is the most inspirational President that I have seen. Kennedy inspired the nation but did not face the troubled aftermath of Vietnam, Watergate, and the economic malaise of the Carter years. Both had a similar quality, a sponge-like mind. Both Kennedy and Reagan could walk in a room and not know their rear end from a hot rock. They wouldn't say a word for five minutes. Then, slowly, each would join the conversation in a way that made you believe they knew what they were talking about. I watched both do it at various times and came away amazed. It will be a long time before we see another President of their wit and charm. But I believe Reagan had the better of Kennedy in one crucial character ingredient—humility. That's an important quality for anyone holding the highest office in the land.

* * *

The most important long-range question before the GOP is how to keep the conservative flame alive in the future. There are many answers and strategies, ranging from solidifying the present coalition to broadening the party base to include more minorities. I don't quarrel with any of them because if one ingredient is crucial in politics, it is flexibility.

In my own view, the two most important factors in the future success of the GOP are young people and principle. I'm convinced that millions of young men and women have joined the Republican Party because they wanted something in which to believe. This is particularly true of working class youth. Many have been turned off by some of the social and moral values in today's permissive liberal outlook. We are also the party of opportunity. In public opinion polls, only 20 percent of the country's young people identify with the Democrats.

Yet, as everyone in politics knows, nothing can be taken for granted. There will forever be a fight for the hearts and minds of younger voters. Their importance to the GOP's future is reflected in these Census Bureau statistics from the national election of 1984. Some 11.4 million voters between the ages of eighteen and twenty-four cast ballots that year, with more than 60 percent for Reagan. The total was 11.2 percent of the entire vote. Yet the entire population of the same age group was nearly 28 million voters. Less than 40 percent of those eligible to vote actually cast ballots! So the GOP must work to win and keep the young.

Republicans have become the country's political innovators. Even Democrats privately concede they have lost their initiative in the past decade. But ingenuity is not enough. I cannot sufficiently stress that principle is the rock-bottom foundation of any great movement. This is reflected not only in our Constitution, laws, religion, and traditions, but in some of the social changes of the past thirty years. The Weathermen and Woodstock are now blips on the American sociopolitical screen. They have been replaced by the wonders of the computer and other technological advances that have offered young people a natural high based on individual opportunity. And more of today's young people are seeking higher social and moral values. Republicans must, above all, be a party of principle.

Compromise is necessary in politics, but there can be no dilution of traditional conservative principles—individual freedom, free enterprise economics, limiting government, and bolstering our national defense. We cannot become a party so splintered by special interests that we have confused and lost our roots, not even to broaden our electoral base. Whether it be the Moral Majority insistence on certain religious stands or minority interests in quotas and similar special considerations, principle cannot be abandoned for momentary electoral advantage. Otherwise we will no longer attract the young and idealistic.

I am optimistic about the outcome. Those now under the Republican umbrella clearly see the Democratic alternative—pandering to a wide variety of interests whose social and moral values are often confused, even contradictory or personally degrading. Also, the old Democratic Big Labor–political patronage coalition has been severely weakened by its failures. The Democrats, now in transition, are groping for a new centrism that they've been unable to define or articulate. They are further hampered by a lack of leadership. There are no real domestic or foreign policy spokesmen for the party.

The Democrats are rethinking the fundamental meaning of liberalism and simply have no new direction or programs to use in redirecting their energies. Even Democrats admit that government has become too big and intrusive. They are trying to untie themselves from their own past, and this cannot be done easily. Their economic and social permissiveness is so discredited that many liberals now want to be known as neoliberals or progressives.

The GOP has an excellent future if it remains the party of opportunity and optimism. It must retain its conservative traditions and not become extreme. We must fight at the grass roots level, and this will improve the quality of our candidates. Our success in attracting young people to help in the 1964 campaign must be repeated in 1992, 1996, and 2000. These years will coincide with a sharp increase in the number of young voters. The post–World War II baby boom generation, born between 1945 and 1960, has been producing what population experts call an echo effect, a sharp rise in births. The U.S. birthrate has not increased, but the number of births has risen because of the number of women now in their childbearing years.

In my life I've personally spoken to and shaken hands with about 20 million Americans. The one question I've been asked more than any other is this: Should a young person go into politics? Unhesitatingly, I've always answered yes. But . . .

You must have the courage to accept considerable criticism, much of it unjustified. You must feel it in your guts and have the courage to accept defeat and continue toward your goals. Finally, you must believe in yourself, in your principles, and in people. Of all this, I considered my belief in people to be my greatest strength. I genuinely liked people and still do. If you don't love people, don't go into politics.

There are a good number of unhappy men and women in politics today. The reason is that they have recognized the selfishness of their lives. They don't really care much for people. It has taken years for some to discover that, yet they find it difficult to admit it, even to themselves. They don't want to surrender the prestige and power they have accumulated. So they play two roles, the false image of the person who cares and the reality of the individual whose only aims are personal.

That's one reason I believe Congress should meet only four to six months a year, five to six days a week. They would then go home. Members would be people again instead of power brokers.

Like and trust the people. No better advice could ever be given to a young person interested in politics. And no more reasonable counsel could be given those who now serve in public office. That, if anything, is my political legacy.

In all parts of the world today, America is under fire economically, politically, and militarily. Yet the roots of most of these problems are here at home. No nation can shape and solidify a successful foreign policy unless its domestic affairs are in order. The secret to our international strength in the year 2000 and beyond is whether the United States can reverse its failures at home on three fronts:

(1) The material and personal cost of government
(2) The idea that forced equality of results can replace equality of opportunity
(3) The steady increase of a massive, uncontrolled bureaucracy.

Government can no longer be allowed to pose as the "honest broker" and manager of our problems. This country is spending one third of its gross national product on government. It's estimated that regulatory agencies add about $150 billion a year to the cost of American products. Our budget deficit is more than $150 billion a year. We are the world's number one debtor nation. This cannot continue.

Nor can government still play political games with minorities—promising giant strides in eliminating poverty and creating educational advancement and then failing. Blacks and others have been duped for far too long by their own politicians, who could not deliver on the false expectations they created.

One of the great challenges of the next generation will

be to come to an understanding of what is meant by equality of opportunity. Instead of opportunity, many in the nation now demand that the law enforce equality of results.

It's nonsense to suggest that a government can guarantee a college degree, a good job, or the "good life." The mental, physical, and other basic characteristics of each individual are all different. Affirmative action quota systems are an attempt at such guarantees. This is Washington-managed social engineering at its most hypocritical because no country can deliver on such promises. Even dictatorships can't do it. No aspect of life operates on the theory of equal results. We have different capacities, whether we practice medicine or hit home runs.

Congress must reassert itself. The unelected bureaucracy has effectively replaced Congress in much of our governing process. The bureaucrats speed up or drag their feet, depending on their own views. The Department of Education and the Legal Services Corporation are notorious examples of independent states within the state. Big business is entering into more and more alliances with the bureaucracy and is even protected by some agencies which are supposed to oversee their operations. This is true of the U.S. Bureau of Land Management, which is deeply involved with ranchers and others, as well as other agencies. The original purpose of regulation and all its red tape was to protect the public from massive corporations. Now, all too often, the large corporation is being protected from the public.

Let us get big business out of government and vice versa. More and more, corporations are calling for centralized federal planning. This is most evident in international competition. The domestic free marketplace is also being replaced by regulation and other corporate-bureaucratic sweetheart relationships that limit competition.

We must cut back on the vast federal bureaucracy. It is out of control. Unlike corporations, federal agencies have no financial bottom line. Inefficiency and just plain stalling are often rewarded. Many live by the old bureaucratic axiom: "Wait the bastards out."

Bureaucrats often sit on their hands until their politically appointed leadership, Congress and the President, see things their way. This is so pervasive in dozens of agencies that a new administration often simply bypasses an agency entirely in order to accomplish its objectives.

I do not delude myself, nor am I trying to deceive anyone. These are the same problems that faced the nation when I arrived in the Senate. Am I and other conservatives total failures? Perhaps not. We have begun to turn the country around. It may take the entire next century to accomplish these goals.

The domestic divisions I have outlined are reflected on the world scene. Today the United States is often a nation at war with itself.

Little by little, we Americans are withdrawing into ourselves. We do not have the will to meet global challenges as we once did. Our adversaries, even our allies, are on the offensive—economically, diplomatically, militarily. We have assumed a defensive, reactionary posture. There are reasons for our withdrawal.

The experiences of Watergate and Vietnam, especially the war, have cost our national leadership dearly, making it much less powerful—and the whole world knows it. Congress has stepped into this partial vacuum of the executive branch and tried to make foreign policy itself.

Friend and foe alike have concluded, as a result of the battle for dominance between our legislative and executive branches, that in future we may not be able to honor our international obligations.

Meanwhile, U.S. corporate executives are in the process of creating a new international order. It is primarily economic but has profound political and military implications. Their mergers and extensive working agreements with foreign firms have formed new international alliances and allegiances. This massive new movement among corporations threatens American economic leadership of the world.

By definition, these new conglomerates have no special loyalty to American workers, products, production plants, or nearby communities—not even to the U.S. government. Profits, international stock prices, and market share are the new order and give rise to new allegiances. The competitive edge has been placed above country and profit above values. International strength and survival come before being a good U.S. corporate citizen.

Corporations are fleeing higher U.S. labor costs and tougher work rules. Their profits increase in the short run, but eventually it will cost the United States and these firms dearly in their abilities to produce and innovate. Yet they expect America to help bail them out—even with U.S. troops—if their creations run into trouble.

Instead of increasing the number of international joint ventures, Americans should be stressing how U.S. companies can strengthen themselves to better compete in the world market.

The answer is not simple. It's clear that the U.S. economy has slipped badly since the early 1970s, and all of us are to blame.

As a nation, we are now consuming about $150 billion more a year than we are producing. Our annual trade deficit is about $170 billion. The servicing of our $2.5 trillion national debt, combined with our trade deficit, eats up whatever slight gains we make in our gross national product.

If we are to extricate ourselves from this swamp, it means that Americans may have to consume less in the foreseeable future. It also indicates that Congress and the Administration must readjust our economic policies to invite more saving and investment instead of consumption. Both Washington and American business must respond to the problems created by the new international order, which threaten our social, economic, and political future. So must U.S. labor, because if unions continue to resist change, more American jobs will drift overseas. Finally, some way must be found to have more U.S. companies move their investments in research and development into production instead of selling off their innovations to foreign firms. We are now losing part of our most powerful tool—Yankee ingenuity.

Our adversaries have sought to exploit this new international economic order and our internal differences. As a matter of policy, they regularly probe for weaknesses in U.S. leadership. This is particularly true of our military alliances. Only our nuclear deterrent prevents Soviet forces from overrunning Western Europe in a conventional war. The Soviet Navy, especially its submarine force, now rivals that of the United States in virtually all the sea lanes of the world. This is particularly true in the Mediterranean gateway to Mideast oil.

If détente is to be the central thrust of our relations with the Soviet Union, I believe we must be much more precise in spelling out to all our adversaries what the United States regards as its legitimate international interests and what we will do to protect them. We must, for example, draw clearer lines around our interests in Central America.

It's obvious that U.S. foreign policy must become more bipartisan. We cannot afford to be torpedoed by having the President and Congress engaged in a jurisdictional war. There must be a clear-eyed understanding of the constitutional powers of each branch and greater consultation between them. Specifically, Congress and the President must agree on the meaning of the War Powers Resolution and the precise role of Congress in shaping foreign policy. That is one of the major lessons of the Iran-Contra hearings of summer 1987. Our foreign power will be bolstered by unified domestic strength.

I am not optimistic that we can achieve such national unity. Many of our political leaders appear much more interested in debating foreign policy than in reaching bipartisan agreement.

* * *

In looking back at the twentieth century, the most important event of our times has not been the atom bomb, communications advances, or the advent of computers. Rather, it has been the rise and international development of communism. Today the term communism represents a number of philosophies embraced by China and Cuba, Romania and Poland, Yugoslavia and the Soviet Union. It is in the process of great change. There is more nationalism among many of these regimes, as well as revisions in economics and other areas in the Soviet Union. These changes are a mixture of good and bad.

Communism is not retreating or withdrawing. It still rules by armed repression. The movement appears, however, to have reached a political plateau with considerable internal ferment about its future directions. Top-level confrontations between the old and new leadership in both the Soviet Union and China have created problems. Such divisions are dangerous because they could spill over to the rest of the world. There could well be economic and political rebellion in Poland and elsewhere.

Despite the uncertainty of grappling with these policy and other problems, the Communists continue to foment troubles around the globe. Juggling turmoil at home and abroad, they are going through a period of high risk. Their troubles create a long-term problem for the entire free world because the Reds may not be able to control the changes they have set in motion.

From our point of view, these risks are worthwhile because the Communists may improve life behind the Iron Curtain and elsewhere. Nevertheless, such changes may lead to unpredictable developments affecting all of us—even war.

Others argue that population, hunger, and disease—such as an AIDS epidemic—are more threatening. I do not entirely believe that, because, among other developments, food production is rising dramatically around the world and medicine has always ultimately managed to meet man's most severe health challenges. AIDS is a health terror, but it is a war which science will win because it must.

Communism is the world's greatest danger because it threatens much more massive human destruction through armed force.

Communism has long and defiantly denied human freedom. Yet millions of men and women are prepared to die for liberty. The seeds of future global conflict have unmistakably already been sown. A Third World War is not unthinkable. It is, indeed, most thinkable if the Soviet Union and China cannot make a peaceful transition from their present uncertainty. It is thinkable because men do not always control events. In politics, events often control men.

Man's greatest weapon against totalitarianism is freedom. I'm reminded of the meaning of freedom every morning. As I sit at my desk, robins and other birds flit back and forth on a ledge outside my study window. Often I watch them for long periods. We have come to know one another since they will sometimes stop and acknowledge my presence.

Freedom has been the watchword of my political life. I rose from a dusty little frontier town and preached freedom across this land all my days. It is democracy's ultimate power and assures its eventual triumph over communism. I believe in faith, hope, and charity. But none of these is possible without freedom.

Epilogue

ON SEPTEMBER 24, 1987, I RECEIVED THE SYLVANUS Thayer Award at West Point. The U.S. Military Academy's Association of Graduates presents the award annually to a U.S. citizen whose service and accomplishments in the national interest exemplify personal devotion to the ideals expressed in the West Point motto, "Duty—Honor—Country."

The award is named in honor of Sylvanus Thayer, class of 1808, who later became an outstanding superintendent at the academy.

I stood on the Plain and reviewed the Corps of Cadets on that bleak, gray autumn afternoon. It seemed that my entire life was passing in review.

Later, after dinner, I told the more than four thousand cadets that their honor code had influenced me more than any other thought except that of freedom itself.

Only my father's illness prevented me from accepting an appointment to West Point and becoming a brother officer in the Army.

In accepting the medal, I never stood taller.

My life had come full circle. I was finally home, where I'd always belonged.

Index